Reconstructing a National Identity

STUDIES IN JEWISH HISTORY
Jehuda Reinharz, General Editor

The Jews of Paris and the Final Solution
Communal Response and Internal Conflicts,
1940–1944
Jacques Adler

Jews in Christian America
The Pursuit of Religious Equality
Naomi W. Cohen

Atlas of Modern Jewish History
Evyatar Friesel

Isaac Bashevis Singer
A Life
Janet Hadda

A Clash of Heroes
Brandeis, Weizmann, and American Zionism
Ben Halpern

Zionism and the Creation of a
New Society
Ben Halpern and Jehuda Reinharz

Between Dignity and Despair
Jewish Life in Nazi Germany
Marion A. Kaplan

The Making of the Jewish Middle Class
Women, Family, and Identity in
Imperial Germany
Marion A. Kaplan

The Making of Czech Jewry
National Conflict and Jewish Society in
Bohemia, 1870–1918
Hillel J. Kieval

The Berlin Jewish Community
Enlightenment, Family, and Crisis,
1770–1830
Steven M. Lowenstein

On Modern Jewish Politics
Ezra Mendelsohn

The Vatican and Zionism
Conflicts in the Holy Land, 1896–1925
Sergio Minerbi

Re-Inventing the Jewish Past
European Jewish Intellectuals and the
Zionist Return to History
David N. Myers

Escaping the Holocaust
Illegal Immigration to the Land of Isreal,
1930–1944
Dalia Ofer

Chaim Weizmann
The Making of a Zionist Leader
Jehuda Reinharz

Chaim Weizmann
The Making of a Statesman
Jehuda Reinharz

Courage Under Siege
Starvation, Disease, and Death in the
Warsaw Ghetto
Charles G. Roland

Reconstructing a National Identity
The Jews of Habsburg Austria during
World War I
Marsha L. Rozenblit

Land and Power
The Zionist Resort to Force
Anita Shapira

The Transformation of Germany Jewry:
1780–1840
David Sorkin

For Whom Do I Toil?
Judah Leib Gordon and the Crisis of
Russian Jewry
Michael F. Stanislawski

Unwelcome Strangers
Eastern European Jews in
Imperial Germany
Jack Wertheimer

The Holocaust
The Face of European Jewry, 1932–1945
Leni Yahil

RECONSTRUCTING A NATIONAL IDENTITY

The Jews of Habsburg Austria

during World War I

Marsha L. Rozenblit

OXFORD

UNIVERSITY PRESS

2001

OXFORD
UNIVERSITY PRESS

Oxford   New York
Athens Auckland   Bankok   Bogotá   Buenos Aires   Calcutta
Cape Town   Chennai   Dar es Salaam   Delhi   Florence   Hong Kong   Istanbul
Karachi   Kuala Lumpur   Madrid   Melbourne   Mexico City   Mumbai
Nairobi   Paris   São Paulo   Shanghai   Singapore   Taipei   Tokyo   Toronto   Warsaw

and associated companies in
Berlin   Ibadan

Copyright © 2001 by Marsha L. Rozenblit

Published by Oxford University Press, Inc.
198 Madison Avenue, New York, New York 10016

Oxford is a registered trademark of Oxford University Press

Library of Congress Cataloging-in-Publication Data
Rozenblit, Marsha L., 1950–
Reconstructing a national identity:
the Jews of Habsburg Austria during World War I/
Marsha L. Rozenblit.
p. cm.
Includes bibliographical references and index.
ISBN 0-19-513465-6
1. Jews—Austria—History.   2. Jews—Austria—Identity.
3. Jews—Cultural assimilation—Austria.   4. Austria—Ethnic relations.   I. Title.
DS135.A9 R69   2000
943.6'0049424—dc21   99-053423

1 3 5 7 9 8 6 4 2

Printed in the United States of America
on acid-free paper

For My Husband,
Kenneth G. Holum

Acknowledgments

As is customary, I would like to thank the people who have helped me and the institutions that extended their hospitality to me during the research and writing of this book. In particular, I would like to thank the staff of the Central Archives for the History of the Jewish People in Jerusalem, especially its director, Hadassah Assouline, and its tireless clerk, Yaakov Zabach, for their assistance, their interest in my project, and for years of friendship; they have always made me feel completely at home when I work there. The staff of the Central Zionist Archives in Jerusalem also treated me cordially, as did the archivists at the War Archives of the Austrian State Archives in Vienna, especially its director, Dr. Rainer Egger, and its associate director, Dr. Peter Broucek. I am likewise grateful to Dr. Erwin Schmidl for enabling me to see the material he collected for his book on Jews in the Habsburg armed forces, now housed at the War Archives, and for his warm friendship and scholarly support over the years. In Prague, Dr. V. Hamáčková of the Jewish Museum graciously arranged for me to see the records of the Prague *Israelitische Kultusgemeinde* and the Refugee Aid Committee even though she was away on vacation, and Dr. Jiřina Šedinová provided me with a pleasant environment in which to work. Finally, I would like to thank Dr. Diane Spielman of the Leo Baeck Institute in New York for her tireless help.

I am fortunate to have an intellectual home in the History Department of the University of Maryland, College Park, where my colleagues for over 20 years have always supported and encouraged my work. I thank both the University of Maryland's General Research Board for granting me two separate semesters off from teaching so that I could devote myself to this project and the Meyerhoff Center for Jewish Studies for funding many research trips to Jerusalem, Vienna, and Prague. Friends and colleagues in Jewish History all over the world have been equally important to me. In particular, I thank my mentor, Paula Hyman, as well as Deborah Dash Moore, Harriet Freidenreich, Hillel Kieval, Albert Lichtblau, Robert Wistrich, and Michael Silber for many fruitful discussions over the years. I have also benefited from my friendships with such eminent Habsburg historians as Gary Cohen, Pieter Judson, and the late William McCagg.

No list of people to whom I am grateful would be complete, however, without singling out István Deák, the influential Habsburg historian and long ago my *Doktorvater* at Columbia University. I thank him most warmly for all our discussions about the Jews of Austria-Hungary, for everything that he has taught me about nationalism in East Central Europe, and for his long and enduring friendship. I am also happy that he and his wife Gloria were in Vienna during my research trip there in the summer of 1994 so that we could share coffee, food, and good times in the Austrian capital.

I also extend my thanks to the people who helped in the production of this book. Chad Shuey, a graduate student in the Department of Geography at the University of Maryland, prepared the beautiful maps. Harriet Freidenreich's close reading of the manuscript and her many suggestions helped me immeasurably. I am grateful to my editors at Oxford University Press—Thomas LeBien, Susan Ferber, Robin Miura, and Kathy Finch—for all their work on this volume.

Finally, I must thank my family. My son Mark's enormous pride in his mother the scholar fills me with happiness. Moreover, his love of history and his ability to understand texts makes me feel successful. My husband, archaeologist and ancient historian Kenneth Holum, has been my most important friend, colleague, editor, and intellectual partner. His probing questions and deep insights during our innumerable discussions of national identity in general and Jewish identity in particular have helped me understand my own subject. His enthusiasm for this book and his supreme confidence in me has sustained me through the years of research and writing. This book has also benefited from his skill as an editor and from the model he provides to me of careful, patient scholarship. For all his help, both in scholarship as well as in our life together, I thank him most affectionately.

Contents

Abbreviations   xi

Place-name Equivalents   xiii

Introduction   3

1 The Jews of Austria-Hungary on the Eve of World War I   14

2 Austrian Jews and the Spirit of 1914   39

3 Mobilizing the Home Front: Patriotic War Work and
   Helping Jewish Refugees   59

4 The Experience of Jewish Soldiers   82

5 Clinging to the Old Identity, 1916–1918   106

6 The Dissolution of the Monarchy and the Crisis of Jewish Identity,
   October 1918–June 1919   128

Epilogue   162

Notes   173

Bibliography   229

Index   245

Photo gallery follows p. 58

Abbreviations

CAHJP	Central Archives for the History of the Jewish People, Jerusalem
CZA	Central Zionist Archives, Jerusalem
IKG	Israelitische Kultusgemeinde
JKor	*Jüdische Korrespondenz*
JMP	Jewish Museum, Prague
JVS	*Jüdische Volksstimme*
JZ	*Jüdische Zeitung*
KA	*Kriegsarchiv* (Archives of the War Ministry), Vienna
LBI	Leo Baeck Institute, New York
LBIYB	*Leo Baeck Institute Yearbook*
MONOIU	*Monatschrift der Oesterreichisch-Israelitische Union*
OW	*Österreichische Wochenschrift* (also known as *Dr. Blochs Österreichische Wochenschrift*)
WMZ	*Wiener Morgenzeitung*

Place-name Equivalents

With the exception of places that are known by English names (Vienna, Prague, Cracow), all locations mentioned in this book have been referred to by their official Austrian, usually German, names. The following list provides the Polish, Czech, Ukrainian, or Magyar names for those places.

Asch	Aš	Bohemia
Bielitz	Bílsko	Silesia
	Bielsko	
Bischofteinitz	Horsovsky Tyn	Bohemia
Boryslaw	Borysław	Galicia
Boskowitz	Boskovice	Moravia
Brünn	Brno	Moravia
Brüx	Most	Bohemia
Budweis	Budějovice	Bohemia
Butschowitz	Bučovice	Moravia
Czernowitz	Czerniwei	Bukovina
	Cernăuţi	
Deutschbrod	Brod Německý	Bohemia
Dorna Watra	Vatra Dornei	Bukovina
Eger	Cheb	Bohemia
Falkenau	Sokolov	Bohemia
Gablonz	Jablonec	Bohemia
Gaya	Kyjov	Moravia
Holleschau	Holešov	Moravia
Jamnitz	Jemnice	Moravia
Karlsbad	Karolovy Vary	Bohemia
Koritschau	Koryčany	Moravia

Krumau	Krumlov	Bohemia
Leipnik	Lipník	Moravia
Lemberg	Lwów	Galicia
	L'viv	
Lundenberg	Brečlav	Moravia
Mährisch Ostrau	Ostrava Moravská	Moravia
Marienbad	Mariánské Lázně	Bohemia
Nikolsburg	Mikulov	Moravia
Olmütz	Olomouc	Moravia
Pilsen	Plžen	Bohemia
Pohrlitz	Pohořelice	Moravia
Pressburg	Pozsony	Slovakia
	Bratislava	
Prossnitz	Prostějov	Moravia
Przemysl	Przemyśl	Galicia
Reichenberg	Liberec	Bohemia
Saaz	Žatec	Bohemia
Smichow	Smíchov	Bohemia
Sniatyn	Śniatyn	Galicia
Strakonitz	Strakonice	Bohemia
Teplitz-Schönau	Teplice	Bohemia
Tischnowitz	Tišnov	Moravia
Troppau	Opava	Silesia
	Opawa	
Ungarisch Brod	Brod Uherský	Moravia
Ungarisch Hradisch	Hradiště Uherské	Moravia
Wiznitz	Wyżnycia	Bukovina
Zablotow	Zabłotów	Galicia
Zizkow	Žižkow	Bohemia

Reconstructing a National Identity

Introduction

This book studies the impact of war and political crisis on Jewish national identity. It focuses on the Jews of Austria-Hungary during and just after World War I to understand how Jews, and by extension ethnic minorities in general, constructed their national, ethnic, and cultural identities—and then reconstructed them when profound political transformations required them to do so. The question is how the Jews understood their relationship to the state in which they lived, both to the multinational, supranational Habsburg Monarchy and to the nation-states that replaced it in late 1918. Their relationship reveals much about the nature of Jewish identity in the modern world, about national identity in East Central Europe, and about the meaning of national, ethnic, and cultural identity in general.

The Jews of Austria-Hungary and its successor states in the early twentieth century make an excellent case study for this exploration of Jewish and national identity. Austria-Hungary was a supranational dynastic state with no real national identity of its own other than loyalty to the Habsburg emperors and their state. Habsburg subjects did not form one nation. Rather, the Habsburg Monarchy consisted of many peoples who differed in language, culture, and ethnicity, or, to use their term, in nationality. These peoples viewed themselves as nations, and some of them hoped for some form of political sovereignty. When Austria-Hungary collapsed at the end of World War I, several nation-states replaced it, in each of which national and political loyalties were equated, and national identity was understood primarily in ethnic terms. This ethnic understanding of national identity would prove problematic for "national minorities," that is, for ethnic groups within the borders of the new states that did not belong to the dominant "nation." This understanding would also prove problematic for the Jews.

Before and during World War I the Jews felt intense loyalty to Austria-Hungary because the supranational state allowed them the luxury of separating the political, cultural, and ethnic strands in their identity. The very structure of the Habsburg Monarchy allowed Jews a great deal of latitude to adumbrate a Jewish ethnic identity, even as they adopted the culture of one or another group in whose midst they lived and articulated a staunch Austrian political loyalty. Jews in Habsburg Austria developed a tripartite identity in which they were Austrian by political loyalty, German (or Czech or Polish) by cultural affiliation, and Jewish in an ethnic sense. Unlike Jews in nation-states like Germany and France, who had to embrace a German or French national identity and felt constraints against revealing Jewish ethnicity, Jews in Habsburg Austria were comfortable with the tripartite identity they had developed in the second half of the nineteenth century. They enjoyed living in a state that defined itself wholly in political, not ethnonational, terms and understood that only such a state allowed Jews the freedom to be as Jewish as they chose.

Jewish loyalty to Austria-Hungary grew during World War I. Jews shared the patriotism and sense of common purpose that galvanized most Habsburg subjects in 1914 and sustained them through four endless years of bloody slaughter. They also felt that Austria's war was a Jewish holy war, a war to defend Austria and save the Jewish people. Because Austria's main enemy in the first two years of the war was czarist Russia, the home of pogroms and state-sponsored anti-Jewish oppression, Austria's Jews regarded their sacrifices at the front and at home as necessary to rescue Jews, including the Jews of Austrian Galicia, from Russian tyranny. World War I thus provided the Jews of Austria with the opportunity to assert their patriotism and their sense of solidarity with other Jews and to demonstrate Austrian and Jewish loyalties at the same time. Moreover, the war legitimized and strengthened the Jewish conviction that they fared best in a multinational, supranational state like Austria. Indeed, when anti-Semitic agitation began to flourish in the last two years of the war in response to food shortages and other wartime hardships, Jews clung ever more tightly to their faith that only multinational Austria could protect them from the anti-Jewish hostility rampant in the various national camps.

The collapse of the Habsburg Monarchy and the creation of the successor states in the aftermath of World War I created a grave crisis of identity for the Jews. These new nation-states would not allow the Jews the luxury of the tripartite identity that had suited them so well. The old Austria had permitted political loyalty to the state without demanding any particular national, ethnic, or even cultural affiliation. The new states, at least in theory, demanded that all inhabitants adopt the identity of the dominant nations of those states. But Jews found it nearly impossible to do so, in part because anti-Semites insisted that Jews formed a foreign element that could never join the nation. Besides experiencing anti-Semitic exclusion, most Jews could not identify themselves as members of the ethnically defined national communities, because they felt that they belonged instead to the Jewish people. They certainly had adopted the cultures of the dominant nations and passionately loved those cultures. But most Jews preferred to remain ethnically Jewish, even if such ethnicity proved problematic in the new political context.

Most Jews hoped that the new states would somehow allow them to continue their old Austrian tripartite identity, to affirm loyalty to the state and affiliation with the culture of its dominant (or another) group while still asserting Jewish ethnicity. Jews, it would seem, did not want to regard the state in ethnonational terms because a true nation-state, or at least the kind of ethnic nation-state so prevalent in East Central Europe, demanded the kind of national identity that they could not share. A state that defined national membership in political, not ethnonational, terms suited Jewish needs far better. Thus, Jews worried greatly about their status and their identity in the new states. In response to the crisis they faced, many retreated ever more assertively into a Jewish ethnic identity.

To understand Jewish identity in Habsburg Austria and its successor states it is necessary to place that identity squarely within the political, social, and cultural context in which it developed. At the same time, theoretical works on nation-hood and ethnicity written by social scientists will prove helpful in clarifying the concepts used so loosely by contemporaries and historians alike. One of the problems inherent in any study of ethnic and national identity is that the very terms of the discourse—nation, nationality, nationalism, citizenship, ethnicity—possess different meanings in different societies. Because of the ways in which states developed, and the political ideologies attending those developments, dif-ferent concepts of the nation emerged in Western Europe, Central Europe, East-ern Europe, and America, not to mention in the rest of the world. The task here is to provide a conceptually clear definition of ethnic group, nation, and nation-ality that is also grounded in the actual situation in Austria-Hungary.

Most social scientists and historians agree that national identity and national-ism are not inherent or natural parts of the human condition but rather are the result of a constellation of political and economic forces that originated in West-ern Europe in the eighteenth century and subsequently spread elsewhere. They also agree that the desire for political sovereignty is central to the modern con-cept of the nation and nationalism. Anthony Smith, for example, defines nation-alism as "an ideological movement for the attainment and maintenance of self-government and independence on behalf of a group, some of whose members conceive it to constitute an actual or potential nation like others."[1] A generation earlier, historian Hans Kohn, who grew up in Habsburg Prague, defined nation-alism as "a state of mind, in which the supreme loyalty of the individual is felt to be due to the nation-state."[2]

The first part of Kohn's phrase is a central feature of the general consensus on nationalism, that is, it is "a state of mind," an idea, not something biological or racial or inevitable, but rather something that results from common consent or will, "a daily plebiscite," in Ernst Renan's famous phrase.[3] In his essay, "What is a Nation?" delivered in 1882, Renan rejected the notion that a nation derived from dynasty, race, language, religion, geography, or even from a community of inter-est. "A nation," Renan argued, "is a soul, a spiritual principle" that possesses "a rich legacy of memories" and desires "to perpetuate the value of the heritage . . . received."[4] More recently, Benedict Anderson, in a work that has influ-enced much of contemporary discourse on nationalism, has argued that a nation is "an imagined political community—and imagined as both inherently limited and sovereign."[5] Such an imagined community could only form after the development of print capitalism—newspapers and books—had created a community of readers. Although linguistic groups do not form nations, "print-language . . . invents nationalism," Anderson insists.[6]

Some contemporary students of nationalism argue that national sentiment builds on preexisting cultural and ethnic loyalties, even if membership in cultural or ethnic groups is voluntary and not determined by biology, geography, or language.[7] A nation, according to Anthony Smith, is "a large, politicized ethnic group, defined by common culture and alleged descent."[8] Smith warns, however, against confusing nations with states, a confusion generated by the specific development of the English and French nation-states. While the state is necessary for the protection and full development of the nation, it is not identical with it.[9] On the other hand, Ernest Gellner defines nationalism as "a political principle which holds that the political and national unit should be congruent," so that "ethnic boundaries should not cut across political ones."[10] A look at the historical development of the nation and the nation-state will help clarify the relationship between ethnic and national identity.

Before the eighteenth century, ethnic and political borders did not coincide. Beginning at that point, nation-states formed in Western Europe, based on the principle that all resident citizens constituted the nation. Liberal principles of popular sovereignty and civil rights provided the foundation for a civic form of national identity here. In these nation-states, common cultural communities also emerged, crafted by the dominant ethnic/cultural group that assimilated other groups under the banner of a common national culture. In Central Europe, on the other hand, nation-states did not develop until later. In the meantime, ethnic groups developed national consciousness and the desire for political legitimation. They based their national identity not on the civic principles of the French Revolution but on concepts of the *Volk,* people or ethnos, and they came into conflict with the existing states.[11]

The clearest analysis of the different concepts of the nation that developed in eighteenth- and nineteenth-century Europe is Rogers Brubaker, *Citizenship and Nationhood in France and Germany*. A political sociologist, Brubaker argues that France, with its long-established, unified territorial state, developed a concept of the nation that was essentially political, state-centered, and inclusive. Building on a territorial base, the French Revolution and its republican ideology invented the idea that the nation was composed of citizens, that is, of all residents of the state, who participated equally in the political process. Borrowing the concept of citizen from the Greek polis and medieval city and broadening it to include all men, France became a nation-state, which understood the nation as a polity ruled by its citizens, not by privileged feudal orders. Wedded to this republican ideology and assuming that republican citizenship required a common French national culture, French elites energetically assimilated all residents of France, including immigrants, into French culture. They felt confident that they could make them all bona fide members of the French nation. Although the late nineteenth century witnessed a surge of xenophobic and exclusionist ethnic nationalism, the predominant national ideology in France remained political and assimilationist.

Germany, on the other hand, was not a unified nation-state until 1871. Indeed, in 1815, there were 39 German states. This territorial fragmentation produced a different concept of the nation in German-speaking Central Europe, one influenced by romanticism and based on ethnicity, culture, and the community of descent. This "ethnocultural" concept of the nation, concerned with the *Volk* and its culture, developed independently of the states, which did not regard themselves as nations. German nationalists sought to create a German nation-state, one in which state and *Volk* would be congruent, but the German *Reich* established in 1871 did not contain all ethnic Germans. For political reasons, the Germans in the Habsburg Monarchy were excluded. Much to the disappointment of German nationalists, moreover, Germany also contained communities of non-Germans, especially Poles in parts of Prussia. Even after the creation of the German nation-state, Germans—both within and without the Reich—continued to understand the German nation in ethnocultural terms as a *Volk*. Although Germany adopted many principles of liberalism, including representative government, most Germans conceived the nation not as a community of citizens but as a community of descent. They could not imagine that non-Germans could assimilate into the German nation.[12]

Thus two competing models of nationhood circulated in Europe, one that viewed the nation as a political collectivity of equal citizens who necessarily participated in a common culture, the other defining the nation as an ethnocultural community of descent with political aspirations. In practice, of course, both models overlapped, even in France and Germany.[13] Moreover, as Anthony Smith argues so forcefully, modern nations can command the ardent support of their populations precisely because they built on loyalty to preexisting ethnic groups, whose members shared a common culture and saw themselves as biologically related.

Social scientists debate the meaning of ethnic identity, but most would agree that ethnic consciousness, like nationhood, is not innate but derives from myths developed to explain the origins and destiny of a particular group, its sense of shared history and culture, and its connection with a specific territory. Agreeing with Renan, these theorists reject the notion that language determines ethnic loyalty, even if language forms part of the shared culture of an ethnic group, along with religion, customs, institutions, laws, folklore, architecture, dress, food, music, and art.[14] Ethnic myths predicated on religious separateness serve especially well to perpetuate ethnic exclusiveness, especially among diaspora ethnic groups. Priesthoods and religious communities, Anthony Smith argues, are even more important than polities or territories in preserving ethnicity.[15] John Armstrong agrees that "the potency of ethnoreligious identity continues to rival the more widespread contemporary ethnolinguistic identity."[16]

Perhaps the most important contemporary theoretician of ethnicity is the Norwegian social anthropologist Fredrik Barth. Barth warns against any simplistic equation of ethnicity and culture and asserts that what is most important is how members of ethnic groups distinguish themselves from nonmembers. Thus it is the boundaries between groups, the definition of insider and outsider, that is crucial in defining ethnic groups. What is central is the "ethnic boundary that defines the group not the cultural stuff that it encloses." Even though individuals may cross the boundaries and disappear into other groups, the boundaries themselves can persist, as they do even when the cultural content of ethnic identity changes over time. What matters, therefore, is the subjective sense of members and nonmembers of who belongs and who does not.[17]

These prevalent theories of nationalism and ethnicity help explain the nature of the Habsburg Monarchy and the anomalous position of the Jews within it. The Habsburg Monarchy was not a nation-state by any definition, not by the political definition developed in France that regarded the nation as a polity of equal citizens who adopted a uniform national culture, and certainly not by the ethnocultural definition developed in German-speaking Central Europe. The Dual Monarchy was an old-fashioned dynastic, territorial state that had adopted many principles of liberalism in 1867 but did not regard itself as a nation and did not create a unified national culture or national identity. Indeed, its ruling elites—the Habsburgs, the bureaucracy, and the army—regarded the Dual Monarchy as a supranational state. The Austrian half of the Monarchy even possessed the profoundly nonnational official name "the kingdoms and provinces represented in the imperial parliament [in Vienna]." One could easily be loyal to this state without adopting any particular culture or national identity. Although the state itself was not a nation, during the nineteenth century many of the Monarchy's subjects identified themselves as members of one or another nation within the borders of the state. Austria-Hungary contained many nations, nations that defined themselves, to use Brubaker's terminology, as ethnocultural communities of descent. They shared a common language and culture, in some cases a separate religion, and in other cases the memory of former political independence. They conceived of themselves as nations, not in the French sense of equal political responsibility, but in the romantic, ethnonational sense that emerged all over Central and Eastern Europe.

Many of these nations also sought some measure of political autonomy, often agitating relentlessly for their goals. In 1867 the Hungarians succeeded in forcing the Habsburgs to recognize their political aspirations, granting them near-sovereignty within the Kingdom of Hungary and parity for Hungary within the renamed "Austria-Hungary." Yet the quest for autonomy, and later sovereignty, of many national groups conflicted with geographical reality. Few of the Habsburg nations were territorially concentrated in a manner consistent with creating homogenous nation-states—states, that is, composed of the members of one nation, defined in terms of the ethnocultural descent they held so dear. Most regions of the Monarchy contained many different nations, whose romantic notions of nationhood prevented them from creating a state based solely on political citizenship, either before or after World War I. Even within Hungary, which fashioned itself a nation-state like Germany, the Magyars formed less than half of all inhabitants, and many of the others resented Magyar hegemony.[18]

Jews did not form one of the nations of Austria. Although officially defined as a religion, Jews formed an ethnic group, most of whose members did not have political aspirations. Barth's definition of ethnicity is especially well suited to describe the anomalous position of the Jews in Austria-Hungary and elsewhere. Jews perceived strong ethnic boundaries between themselves and their Gentile neighbors, a perception shared by those neighbors. Even as Jews acculturated in the nineteenth-century, abandoning many or even most of the features of traditional Jewish culture in favor of the social and cultural mores of the European bourgeoisie, they continued to regard themselves as an ethnic group within the larger society. Jews in nineteenth century Habsburg Austria felt comfortable adopting the culture of one or another of the nations in whose midst they lived while still adhering to a sense of Jewish ethnic solidarity. To be sure, there were Jews who longed to abandon Jewish identity altogether, but most Jews understood that they formed a separate group in society. Their Gentile neighbors agreed that Jews remained Jews despite adopting German, Czech, or Polish culture.

Of course, Barth's emphasis on boundaries over cultural content in forming ethnic identity is too strong. For most ethnic groups, common culture, a sense of shared history and destiny, and sometimes religious ritual also contributed to separate identity. Such was surely the case for Jews, who despite their acculturation continued to believe that they shared a common past and future and that they were bound together by a common religion, even when they did not observe its regulations. Indeed, Jews have long formed a quintessential religio-ethnic group, whose distinctive and traditionally despised religion helped preserve a sense of separate identity.

Habsburg Austria proved most receptive to Jewish ethnic identity.[19] The multinational, supranational character of the state provided a relatively congenial atmosphere for the Jews, allowing them to retain their ethnic attachments even as they adopted the culture of one or another nation and espoused a fervent state patriotism. Indeed, the very fact that the state was only a political construct and not a nation made it very easy for the Jews to adumbrate a staunch Austrian loyalty without having to adopt any particular national identity. The supranational state permitted the Jews to develop a tripartite identity that suited them very well. They could adopt German (or Czech or Polish) culture without having to join the German, Czech, or Polish nation. Because of their sense of Jewish ethnicity, most Jews did not want to join those nations except in a cultural sense. Members of nations that understood identity in terms of (alleged) descent were generally not eager to welcome the Jews as full-fledged members of the national community. Anti-Semitism may have flourished in late Habsburg Austria, but Jews nevertheless appreciated the space the political system gave them to be as Jewish as they chose.

During World War I, Jewish patriotism and Jewish ethnic solidarity surged. Fighting in the army allowed Jewish men to demonstrate in the most concrete way their utter loyalty to Kaiser and Reich. About 300,000 Jewish men served in the Habsburg armed forces during the war; they suffered high casualties and received large numbers of medals for their bravery. In the war against Russia, they also fought for a Jewish cause and against an enemy of the Jews. On the home front, Jews—and especially Jewish women—mobilized to do patriotic war work and demonstrate their loyalty to the Habsburg Monarchy. Since most who benefited from their effort were fellow Jews, however, those who did war charity also experienced the intertwining of Austrian patriotism and Jewish solidarity. They provided desperately needed help to large numbers of Galician Jewish refugees who fled their homes in the face of the Russian invasions of 1914 and 1916, refugees who were simultaneously Austrian citizens, victims of Austria's war, and fellow Jews in distress. Thus both the military front and the home front reinforced both the Austrian and Jewish loyalty of the Jews.

Political events in the last two years of the war, however, presented the Jews with a grave crisis. Not only did anti-Semitism proliferate in a war-weary and hungry population, but nationalist politicians increasingly lobbied for greater autonomy and for a reconfiguration of Austria-Hungary's political arrangements. In a period of uncertainly about the future of the Monarchy, especially after the death of the old emperor Franz Joseph at the end of 1916, Jews desperately clung to their old tripartite identity and vigorously insisted that only the continuity of the Dual Monarchy served the interests of all its subjects, not least of all the Jews. Fearful of the fate of the Jews in independent nation-states, in which nationalist, anti-Semitic leaders could govern unchecked by the more tolerant Austrian central government, Jews prayed that the Habsburg Monarchy would persist. When it collapsed in November 1918, they mourned deeply.

The dissolution of the Monarchy and the creation of successor states eradicated the foundations of the comfortable tripartite Jewish identity. The new states regarded themselves as nation-states, even if they still contained sizeable ethnic minorities, and thus would not tolerate the separation of cultural, national, and political identities. They demanded that the Jews identify with the dominant nation, not only in the cultural sense, but in the national sense as well. Unfortunately, though, anti-Semitism flourished in most of these states, and radical anti-Semites denied that Jews could ever become part of the nation in any sense at all. The Jews in these states had to refashion an identity for themselves, consonant with Jewish tradition and with the new political realities. Such a reconstruction was extraordinarily difficult. In the period between November 1918, when the Monarchy collapsed and the successor states declared their independence, and June 1919, when the Versailles Treaty and treaties with the new states were concluded, Jews engaged in soul-searching debate about their identity and their relationship to the new nation-states. Many Jews responded to the crisis by hoping to preserve as much of the old tripartite identity as possible, even if it was no longer politically realistic to do so.

This book begins with discussion of the Jews in the late Habsburg Monarchy, in an effort to understand how and why Jews developed this tripartite identity in the first place. Subsequently, it focuses on the impact of World War I on the Jews, both on their actual behavior on the front and at home and on the ideologies that Jews created to give meaning to their experience in the war. Finally, the book analyzes how the Jews confronted the political turmoil and growing threat to the continuity of Austria-Hungary in the last two years of the war and how they reacted to the crisis generated by the collapse of the Monarchy and the creation of the successor states. A study of the impact of war and political disintegration on Jewish identity, the book covers the period from the summer of 1914, when the assassination of Habsburg heir-apparent Franz Ferdinand in Sarajevo led to the outbreak of hostilities, until June 1919, when the Versailles Treaty ushered in a new period in European history. How the Jews in the successor states fully realized the identities they cautiously began crafting in the months after World War I would be the topic of another study.

This book limits itself to the German-speaking Jews in the Austrian half of the Dual Monarchy. Numbering over two million, the Jews of Austria-Hungary were an extremely diverse group, and although all of them felt loyal to the Monarchy, not all experienced the crisis of its collapse in the same way. As will be discussed in the next chapter, the Jews in the Hungarian half of the Monarchy had adopted a Hungarian national identity in the second half of the nineteenth century. After the compromise of 1867 gave Hungary sovereignty in most areas, Hungary fashioned itself into a nation-state and undertook to assimilate non-Magyars, including Jews, into the Magyar nation. Thus the collapse of the Habsburg Monarchy did not cause a crisis for Hungarian Jews, who had already adopted Magyar culture and national identity and could easily adjust to the new Hungary. Despite anti-Semitism in interwar Hungary, the Jews who lived there were comfortable with their Hungarian national identity. Similarly, in Bohemia and Moravia, some Jews already had adopted a Czech identity before the war, and they felt vindicated by the creation of independent Czechoslovakia. On the other hand, the large community of Yiddish-speaking Jews of Galicia and Bukovina, many of whom still adhered to traditional, religious Jewish culture, certainly mourned the demise of the Habsburg Monarchy and feared for their physical safety in the face of virulent Polish, Ukrainian, and Romanian anti-Semitism. Because the war had destroyed their homes, however, while the economic basis of their existence lay in shambles, and vicious pogroms endangered their very lives, they hardly had the luxury of debating their identity or constructing a new one in the chaotic months after the war. Indeed, the virulence of anti-Semitism in interwar Poland and Romania, combined with the persistence of traditional Jewish culture and the popularity of Zionism in those countries, guaranteed that Jews living there had little interest in adopting a Polish or Romanian identity. They continued to identify primarily as Jews.[20]

This book will focus on the German-speaking Jews of Austria because it was these Jews who faced most acutely the crisis of identity both during and after the war. It was the Jews who had identified with German culture, whether they lived in the Czech lands, in Bukovina, or in Vienna, who endured the gravest challenge after the dissolution of the Monarchy. In Czechoslovakia, Jews who had associated with German culture now had to craft a new identity for themselves in a state dominated by Czechs. Fortunately, interwar Czechoslovakia was relatively tolerant of ethnic minorities, and so the Jews there had some latitude in forging their new identity. The opposite was the case in interwar Romania, where the government pursued an anti-Semitic policy. The German-speaking Jews of Bukovina had no desire to become Romanians and increasingly turned to Jewish nationalism. Above all in the German-speaking lands of the Monarchy, in the rump state called German-Austria (*Deutschösterreich*), Jews faced a terrible dilemma. They already adhered to the dominant culture, but they did not really see themselves as part of the German *Volk* in a country that now saw itself as a true nation-state in which culture, *Volk*, and state were one. Here, too, anti-Semites refused membership in the German nation to the Jews. Jews now had to reconstruct a new kind of identity as they mourned the old one that had fit their needs so perfectly.

In all three areas, Jews hoped that the new nation-states would nevertheless allow them the luxury of the old tripartite identity, which combined political loyalty to the state with cultural affiliation with its dominant group and a sense of Jewish ethnicity. The political and economic traumas of the interwar period rendered such an identity problematic, but it was one the Jews preferred.

The analysis of Jewish ideology and behavior presented here is based on a close reading of memoirs—published and unpublished—and of the extensive Habsburg Jewish press. These newspapers, which served primarily as a forum for debate on current issues, reflected a wide range of political ideologies. Although newspapers do not reflect the views of all individuals, they are nevertheless crucial sources because, as Benedict Anderson so cogently argues, they create the community of readers central to the development of ethnic and national identity. Indeed, Jewish newspapers, along with other publicistic sources like pamphlets and sermons (also used here), served to construct and reconstruct Jewish identity in this period. In the memoirs they wrote many decades later, former Habsburg Jews remembered that identity with great fondness. While it is true that these memoirs, written mostly after the Holocaust, tend to view the pre-World War I period in idyllic terms, especially in contrast to what came later, there is no reason to doubt their veracity on basic issues of identity. This study also relies heavily on the archives of the Jewish communities of Vienna and Prague, the Central Zionist Archives, and the Austrian War Archives.

A Note on Place-names

Habsburg historians are bedeviled by the fact that many towns and cities have more than one name. The authorities in Vienna gave German names to most places, but the national groups often used different names in their own languages. In addition, Hungarian authorities gave Magyar names to places even if non-Magyars lived in them. The successor states used the names preferred by the dominant nationalities of those states, even for cities and towns in regions inhabited by national minorities. Nationalist pride further complicated nomenclature. After 1918 it became politically incorrect to use the old Habsburg, German names for cities and towns in Poland, Czechoslovakia, Romania, and Yugoslavia, whose citizens regarded those names as symbols of the Habsburg oppression they had successfully thrown off. The changing borders of those states and the resulting shift in dominant nation groups made the situation even more complex.

Some examples are in order. The city in eastern Galicia that the Habsburg authorities called Lemberg was called Lwów by the Poles, both before 1918 and in independent Poland between 1918 and 1939. But, this city, which contained a mixed population of Poles, Ukrainians (and Jews before World War II), became part of the Ukrainian Soviet Socialist Republic in 1944, and is now part of independent Ukraine, whose leaders call it L'viv, a name long used by its Ukrainian inhabitants. Similarly, the Habsburg authorities called the city in western Slovakia Pressburg, but since Slovakia was part of the Kingdom of Hungary, the local authorities called it Poszony. The city was inhabited by Magyars, Germans, and Jews, but when Slovakia became part of interwar Czechoslovakia, its new masters gave it the Slovak name Bratislava. In Bohemia and Moravia, many places had both German and Czech names, the German names used by the Habsburg authorities and the German minority, and the Czech names used by the Czechs and later by the Czechoslovakian government. What the Germans called Budweis, for example, the Czechs knew as Budějovice.

Many historians, sympathetic to national self-determination and not wanting to offend nationalist sensibilities, have opted to use the names preferred by the Habsburg successor states rather than the Habsburg German (or Hungarian) names. I find this method disturbingly anachronistic. Moreover, a study of the Jews, especially one that focuses on the German-speaking Jews in the Austrian half of the Monarchy, on their Habsburg loyalty, and on the crisis they experienced with the collapse of the Monarchy, should certainly use the place-names used by the Jews themselves. Most Jews in Austria used German place-names. Not only German-speaking Jews did so, but so did the large numbers of Yiddish-speaking Jews of Galicia and Bukovina, whose Yiddish place-names resembled the German ones. Thus this book will use the German names for all places, with the exception of cities that have English names, like Vienna, Prague, and Cracow. I hope that I will not offend any national sensibilities in my desire for historical accuracy. See "Place-name Equivalents" (p. xiii) for a list of alternate names for the cities and towns discussed here.

1

The Jews of Austria-Hungary on the Eve of World War I

Numbering over two million, Austro-Hungarian Jews in the early twentieth century were a group that defies simple description. They were not monolithic with a universally held identity or life-style. As the Dual Monarchy itself was a complicated mosaic of disparate national, ethnic, religious, linguistic, economic, and social groups, so the Jews of the Monarchy embraced a whole range of radically different identities. These identities all took Jewish tradition as a starting point, but they developed differently depending on the region of the Monarchy in which the Jews resided, on the degree to which Jews had experienced socioeconomic modernization, and on the dynamics of Jewish involvement in the contentious nationality politics of Austria-Hungary. The Jews of Austria-Hungary did not share an occupational profile, even if they all differed from the prevailing economic patterns. They did not have a common language, although many did share a second or third tongue. They did not live in the same region, even if they concentrated in a few provinces, or hold a common political ideology, even if they agreed on some issues. They did not even all practice the religion of their ancestors.

Nevertheless, Jews and non-Jews alike considered the Jews of Austria-Hungary to be a separate, identifiable group. Such an evaluation should not be surprising. The Jews, after all, often differed from their neighbors in economic preferences, in political loyalties, and in social affiliations. Moreover, historically the Jews had formed a distinct group in Europe, pursuing different occupations and, more importantly, a different, and detested, religion. Despite decades of assimilation into the dominant cultures of the region, the Jews remained different, although whether one evaluated that difference positively, negatively, or neutrally depended on one's point of view. The Jews themselves had a sense that they formed a distinct group in Austro-Hungarian society, one that was bound by a common history, common problems, and a sense of belonging to the same people. Virtually everyone else in Austria-Hungary agreed.

Jews were almost equally divided between the two halves of the Dual Monarchy (see Map 1). The Kingdom of Hungary contained 932,458 Jews in 1910, and Jews formed 4.5% of the total population.[1] In "Austria," or, as it was officially known, "the kingdoms and provinces represented in the imperial parliament" (in Vienna), 1,313,687 Jews resided, forming 4.6% of the total population in 1910.[2] Jews did not live all over Cisleithanian Austria, as the Austrian half of the Monarchy was often called. Indeed, most regions of Austria, in particular the Alpine and coastal provinces, had almost no Jews at all. The vast majority, about three quarters of "Austrian" Jews, lived in the northeastern provinces of Galicia and Bukovina. Jews formed a substantial minority in Galicia. Numbering 871,906, they formed 11% of the total population in 1910. In that year, Bukovina contained 102,919 Jews, who formed 13% of the total population.[3]

Virtually all of the rest of the Jews of "Austria" lived in Bohemia, Moravia, and Silesia, or in the capital, Vienna. In 1910, 85,826 Jews lived in Bohemia, 41,158 in Moravia, and 12,442 in Silesia.[4] By far the largest Jewish community in Austria was the Jewish community of Vienna, one of the largest urban Jewish communities in Europe. In 1910, 175,318 Jews lived in the imperial capital, forming 9% of the total urban population of over two million.[5] Almost all of these Jews were immigrants to the city or the children of immigrants from Hungary, Bohemia, Moravia, and Galicia, who arrived after 1848, when the government ended traditional restrictions on Jewish residence in Vienna.[6]

The situation of the Jews in Austria-Hungary can best be understood within the context of general political developments in the Monarchy. The Habsburg Monarchy was a supranational, dynastic state that contained a patchwork of territories acquired over centuries for a variety of dynastic, military, and family reasons. In addition to their hereditary lands, such provinces as Upper and Lower Austria, Styria, Carinthia, Salzburg, Tyrol, and Vorarlberg, the Habsburgs acquired the Bohemian lands in the sixteenth century, the kingdom of the Crown of St. Stephen—that is, Hungary—in the seventeenth century, and Galicia in the eighteenth century, as part of the partitions of Poland. As was the case in most premodern dynastic states, different rules applied in different parts of the realm, and local noblemen jealously guarded their hallowed rights to administer their own territory. At the end of the eighteenth century, the enlightened, reforming Habsburg emperor, Joseph II, embarked on a campaign to centralize, bureaucratize, and Germanize his realm. While extraordinarily important for Jewish modernization, Joseph's efforts met with much resistance in some places, especially in Hungary.[7]

The forces of liberalism and nationalism transformed the Habsburg Monarchy in the nineteenth century. In 1867, after Habsburg defeat in the Austro-Prussian war of 1866 made it clear that Austria would be excluded from a unified German empire, the emperor bowed to liberal demands and transformed the realm into a constitutional monarchy with a representative government. At the same time rising national consciousness in Hungary allied with traditional aristocratic privilege forced the Monarchy into the historic compromise, the *Ausgleich* of 1867. This agreement created "Austria-Hungary" and made Hungary a sovereign country, united with the rest of the Monarchy only by a common foreign

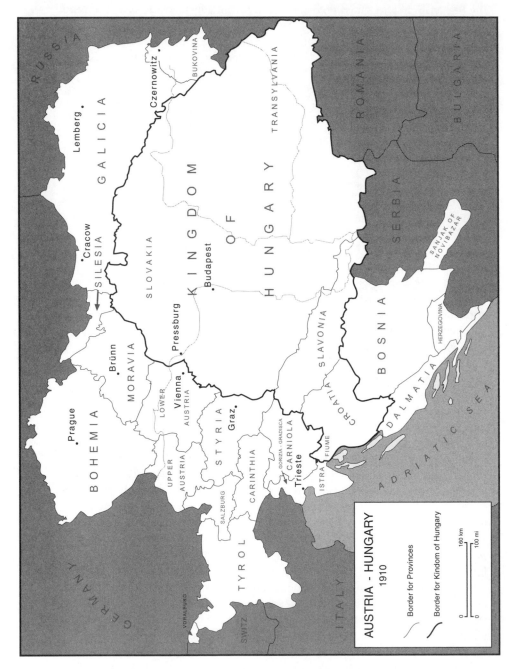

AUSTRIA - HUNGARY
1910

Border for Provinces
Border for Kindom of Hungary

0   160 km
0   100 mi

MAP I

policy, common army, common foreign trade, and allegiance to the person of the monarch, whom the Hungarians recognized as king, not as emperor. In all other respects, Hungary and "Austria"—that is, all Habsburg domains except Hungary—were foreign countries.

The Compromise of 1867 assuaged Hungarian national demands, but other aspiring national groups in Austria soon wanted a similar arrangement or at least a far larger measure of national autonomy than they had traditionally enjoyed. The final decades of the Habsburg Monarchy, from 1867 until the dissolution of the Monarchy at the end of World War I, witnessed an outpouring of nationalist agitation in Austria.[8] Nationalist politicians had no interest in transforming Austria into a unitary nation-state like Hungary, which sought national uniformity at the expense of her own numerous national, linguistic, and religious minorities. On the contrary, spokesmen for different national groups in Austria wanted "national rights" for their own groups. While these groups did not mention sovereignty until 1918, they certainly sought linguistic and cultural rights. The dilemma of Austrian politics at the end of the nineteenth and beginning of the twentieth century was how to balance the political demands of all of the national groups with each other and with the needs of a state that remained supranational. The government neutralized Polish nationalism in Austria by allowing the Polish nobility in Galicia a large measure of home rule.[9] Other national groups, especially the Czechs, felt increasingly aggrieved by their perceived inferior status in the Monarchy, and they escalated their demands to the point that normal parliamentary politics became impossible.[10] The Germans, who had traditionally considered themselves the *Staatsvolk,* felt beleaguered when the government acceded to demands of the Czechs and other Slavs for linguistic parity.[11] Indeed, the issue of language became the focal point of nationalist agitation and the symbol of national identity.

Throughout these decades of rising national consciousness among Austria's nationalities, the Austrian state, at least in theory, remained above the nationalist fray. It is true that the government and its institutions—the bureaucracy, the army, and so forth—used the German language, but the government did not think of itself as German in a national or ethnic sense. Indeed, the Emperor Franz Joseph, who reigned from 1848 until 1916, his army officers, and his upper level bureaucrats thought of themselves as loyal to Austria and to the Habsburg dynasty, not to an ethnically defined German nation.[12] They were patriotic, to be sure, but to a supranational Austria, a territorial, dynastic state, not a nation either in the French sense of a nation of equal citizens or in the ethnonational sense so pervasive in Central Europe.[13]

State patriotism in Austria—which existed not only in the upper ranks of officialdom, but to judge from the outpouring of enthusiasm in August 1914 was also diffused in the population at large—was therefore not coterminous with national identity as it was in either France or Germany. There was no Austrian national identity, even if there was an Austrian state identity because in Austria, unlike in Western Europe, state and nation were not the same. Instead, the Monarchy recognized that within its borders lived at least eleven different nations, not defined in a political sense as peoples possessing sovereignty, nor defined in territorial terms as the inhabitants of a province or region, but rather defined in ethnic, cultural, or linguistic terms, or as "ethnocultural communities of descent," to use Brubaker's term.

In its constitution of 1867, Austria, which considered itself a nationalities-state, not a nation-state, recognized the equality of its nationalities and guaranteed to them the right to use their national languages in public life.[14] To simplify matters, the authorities determined affiliation with one or another nation—officially called *Volksstämme* (national-ethnic groups)—through language, and specifically through *Umgangssprache,* the language of daily speech, not mother tongue. Language is not necessarily the most accurate gauge of national affiliation, but it is easily measured, at least in theory, and the nationalities of Austria themselves regarded it as the symbol of their national identities and struggles.

The Monarchy as a whole contained eleven official nationalities: Germans, Hungarians, Czechs, Poles, Ruthenes, Romanians, Croats, Serbs, Slovaks, Slovenes, and Italians. Within Hungary, which considered itself a nation-state, the Magyars, who formed only 48% of the total population, dominated politics and culture, and they attempted to Magyarize the other national groups in Hungary, including Slovaks in the north, Serbs and Croats in the southwest, Romanians in Transylvania in the southeast, and Germans and Jews throughout.[15] In Austria the situation was far more complicated. The Germans considered themselves the *Staatsvolk,* but in 1879 the government came to rely on Slavic support, especially on Poles, and Germans no longer dominated politics in Austria. Yet Germans continued to play a leading role in the economic and cultural spheres. The German language was the language of government, the economy, and high culture, providing a common medium of communication among all of Austria's (indeed all of Austria-Hungary's) educated inhabitants. Even as measured by the standards of Austria's census, the Germans—that is, people who said their language of daily speech was German—counted for only 36% of the population of Austria. In 1910 they formed virtually the entire population in Upper and Lower Austria, Salzburg, and Vorarlberg, almost 80% of the population of Carinthia, and 70% of the population of Styria. In Tyrol, German-speakers accounted for 57% of the population, sharing that province with Italians. Germans were a very important minority in the Czech lands, providing 37% of the population of Bohemia, 28% of the population of Moravia, and 44% of the population of Silesia in 1910. Elsewhere their numbers were far lower. Germans were a negligible proportion of the populations of Carniola, the Dalmatian coastal provinces, Trieste, and Galicia, but they did form 21% of the population of Bukovina.[16]

Various Slavic peoples inhabited much of Cisleithanian Austria. According to the Austrian census, which measured national affiliation by language of daily speech, the Czechs predominated in Bohemia and Moravia, forming 63% and 72% of the populations of those provinces, respectively, and 24% of the population of Silesia. Poles provided 52% of the population of Galicia and 32% of the population of Silesia. The number of Poles in Galicia was skewed by the fact that the authorities did not count Yiddish as a language and arbitrarily counted the masses of Yiddish-speaking Jews in Galicia as Poles. Ruthenians—Ukrainians who practiced the Orthodox rite but recognized the authority of the Pope in

Rome—formed 40% of the population of Galicia and 39% of Bukovina. In addition, Austria was home to Slovenes in Carniola, Gorizia-Gradisca, Styria, Carinthia, Trieste, and Istria, and to Serbs and Croats (counted together) in Istria and Dalmatia. Finally, two non-Slavic groups (besides the Germans) also inhabited Austria: Italians in Trieste, Gorizia-Gradisca, Istria, and Tyrol; and Romanians in Bukovina, who formed 34% of the population there.[17]

Self-appointed leaders of each of these nationalities tirelessly articulated cultural and political programs. It is less clear exactly how ordinary Germans, Czechs, Poles, Ruthenes, or Italians understood their national identity and how they integrated their national identity with their loyalty to the supranational Dual Monarchy. Before the last third of the nineteenth century, national identity was fairly fluid, and many residents of the Habsburg Monarchy switched national identity simply by learning a new language and adopting a new culture. Germans and Jews in Hungary, for example, Magyarized and became Hungarian. In Bohemia and Moravia, the barriers between Germans and Czechs were easily crossed in both directions.[18] Only at the end of the nineteenth century, when the nationality struggle intensified, nationalist ideas proliferated through increasingly accessible education, and racially determined notions of national identity flourished, did belonging to a nationality become more rigid. Even so, it remained unclear exactly what "Czech-ness" meant to a Czech or "German-ness" meant to a German, even if the radical nationalists among them had clear, exclusivist notions of Czech or German nationalism. Migration further complicated the issue of national identity by creating mixed populations in many cities. Migrants assimilated into the dominant cultures of their new homes, but their identities often remained ambiguous.[19]

Neither in Austria nor in Hungary—nor indeed in any country of the Western world—did the government regard the Jews as a nation. Possessing no territory, no common spoken language, no normal economic distribution, and no political aspirations, to the nineteenth century observer the Jews did not display the usual attributes of a nation. Thus Austrian authorities did not count the Jews as a *Volksstamm,* a nationality, according to article 19 of the constitution. They also did not accord Yiddish the status of a language, a *Volkssprache,* because not all Jews in Austria spoke it. Instead, Habsburg authorities (like all other Western governments) regarded the Jews solely as adherents of a particular religious confession: Judaism. Jews, then, were members of a religious community, akin to Catholics, Protestants, members of the Orthodox churches, and Muslims.[20]

This religious definition of Jewishness was itself the product of the modern age and of the process of emancipation begun in the eighteenth century. Traditionally, Jews regarded themselves as a nation in exile. That is, medieval Jews believed that they had been exiled for their sins from the land of Israel, their ancient homeland, and they expected to return there in the messianic future. Redemption, for which they prayed three times a day, included not only the creation of a perfect world of justice and love, but also their reconstitution as a political nation in the land of Israel and the restoration there of the Davidic dynasty. European society and rulers in the Middle Ages agreed that the Jews constituted a separate, foreign "nation," and they granted the Jews charters that spelled out their rights, duties, and obligations, including self-government and the right to live according to Jewish law. Because of traditional Christian antipathy to Judaism, European states also severely restricted the Jews economically, by residence, and politically, isolating them and burdening them with extra taxes. Expelled from most of Western and Central Europe in the course of the late Middle Ages, the Jews encountered hostility at all levels of European society. Christian antipathy to Judaism as a religion generated most of that hostility, but social and economic tensions between Jews and Christians also contributed to it. Before the modern period, everyone understood that the Jews and Judaism were coterminous, but no one defined the Jews strictly as a religious group. Indeed, the Jews were a foreign "nation" whose boundaries were defined by religion.[21] No one, however, considered the Jews a nation in the modern, political sense of that word. Rather, the Jews formed a religio-ethnic group, a diaspora ethnic group, a pariah ethnic group.[22] Jews and non-Jews reinforced the boundaries between them, and Jewish ethnicity found secure support in a complex system of religious law and custom. Yet because the Jews remembered a time of political independence and wished for its reconstitution, they formed not just an ethnic group, but also a potential nation.

Beginning at the end of the eighteenth century, and accelerating in the nineteenth century, intellectual movements like the Enlightenment and political movements such as liberalism called for an end to the complicated web of restrictions that had separated Jews from Christians in Europe. European liberals sought to make the Jews equal citizens of the lands in which they lived, to subject them to a uniform code of law, and to integrate them into civil society. In exchange for this emancipation, liberals demanded that the Jews abandon Jewish national identity and adopt the national identity of the countries in which they lived. Thus, for example, when France emancipated her Jews during the French Revolution, those who proposed such emancipation made it clear that the Jews had to observe French, not Jewish law, and had to be French, not Jewish, by national identity, although if Brubaker is right about French national identity, the revolutionaries only demanded that Jews join the nation of citizens and adopt French culture. In the German states in the nineteenth century, liberals who supported emancipation vigorously demanded that Jews renounce their "foreign" Jewish identity and become "Germans," adopting not only German culture, but joining the German national community as well. Although some emancipators in both France and Germany hoped that Jewish group identity would dissolve completely, most assumed that Jewish identity in the future would consist entirely of a religious identity. Jews would differ from their compatriots solely in the matter of religious faith, and Judaism would be reduced to a religious confession.[23]

For their part, Jews in Europe who sought emancipation and integration into European society and culture eagerly embraced this new definition of Jewish identity. Jewish leaders in nineteenth-century France and Germany publicly asserted that Jews were French or German by culture and national identity and Jewish only in religious faith. Nineteenth-century Western and Central European Jews "assimilated," or rather, "acculturated," adopting the culture and political loyalties of the countries in which they lived, even if the process of social transformation was slower than many of the emancipators had hoped. They abandoned traditional Jewish occupations in petty trade and entered more respectable positions in commerce and the professions, exchanging extreme poverty for middle-class status in the process. They learned the languages of the countries in which they lived, obtained secular education—and increasingly neglected to observe traditional Jewish ritual. In Germany, where emancipation was protracted, Jewish reformers stripped Judaism of its national elements by removing from the liturgy those prayers that called for the restoration of Jewish sovereignty in the land of Israel.

By the end of the nineteenth century, emancipated, modernized German or French Jews agreed that Jewish identity rested solely on religion and contained no national dimension. Nevertheless, most German and French Jews continued to feel solidarity with other Jews and a sense of Jewish group identity that transcended religion. Although they identified as German or French by nationality and culture, they continued to act as members of a Jewish ethnic group in societies that eschewed ethnic diversity. Moreover, the Jewish desire for continuity and the influence of ever-present anti-Semitism meant that Jews tended to socialize with and marry other Jews, thus guaranteeing the persistence of Jewish ethnic distinctiveness. Of course, this Jewish ethnicity received its legitimacy through religious tradition, even if many Jews no longer practiced the rules of that tradition.[24]

The Jewish identity of German or French Jews was, therefore, not merely religious, even if Jewish public pronouncements asserted the solely religious basis of Jewish separateness. At the same time, however, the Jews in France or Germany did feel themselves to be part of the French or German nation, not just because they had adopted French or German culture and political loyalty, but because they had become French or German in the national sense. Loyalty to France and Germany was not just political loyalty to a state; it entailed membership in the national community, whether determined politically or ethnoculturally. Jews in those countries, therefore, were members of a Jewish ethnic group and part of the French or German nation at the same time—or at least so they thought. The emergence of radical antisemitism at the end of the nineteenth century, especially of its racist version, signified that some Frenchmen or Germans refused to grant Jews membership in the nation. The antisemites regarded the Jews as dangerous foreigners, or worse, as racial enemies, who sought the destruction of the nation, defined by blood. Despite the proliferation of anti-Semitic groups and parties at the end of the century, the Jews continued to consider themselves Frenchmen or Germans and Jewish only in matters of religion. In 1893 the founders of the main organization created to combat anti-Semitism in Germany named it the *Centralverein deutscher Staatsbürger jüdischen Glaubens,* the Central Organization of German Citizens of the Jewish Faith. It is telling, however, that the founders spoke of German citizens, thus emphasizing their loyalty to the German nation as a polity, not a *Volk.*[25]

In nineteenth-century Austria-Hungary the situation was similar, yet very different. In both parts of the Monarchy, liberalism prevailed in 1867. The liberals emancipated the Jews and fully expected them to modernize, assimilate, and become loyal citizens. They defined the Jews as a religious group and declared traditional Jewish national aspirations unacceptable. But the Dual Monarchy did not resemble France and Germany, and Austro-Hungarian Jewry differed profoundly from the Jewish communities of European countries farther west. The Monarchy was not a nation-state in which the state, the nation, and the national culture were coterminous, but rather was a multinational state containing at least eleven nations, defined in an ethnic, cultural, and linguistic sense, all clamoring for recognition. There was no single national identity uniting the country.

Into what nation, therefore, should the Jews integrate and assimilate? The situation was simple in Hungary, which did have pretentions to be a nation-state. There, Jews Magyarized and adopted Hungarian patriotism and national identity, in much the same manner as the Jews in Germany became German. In Austria, however, Jewish national identity became a highly contested issue. The Jews could and did identify as Austrians, but there was no Austrian national identity in Austria. Austrianism was a political identity shared by the emperor, the bureaucrats, the army officers, and others, an identity whose essence was loyalty to the state and dynasty. Such an identity had no cultural or ethnic-national component in a country in which ethnic nationalism came to dominate by the end of the nineteenth century. Austrian identity, then, did not suffice. Should the Jews become Germans? Assimilating to German culture and society certainly made sense, given the significance of the German language in the political, economic, and cultural life of the Monarchy and the ease with which Jews, who traditionally spoke Yiddish, could acquire German. The first generations of modernizing Jews all over the Monarchy did Germanize, but German identity began to prove problematic as nationalism spread. The Germans were not the majority of the population, and many of the nations came to resent all things German. The German identity of Jews aroused the anger of the non-Germans in whose midst Jews lived. At the same time, affiliation with one of the other nationalities—the Czechs or Poles—smacked of opportunism. Moreover, the growth of radical anti-Semitism in many of the national camps, above all among the Germans, Czechs, and Poles, compounded the problem of national affiliation. The anti-Semites in each of these camps refused to admit Jews as members, no matter how hard the Jews declared their undying commitment to that particular nation.[26]

The situation was further complicated in Austria-Hungary by the very nature of the Jewish community itself. Despite emancipation and equality, the vast majority of Austro-Hungarian Jewry never experienced social and economic modernization. In Galicia and in Hungary, many Jews remained enmeshed in their traditional economic roles as middlemen in the rural economy and as craftmen. They continued to speak Yiddish and to follow punctiliously the rules and regulations of Judaism, many of them adepts of the pietistic, mystical Hasidic movement and steadfastly loyal to charismatic Hasidic *rebbes*. Whether Hasidic or not, the majority of Jews in Galicia and Hungary held fast to a traditional Jewish identity, regarding themselves as a nation in exile awaiting redemption. Yet many Jews in Austria-Hungary—in particular the Jews in Bohemia and Moravia, a substantial number of Jews in Hungary, some Jews in Galicia and Bukovina, and the

Jews of Vienna—did experience modernization and secularizataion. They pursued modern, urban occupations, spoke the languages of the regions in which they lived, obtained secular education, and acculturated into one or another of the national groups in the Monarchy. It is these Jews, the modern Jews of the Monarchy, who faced the dilemma of national identity most acutely.

The multinational nature of Austria-Hungary, its inability to become a nation-state on the Western European model, combined with the persistence of a traditional Jewish community alongside a modern one, created a situation in which the Jews of the Monarchy, and especially the Jews of Austria, did not have to abandon or submerge the ethnic component of Jewish identity as they modernized. Indeed, Jews could comfortably assume a tripartite identity in which they espoused a fervent loyalty to the state, adopted the culture of one or another people in whose midst they lived, and unselfconsciously behaved as a separate ethnic group. Although the government only recognized them as members of a religious faith, Jews functioned as a separate ethnic group that did not have to hide its ethnic behavior behind a public rhetoric that emphasized religious difference. Austria gave the Jews room to be as ethnically assertive as they pleased, and Jewish behavior ranged from militant affirmations of Jewish ethnic pride, to the simple assumption of ethnic difference, to indifference, even hostility, to the issue. No matter how they understood their Jewish ethnicity, however, they did not feel as strong a need as Jews in Germany or France to insist that they fully belonged to the national communities whose culture they had adopted. This tripartite identity proved comfortable to the Jews, who appreciated the opportunity the multinational state gave them to be patriotic citizens, adherents of German, Czech, or Polish culture, and Jews all at the same time.

Habsburg Jews adopted many new languages and cultures in the course of the nineteenth century. In Hungary, most Jews, including the ultraorthodox, learned the Magyar language. Modernizing Bohemian and Moravian Jews chose to affiliate with German culture, but by the turn of the century, some Jews in the Czech lands had adopted Czech culture. In Galicia, modernizing Jews adopted Polish culture as their own, and in Bukovina, which had a sizeable German minority, modern Jews participated in German culture. Naturally, Jewish immigrants to Vienna learned German or had already Germanized before they migrated.

This cultural assimilation, however, did not correspond to a concomitant ethnic-national assimilation. Jews who adopted German language and culture, for example, did not become Germans. Germanization, historian William McCagg correctly insists, meant "an escape from the mud and dialects of the village world" into the realm of civilization and culture.[27] Jews who assumed a German identity affiliated with the German *Kulturnation,* with the German people as defined by German culture. They did not become members of the German *Volk,* the German nation as defined in ethnic, biological, or racial terms, a definition which became increasingly popular at the end of the nineteenth century.[28] Jews in Germany probably also did not see themselves as members of the German *Volk,* but they did see themselves as participants in the German national community. Austrian Jews were simply Germans by culture, not by national identity.[29] Such an affiliation derived not only from the historical circumstance that Jews began the process of Germanization when enlightenment, cultural views of German identity prevailed, but also from the fact that such a cultural Germanism suited the Jews perfectly. Moreover, since those Jews who adopted German culture were men and women who aspired to middle-class status, Jews who Germanized adopted not the culture of German peasants in the Sudetenland or of German artisans in provincial cities but rather the culture and life-style of the German bourgeoisie.

Some historians have recognized that the German identity of Austrian Jews was mainly enthusiasm for German culture, but these historians assume that such enthusiasm was for German high culture and especially the humanistic, cosmopolitan values of the German Enlightenment.[30] Enlightenment ideas were indeed important for the Jews, but German culture included far more than the tolerant views of Goethe and Schiller. Upwardly mobile Jews sought to acquire *Bildung,* that untranslatable Enlightenment term meaning culture, education, manners, cultivation, self-formation, reason, aesthetic taste, and moral individualism, but most Jews were not intellectuals concerned with Enlightenment philosophy. If we understand *Bildung* in the broader sense that Marion Kaplan advocates, that is, as the acquisition of middle-class respectability, good manners, and refined family life along with a patina of high culture, then surely Germanization for Austrian Jews included *Bildung.* To identify as German meant to speak German and to display middle-class manners, life-style, and education.[31]

Becoming "German" also had a political dimension. It signified staunch loyalty to the central government, to the dynasty, and to the multinational state itself. Adopting German culture was thus a statement of support for Austria.[32] Jews felt that the central government fully deserved such support, since it had emancipated them and protected their rights. Moreover, most Jews associated German identity with political liberalism because the German liberals had advocated Jewish emancipation. Indeed, Jews in the Monarchy generally supported liberal parties in the late nineteenth century.[33] Such a German identity, one based on German culture, middle-class values, and Austrian political loyalty, did not require the Jews to abandon a Jewish ethnic identity.

Whether they adopted German, Czech, or Polish cultural identity or continued to adhere to traditional Jewish culture, all Jews in Habsburg Austria identified themselves fervently with Austria. Indeed, Jews all over the Monarchy enthusiastically supported the dynasty and the supranational state, which best protected them from the anti-Semitism of the various national camps. The Austrian identity of Jews in Austria was primarily political, involving patriotism to the Austrian state, the *Gesamtstaat,* and not to an Austrian national or ethnic culture, which did not exist. Indeed, precisely because Austria did not develop a national identity, Austrian Jews could adopt the culture of one of the nations of Austria and could embrace an Austrian political identity while still asserting Jewish ethnicity. The very nature of Austria allowed for the persistence of Jewish ethnic attachments.[34]

Jews in Habsburg Austria could thus be Austrians by political loyalty, Germans (or Czechs or Poles) by culture, and Jews by ethnicity, all at the same time. More free to express their ethnic identity, they did not experience the same dissonance as Jews in France and Germany did between an ideology of assimilation to a national community and the reality of Jewish ethnicity. The Jews may not have formed one of the nations in Austria, but they certainly constituted an identifiable ethnic group.[35] Some Jews, of course, eschewed Jewish ethnicity and attempted total assimilation into one or another of Austria's nations, but most Jews felt comfortable with a tripartite identity that allowed them to be Austrians, Germans (or whatever), and Jews at the same time.

This tripartite identity developed slowly, beginning at the end of the eighteenth century, when the Austrian emperor Joseph II sought to make his Jewish subjects more "useful" by lifting some of the economic and residential restrictions under which they suffered and by urging them to acquire secular culture. In his Edict of Toleration of 1781/82, Joseph II not only granted the Jews the freedom to pursue all branches of commerce, but also required that they establish modern, German-language primary schools for their children or send them to Christian schools, newly opened to them. The Edict also permitted Jews to attend secondary schools and reminded them that they could enroll at the university. Finally, Joseph prohibited the Jews from keeping their commercial books in Yiddish or Hebrew. Subsequent Josephinian legislation abolished the autonomy of the Jewish community, required Jews to adopt German family names, made the Jews liable to military conscription, and demanded that Jewish religious functionaries obtain secular education.[36]

The Edict of Toleration was part of Joseph's attempt to centralize and Germanize his realm, and it succeeded only in part. In both Galicia and Hungary, Jewish traditionalist opposition to modern education combined with resistance of Polish and Hungarian aristocrats to Vienna's interference in their authority. As a result, few modern German-language schools came into existence, and few Jews adopted modern culture at that time.[37] In Bohemia and Moravia, on the other hand, local Jewish religious leaders cooperated with sympathetic Austrian bureaucrats to create an extensive network of modern German-language Jewish schools that provided a German cultural and Austrian political identity to generations of Jews in the Czech lands.[38] The fact that Jewish children in Bohemia and Moravia in the nineteenth century obtained their secular education, German culture, and Austrian patriotism in a Jewish social context, one that incorporated traditional religious values, surely provided significant underpinning to a sense of Jewish ethnicity in this region.

In the course of the nineteenth century, Jews in Bohemia and Moravia experienced urbanization, secularization, and changes in occupation as the Austrian authorities slowly lifted the restrictions on their residence, movement, and economic opportunities and then, in 1867, granted them emancipation. Traditional Jewish schools, the heder and yeshiva, disappeared, and even the number of modern Jewish schools declined at the end of the century, because the Jews increasingly attended public schools. Throughout the nineteenth century and into the early years of the twentieth, the Jews in these provinces identified with German culture. It was natural that the Jews opted for a German affiliation. German language assimilation, after all, had opened up European culture, secular society, and economic opportunity to the Jews. Moreover, it was the German liberals who had enacted Jewish emancipation. Finally, since German was the language of the Habsburg authorities, Jews equated German identity with Austrian loyalty. It was also relatively easy for Jews to make the transition from Yiddish to German.

Only at the very end of the century did some Bohemian and Moravian Jews adopt Czech culture. In 1890, two thirds of the Jews in Bohemia, and in Prague three quarters of the Jews, declared German to be their *Umgangssprache* for the census, but in 1900, a mere ten years later, half of Bohemian Jewry listed Czech as their language of daily speech, thus counting themselves as Czechs.[39] Scholars disagree about the extent, cause, and significance of the new-found Czech identity of Bohemian Jews. Hillel Kieval, for example, argues that a substantial percentage of Bohemian Jewry, especially Jews from small towns in Czech-speaking regions of the province, genuinely identified as Czechs by the last decades of the century. Always bilingual, they increasingly attended Czech-language secondary schools and naturally came to identify with Czech culture and the Czech national movement. Czech nationalist pressure on the Jews to affiliate as Czechs also played a significant role in the "Czechification" of Bohemian Jewry.[40] Gary Cohen, on the other hand, in his impressive study of Prague Germans, argues that while some Prague Jews did assimilate to Czech culture by the 1890s, especially the poorer ones, the vast majority persisted in their German cultural identity, largely because of the value of such identity in Austria as a whole. Moreover, Germans in Prague—unlike Germans in some other regions of the Monarchy—fully accepted the Jews as Germans, and Czech nationalist anti-Semitism offended the Jews. Cohen argues that the census statistics do not reflect a sudden, genuine turn to Czech culture and national identity, but rather reflect the political sagacity of the Jews, who understood the strength of the Czech national movement and therefore identified as Czechs.[41]

Other recent studies extend Cohen's findings for Prague to the rest of Bohemian and Moravian Jewry.[42] All over the Czech lands Jewish institutions remained German, and Jews continued to prefer German schools over Czech ones. In the 1880s, for example, 80% of Jewish secondary school students in Bohemia attended German schools, and as late as 1912, 70% of all Jewish students still did so. Jews also overwhelmingly attended the German university in Prague, not the Czech one. In 1910, 89% of all Jewish children in Prague attended German elementary schools.[43] In Moravia and Silesia Jews remained even more loyal to German culture than in Bohemia. According to the 1910 census, 78% of the Jews in Moravia and 84% of the Jews in Silesia indicated that German was their language of daily speech.[44]

Memoirs of Jewish life from late nineteenth-century Bohemia and Moravia certainly indicate persistent Jewish loyalty to German culture. With some exceptions, they also reveal that Jews understood their German identity in cultural, not ethnonational terms. Enoch Heinrich Kisch, for example, asserted that "with my whole heart [I am] a good Austrian, black and gold down to my toes, and German through education and conviction."[45] Eric Fischer, a Viennese Jew of Moravian background, described the intense German loyalty of his Aunt Paula in Brünn. Growing up in the liberal era, she assumed the superiority of German culture, looked down at the Czechs, and was active in a wide array of German cultural organizations. When others "Czechified" later, "Aunt Paula stuck to her early convictions, . . . proud of her 'superior' German education."[46] In his memoirs, Friedrich Bill, an engineer who grew up in Brünn, described the absolute separation of Czechs and Germans in the city of his childhood, noting that the "Jews, with few exceptions, belonged to the German cultural community (*Kulturgemeinschaft*), which they maintained at great financial sacrifice and with total passion."[47] Arnold Höllriegel, a journalist who grew up in Prague, similarly asserted that in the German-Czech conflict he stood "naturally and unconditionally on the German side," although the vituperative atmosphere of the conflict and the aridness of nationalism upset him a great deal. At the same time, however, he told a friend: "I feel that I am neither Czech nor German, but rather both, a Bohemian." In fact, Höllriegel understood that he was an Austrian, and above all a Jew, despite the fact that "my Judaism meant little to me."[48] A generation earlier, the writer Fritz Mauthner, who became a German nationalist and moved to Germany in the 1870s, felt that as a Jew in Prague, speaking High German instead of a German dialect, he lacked the essential ingredients to belong fully to the German people.[49]

Even if not part of the German people, Jews from Prague asserted their absolute identity with German culture. In their memoirs written after the Holocaust, when the Nazis had denied them the right to be German, they proudly if somewhat nervously recalled their old commitments. Elsa Bergmann noted in her memoirs that "the Jews then had no inkling that anyone ever could doubt their true Germanness."[50] Olly Schwarz insisted that her assimilated family "belonged to the most ardent Germans." Indeed, the high point of her girlhood was when she served as a "flag virgin" in the celebration of the fiftieth anniversary of the oldest German student club in Prague, a symbol of the German cause and of freedom and enlightenment.[51] Grete Fischer described her passionate love for German language and culture, but admitted that "the Prague German identity to which we were raised seemed a matter of course to us as long as we had no contact with the outside world."[52]

Many of those Jews who did speak Czech in public still valued German culture in private. Hugo Herrmann movingly described how Jews living in Czech areas of Bohemia became latter-day Marranos, speaking Czech in public but returning to the comfort of German at home, ostentatiously carrying the Czech papers in the street, but reading the German ones in private.[53] The historian Hans Kohn, born in Prague in 1891, pointed out that his parents came from "Jewish families who had lived for generations in the Czech countryside." They spoke both Czech and German but "the language used in their families' homes was predominantly German." Moreover, Kohn insisted, "German became or remained the main language" of Jews who migrated from the Czech countryside to the cities.[54] Similarly Joseph Wechsberg, born in Mährisch Ostrau, Moravia, in 1907, recalled in his memoirs that Jews spoke Czech at the tax-collector's office, watered-down Polish to the servants, and German among themselves.[55]

Bilingualism was certainly widespread, and a minority of Jews did affiliate with Czech culture, especially in Bohemia. Yet virtually all the memoirs make clear that before the creation of Czechoslovakia, affiliation with Czech culture was the exception among the Jews. Memoirists often mention only one relative, or one person in their hometown, who possessed a Czech identity, and they do so to make the point about the unusual nature of such behavior in the late nineteenth century.[56] Moreover, even those who embraced Czech identity admitted the continued hold of the German language. Gisa Picová-Saudková, from Kolín, Bohemia, for example, lamented in her diary that despite her valiant efforts to speak Czech, she did not always manage to think in that language.[57] Prague-born Hella Roubicek Mautner insisted that her first language was Czech and that her family only spoke Czech at home. Yet, she attended German schools, regularly went to the German theater, and preferred the German newspapers. Despite her claim that all Czechs spoke German with horrible Slavic accents, she implies that she herself had no such accent.[58] The sources leave the impression that Jews in small towns in Bohemia were the most likely to possess, in public at least, a Czech cultural identity, while Jews in Prague, and especially in Moravia, were the most devoted to German culture.[59] Even those who strove for Czech identity still linked themselves with the world of German culture.

Whatever their cultural orientation, the Jews of Bohemia and Moravia expressed loyalty to the emperor and Austria. Hans Kohn, for example, asserted that "Prague was my home, the Austrian monarchy my fatherland, and not unreasonably, I felt a sentimental loyalty to both."[60] Kohn regretted that Emperor Franz Joseph never managed to parlay the intense loyalty of his subjects into a unifying Austrian national idea that might have saved the Monarchy from dissolution.[61] Arnold Höllriegel related how all of his relatives behaved like "good Germans, good Austrians" and how his Prague teachers infused him with an Austrian identity and great respect for the old Kaiser.[62] Gertrude Hirsch recalled how much she loved celebrating the Kaiser's birthday and singing the national anthem, which gave her "the ever recurrent revelation of belonging to the country where I was born, grew up with its flowers, trees, its customs, and having inhaled with everybody else the air of its old inheritance—Austria!"[63] Moravian Bertha Landre remembered her excitement as a child when Franz Joseph visited her city,[64] and Hella Roubicek Mautner also recounted how she and her siblings "adored the Austrian Kaiser Franz Joseph."[65]

Such allegiance to the emperor and to the Monarchy was widespread among the Jews of Galicia and Bukovina, who understood well that their legal status—as emancipated Jews with equal legal and civil rights—far surpassed the status of fellow Jews across the borders in the Russian Empire and in Romania. The writer Manès Sperber, born in Zablotow, Galicia at the turn of the century, who fled with his family to Vienna during the war, recalled:

> Emperor Franz Joseph I meant far more to all the shtetl Jews throughout the monarchy than to any other subjects, for the Jews viewed him as the guarantor of their civil rights, their protector against hatred and despotism.[66]

Indeed, a veritable cult of Franz Joseph arose among the Jews, especially in Galicia, to the point where they even credited him, rather than the German liberals, with granting them emancipation.[67] Joachim Schoenfeld, from Sniatyn, remembered that the Galician Jews loved the Kaiser, gave him the affectionate Yiddish nickname Froyim Yossel, and celebrated his birthday with great joy every year.[68] Minna Lachs, who came to Vienna during the war as a small child from her native Trembowla, noted that her grandmother considered it extremely significant that she shared a birthday with Franz Joseph. In Trembowla, her father read the Viennese *Neue Freie Presse* daily and, like many Galician Jews, kept a picture of the emperor, "our good, old Kaiser," on the living room wall.[69]

The loyalty of Galician Jews to Austria derived largely from their conviction that Austria protected them from the anti-Semitism of the Poles and Ruthenians among whom they lived. Although the Polish aristocracy controlled Galicia, the presence of the imperial bureaucracy and Austrian law shielded the Jews from anti-Semitic excess. Indeed, at the end of World War I, when Austria lost control in the province, pogroms erupted and large numbers of Jews were killed. Even during more peaceful times, however, Poles, Ruthenians, and Jews formed three distinct, often antagonistic groups within Galician society.[70]

Loyalty to Austria did not preclude a Polish cultural identity among the modernizing Jews in Galicia. Although the primary language of the vast majority of Jews in the province was Yiddish, and many Jews also knew German, a growing number of younger Jews and modern Jews acquired Polish culture by the turn of the century.[71] The linguistic situation among Galician Jews is not reflected in the Austrian census. Austrian bureaucrats did not count Yiddish as a language and for political reasons considered the Jews of Galicia to be Polish speakers. Thus 93% of Jews in the province appear as using Polish as their main language, which was certainly not the case.[72] Nevertheless, a growing number of modernizing Jews did send their children to Polish schools by the end of the century. In 1875 very few Galician Jews sent their sons to secondary school (730), but 32% of those who did school their sons sent them to the German *Gymnasium* in Lemberg. In 1895, 2390 Galician Jews attended *Gymnasien,* virtually all of them Polish-language.[73] By the eve of World War I, many Jews in the province had received a Polish education, so the Jews of Galicia were the most Polonized of all Jews in the newly formed Polish republic after the war.[74] Although Ruthenians (Ukrainians who followed the Orthodox rite but respected the authority of the Pope) formed two fifths of the population of Galicia and were an overwhelming majority in East Galicia, home of the majority of the Jews, few Jews in Galicia learned Ruthenian or adopted a Ruthenian cultural identity. It was only natural for the Jews to avoid Ruthenian culture. Most Ruthenians were peasants, while Jews lived in cities and towns, inhabited largely by Jews and Poles. Jews perceived no advantage in adopting Ruthenian culture in a province dominated politically, culturally, and economically by Poles.[75]

In their memoirs, many Galician Jews expressed a great deal of affection for Polish language and literature, including Norman Salsitz (Naftali Saleschütz), who came from a Yiddish-speaking, Hasidic family in Kolbuszowa.[76] The father of psychoanalyst Helene Deutsch had received a German education, but she, born in Przemysl in 1884, attended Polish private schools. Later estranged from Poland by its anti-Semitism, she nevertheless loved Polish literature, "identified intensely with Poland," and insisted on her Polish national identity.[77] Most Jews who adopted Polish language and culture did not consider themselves Poles. Indeed, Polish antisemitism and the social distance between Jews and Poles combined with a rich Jewish cultural life in Galicia (and elsewhere in Poland) to create a situation in which Jews did not feel part of the Polish nation even if they had adopted Polish culture. In Galicia even more than in Bohemia and Moravia, Jews felt themselves to belong to the Jewish people. Whether traditionally religious or followers of the rapidly growing Zionist and Jewish diaspora nationalist movements, the primary identity of most Galician Jews was as Jews.[78]

The situation was even more complicated in Bukovina, with its mixed population of Ruthenians, Romanians, Germans, and Jews. Most Jews in Bukovina, like Jews in Galicia, remained traditionally religious and Yiddish-speaking, and continued to pursue traditional occupations in petty trade and the crafts. Those that modernized, however, eschewed both Ruthenian and Romanian culture, choosing instead to affiliate with German culture, largely because of the presence of a significant German minority in the province. Also, a German identity brought economic and cultural advantage in Austria generally, while Romanian or Ruthenian culture did not provide benefit in a province in which the two groups were evenly balanced. Official statistics from Bukovina, which did not count Yiddish as a language, exaggerate the German identity of Bukovinian Jews. According to the 1910 census, 93% of Jews indicated a German *Umgangssprache*.[79] Even though most Jews in the province actually spoke Yiddish as their primary language, a growing number of modern Jews choose to affiliate with German culture. Adolf Mechner, a doctor born in Czernowitz in 1897, describes his childhood in the Bukovinian capital as "a paradise." The son of a middle-class family, he attended German schools, loved German language and literature, and became a devotee of the German theater.[80] Modernized, middle-class Jews in the province overwhelmingly sent their sons to the German-language *Gymnasien*.[81]

This German cultural affiliation did not mean that Jews had become Germans. On the contrary, a large percentage of Jews in Bukovina affiliated with the Jewish nationalist movement at the end of the nineteenth century and asserted that the Jews formed their own nation. In 1909, the Bukovinian Diet agreed to recognize the Jews as one of the nationalities of Bukovina, granting them a Jewish national curia for future elections, similar to those established for Germans, Romanians, and Ruthenians. The Austrian authorities rejected this recognition of Jewish national rights, adhering to the liberal notion that Jews constituted only a confessional group. Moreover, the central government worried about the anti-Semitic consequences of separating the Jews as a nation and undoubtedly preferred not to diminish the political clout of Germans in the province. Nevertheless, the local authorities, with imperial approval, connived to grant the Jews *de facto* national representation through gerrymandered voting districts. In provincial elections in 1911, Jewish nationalist candidates won ten mandates.[82]

In Hungary, on the other hand, not only had the Jews Magyarized, adopting the Magyar language and culture by the second half of the nineteenth century, but many also identified with the Hungarian nation, much the same as the Jews of Germany identified as Germans. Most remarkable about the situation in Hungary is that this process of Magyarization and Magyar national identity affected not only the modernizing, upwardly mobile Jews in Budapest and other cities, but also large numbers of Orthodox Jews who were economically, socially, and religiously traditional. The Magyar elite of Hungary—composed almost entirely of artistocrats and gentry—wanted Hungary to be a nation-state with Magyar language and culture dominant and synonymous with the nation. Given the fact that Magyars did not account for the majority of the population, Magyar leaders needed to co-opt non-Magyars into the Hungarian nation. Thus they welcomed Jews, Germans, and others as Hungarians, and Jews eagerly accepted their hospitality. Later, in drastically reduced interwar Hungary, Hungarian leaders no longer needed the Jews to bolster the number of Magyars, and the antisemitic notion that the Jews could never be true Magyars prevailed. In the prewar period, even though anti-Semitism flourished and social separation existed between Jews and Gentiles, Jews identified as Hungarians by culture, patriotism, and national identity in much the same way as German or French Jews identified with the German or French nation.[83]

The intensity of Jewish identification with the Magyars is especially interesting, because in Hungary, the first generations of Jews to modernize did so through the medium of German culture, in much the same manner as did Jews in Bohemia, Moravia, or Galicia. Indeed, one historian of Hungarian Jewry has even called the Jews of Hungary before 1880 "the largest German-speaking Jewish community in Europe."[84] German cultural orientation was normal given the political realities of the Austrian Empire before 1867, when the Habsburg authorities sought to Germanize their realm. There were obvious economic and cultural advantages of knowing German, and Yiddish-speaking Jews could learn the language with relative ease. Although Joseph II's attempt to introduce modern, German-language Jewish schools in Hungary did not succeed, large sectors of Hungarian Jewry nevertheless learned German by mid-century.

Beginning at that point, however, influenced by rising Magyar nationalism, the Jews in Hungary began to Magyarize. By the eve of World War I, most Hungarian Jews spoke Magyar either as a first or a second language. Indeed, Jews Magyarized more completely than any other minority group in Hungary. In 1880, 57% of Hungarian Jews had indicated that Hungarian was their mother tongue. On the 1910 census, 76% declared Hungarian as their mother tongue.[85] It is not unlikely that this figure is somewhat inflated by bilingual Jews who knew it was better to say that Magyar was their first language. Victor Karady estimates that only 44% of Jews in Hungary indeed had a Magyar mother tongue. Not surprisingly, Magyar prevailed more among Jews in regions in which Magyars formed the majority and less in non-Magyar or mixed regions. In 1910, well over three quarters of the Jews in the Central Hungarian plain, in Budapest, Transdanubia, and the eastern plain regions, and about half of the Jews in eastern Slovakia and Ruthenia spoke Magyar natively. In western Slovakia, in the region between the Tisza and Maros rivers and in Transylvania, the percentage of Jews whose mother tongue was Hungarian was far lower, ranging between 25 and 33%.[86]

Most Hungarian Jews were bilingual, speaking Magyar and German or Yiddish and Magyar. Raphael Patai, born in Budapest in 1910 to a fully Magyarized, middle-class Jewish family, recalls in his memoirs how when he was four or five years old his parents, "both of whom spoke German as fluently as Hungarian," hired a German governess so that the children could learn German perfectly. They did so, he asserts, because all middle-class Hungarians, especially the Jews among them, regarded German as "the key to European culture." Thus the family always made a point of speaking only German at dinner.[87] His mother's experience reflected the transition from Germanization to Magyarization. Growing up in Nagyvárad, she attended Hungarian schools, but her family spoke only German at home.[88] Although Jews successfully Magyarized, they nevertheless did not abandon German. Other Jews in Hungary, especially the masses of Hasidic and non-Hasidic Orthodox Jews, learned Hungarian but continued to speak Yiddish among themselves. Many Jews in Hungary were trilingual, speaking Magyar, German, and Yiddish.

In Hungary, Magyar language and Magyar national identity went hand in hand. As a result, the majority of Jews in the Magyar-speaking parts of Hungary identified as members of the Hungarian nation. When Zionism, which emphasized that the Jews constituted their own nation, emerged at the end of the nineteenth century, Hungarian Jews steadfastly opposed it. Miksa Szabolcsi, the editor of the most influential Hungarian Jewish newspaper, *Egyenlöség,* rejected Zionism and affirmed the merger of the Jews in the Magyar nation in language never used by Jews elsewhere in the Monarchy. He declared:

> We . . . are Hungarians because our heart, our feeling is Hungarian, because we cannot be anything else, because we do not want to be anything else. The love of fatherland often breaks through without our wanting it. Because it has become our blood, because it has struck deep roots in our hearts . . . Don't forget that we have become Magyars not only in language and feelings but also in temperment.[89]

In other regions of Hungary, in Western Slovakia or parts of Transylvania, on the other hand, the masses of Orthodox Jews may have felt Hungarian patriotism but not a Hungarian national identity.[90]

Hungarian Jews combined Hungarian patriotism and national loyalty with devoted allegiance to the Habsburg Monarchy and especially to Franz Joseph, the emperor of Austria and king of Hungary. The Hungarian-born American journalist Charles Fenyvesi recalled that his grandfather Karl Schwarcz, a landowner in Gyulaj, Szabolcs County, was a Hungarian patriot who believed "ardently in the need for a confederation of Danubian states . . . under the rule of a thoughtful Habsburg." Schwarcz admired Franz Joseph because he "personified not only decency and fairness, but also predictability" and other bourgeois virtues. To the Jews, Franz Joseph meant peace and equality. He "helped make our world whole."[91] Every year during a trip to Vienna, Karl Schwarcz made a point of waiting for Franz Joseph's carriage so he could shout, "Long live the King of Hungary!"[92]

In many ways, the Jews who migrated to Vienna from Hungary, Bohemia, Moravia, Galicia, and Bukovina had the easiest task of all with deciding their national affiliation. Naturally, the Jews of Vienna adopted German language and culture as they adapted to urban life. Yet while Vienna was a German city, many of its "Germans" were recent immigrants from Bohemia, Moravia, and Hungary.[93] Sigmund Mayer, a wealthy Viennese Jewish textile manufacturer born in Pressburg in 1831, argued in his memoirs that Vienna did not have a profoundly "German atmosphere." He attributed this absence to the presence of large numbers of immigrants who lost their original national culture and became Viennese, "but not quite German."[94] More important, as home of the emperor, army, government, and imperial bureaucracy, Vienna was utterly Austrian, the center of supranational Austria. As a result of their identity as residents of the Austrian capital, and because they succeeded in Germanizing immigrants, the Viennese were less obsessed with their German national identity than were many Germans in the Habsburg borderlands.[95] Precisely because Viennese were less worried about their "German-ness," Germanization in Vienna did not necessarily entail a merger with the German *Volk*. Here Jews could most easily be Germans by culture, Austrians by political loyalty, and part of a Jewish ethnic group all at the same time.[96]

Jews immigrated to Vienna in increasingly large numbers in the second half of the nineteenth century and modernized, abandoning traditional Jewish occupations for urban careers as clerks, salesmen, managers, respectable businessmen, and professionals. They adopted secular German culture, spoke German, sent their children to the public schools, and adopted German names and a respectable bourgeois life-style, if they were lucky enough to become prosperous. Yet the structure of their lives remained intensely Jewish. By living in largely Jewish neighborhoods, joining mostly Jewish organizations, and befriending and marrying mostly fellow Jews, Jews in Vienna retained their ethnic coherence and a strong sense of Jewish group persistence. Jewish tendencies in this direction, together with vigorous anti-Semitism in Vienna, guaranteed the maintenance of strong ethnic boundaries between the Jews and other Viennese.[97] The immigrant composition of the community and the relaxed sense of German identity in the capital enabled the Jews of Vienna to freely assert their ethnicity, even as they proudly proclaimed their allegiance to German culture and the Austrian state.[98]

The writer Stefan Zweig, who grew up in late Habsburg Vienna, introduces his memoirs by telling his readers that he was "an Austrian, a Jew, an author, a humanist, and a pacifist."[99] It is interesting that he omits saying he was a German, although he was educated in German culture and belonged to it. Writing his memoirs in exile during World War II and depressed over Nazi success in Europe, it is natural that Zweig might choose not to announce a German identity. Yet, it is striking that unlike Bohemian Jews, Viennese Jews never discuss their German identity in their memoirs, even when they parade their love for German language, music, art, and literature.[100] Taking their German culture for granted, they emphasize instead their identity as Viennese, as Austrians, and as Jews. George Clare, born in Vienna just after World War I, repeatedly emphasized the "wholly Austrian" identity of his parents and grandparents, all of whom originated in Galicia and Bukovina. His father and his siblings, the grandchildren of an Austrian army doctor who settled in Vienna in 1868, were "fully integrated Viennese. . . . They were born and grew up as Austrians among Austrians." His paternal grandmother, born in Czernowitz, was likewise "totally Viennese." His family, he concluded, was "not just Austrian, but German-Austrian," participating in German culture, but Austrian, not German.[101] Erna Segal bluntly declared that Vienna was her eternal homeland.[102] Viennese Jews articulated a strong Habsburg dynastic loyalty and Austrian patriotism as well.[103]

At the same time, the Jews in Vienna persisted in their ethnic loyalties as Jews, even if they abandoned many or even all Jewish religious traditions and assimilated into German culture. Sigmund Mayer admitted that he had not thought much about his Jewish identity until reminded of it by the anti-Semites, but insisted that Jews could easily be members of one of the "culture-nations" of Austria and continue to feel Jewish, not as members of a Jewish nation but as part of the Jewish *Volk*.[104] Similarly, the playwright Arthur Schnitzler, whose family had already abandoned Jewish rituals by the 1870s, emphasized the family's "stubborn emphasis on racial solidarity" with other Jews.[105] Otto Ehrentheil described in his memoirs how he and his wife felt "that we are children of the tribe which has existed for four thousand years," a tribe formed by "historical circumstances" and by "blood relationships" and generating "certain attitudes . . . which are of value."[106] Max Kriegsfield, who grew up in Carinthia, voiced similar views when he said, "I am Jewish, not much of a practicing Jew, but Jewish nonetheless, by birth, ethnic background, heritage, and belief."[107]

These memoirists reiterate on an intimate level what Viennese Jewish leaders posited more formally throughout the nineteenth century. Jewish spokesmen proclaimed that the Jews formed a unique people, bound together by a common history and destiny and united by a common religion. Refusing to regard the Jews merely as a community of faith, a *Confessionsgemeinschaft,* as liberal ideology proposed, Viennese Jewish spokesmen freely used terms like *Volk* or *Stamm* (literally tribe, but best translated as ethnic group), or occasionally even *Nation,* to describe the Jews. These spokesmen certainly did not think that the Jewish *Volk* was a modern, political nation. Indeed, virtually all of them rejected the Zionist movement, which arose at the end of the nineteenth century and called for the restoration of a Jewish state in the Land of Israel. But they did regard the Jews as an ethnic group with a unique culture, a culture that they agreed derived from the Jewish religion. Thus they believed the Jews were a religio-ethnic group, not just a religious community, and they regarded themselves as German by culture but not as members of the German *Volk*.

Vienna's chief rabbis in the nineteenth-century—Isak Noa Mannheimer, Adolf Jellinek, and Moritz Güdemann—regularly articulated this ideology of Jewish religio-ethnic distinctiveness.[108] Mannheimer, a moderate reform rabbi in Vienna from 1825 to 1865, made it clear that while he considered Jewish religion and its belief in God the essence of Jewish identity, he nevertheless remained committed to Jewish peoplehood. In a rabbinic opinion he wrote on circumcision in 1844, he declared that what was most important in Judaism was not an idea or philosophical principle, but rather the Jewish "sense of belonging together."[109] Adolf Jellinek, rabbi in Vienna from 1858 until his death in 1893, similarly assumed a religious basis for Jewish distinctiveness, even though he regularly used words like *Volk* and *Stamm* to describe the Jewish people. In his 1869 tract, *Der jüdische Stamm,* Jellinek denied any national basis for Jewish identity, but he admitted that the Jews do have ethnic qualities (*Stammeseigenthümlichkeiten*).[110] Similarly, in an 1884 article, Jellinek asserted that Jews have always maintained a strong ethnic consciousness, a *Stammesbewusstsein,* despite their dispersal.[111] Jellinek presented his clearest statement of Jewish identity in 1893. Although the Jews did not form a nation, because they possessed neither territory nor sovereignty, Jellinek nevertheless insisted that "they belong to one and the same *Stamm* [and] profess the same articles of faith."[112]

Moritz Güdemann, Vienna's traditionalist chief rabbi from 1866 to 1918, also defined Jewish ethnicity in strictly religious terms. In 1871, during the controversy over implementing reforms in Viennese synagogues, Güdemann defended the retention of prayers for a Jewish return to Zion. He made it very clear, however, that he did not envision a Jewish state. For him, Zion was a symbol of the ultimate redemption of mankind by God.[113] Although initially intrigued by Theodor Herzl, he rejected the Zionist movement as antithetical to Judaism. In his 1897 anti-Zionist pamphlet, *Nationaljudenthum,* Güdemann reiterated his conviction that the concept of the Jewish people (*Volksbegriff*) was inseparable from its concept of God.[114] Yet Güdemann's sermons urged Viennese Jews to feel themselves part of the Jewish people, which he labeled their *Volksheimat.*[115]

The most indefatigable propounder of Jewish ethnic consciousness in Vienna was Josef Samuel Bloch, a Galician-born rabbi in the suburb of Floridsdorf, member of parliament from Galicia, tireless fighter against anti-Semitism, and founder and editor of the most widely read Jewish newspaper in Austria, the *Österreichische Wochenschrift.* He created the newspaper in 1884 to arouse Jewish national feelings

> to rouse a feeling of kinship among all who belonged to the Jewish race and to make them conscious of their inescapable common fate, as well as at the same time arousing a noble pride in their common past of four thousand years unparalleled alike in suffering and glory.[116]

When Bloch used the term "national feelings" he did not mean modern, political nationalism. Indeed, Bloch opposed Zionism and Jewish nationalism, even if he appreciated the fact that these movements raised Jewish consciousness.[117] Bloch wanted to arouse Jewish ethnic identity in Austria. He railed against Jewish efforts to affiliate with any of the nationalities and firmly advocated a staunch Austrian loyalty. Indeed, he chose the name of his paper, the "Austrian Weekly," in conscious contradistinction to Heinrich Friedjung's German nationalist *Deutsche Wochenschrift.*[118]

A strong sense of Jewish consciousness and Austrian patriotism dominated the largest Jewish organization in Vienna, the *Österreichisch-israelitische Union* (Austrian Israelite Union). Founded in 1886 to combat rapidly escalating anti-Semitism through legal actions and public propaganda, the Union worked to bolster Jewish pride and solidarity in the face of hostility. At the same time, it insisted on the Austrian identity of Austrian Jews, and later vigorously opposed Jewish nationalism. At the founding meeting, spokesman Sigmund Zins declared:

> We find that the patriotism and national feelings of Austrian Jews of the different kingdoms and provinces does not preclude Jewish consciousness and its

preservation; indeed it can be harmoniously tied to this consciousness, just as the enthusiastic patriots and hottest nationalists of the Aryan race correctly understand that their patriotism and their national feelings are not impugned by their Christianity. We stress the duties of Austrian Jews to a sincere Austrian patriotism and to political brotherhood with the peoples and nations amongst whom they are born and raised, in whose literature they are educated, and in whose economic and cultural life they participate. But we also recognize our holiest duty as Jews, to uphold . . . our ancient heritage.[119]

The Union did not consider the Jews to be one of the nations of Austria, and it posited a religious basis for Jewish solidarity. It also assumed that Jews in Austria could be Germans, Czechs, or Poles, but it regarded "German-ness" or other "national" identities in terms of education and culture not ethnicity or race. Nevertheless, although the leaders of the Union were not quite as insistent on Jewish *Stammesbewusstsein* as Bloch, who had initiated the founding of the organization, they came to uphold a large measure of Jewish ethnic consciousness. Given the fact that the leadership cadres of the Union and the *Israelitische Kultusgemeinde* (Jewish religious community, IKG) overlapped significantly, the Union's concern for Jewish consciousness dominated the leadership of Viennese Jewry at the end of the nineteenth century.[120]

Austrian Jewry thus was extremely diverse. It contained large numbers of Jews who continued to adhere to traditional Jewish culture, especially in Galicia, Bukovina, and Hungary, as well as significant numbers of modern Jews who had adopted the culture of one or another nationality. In addition, Austrian Jewry also contained a sizeable contingent of Jewish nationalists. Influenced in large measure by the vociferous nationality conflict that engulfed their country, angered by the anti-Semitism that many of the nationalities displayed, and convinced of the distinctiveness of Jewish culture, Jewish nationalists asserted that the Jews formed a nation, one of the nations of Austria, and deserved legal recognition as such. Some of these Jewish nationalists were Zionists who sought to create a Jewish homeland and state in Palestine. Others were diaspora nationalists who demanded Jewish national/cultural autonomy in a reorganized Austrian federation of nationalities.[121]

Zionism first emerged in the early 1880s. A group of students, angered by the rising anti-Semitism of the German nationalist fraternities at the University of Vienna, created *Kadimah,* a Jewish nationalist dueling fraternity. At the same time, Jews in Galicia and Bukovina formed Zionist groups similar to the Lovers of Zion associations in Russia. Zionism grew rapidly after the Viennese journalist Theodor Herzl issued his call for a Jewish state in 1896. Zionism attracted both middle-class, modernized Jews who had become disillusioned with the possibilities of Jewish integration as a result of anti-Semitism and traditional Jews who were attracted by the romantic appeal of rebuilding the ancient Jewish homeland. Although the strength of Austrian Zionism always lay in Galicia and Bukovina, Zionism also appealed to growing numbers of Jews in Vienna and in the Czech lands.[122]

For Jews in Bohemia and Moravia in particular, Zionist affiliation offered a perfect opportunity to remain neutral in the escalating conflict between Czechs and Germans. Zionists could say they belonged neither to the German nor to the

Czech national camp but to the Jewish one. Influenced by cultural Zionists like Ahad Ha'am and especially Martin Buber, and by Czech and German nationalism, the members of the Prague student group Bar Kochba sought Jewish spiritual and cultural renewal through a focus on Jewish national identity. Coming mostly from families that had identified with German culture, they took that culture for granted but refused to identify with the German nation.[123] Max Brod, a member of the Prague Zionist circle, described his relationship with German culture as *Distanzliebe,* love from a distance, with no desire to meld into the German *Volk.*[124] Zionism offered Jews in Galicia and Bukovina a similar respite from the nationality struggles that raged in those provinces. Asserting membership in the Jewish nation meant that Jews did not have to affiliate with the Poles or Ruthenians but could simply be Jews. Such assertions did not always please their neighbors, who often demanded Jewish national affiliation while at the same time declaring its impossibility, but Zionism did provide Jews in these regions with a coherent ideology and identity.

Whether Zionist or diaspora-centered, Jewish nationalists all agreed that members of the Jewish nation might be culturally German, Czech, or Polish. At the same time, unlike many nationalists in Austria, they all emphasized their utter devotion to the Austrian *Gesamtstaat.* Heinrich York-Steiner, for example, in a 1907 article entitled, "We are no Germans," insisted that by nationality the Jews were not German, Czech, French, or English, but rather Jews. "We are Jews of German culture," he insisted, not Germans but Jews.[125] The author of an article in the Viennese Jewish nationalist weekly *Jüdisches Volksblatt* asserted that "the national activity of Jews in no way stands in opposition to our effectiveness as persons of modern culture and as Austrian citizens."[126] Indeed, the very hallmark of the Jewish nationalist program—the reorganization of Austria into a federation of autonomous nationalities based on personal affiliation, and the recognition of the Jews as one of the autonomous nations in the new Austrian *Völkerstaat*—presupposed the continuity of supranational Austria.[127] Austrian Zionists enthusiastically adopted this program in their own Cracow Program of 1906, emphasizing that Jewish nationalism and international Jewish unity in no way contradicted the state patriotism of the Jews. On the contrary, Austrian Zionists affirmed their staunch support for Austria because they understood that only within such a state could they demand Jewish national autonomy[128]

Jewish nationalists succeeded in convincing neither the Austrian authorities nor the majority of their fellow Jews that the Jews should gain autonomy, but their version of Jewish identity increasingly appealed to the younger generation, especially in Galicia and Bukovina, but also in Bohemia, Moravia, and Vienna. Jewish nationalists ran candidates for parliament in 1907 from areas with large numbers of Jewish voters, and four of them—Adolf Stand, Benno Straucher, Heinrich Gabel, and Arthur Mahler—won mandates in Galicia and Bukovina. These men formed a "Jewish Club" in parliament and used their positions to lobby on behalf of Jewish interests.[129] The nationalists also tried to take control of local Jewish communities, presenting slates in IKG elections. The Zionists and Jewish nationalists did not win these elections before the war, but they did attract a significant minority of voters and assumed that if they extended the suffrage, they would surely dominate.[130]

The existence of Zionists and Jewish nationalists, of large numbers of religious Jews with a traditional understanding of Jewish identity, and of ordinary Jews who asserted their Jewish ethnicity consciously or unconsciously while considering themselves members of other cultures, should not obscure the fact that there were Jews in Austria-Hungary who did see themselves as full-fledged members of the German, Czech, or Hungarian nations. Others—especially those involved in the Socialist movement—had no interest in Jewish ethnicity at all or were only nominally Jewish. Moreover, there were also Jews who tried to assimilate fully, to divorce themselves from any connection to the Jewish people, by converting to Christianity or to the neutral category, "without religion." Many converts did so to further their careers or to marry and not necessarily with the express purpose of divorcing themselves from the Jewish people. For some of these people and their offspring, Jewishness continued to have some significance, positive or negative. Moreover, the high level of anti-Semitism in late Habsburg Austria, coupled with the increasing popularity of racial notions, led many people to regard these converts and their children as Jews.[131] Most Austrian Jews, however, had a far stronger conception of Jewish identity than did the converts or other Jews who sought full assimilation.

It is obvious that the Jews of Austria did not merely form a religious community. Instead, most Jews perceived themselves and were perceived by others to be a religio-ethnic group par excellence that maintained its ethnic boundaries effectively, helped, of course, by the persistence of both anti-Semitism and Jewish traditionalism. Jews could assert or simply assume their ethnic distinctiveness because of the unique constellation of political forces in Austria-Hungary. Multinational Habsburg Austria allowed the Jews to assert their Austrian patriotism, to declare their love for the culture of one or another of the national groups, and at the same time to feel part of the Jewish people. In particular, the German-speaking Jews of Bohemia, Moravia, Bukovina, and Vienna, the subjects of this book, could be loyal Austrians, devotees of German culture, and members of a separate Jewish ethnic group.

World War I provided the Jews of Austria-Hungary with an opportunity to demonstrate their Austrian loyalty and Jewish ethnicity. By serving in the army, by donating money, and by helping the victims of war, Jews asserted that they were Austrians, loyal to the Austrian cause, ready to sacrifice their *Gut und Blut,* their lives and their fortunes, for Austria. Such patriotism expressed the genuine convictions of the Monarchy's Jews, who remained committed to the existence of the supranational Monarchy until the very end. Moreover, because Austria fought against Russia, which persecuted the Jews, fighting for Austria also assumed a Jewish dimension. Jewish soldiers would help defeat the great enemy of the Jews and liberate Russian Jewry. Austrian Jews could therefore combine their Austrian patriotism with Jewish ethnic loyalties.

Ultimately the war would lead to the dissolution of the Habsburg Monarchy and to the end of the comfortable tripartite identity of Habsburg Jewry. In 1914, of course, no one knew that the war would have such profound impact. At that time, caught in the vortex of patriotic enthusiasm that accompanied the outbreak of hostilities, Austrian Jews embraced a war they universally felt would confirm their identities as Austrians and as Jews.

2

Austrian Jews and the Spirit of 1914

In August 1914, Europe erupted in a patriotic frenzy. Without any real sense of what modern, industrialized warfare meant, and utterly convinced that the fighting would last only a short time, soldiers in all the belligerent countries marched off to war excited by the prospect of adventure and were wildly cheered on by adulatory crowds. On both sides of the conflict, men and women of all social classes and all political persuasions joined forces to defend their fatherlands from what they perceived was an unjust attack by evil enemies bent on their destruction. Even the Socialists, who had long vowed to oppose war, rushed to the defense. In England, France, and czarist Russia on the one side, and in Germany and Austria-Hungary on the other, patriotic excitement reigned in the first months of World War I. Such patriotism seemed to dissolve traditional social, religious, and political antagonisms in the warm glow of national purpose, solidarity, and brotherhood. In war, the true nation could be forged, it was thought, and a true national community would emerge.[1]

Jews all over Europe—with the probable exception of Russia—participated in August 1914 in the outpouring of patriotic enthusiasm. Indeed, the war offered them the perfect opportunity to demonstrate with their blood their utter loyalty to the nations in whose midst they lived. It was a chance to participate in the great national effort and prove their membership in the national community. For decades, anti-Semites in Western and Central Europe had vilified the Jews as crafty, rapacious foreigners who undermined French or German national culture. By fighting and dying for the Fatherland, Jews hoped not only to disprove traditional stereotypes of Jews as cowards, but also, and more importantly, to win full acceptance as Frenchmen or Germans. Through their heroism they could attest to their profound sense of belonging to the French or German nation.[2]

In Austria, too, patriotic enthusiasm was widespread, far more widespread than many had predicted given the intensity of the nationality conflict. As in France,

England, and Germany, enthusiastic crowds cheered soldiers valiantly going off to war to fight evil enemies. Many national groups, especially the Germans, Magyars, Croats, and Poles, supported the war energetically. Habsburg authorities worried about the loyalty of some of the Slavs, in particular the Serbs, Ruthenians, and Czechs, but in fact the overwhelming majority of all the nationalities loyally supported the Habsburg war effort until 1918. Despite the fact that some Czech nationalist parties had flirted with Russia and Pan-Slavism before the war, Czech troops did their duty for the Habsburg Monarchy during the war, even if somewhat less enthusiastically than the authorities would have liked. Fervent patriotism may not have been universal, but it was widespread in 1914 and throughout most of the war.[3]

The Jews of Austria did far more than their duty. They embraced the war effort with passion and conviction. All over the Monarchy, Jews of all political and religious persuasions supported Austria's war in 1914. One can detect absolutely no regional differences in the patriotic fervor of Austria's German-speaking Jews. Whether they lived in Vienna, or among the somewhat less enthusiastic Czechs in Bohemia and Moravia, or in the eastern provinces, Austrian Jews rallied to defend the fatherland. To some extent, they supported the war for the same reasons as did other European Jews. They too wanted to dispel anti-Semitic myths about Jewish cowardice and to prove the loyalty of Jews to the state. The war provided these Jews with the perfect opportunity to affirm their loyalty to Austria, to the supranational state in which they had flourished. By fighting and dying for the fatherland, Jews could prove their absolute devotion to the Habsburgs and to the Habsburg Monarchy.

The extraordinary enthusiasm of Austria's Jews for the war in 1914 derived not only from their acknowledged Habsburg loyalties: Jews in Austria fervently supported the war because for them it was also a Jewish war. Austria, after all, was fighting czarist Russia, a country that systematically persecuted its Jewish inhabitants. To join the struggle against Russia, the Jews believed, would lead to the liberation of the Jews of Eastern Europe. By participating in Austria's war, therefore, Jews could demonstrate their loyalty to Austria and work for a Jewish cause at the same time. The identity of Austrian and Jewish interests on the Eastern Front guaranteed overwhelming Jewish support for the war. In none of the other belligerent states could Jews support the war so wholeheartedly.

Jews therefore did not experience any dissonance between their Austrian and Jewish identities during World War I. Indeed, the war served to strengthen the Austrian identity of Austrian Jews and their commitment to the continuity of the multinational Monarchy. At the same time, the war reinforced their Jewish loyalties and convinced them that Jewishness flourished best in Habsburg Austria. Unlike some of Austria's nationalities, Jews faced no conflict between their group loyalty and their desire to serve the fatherland. On the contrary, the war reinforced the Jewish notion that they could be good Austrians and good Jews at the same time.

Jewish enthusiasm about the war probably also derived from the realization that a war for the fatherland as a whole could mute pressure on the Jews to join one of Austria's nationalities. Thus Jews could continue to insist that they had adopted one of the cultures of the land but still belonged to the Jewish people. Unlike Jews in France or Germany, who hoped the war would lead to their full membership in the French or German nation, the Jews in Austria thought that the war would confirm their tripartite identity as loyal Austrians who adhered to the culture of one of the nationalities but who remained devoted to the Jewish people. They prayed for the continuation of the Monarchy because they knew that only such an Austria allowed them this comfortable identity.

The Beginning of War

On June 28, 1914, Bosnian Serbs, probably backed by the Serbian government, assassinated Franz Ferdinand, the heir to the Habsburg throne, in Sarajevo, a city in Austrian Bosnia. This assassination impelled the Austro-Hungarian government, eager to punish Serbia for supporting anti-Habsburg movements in Bosnia, to issue an ultimatum to Serbia. Dissatisfied with the Serbian response, the Dual Monarchy declared war on Serbia on July 28, despite the fact that the alliance system of Europe guaranteed that an Austrian-Serbian war could not remain a localized conflict. Habsburg military leaders either hoped to defeat Serbia before Russia intervened or invited war with Russia in the expectation of undermining Russian power before she posed too great a threat to the security of the Monarchy. Austria's ally, Germany, encouraged Austrian bellicosity because of its own designs on Eastern Europe.

When Austria-Hungary declared war on Serbia, Russia mobilized against the Monarchy, and Germany declared war on Russia. Germany's war planning called for her to invade Belgium and France in the event of war with Russia. As a result, Great Britain and France, in alliance with one another, declared war on Germany. By the middle of August 1914, Europe, which had known only peace for decades, found itself engaged in a massive war, pitting England, France, Russia, Serbia, later Romania and Italy, and still later the United States, against Germany and Austria-Hungary, joined by Turkey and Bulgaria. The war, which was to last over four years, would claim the lives of millions and transform politics and society in Central Europe.[4]

Like other Austrians, most Jews did not expect that war would result from the assassination of Franz Ferdinand. Adolf Mechner, a seventeen-year-old in Czernowitz at the time, noted in his memoirs that "practically nobody thought that war may result. Especially we young people did not think about it."[5] Many Jews worried about the possibility of war,[6] but such worries did not stop middle-class Jews from going on vacation in July 1914.[7] Lillian Bader of Vienna, twenty-one years old in 1914, poignantly expressed in her memoirs the dominant mood of Austrian Jews upon hearing the news. Not liking Franz Ferdinand, they were shocked but not surprised that someone had killed him. Instead, they felt sorry for the old emperor, Franz Joseph, who had to bear so much sorrow in his lifetime. Bader noted: "The sympathy of the nation went out to the old emperor . . . but our feeling did not rise beyond the feeling of sympathy toward this 84 year old sovereign."[8]

Such views were reiterated in the Jewish press. The widely read Viennese liberal Jewish newspaper *Österreichische Wochenschrift* spent very little time discussing Franz Ferdinand himself. Instead, it extended its sympathy to Franz Joseph for having to bear another loss, praising the old emperor as a man of peace. The paper lauded Karl, the new heir apparent, as a friend of the Jews and blamed Russian machinations for the assassination.[9] The Zionist press sounded the same note. The Vienna-based *Jüdische Zeitung* extended its sympathy to Franz Joseph and hoped that the avowed loyalty of his Jewish subjects would help to lessen his pain.[10] Similarly, Prague's *Selbstwehr* barely mentioned Franz Ferdinand in its rush to express its deep sympathy with the monarch. It wrote:

> With sincere sorrow we Jews of Austria share in the pain of our oft-tried monarch and unite in this hour with the other peoples of Austria in wishing that for Austria's sake, fate will divert all trouble from its sovereign and the Reich will remain under the wise care of Kaiser Franz Josef for a long time.[11]

In Brünn, the *Jüdische Volksstimme* extended its heartfelt sympathy to the Kaiser while admitting that it had opposed Franz Ferdinand's policies.[12] All over Austria, Jews held prayer services mourning the slain successor to the throne and affirming their loyalty to emperor and Reich.[13] In July 1914, none of the Jewish newspapers gave any hint that they thought war was imminent.

The outbreak of war, especially the Kaiser's July 31 order to mobilize the army against Russia, galvanized Austrian Jewry. Every memoirist recalled exactly what he or she was doing and exactly how he or she felt when the war began. It was one of those moments that define an entire generation, and it was etched clearly on everyone's memory. Minna Lachs, who was seven years old, remembered that her father took her downtown at night (in Trembowla, Galicia) to see "how a war begins." At the city hall, Austrian and Galician flags waved in the breeze, torches glowed, a man read Franz Joseph's manifesto to his peoples, everyone sang and cheered the Kaiser, and she felt that she had witnessed "an historical, world-shattering event."[14] Similarly, Manès Sperber, nine years old at the beginning of the war, recalled that Max the trumpeter, who announced the mobilization in the Galician town of Zablotow, appeared intensely joyful as he announced the great news. "Looking at him," Sperber wrote, "you would have thought he had announced that the Messiah had come."[15] On vacation in Styria, the Viennese Lillian Bader felt that "We had been struck by lightning and our very souls were left burning." Back in Vienna, she recalled, "I was in a state of constant ecstasy."[16]

Memoirists all attest to the intense excitement for war that gripped Austria in August 1914 and in which they shared. They describe trains full of soldiers, torchlit parades, crowds lining the tracks waving Austrian flags and cheering, masses of people everywhere singing, hugging soldiers, and generally "electrified."[17] Fritz Lieben, who had just completed his medical studies and had hurried back to Vienna from vacation in England, described his mood in early August: "In those two weeks in Vienna I felt the strong surge of patriotic feeling that undeniably gripped the city and country at that time."[18] The writer Stefan Zweig, who claimed that he was "inoculated" from this excitement by his anti-war ideology, nevertheless was deeply moved by it. He noted in his memoirs that

"there was a majestic, rapturous, and even seductive something in this first outbreak of the people." He admitted that "I should not like to have missed the
memory of those first days."[19] Arnold Höllriegel, as well, who feared that the
war would mean an absolute break in his life and in the cultural life of Europe,
walked around Vienna "dumbfounded," sharing in the "prevailing war enthusiasm."[20] Many recalled that war enthusiasm united people of different classes,
ranks, nationalities, religions, and languages, making them forget particularist interests in a surge of national solidarity.[21]

For many the war may have appeared as "a rapid excursion into the romantic,
a wild manly adventure," in the words of Stefan Zweig.[22] But not everyone
shared this naive view of war. Manès Sperber's father, for example, understood
immediately that the war would bring only disaster. "For us," he told Max the
trumpeter, "every war is a disaster." The Jewish women of his Galician hometown ran to the cemetery to pray and weep at the graves of their ancestors, beg-
ging God for intercession on their behalf.[23] Many women, fearing for the lives of
their sons and husbands, wept as they sent them off to war. Bertha Landre from
Ostrau, Moravia, recalled that her mother cried bitterly at the onset on the war
because she could not understand how people could celebrate when young men
would be slaughtered.[24] When Erna Segal, a teenager from a religious family in
Vienna, accompanied her brother to the train station upon his departure for the
front in 1914, she was distraught, not only worried about his safety, but also convinced of the horrors of war. "I hated the war from the depth of my soul before
it had even begun."[25]

One cannot argue, as some theorists have, that men embraced war as "manly
adventure" while women, realistically understanding the meaning of war, wept
helplessly. This sterotypical notion of valiant men and crying women is not born
out by the facts. Many women wept, but other women shared in the war enthusiasm, throwing flowers and kissing soldiers, embarrassed by women who cried.
Twelve-year-old Landre, for example, was ashamed of her mother's tears.[26] Lillian Bader was "disgusted" with her mother for worrying when she herself was
enraptured with the war.[27] Some men cried when their sons departed for war.[28]
Moreover, some men realized that war would lead only to slaughter. Joseph Floch
from Vienna remembered his feelings at the outbreak of the war: "People want to
assassinate each other until their annihilation. All what is young and powerful
must leave for the slaughter. . . . Did this have to happen? Did the abcess [sic]
have to burst?"[29] Of course, at the time, everyone assumed the war would be
short. "In 1914," Hans Kohn noted, "no one foresaw that the war would become
a protracted holocaust."[30]

A Jewish War

Even if they understood its likely consequences, Austrian Jews utterly embraced
the war in 1914. For them, the war presented no moral dilemmas. They not only
felt compelled to do their patriotic duty,[31] but recognized immediately the Jewish dimension of the war. A war with Serbia, of course, would never have galvanized the Jews of the Monarchy. Because Russia mobilized and invaded Austria,

however, Jews could focus on Russia, which was simultaneously an enemy of Austria and of the Jews. From the beginning, Jews viewed the war solely as a war to defeat Russia, a task necessary in part to check Russian despotism but mostly to liberate the Russian Jews.[32]

At the very beginning of the war, official Jewish spokesmen rushed to express their patriotic fervor. The *Israelitische Kultusgemeinde* (organized Jewish community) of Vienna called on all Austrian Jews "to be ready to sacrifice *Gut und Blut* for Kaiser and Fatherland," to fight "shoulder to shoulder with the other loyal sons of the Reich" for Austrian victory.[33] The Jewish press immediately coupled this patriotism with the hope that Jewish valor would once and for all dispel anti-Semitic invective. The *Österreichische Wochenschrift* proudly announced on July 31 that Jews would bravely serve the land and dynasty they loved in the fervent hope "that Waidhofen lies would be utterly demolished by courageous deeds on the battle field."[34] Even more boldly, the organ of the Austrian Israelite Union described the Jews as the most loyal, most devoted, and most willing to sacrifice of all Habsburg subjects, all ready to give their lives for the honor and glory of the fatherland. Despite prewar anti-Semitism, Jews would gladly risk their lives to thank the Kaiser for his beneficence toward them. At the same time, they expected that "the blood of our sons dedicated to the fatherland" would entitle the Jews to "full, undiminished equality, to unreserved recognition of our citizenship rights."[35] Similarly, the Zionist *Jüdische Zeitung* emphasized how Austrian Jews were second to none in their readiness to sacrifice their lives for the fatherland and how delighted they were to express their *Reichstreue,* their "true, deep, and clear" patriotism, thereby dispelling anti-Semitic myths about Jewish cowardice and lack of devotion.[36] Like the Jewish liberals, Zionists assumed that Jewish loyalty and patriotism would be rewarded after the war.[37] Despite their continuing concern with anti-Semitism, however, Austrian Jews never focused exclusively on the use of the war to dispel anti-Semitism. Unlike the Jews in Germany, for whom rising anti-Semitism became the central issue of the war, Jews in Austria took anti-Semitism in stride and devoted themselves to the Austrian war against czarist Russia.

In August 1914, Austrian Jews developed an ideology that infused the war with meaning and lasted at least through the end of fighting on the Eastern Front in 1916. Focusing exclusively on the war with Russia, Austrian Jews of all political and religious persuasions firmly believed that Austria was fighting a just war on behalf of culture and civilization against an utterly evil enemy, the epitome of barbarism, despotism, and tyranny. The Austrian propaganda machine regularly churned out such statements for the population at large, but they had a special meaning for the Jews. Austrian Jews regarded the war as a Jewish holy war, a war of revenge for Kishinev, the scene of the most bloody pogrom in 1903, and for all the other anti-Jewish pogroms that had erupted in Russia since the end of the nineteenth century. With such an understanding of the war, Austrian Jews could do battle for European culture, the Monarchy, and at the same time for the Jewish people.[38]

In an *Österreichische Wochenschrift* article in early August 1914, Moritz Frühling, who later published several books on Jews in the war, set the tone. He declared that Austrian Jews needed to throw the "hereditary enemy" of the Monarchy and of "human morality" back to the steppes of Central Asia where it belonged so that European freedom could be guaranteed by Austria-Hungary and Germany. Jewish soldiers, he insisted, had a special Jewish reason for fighting the "northern barbarian." Invoking the biblical injunction to remember Amalek, the traditional enemy of the Jews, Frühling asserted that Jewish soldiers "must take revenge for all of the atrocities committed against our brothers, must make expiation for our raped and murdered sisters." Thus Jews had the duty to fight barbarism in this most just of all wars, in this "holy war," as another writer put it the following week.[39] In a telegram to its American brother organization, the Austrian Bnai Brith declared that the war was "a battle of freedom against slavery," a battle on behalf "of the millions of our horribly oppressed and persecuted co-religionists (Glaubensbrüder)."[40] Explaining the outbreak of war for young readers, the Prague-based Jung Juda confidently asserted that the Monarchy and Germany were fighting "a battle for the just cause" against "the kingdom of darkness," czarist Russia, to guarantee European freedom and to liberate the Jews.[41] The fact that the Jewish press usually called the Russians "Cossacks" reinforced the notion that all Russians were pogromchiks intent on murdering Jews.

Jewish newspapers regularly published letters by Jewish soldiers expressing their feeling of engagement in a Jewish holy war against Russia. David Sternberg, for example, movingly described his emotions to his brother in Prossnitz, Moravia at the beginning of the war:

> The fatherland calls. With all my strength I fight against Russian tyranny. There will be no victory more beautiful, and if necessary no death more sweet, than to live with the consciousness of fighting and dying for the just cause."[42]

Similarly, but more graphically, another soldier's letter asserted:

> It is a very sweet feeling . . . to be able to go to war against an enemy like Russia. Oh may we be able to take revenge for the mutilated bodies of Kishinev, for the most shameful atrocities of Zhitomir, for the eyes put out in Bialystok, for the defiled Torah scrolls, for the pogroms, and for the innumerable murdered innocent children.[43]

Even if these letters exaggerated the feelings of soldiers for propagandistic purposes, they reflect the widely held Jewish commitment to a holy war against Russia.

The most eloquent and graphic spokesman for the Jewish holy war against Russia was Rabbi W. Reich, from the Viennese resort suburb of Baden. In a series of articles in the Österreichische Wochenschrift in the summer and fall of 1914, Rabbi Reich painted gruesome images of an evil, rapacious Russia, a Russia with the blood of Jews on its hands. Reich depicted the war as a Manichean struggle of light against dark, good against evil, culture against barbarism. Germany and Austria-Hungary, the home of cultivated, educated people, were fighting to save Europe from the inhuman, barbaric, and illiterate hordes of Russia who only wanted to impose tyranny and deprive Jews of their rights. Russia, Reich warned, was a land of robbery, rape, murder, brutality, and pogroms, while

Germany and Austria were the bastions of culture, progress, and humanity. As far as he was concerned, "this war is a holy war for us Jews." Using biblical images, and evoking a mood of messianic urgency, he declared his supreme confidence that the Central Powers would emerge victorious. Such a victory, he insisted, was inevitable because culture had to triumph over barbarism, and God would surely help Austria and Germany save humanity from the despotic, hypocritical Cossacks, those "heroes of the pogroms."[44]

Rabbis all over Austria reiterated these themes in sermons they delivered at the beginning of the war. In a sermon to celebrate the Kaiser's 84th birthday in August 1914, Rabbi Rubin Färber of Mährisch Ostrau contrasted Austrian righteousness, tolerance, and culture with the evil of Russia, a country that spilled the blood of innocent people. Thus he viewed the war as "a battle of good against evil, of light against darkness, a battle of morality against immorality, of virtue against wickedness and brutality, of law against lawlessness and barbarism." Urging his congregation to remember Amalek, he too declared that God would help Austria and her Jews destroy the terrible enemy.[45] In a Chanukah sermon in December, Färber repeated his belief that the Austrians would triumph against "Russian darkness" because true culture and light "must triumph" over barbarism and dehumanized Cossacks.[46] In August 1914, Rabbi D. Herzog from Graz similarly depicted Russia as "an evil, malicious, underhanded enemy" that wanted "to annihilate several centuries of progress and culture." He too viewed the war as a battle of "culture against barbarism, light against darkness, human happiness against human oppression." Thus, he concluded, "it is the holy duty of every man of culture to fight this barbaric people." For Jews in particular, he insisted, the destruction of this enemy was of primary importance. The "screams of pain" of Russian Jewry "compel us to participate in the annihilation of this enemy."[47] In articulating such an anti-Russian position, rabbis reflected not only the views of Austrian Jews, but also of clergymen in Germany who sermonized regularly about Russian barbarism.[48]

Zionists as well viewed the war in starkly moral terms as an Austrian and Jewish war against Russian villainy. Russia, the Russia of darkness and cruelty, of innocent Jewish blood, of pogroms and "horrible diaspora suffering" was the true enemy, the editors of *Selbstwehr* declared in late August. Indeed, the purpose of the war was to liberate the Jews of Russia from "barbarous despotism." Thus the Jews of Austria found themselves in an envious situation: "For us the battle for the fatherland is at the same time a battle for the just cause and also a holy war against the hereditary enemy of the Jews."[49] Similarly, the *Jüdische Volksstimme* in Brünn understood the war to be a war of liberation for Russian Jewry.[50] The Jewish National Party of Bukovina urged the Jews to remember the pogroms of Homel, Kiev, Odessa, and Kishinev as they fought for an Austrian victory and Russian Jewish freedom.[51]

The Jewish festival of Chanukah provided an opportunity to assert the identity of Austrian and Jewish goals in the war. Liberal Jewish spokesmen in particular insisted that Jewish soldiers—indeed all Austrian soldiers—were the heirs of the Maccabees, not only because of their courage and valor, but because they fought a just war against oppression and religious persecution. As the Maccabees had triumphed over the Seleucid Greeks, so the modern-day Maccabees would triumph over the Russians.[52] At a 1915 Chanukah service for soldiers, for example, Chaplain Albert Schweiger declared that Austrian troops fought against "a world of enemies" but would surely triumph because, like the Maccabees, they "were filled with enthusiasm for their just cause."[53] Several rabbis even compared Franz Joseph to Mattathias, the elderly father of the Maccabees who had urged them to fight oppression "in a holy struggle for the fatherland."[54] Passover offered another opportunity to integrate the war into Jewish tradition. In March 1915 *Jung Juda* urged its young readers to regard the Russian czar as a cruel Pharoah who oppressed the Jews and deserved defeat. It envisioned future seders in which Jews would recount the brave deeds of Jewish soldiers who had spilled their blood for "God, Kaiser, and fatherland."[55]

Imagining the war in such stark moral terms as a war of good versus evil, Austrian Jews confidently expected that Austria would emerge victorious. Austria would triumph "because our cause is holy," because "justice is on our side," and because righteousness and culture had to triumph over barbarism and slavery.[56] Not only justice, but God Himself was on the side of Austria-Hungary, Jewish spokesmen insisted. Rabbis in particular regularly asserted that God would ensure an Austrian victory.[57] Some, like Rubin Färber of Mährisch Ostrau and W. Reich of Baden bei Wien, even viewed Franz Joseph as the agent of God.[58] The liberal Jewish press regularly stressed that God would ensure an Austrian victory. *Jung Juda* declared that God would lead Austria and her allies to victory because theirs was a just cause.[59] The editors cited a postcard from a Jewish girl in Vienna to her uncle on the Russian front that quoted the psalmist, "The Lord is with me, I shall not fear," and declared: "Surely our victory is certain. This straightforward belief in God will soon let us triumph over our enemies."[60] Such views were common in all of the belligerents,[61] but Austrian Jews thought that Russian persecution of the Jews gave them a special reason to believe that God was truly on their side.

Jews in Austria did not face the terrible dilemma of Jews in all of the other belligerent states. They did not need to justify a war fought alongside an ally they regarded as evil or against countries they admired. Jews in England and France faced the difficult task of fighting on the same side as Russia, a country they detested for persecuting the Jews. Jews in Germany, like Jews in Austria, could regard World War I as a war of revenge for Kishinev, a holy war against the traditional enemy of the Jews. Most German troops, however, fought England and France on the Western Front and thus had to justify a war against two countries that Jews respected. Jews in England, France, and Germany defended their participation in a morally ambiguous war by invoking their loyalty to the states in which they lived and by villifying their enemies for jealousy, perfidy, or militaristic aggression. Nevertheless, the war presented them with a conflict between their national and Jewish loyalties.[62]

In contrast, Austrian Jews felt no such conflict between their loyalty to the fatherland and their loyalty to the Jewish people. Austria's primary enemy in the first half of the war was Russia, so Austrian Jews fought in the war absolutely convinced of the justice of their cause. They did not have to worry about justifying a war against respected enemies. Although technically at war with England and France, Austria sent virtually no troops to the Western Front. Not having to confront the English and French in battle, the Jews in Austria could easily ignore the fact that their fatherland was at war with two countries that they traditionally admired as the bastions of democracy and Jewish rights. On the rare occasions when Jewish polemicists mentioned England and France, they mouthed conventional pieties about English jealousy of German wealth, or they blamed Russia for exerting an evil influence on her allies. Thus they transformed a discussion of the Western democracies into another opportunity to lambast Russia.[63]

The course of the fighting on the Eastern Front in 1914 and 1915 reinforced the Jewish conception of the war as a holy war against Russia. In August 1914, Russian troops overran the Austrian provinces of Galicia and Bukovina and imposed their first military occupation. It lasted until June 1915, when German and Austrian troops defeated the Russians and restored most of Galicia and Bukovina to Austrian control (See Map 2).[64] The Russian invasion of these provinces underscored that Austrian and Jewish goals in the war were identical. The Jews not only had to defend the fatherland from invasion and help it regain conquered territory, but also to rescue fellow Austrian Jews from the clutches of an enemy bent on persecuting them as Austrians and as Jews. Throughout 1914 and 1915, Jewish newspapers all over the Monarchy villified Russia endlessly as the barbaric opponent of culture and civilization, often using extremely vivid language. They referred, for example, to "the barbarism of our truly cannibalistic enemy." More importantly, the Jewish press regularly presented gruesome reports of Russian atrocities against Jews in Galicia, many of them exaggerated, depicting Russian policy as a "war of annihilation against all that is Jewish." The war, then, was not only a *Rachekrieg für Kishinev* but was fought for the liberation of Galician and Bukovinian Jewry, simultaneously on behalf of the Habsburg Monarchy and Austrian Jewry.[65]

Jewish spokesmen all agreed on the identity of Austrian and Jewish goals in the struggle to liberate Galicia and Bukovina. Rabbi Adolf Altmann in Meran, later a military chaplain, boldly declared in early 1915 that the war against Russia was a war against Amalek, "the hereditary enemy of Jewry and perhaps no less the hereditary enemy of our fatherland."[66] Similarly, Heinrich Schreiber declared in May 1915 in the pages of the *Österreichische Wochenschrift* that "we struggle bravely for the ideals of our fatherland, and we feel as one with the masses of our fellow Jews (*Glaubensbrüder*) who are threatened by the enemy hordes and their pogroms."[67] Zionists too delighted that in Galicia they could fight for Austria and the Jewish people at the same time. A writer for the Brünn-based *Jüdische Volksstimme* reminded his readers in March 1915 that "we do not forget that we are fighting against the descendants of Esau," against a country that murders and tortures Jews, for the liberation of millions of Jews, and for the creation of a new, more moral world.[68] Like all Jews, Zionists used inflated language to describe the war as a struggle between Western culture and Asiatic barbarism, a conflict against an enemy who had embarked on a "war of annihilation" against the Jewish people.[69]

During the course of the fighting with Russia, Jewish spokesmen always em-

The Fighting in Galicia During World War I

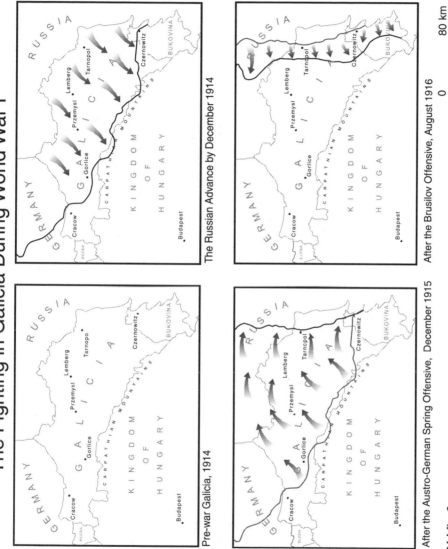

Pre-war Galicia, 1914

The Russian Advance by December 1914

After the Austro-German Spring Offensive, December 1915

After the Brusilov Offensive, August 1916

MAP 2

phasized the Austrian identities of the Jews in Galicia and Bukovina. At the beginning of the war, the Jewish press was filled with articles attesting the supreme devotion of Galician Jews to the Austrian cause, demonstrating how Jews all over the province rushed to provide advancing Austrian soldiers with food, drink, assistance, and good wishes, even on the Sabbath.[70] One writer in the *Österreichische Wochenschrift* asserted that Galician Jews were utterly "ready out of inner conviction to fight for the victory of Austria." Their patriotism was "healthy" and "instinctive," causing them to take their sons out of Talmud study houses so they could sacrifice their lives for their beloved land against "the greatest enemy of mankind."[71] The Zionist *Jüdische Zeitung* proudly reported that during the Russian siege of Czernowitz, Bukovina, Salo Weisselberger, the city's Jewish mayor, refused to remove the Austrian flag from the city hall.[72] One Jewish chaplain summed up the Jewish position claiming that "the Galician Jews are one of the most loyal groups of inhabitants of Austria. They have sacrificed a great deal, lost the most, and suffered the most in this war."[73] The Jewish press delighted in reporting that Crown Prince Karl praised the Jews of Galicia and Bukovina for their patriotism and loyalty to Austria during the Russian occupation and promised them reparations for their losses.[74]

When Russian troops conquered most of Galicia and Bukovina in the summer of 1914, hundreds of thousands of Jews fled the provinces fearing for their lives at the hands of the Russians. Those who remained suffered under the Russian occupation, although, despite exaggerated reports about Russian atrocities, for the most part the Russian army maintained order.[75] Austrian Jews universally argued that the Russians persecuted Galician and Bukovinian Jews because of their Austrian loyalties. In September 1914, a writer for the *Österreichische Wochenschrift* asserted that the Russians attacked the Jews in eastern Galicia "as loyal Austrians, bitter enemies of . . . Russia, and as Jews."[76] In an article on Russian atrocities in the Bukovinian town of Sadagora, the author similarly declared that the Jews had suffered specifically because of their loyalty to Austria.[77] Angry with anti-Semitic slander, in early 1915, the newspaper declared that Galician Jews were "the staunchest and most loyal protectors of the fatherland and the dynasty," whom the Russians treated "as their worst opponents" in the war. One writer simply stated: "The Russians persecuted the Jews for their notorious Austrian sympathies, their loyalty to the Kaiser, the love and respect for His Majesty Kaiser Franz Joseph."[78] Jewish spokesmen agreed that the Jews of Galicia and of Russian Poland viewed the Austrian troops as their liberators.[79]

Austrian Jews understood, of course, that anti-Semitism played a significant role in Russian persecution of the Jews in Galicia and Bukovina. Nevertheless, Austrian Jews preferred to emphasize that Russians wanted to punish Jews for their staunch identification with Austria. Such arguments served to bolster the Jewish conviction that they were the most loyal of all Austrians. Moreover, if the Galician refugees had suffered as Austrians, surely they deserved public assistance and sympathy. Most importantly, arguing that Russia persecuted Galician Jews as Austrians reinforced the Jewish commitment to fight against Russia both as loyal Austrians and as good Jews.

At the same time, Jewish spokesmen always admitted that Jews cared about the

war not only because they loved the fatherland, but because the war would rescue Jews. In June 1915, Chaplain Majer Tauber wrote a lengthy report about Jewish bravery during the Austrian offensive in Galicia. Jewish soldiers, he noted,
fought valiantly for the fatherland "and also with the consciousness that they
were fighting the oppressor of the Jews."[80] The Jewish press singled out for praise
Galician Jewish soldiers, who fought to avenge loved ones persecuted by the
Russians. In May 1915, for example, the *Österreichische Wochenschrift* attributed the
courage of a Galician Hasid to the fact that the Russians had raped his sister and
taken his father hostage. The author concluded, probably exaggerating for propaganda purposes, that "all the Galician Jewish soldiers are as courageous and determined [as this one]. With insane fury they attack, and their hatred of the Russian
murderers, who have treated their families so brutally, is the best stimulus [for
their valor]."[81]

Given these assumptions, it was only natural for Austrian Jews to exult over
German and Austrian military successes in Galicia in the spring and summer of
1915. Beginning with the breakthrough at Gorlice in April, the Central Powers liberated most of Galicia and Bukovina by June and advanced deeply into Russia, oc-
cupying Russian Poland and the Baltic region by the summer.[82] Austrian Jews responded with a joyful cheer as they sent innumerable congratulatory telegrams to
political leaders, held countless prayer services and torchlit parades all over the
country, and expressed their happiness and relief that the Russians had been defeated and Galician and Polish Jewry liberated. Refugees especially held patriotic
demonstrations to celebrate the liberation of Przemysl, Lemberg, and other cities
in Galicia.[83] The IKG of Vienna sent a telegram to Archduke Friedrich congratulating him for the Austrian reconquest of Przemysl, stating that:

> Austrian Jewry is proud that its sons, filled with burning love for Kaiser and
> fatherland, permeated with [the conviction of] the justice of our cause, fight
> devotedly and contemptuous of death alongside their fellow citizens under
> your imperial and royal majesty's command for the defense of the fatherland.
> May God's protection continue to accompany our glorious army to a final
> victory.[84]

IKG President Alfred Stern repeated these sentiments in his speech at the religious service held on June 24 to rejoice over the liberation of Lemberg by Austrian troops. Stern lauded the Jews who fought with all their hearts as Austrian
soldiers for Kaiser and Reich alongside their comrades, to defeat czarist Russia,
the most terrible enemy of humanity, and thus to guarantee that "Europe will
not be Russian."[85]

Moritz Güdemann, the elderly chief rabbi of Vienna, also rejoiced over the
Austrian liberation of Lemberg. He noted in his diary: "Oh great, obstinate, im-
penitent Russia of terror and pogroms, how dearly you and your czars must still
pay for your persecution of the Jews."[86] His colleague in Graz universalized the
point in a sermon on June 26. The reconquest of Lemberg, he declared, was a
victory of culture over barbarism, "a day of salvation for mankind," proof of the
triumph of God and justice.[87] The editors of *Jung Juda* simply announced:
"Almighty God has obtained victory for our just cause."[88]

Zionists too extended their fervent congratulations to the Kaiser, expressing their "jubilant joy" over the liberation of Lemberg and reiterating their "traditional dynastic loyalty and patriotic feelings."[89] The editors of Prague-based *Selbstwehr* declared the "overwhelming joy" of "we Austrian Jews," noting: "Lemberg conquered. These two words encompass the enormous measure of our happiness that no one will forget his whole life long."[90] Benno Straucher, the Jewish nationalist parliamentary deputy from Bukovina, announced that the victory of the Central Powers in Galicia and Russian-Poland would prevent the oppression of Europe by wild, barbaric Cossacks.[91] Similarly, Brünn Zionists declared that "the liberation of Galicia from the yoke of the Cossack hordes" represented the triumph of freedom and humanity over barbarism.[92] Many Jews hoped that their victories over the Russians in Galicia and Poland meant that the war would soon be over, with Austria and her allies victorious.[93]

The lead article in the *Österreichische Wochenschrift* on June 25, 1915, summed up the attitudes of Austrian Jews quite well. Entitled "The Liberated Land," the article detailed Russian atrocities against the Jews, expressed deep satisfaction that Galician Jewry had been liberated from Russian oppression, and asserted its happiness that "Galicia is once more Austrian."[94] All summer, the Jewish press printed articles about Russian atrocities, vilified the Russians, and claimed that Russians had persecuted Galician Jews because of their Austrian loyalty.[95] More importantly, the press made it clear that Austrian Jews fervently wished that Galicia remain Austrian, no matter what plans Germany and Austria might have for the future of Poland.[96] Jewish appeals for aid to the suffering Jews in liberated Galicia assumed the continuity of Austrian sovereignty in the province and viewed the Austrian central authorities the only possible source of fairness and justice in an anti-Semitic region.[97] While the *Burgfrieden* prevented Jewish newspapers from lambasting Poles for their anti-Jewish activities in Galicia in 1915, internal Jewish reports on the situation in Galicia indicated high levels of Polish anti-Semitism and mistreatment of Jews in the province. The Jewish mayor of Boryslaw, Galicia, reported to Viennese Zionist leader Robert Stricker in July 1915 that "the officials [in Galicia] of Polish nationality are fanatical Jew-haters and do everything in order to bring despair to the Jewish population."[98] No wonder Austrian Jews wanted to retain Austrian control in Galicia.

Zionists articulated their hopes for Austrian Galicia most forcefully. The Executive Committee of Austrian Zionists wrote to the new governor of Galicia, General von Colard, to tell him that "a fortunate Galicia in indivisible bonds with a strong Austria is the goal of all truly patriotic hopes, and therefore also the wish of nationally-minded Jews in Galicia."[99] The Executive Committee also appealed to the Austrian Minister President to ensure that the central government, not local authorities, supervise the reconstruction of Galicia. After all, Zionists argued, Galicia had been reconquered with the blood of the supranational Austrian army for the *Gesamtmonarchie*. Jews in Galicia and Bukovina had suffered more than any other Austrians because of "their unshakable love of the fatherland and their adamant loyalty to the state." As "bearers of the Austrian state idea in the East," they had suffered for Austria and deserved to remain in Austria.[100] Zionist newpapers also demanded that Galicia remain Austrian. The Brünn *Jüdi-*

sche Volksstimme insisted in July 1915: "Jewish national interests and Austrian imperial interests urgently require that Galicia be tightly united with the other parts of
the Monarchy and that Galicia be ruled from Vienna for all eternity."[101] All the
Zionist papers emphasized that the Austrian victory was a victory for a multinational, united Austria and expressed their absolute desire for the continuity of the
supranational state.[102]

The Kaiser's 85th birthday in August 1915, soon after the decisive victories of
the Central Powers in Galicia and Poland, gave Austrian Jews an opportunity to
reiterate their deeply held convictions about the war. Praising the Kaiser as a man
of peace defending his people from hostile attack, Jews pointed out how the
peoples of the Monarchy, united in defense of the fatherland, had defeated
czarism and saved the Jewish people. They also used the opportunity to repeat
how the Jews were the most patriotic of all Austrians.[103] These views were ele-
gantly articulated by Rabbi Isaak Hirsch in his sermon in Wiznitz, Bukovina,
commemorating Franz Joseph's birthday. Depicting the war with Russia as a war
"to put a stop to this insatiable, cannibalistic angel of death" and "to throw its
wild Cossack army back to the desolate steppes of Asia," Rabbi Hirsch rejoiced
over the Austrian and German victories and wished Franz Joseph, "our protect-
ing angel," long years on the throne. Hirsch even compared the feelings of returning Galician refugees seeing their ruined homes to traditional Jewish feelings
about the ruins of Jerusalem![104] Similarly, to celebrate the 67th anniversary of
Franz Joseph's ascension to power, Jews expressed their thankfulness that Austrian
troops had chased the Russians out of Galicia and had reintroduced "justice,
righteousness, culture, and freedom" in the province.[105] Naturally, on the anniversary of the liberation of Galicia, Jews also repeated their conviction that justice would inevitably triumph against Russian despotism.[106]

When Russian troops invaded Galicia and Bukovina again in the Brusilov Offensive in the summer of 1916 (see Map 2),[107] Austrian Jews repeated their confidence that the Central Powers, the representatives of freedom and culture,
would surely drive out the evil Russians once again because "justice must and
will triumph in this war." Moreover, the editors of the Orthodox *Jüdische Korre-
spondent* reminded its readers, "the war with Russia is and remains the holiest and
most noble task of all Jews,"[108] and they remained utterly confident in Austria's
victory.[109]

Romania's declaration of war on the Central Powers in the summer of 1916
provided Austrian Jews with yet another opportunity to articulate their wartime
ideology. Because Romania had persecuted her Jews vigorously, Austrian Jews
could consider Romania "next to Russia, our worst, most malicious enemy." War
with Romania was thus also a Jewish war, "a war of revenge for all the abomi-
nable, brutal, and criminal acts . . . that this country has committed, unpun-
ished, against our brothers for decades."[110]

The rest of the fighting war held absolutely no interest for the Jews. Although
they regularly asserted their patriotic fervor and did their duty on the Italian
Front, the war with Italy was not a Jewish war and Jewish polemicists simply ignored it. Indeed, many Jewish newspapers did not even bother to mention the
outbreak of war with Italy in May 1915. Those that did mouthed conventional

pieties about Italy's "perfidy" for having broken her treaty obligations with Germany and Austria-Hungary in order to join the war on the side of England and France. Prague Zionists used the opportunity of Italy's declaration to express their sympathy for Franz Joseph for having to bear yet another sorrow and to declare the absolute loyalty of Austrian Jews. Similarly, the monthy periodical of the *Österreichisch-Israelitische Union* downplayed the significance of the new front with Italy in the face of the victories of the Central Powers in Galicia and Poland and their faith in an imminent victory.[111] Memoirists also rarely mentioned the war with Italy, and when they did it was just to denote Italian treachery.[112] Although the war with Italy was generally popular in Austria, serving to allow the different national groups to work together for a larger Austrian goal,[113] Jews seem not to have cared very much about it, probably because it was not a Jewish war like the war with Russia.

The Goals of Jewish Patriotism

Throughout the war, the Jews of Austria endlessly asserted their patriotic devotion to the fatherland and their conviction that they had contributed as much if not more than any other people in Austria to the war effort. Not only did they valiantly serve in the armed forces—ultimately 300,000 Jews served in the Austro-Hungarian army during the war[114]—but they were exemplary soldiers who fought hard, were frequently decorated, and died for the fatherland. In addition, Jews contributed significantly on the home front, donating much money for war loans and war welfare and volunteering their time to help soldiers and their dependents. Thus Jews gave their *Gut und Blut,* their lives and their money, to the war. They did so, Jewish spokesmen argued, out of deep gratitude to the Kaiser and out of fervent love for the fatherland. They also had uniquely Jewish reasons for such patriotism. As we have already seen, they viewed the war as a Jewish holy war to liberate fellow Jews, and they hoped that their loyal service would dispel anti-Semitic myths. In addition, Jews felt compelled to assert their patriotism so loudly because they hoped that it would ensure the continuity of the supranational Monarchy. Convinced that only Habsburg Austria could protect them from anti-Semitism, Austrian Jews also knew that only such a supranational state permitted them their comfortable Jewish identity.

At the beginning of the war, Jewish spokesmen coupled their assertions of patriotism with confidence that the war would lead to Austrian brotherhood and unity. An article in September 1914 in *Jung Juda,* for example, reminded its young readers that Jewish soldiers fought "in true brotherhood of arms, shoulder to shoulder with their comrades to defend the fatherland bravely and courageously, happily fulfilling their duty to their common fatherland."[115] Similarly, Prague Zionists asserted in November that Jewish soldiers were fighting "shoulder to shoulder with the other citizens for the good of Austria, so that in the field there was no difference between Jews and non-Jews."[116] Writers for the Viennese *Österreichische Wochenschrift* also hopefully assumed that the war would lead to internal Austrian unity and the creation of an Austro-Hungarian nation.[117]

Even while they hoped that their effort would erase differences between groups, Jewish polemicists assumed that Jews had a particular gift for patriotic sacrifice. Insecurity in the face of anti-Semitism induced Jewish spokesmen to insist that Jews were the most patriotic of all Austrians. In October 1914, Heinrich York-Steiner wrote that among all the nations of Austria, the Jews were unparalleled in loyalty to Kaiser and Reich, in absolute devotion to Austria's victory, in willingness to sacrifice their lives and their energy for the Austrian cause, and in their fervent prayers for an Austrian victory.[118] Zionists also regularly asserted that Jews, fighting courageously for freedom and the fatherland, were the staunchest supporters of the Monarchy and the idea of a unified Austria.[119]

Jewish appeals to purchase war bonds emphasized Jewish patriotism and the special Jewish obligation to support the war. In May 1915, the editors of the *Österreichische Wochenschrift* argued that buying bonds was just as significant as fighting on the battlefield and urged people to sign up to prove "that the peoples and nationalities of the Monarchy, with loyal resolve, flock to defend with their lives and their money the Habsburg throne, their honor, and their future."[120] Most appeals, like that of Vienna's chief rabbi Moritz Güdemann for the third war loan, urged Jews to contribute because it was their duty both as Austrians and as Jews.[121] Zionists especially emphasized the Jewish dimension in their appeals for Jews to buy war bonds. Urging readers to sign up for the second war loan in May 1915, the editors of *Selbstwehr* argued that Jews had to support Austria not only because it would liberate East European Jewry, but because only a supranational Austria could hold anti-Semitism in check. Bohemian Jewry, *Selbstwehr* warned, should remember that "its future and its well-being are inseparably bound up with that of Austria."[122] The Zionist Party of Austria reminded its adherents that supporting Austria financially was necessary for the further development of Zionism and Jewish nationalism.[123] No doubt Zionists understood that they could only achieve Jewish national autonomy in a multinational Austria, not in any of the unitary nation-states that might replace it.

Reports of Jewish bravery underscored Jewish devotion to the fatherland. The Jewish press delighted in reporting how the archdukes who commanded the Austrian armies singled out Jewish soldiers and praised their bravery. In January 1915, the *Österreichische Wochenschrift* reported how Archduke Josef praised Jewish soldiers under his command, saying that "their courage is admirable, their devotion deserving praise."[124] Similarly, Archduke Peter Ferdinand asserted that his Jewish soldiers, including the traditionally religious among them, "are all extraordinarily . . . brave. The Jews in my division fight courageously, and I am very satisfied with them."[125] Throughout the war, all Jewish newspapers published weekly reports about Jewish acts of heroism and lists of Jews who received military decorations for valor. They also published the names of Jewish officers and men who lost their lives fighting for the fatherland. Periodically, a *Jüdisches Kriegsgedenkenblatt* appeared that provided long reports of the bravery of individual fallen Jewish soldiers, especially Jewish officers. Such lists of honor reminded Jews of their significant contribution to the war effort and confirmed to them their absolute loyalty to the Monarchy.

At the same time, these reports and lists bolstered the Jewish hope that their deaths on the battlefield would eliminate the scourge of anti-Semitism. Reports often mentioned how non-Jewish soldiers were impressed with Jewish bravery in battle or how Jewish soldiers were second to none in courage and daring. Discussions of Jewish bravery were regularly coupled with the hope that Jewish heroism would dispel anti-Semitic prejudice about Jewish cowardice.[126] The Zionists organized an archive to collect information about Jewish bravery and patriotism and, with the financial help of the *Israelitische Kultusgemeinde* of Vienna, published a journal, *Jüdisches Archiv,* specifically to combat anti-Semitism with reports of Jewish heroism.[127] Zionists understood that Jewish soldiers were representatives of the Jewish people fighting for Jewish honor as well as for a Jewish and Austrian cause.[128]

Despite Jewish hopes for solidarity and brotherhood emerging from the comradeship of war, and despite the *Burgfrieden,* the wartime ban on inciting national, religious, or political animosity, anti-Semitism did not diminish. Indeed, during the last two years of the war anti-Semitism grew enormously, as many segments of the war-weary population blamed the Jews for the severe food, fuel, and housing shortages. Throughout the war the Jewish press tracked anti-Semitism, always worried about it, and hoped that it would somehow dissipate. Jewish spokesmen expressed their annoyance that Jewish devotion to the war effort and bravery in the field had not stilled the anti-Semites, who continued to charge the Jews with cowardice, treason, and shirking military responsibility despite mountains of evidence to the contrary. They complained that the censor was not more vigilant in preventing anti-Semitic invective in the press. Zionists in particular, who traditionally believed that the only solution to the problem of anti-Semitism was the creation of a Jewish state, but who nevertheless had hoped that Jewish bravery would dispel anti-Semitic myths, became pessimistic that the blood of Jewish soldiers and the sufferings of Jewish refugees might have any effect on anti-Semitism.[129]

In their expectation that the war would end anti-Semitism and bring full equality, and in their disappointment with rising anti-Semitism in the second half of the war, Austrian Jews resembled Jews in Germany. In that country too, all Jews, from the liberals to the Zionists to the Orthodox, had greeted the advent of the war with patriotic enthusiasm and hope that the war would erase anti-Jewish antagonisms in a swell of patriotic brotherhood. There too, disappointments with an endless, bloody war, combined with terrible privations and political problems on the home front, led to rising anti-Semitic agitation from 1916 on. In both countries, anti-Semites charged the Jews with war profiteering, shirking military responsibility, and undermining the war effort. Jews in both Germany and Austria responded to that anti-Semitism with ever greater assertions of patriotism and reminders of their heroism and sacrifice.[130] In both countries, the war experience generated greater Jewish ethnic consciousness.

Yet the similarities between Austrian and German Jews should not obscure some very significant differences. In the first place, because of their belief that the war would allow them to merge fully into the German nation, even into the German *Volk,* German Jews were probably more disappointed than Austrian Jews by anti-Semitism because it made it clear that Jews could never be full members of the national community.[131] Austrian Jews, on the other hand, had generally not sought merger in any particular *Volk,* but rather had only wanted to assert their loyalty to the multinational Austrian state, and the state itself had not disappointed them. Although anti-Semitism flourished in Austria, neither the government nor the army discriminated against the Jews. Jews therefore remained convinced that the multinational state provided them with the best protection against anti-Semitism. In Germany, not only did anti-Semites prohibit Jews from merging into the nation, but even the state seemed to reject Jewish patriotism and became involved in anti-Semitic acts. It remained nearly impossible during the war for the Jews to receive officers' commissions in the German army. More importantly, in 1916, the German government bowed to anti-Semitic pressure and conducted a military census to determine if indeed Jews had shirked their military responsibilities. Although the government insisted it conducted the census only to dispel anti-Semitic charges, the fact that it conducted it at all supported anti-Semitic contentions about the Jews. Thus the Jews of Germany felt betrayed by the very fatherland for which they so valiantly fought.[132] Jews in Austria felt no such betrayal and therefore remained loyal supporters of the multinational state to the very end.

A second difference between the Jews of Germany and Austria during the war has to do with the issue of Jewish ethnicity. Both Jewish communities experienced rising Jewish solidarity and much greater emphasis on Jewish peoplehood. Historians argue that the major impact of World War I on the Jews in Germany was a new emphasis on their ethnic consciouness, a consciousness generated by wartime anti-Semitism, especially the military census, and by the encounter of German Jews with East European Jews during the German occupation of Russian Poland after 1915.[133] Austrian Jews also experienced a deepening of Jewish ethnic consciousness during the war years. Rising Jewish self-consciousness in the Monarchy, however, had little to do with the encounter with East European Jews, since Austrian Jewry always included large numbers of East European Jews in Galicia and Bukovina, many of whom had migrated elsewhere in the Monarchy and all of whom were Austrian citizens. Anti-Semitism played an important role in augmenting Austrian Jewish solidarity, but the main reason for rising Jewish consciousness was the escalating nationality conflict after 1917 and the need for the Jews to position themselves within it. Just as Austrian Jewry had always been freer than other Western European Jews to assert Jewish ethnicity because Austria was not a nation-state but a conglomeration of national groups, so too during the war, nationality politics created a situation in which Jews felt compelled to assert their ethnic identity. Moreover, while German Jews still felt tied to the German nation that spurned them, Austrian Jews increasingly belonged to none of the nationalities of Austria at all. Indeed, at the end of the war, the collapse of the Monarchy also deprived them of a political identity, and they were truly cast adrift.[134]

World War I thus served to fortify the staunch Austrian identity of Austrian Jewry. The war, especially the first two years of it, did not create a break in Jewish attitudes, but rather reinforced long-cherished ideas. Because Austria fought Russia, the traditional enemy of the Jews, and because Russia invaded Austria and persecuted Jews in Galicia and Bukovina, Austrian Jews could easily regard the war as a Jewish holy war. They could passionately support the Austrian war effort, convinced that they served "a just cause." Because they were fighting for the Jews at the same time as they struggled on behalf of Austria, the war also served to fortify the Jewish consciousness of Austria's Jews. Only in the supranational Monarchy, of course, could the Jews so confidently assert their Austrian and Jewish loyalties at the same time.

Jews supported the Austrian war effort both on the battlefield and on the home front. Indeed, their work on the home front in particular reinforced the identity of Austrian and Jewish concerns in their minds. Jewish men and women participated actively in patriotic war work, but from the beginning they devoted their special attention to the plight of the refugees from Galicia and Bukovina who flooded into Vienna, Bohemia, and Moravia. By working with these refugees, Bohemian, Moravian, and Viennese Jews assisted the victims of Austria's war with Russia at the same time as they helped fellow Jews. Such assistance not only reinforced their convictions about the necessity of the war but also made them acutely aware of their commitments to the Jewish people and to the continuity of Habsburg Austria.

Galician refugees in Brünn. *Courtesy CAHJP, PL 474.*

Anitta Müller's "Soup and Tea Institute," for Jewish refugees, Vienna. *Top:* Waiting in line to get in; *bottom:* Indoors. *Courtesy CAHJP, AW 2318.*

Anitta Müller's trade school for Galician Jewish refugee girls and women, Vienna. *Courtesy CAHJP, AW 2318.*

Celebrating the Jewish holiday of Simchat Torah on the Italian Front, 1917. *Courtesy CAHJP, Au 258, 6a.*

Celebrating Passover on the Italian Front, 1918. *Courtesy CAHJP, Au 258/11.*

Junior Reserve Officer
(Zugsführer) Moritz Pollack
from Prossnitz, Moravia.
Courtesy CAHJP, CS 190.

Medic Teofil Reiss (on right)
before a sign asking people to
subscribe to the seventh war
loan. *Courtesy Erwin Schmidl.*

Soldier Weiss, card sent to
his wife describing the scene:
"Succoth in the Field, 5658
(sic: 5678)–1917, after services,
in front of the 'temple.'"
Courtesy CAHJP, Au 258/26.

Three Austrian Jewish chaplains. *Courtesy CAHJP, Au 258/4.*

Josef Samuel Bloch, editor, Österreichische Wochenschrift, picture from his Polish passport, 1921. Born in Galicia, Bloch did not receive Austrian citizenship in the Republic, despite living in Vienna for decades. *Courtesy CAHJP, P150/1.*

3

Mobilizing the Home Front

Patriotic War Work and Helping Jewish Refugees

For all the belligerents, World War I was a total war, mobilizing not only young men in the armed forces, but all sectors of society, who regarded work on the "home front" as a significant contribution to the war effort and as an expression of patriotism analogous to the efforts of men on the battlefield.[1] Like Jews in Germany, France, and England, Jews in Austria participated actively on the Austrian home front in the First World War, their actions demonstrating their loyalty to the state in which they lived. They not only sent their sons to die on the field of honor but also gave their money, time, and devotion to help their country fight its enemies. Middle-class Austrian Jews believed that their patriotic war work—buying war bonds, preparing linens and woolens for soldiers, working for the Red Cross, volunteering as nurses, caring for the widows and orphans of the millions of fallen soldiers—demonstrated their support for the Austrian war effort. They hoped that, like valor on the battlefield, war work would dispel anti-Semitism and prove their loyalty to Austria.[2]

The very nature of the war in Austria, however, created a situation in which Jews devoted most of their patriotic war work to the needs of fellow Jews. Middle-class Austrian Jews attended to the religious needs of Jewish soldiers in the army. More importantly, the enormous influx of Jewish refugees from Galicia and Bukovina compelled the Jews in Vienna, Bohemia, and Moravia to devote the bulk of their wartime charitable efforts to aid suffering Jews from the East. They regarded such traditional Jewish charity primarily as an act of Austrian patriotism, because these refugees were Austrian citizens, victims of Austria's war with Russia. Jewish work on the home front thus reinforced the identity of Austrian and Jewish interests during World War I.

The fact that Austrian Jews, particularly Jewish women, spent so much time helping fellow Jews also reinforced Jewish solidarity. While they may have justified their behavior in terms of Austrian patriotism, the work itself led to a greater sense of Jewish peoplehood. Even when German-speaking Jews living in "western" Austria—that is, Vienna, Bohemia, and Moravia—felt superior to Jews from the East, they nevertheless understood the need for Jewish unity, especially in the face of increasing anti-Semitism in the last two years of the war. Such unity underscored the anomolous position of the Jews as a separate people in Austria and at the same time served to strengthen the commitment of Austrian Jewry to the continuity of a unified, multinational Austrian state.

Patriotic War Work

When the war broke out at the end of July 1914, Austrian Jewish leaders loudly proclaimed the eagerness of Jews to contribute to the war effort on the home front. Jews immediately donated money and volunteered their services to help soldiers and their families, without any regard to the religion or national identity of those they aided. Indeed, Jews delighted in working for the Red Cross and the various governmental agencies set up to provide welfare assistance, because such work affirmed their integration into Austrian society. It also contributed to the spirit of brotherhood and solidarity that marked the early months of the war.

Jewish communities all over Austria rushed to donate money for the war effort as well as hospital beds for the wounded.[3] Throughout the war, they donated money to the Red Cross and government War Relief as well as to organizations that provided assistance to wounded soldiers or to impoverished military dependents.[4] They even donated the copper from the roofs of synagogues to help produce armaments.[5] Humanitarian Jewish organizations like the Bnai Brith also donated space for military hospitals and paid for the care of those treated there. They fed thousands of people rendered unemployed by the war.[6]

At the very beginning of the war, Jewish communities hoped to prevent a confessionalization of relief work. Since they perceived their generosity as an act of Austrian patriotism in the spirit of August, they did not want to target Jewish soldiers or their dependents as the recipients of Jewish charity. On August 17, 1914, the Jewish community of Vienna assembled 123 representatives of Jewish charitable organizations to coordinate their war relief efforts. With millions of men drafted into the military, many families were left without any means of support beyond the meager government allotment provided to soldiers' dependents. Gustav Kohn, the vice president of the IKG, announced that it was "unwise" to place relief on a confessional basis. He urged that Jewish organizations simply assist *anyone* impoverished by the war. Kohn's advice reflected both his commitment to Austrian brotherhood and his concern, despite the spirit of August, that if Jews targeted Jewish recipients for aid, official relief organizations might not adequately attend to Jews.[7]

Like the Jewish communities, the humanitarian organization Bnai Brith also insisted at the beginning of the war that it engaged in war welfare "without distinguishing between nationalities or religions." Reports of Bnai Brith activities repeatedly stressed that members worked without any consideration to the national or religious background of the recipients of their charity.[8] Even the Zionists, normally focused on Jewish solidarity, emphasized that their patriotic war work served the common welfare. In August 1914, the Austrian branch of the Jewish National Fund, which collected money to support Jewish settlements in the land of Israel, declared that the terrible economic problems created by the war impelled it "in the interests of humanity" to collect money for war wounded, widows and orphans of fallen soldiers, and families made needy by the war.[9] Zionist youth groups helped harvest the crops, distributed food to soldiers, and volunteered for the Red Cross.[10] As the war progressed, Jewish charitable organizations continued to do general war work on an interconfessional basis, despite their increasing attention to the needs of fellow Jews.[11]

The outpouring of time, money, and effort by Jewish individuals to war work was impressive. Many earmarked their contributions for synagogue honors to war relief or, following traditional Jewish custom, donated money on special occasions to help soldiers and their dependents. Until 1916, the majority of such special donations to the Vienna Jewish community were specifically directed toward general war work.[12] The *Österreichische Wochenschrift* sent its income from New Year's ads, which it had urged people to take out instead of sending cards, to Austrian War Relief.[13]

From a financial point of view, the most significant contribution of Austrian Jews to the war effort was the buying of war bonds, which actually meant contributing to the war loans. The Austrian government conducted eight campaigns for war loans between 1914 and 1918. Each time, the *Israelitische Kultusgemeinde* of Vienna contributed 500,000 crowns, and considered the financial sacrifice to be a patriotic duty.[14] Other Jewish communities did so as well. In the spring of 1916, the tiny Jewish community in St. Pölten gave 225,000 crowns to the fourth war loan, and the Jewish communities of Bohemia jointly provided 500,000 crowns.[15] The Prague Jewish community regularly contributed to the war loans, generally between 150,000 and 250,000 crowns.[16] Individuals and organizations also contributed generously to the war loans. The Agudas Yisroel Society, an organization of Orthodox Jews in Vienna, for example, raised 235,000 crowns for the fourth war loan and 304,000 crowns for the fifth, mostly from men and women of modest means.[17] Campaigns among Jewish school children also netted contributions.[18]

Such financial commitment helped those at home to equate their service to the fatherland with the valor of those fighting on the front. In the spring of 1916, the IKG of Vienna circulated an open letter urging Jews to contribute to the fourth war loan and suggesting that such sacrifice manifested patriotism at the same time as it helped assure an Austrian victory. These communal leaders declared:

> Jewish Fellow Citizens: In fulfillment of their obvious duty, our fathers, brothers, and sons devote their blood and their lives as brave soldiers in our glorious army. With similar consciousness of duty, those who remain at home also have happily sacrificed their property on the altar of their beloved fatherland. Thus now again the call of the state should arouse a patriotic echo in all of us! . . . In this way each of us helps ensure the complete victory of our heroes at the front and does his part to shorten this war, inflicted upon us by our enemies.[19]

The work performed by women was by far the most conspicuous aspect of Jewish patriotic war work—indeed of the home front in general. All over Europe, middle- and upper-class women devoted their money, time, and energy to help soldiers and their families. These women considered such work an extension of the traditional female roles of mother and nurturer and thus felt no conflict between their obligations to their own families and their public service. Moreover, such work on the home front made them feel that they too contributed to the national cause. While no one ever really believed that the home front was as important as the military front, women nevertheless viewed their relief work as analogous to the sacrifices of men in battle and necessary for a successful conclusion of the war.[20]

At the very beginning of the war, Jewish activist Clothilde Benedikt called on Austrian Jewish women to help the war effort by aiding the families of soldiers called to military service. She urged women to support soup kitchens to feed the poor and advised girls to care for the children of mothers forced by the conscription of their husbands to seek work.[21] Benedikt did not presuppose a specifically Jewish clientele for this charitable effort. Neither did the IKG of Vienna when it proudly announced that Jewish women and girls enthusiastically volunteered to do *Samariterdienst,* helping soldiers and those who remained behind.[22]

Middle-class Jewish women's organizations in Austria responded to the outbreak of war in 1914 by mobilizing their resources to help soldiers and their destitute families. At the end of July, Jewish women's philanthropic organizations in Vienna united to form *Weibliche Fürsorge* to coordinate their relief activities.[23] Throughout the war, *Weibliche Fürsorge* worked tirelessly on behalf of women and children impoverished by the conflict.[24] With such a clientele, the members of this umbrella organization could easily view their work as an extension of their traditional roles.

At the beginning of the war, many female Jewish charitable organizations felt that patriotism impelled them to contribute to the Austrian war effort as a whole and not focus on the special needs of Jews, their normal clientele. Jewish women's organizations collected money and held benefits to help invalid soldiers or the families of soldiers at the front.[25] The Society for the Establishment of Kosher Soup Kitchens in Vienna responded to the war crisis by providing hundreds of thousands of free or low-cost meals at its soup kitchens in Vienna's second and twentieth districts to the wives and children of soldiers, regardless of their religion. In the summer of 1915, the Society opened a special soup kitchen in the Inner City for suffering members of the middle class, serving about 500 people a day an inexpensive meal on tables with tablecloths and flowers. Although this society was not technically a women's organization, it was dominated by its soup kitchen supervisor, Hermine Kadisch, and by its army of female volunteers, and thus was associated in the public mind with women's war work.[26] Women's auxiliaries of the Bnai Brith also worked for the Red Cross, fed soldiers and their families, and donated to general war relief.[27] Zionist women's groups did likewise.[28]

Individual Jewish women donated money, formed committees to provide food to soldiers' children, and knitted socks and scarves for soldiers on the front.[29] Many women volunteered as nurses' aides in the Red Cross, and Jewish organizations offered courses to prepare them for their duties.[30] Women also visited soldiers in the hospitals, bringing them food, newspapers, and books.[31]

The Jewish women who volunteered their services to the war effort, and their families, understood this work as a patriotic contribution to the Austrian war effort and analagous to fighting at the front. Esti Freud, who came from a wealthy family and later married Sigmund Freud's son Martin, remarked in her memoirs that "my father had no son to sacrifice on the altar of the Fatherland. He was a good Austrian patriot so he suggested that I become a volunteer nurse."[32] One mother wrote to her son in the army describing how the girls in town made bandages. She concluded that "everyone has to fight, loyal to the dear fatherland."[33] In a December 1914 article in the Viennese *Österreichische Wochenschrift*, Rahel Edelstein compared female war relief to Moses holding his arms in the air when Joshua and the Israelites fought Amalek. Just as Moses' outstretched arms guaranteed an Israelite victory, so too the dedication of middle-class Jewish women, "sacrificing their *Gut und Blut* (money and their blood) on the altar of the fatherland," would lead to the victory of Austria.[34] In her reports on women's war work, Clothilde Benedikt spoke about "a second female army in the service of philanthropy."[35]

Although Jews eagerly participated in general patriotic work, both to win acceptance and assert their Austrian loyalties, the overwhelming majority of Jewish war work in fact was directed at fellow Jews. Jews may have hoped to prevent a confessionalization of wartime charity, but from the beginning they had to attend to the needs of other Jews. In particular, Jews all over the Monarchy felt compelled to provide for the religious needs of Jewish soldiers. Jewish communities, Jewish organizations, and Jewish individuals provided soldiers with prayer books and other religious supplies. They distributed Chanukah presents, held Chanukah parties, and arranged kosher food, at least for Passover and the High Holidays, for Jews serving in the Monarchy's armed forces. By attending to the religious needs of Jewish soldiers, Austrian Jews reminded themselves that Jews served the fatherland with utmost devotion. Thus work on behalf of Jewish soldiers reinforced Austrian patriotism at the same time as it encouraged Jewish solidarity.

Jewish communities, especially Vienna, responded generously to the countless requests of Jewish soldiers for prayer books, prayer shawls, phylacteries, High Holiday prayer books, shofars, scrolls of the Book of Esther for Purim, Jewish religious literature, and Jewish calendars.[36] Indeed, the Vienna Jewish community felt great sympathy for the many deeply religious Jews from all over Austria who turned to it for such supplies and willingly spent money helping Jews who were not members of the Vienna IKG.[37] Jewish army chaplains also turned to Vienna and other Jewish communities to help arrange religious services for the soldiers under their care, and the IKG gladly complied.[38] The Jewish community of Vienna prepared a special prayer book for Jewish soldiers, which it distributed to soldiers from all over the Monarchy. Partly subsidized by the War Ministry, this 56-page booklet contained most of the basic prayers of the daily and Sabbath service as well as a few highlights from the High Holiday services, along with devotions for the Kaiser and the Monarchy.[39]

The generosity of the Vienna IKG surely derived from the fact that it saw itself as the leader of the Monarchy's Jews. The IKG of Prague, on the other hand, did not make a similar claim, and proved less willing to send prayer books or religious supplies to Jewish soldiers elsewhere.[40] It did, however, arrange for religious services for Jewish soldiers stationed in its vicinity.[41]

Jewish communities all over Austria held special High Holiday services for soldiers. The Vienna IKG rented large halls for services and asked the military authorities to release all Jewish soldiers so they could attend.[42] Even small Jewish communities, like the one in Klagenfurt, held services and provided food for the High Holidays, usually with the assistance of women's organizations.[43] In addition, local rabbis supplemented the work of Jewish chaplains by visiting the wounded and sick soldiers in hospitals in their vicinity and attending to their religious needs. These rabbis often helped soldiers locate and correspond with relatives, an especially difficult task given that many Jews had fled from Galicia and Bukovina. Some rabbis volunteered for such duty, but the organized Jewish community, at least in Vienna, also assigned rabbis to these tasks and tried to coordinate such activities with the military chaplains.[44] Rabbi Béla Fischer worked directly with the Red Cross, distributing prayer books, other religious necessities, and cigarettes to Jewish soldiers.[45]

Of all the activities on behalf of Jewish soldiers, surely the most important in terms of effort, expense, and significance were the seders and kosher Passover food that Jewish communities all over the Monarchy provided to soldiers in their vicinity. For the first Passover of the war, in 1915, the IKG of Vienna tried to enlist the assistance of all major Jewish communities in providing free matzah to all Jewish soldiers in the armed forces. Such an effort foundered on the unwillingness of the Hungarian government to provide the necessary flour and the fact that most Jewish communities were overextended helping Galician Jewish refugees. Instead, Vienna advised other Jewish communities to provide matzah to Jewish soldiers in their vicinity, and most complied, sometimes with financial assistance from Vienna.[46] The IKG of Vienna itself undertook to feed all Jewish soldiers in the Vienna area three meals a day for all eight days of Passover, in coordination with the military authorities, who provided the IKG with the money that it would normally spend on food for those soldiers, and local kosher soup kitchens, which provided the food. Since food shortages were not yet a problem, these soup kitchens, largely run and staffed by female volunteers, fed soldiers kosher sausages, eggs, and matzah for breakfast; and soup, meat, potatoes, prunes, and matzah for dinner and supper, at a cost of 2.60 crowns a day per soldier. The army contributed 1.42 crowns for each man. That Passover, the Vienna Jewish community provided Passover food to 2153 Jewish soldiers in hospitals or convalescent homes and to 419 soldiers in the Vienna garrison at a cost of over 16,000 crowns, partially defrayed by a generous contribution by Baron von Rothschild.[47] In addition, the IKG of Vienna sent either matzah or money to Jewish soldiers elsewhere who requested it.[48]

Other Jewish communities, assisted by Jewish women's philanthropic organizations, also provided Passover food and seders to Jewish soldiers stationed in their vicinities.[49] Jewish women's organizations often took it on themselves to organize seders for local soldiers.[50] Even as the war dragged on and food became increasingly scarce, Jewish communities continued to arrange for Passover food, usually—as was the case in Vienna—by subsidizing local kosher soup kitchens.[51]

Providing Jewish soldiers with Passover food, visiting wounded Jewish soldiers, and providing all Jewish soldiers with gift packages (*Liebesgaben*) for Chanukah surely reminded Jews that they served Austria loyally as self-conscious Jews. In Vienna, Margarethe Grunwald, wife of the rabbi of the Leopoldstadt Temple, coordinated a major Chanukah gift campaign every fall as well as Purim and Passover gift campaigns, working closely with Jewish chaplains in the field.[52] Orthodox Jews collected prayer shawls and phylacteries to send to soldiers.[53] Zionist groups—especially Zionist girls—prepared special gifts to send to comrades in the army and visited Jewish war wounded in the hospitals.[54] Jewish women's organizations also held Chanukah and Purim parties for soldiers.[55] That such work bolstered Jewish solidarity was made clear in Elsa Köhler description of one such Chanukah party in 1917. She felt that the wounded soldiers, who had the blood of the Maccabees in their veins, were fighting for Judaism. With them she shared a *Heimat* of faith.[56]

Assisting Galician Jewish Refugees

Patriotic war work was important to Austria's Jews as a means of asserting their Austrian identity during World War I, but Jewish refugees quickly became their primary concern. In 1914 and again in 1916, hundreds of thousands of Jews fled from Galicia and Bukovina in the face of the advancing Russian army. Although the Austrian government provided financial asssistance to all the refugees, such aid proved inadequate to meet the overwhelming need. The Jewish establishment in Vienna, Bohemia, and Moravia, where most of the refugees had fled, attempted to fill the gap, providing charitable assistance to thousands of Galician and Bukovinian refugees. Work on behalf of Jewish refugees became the most important patriotic war work undertaken by Jewish groups. Not only did it consume most of their time and money, but work on behalf of refugees also served to reinforce the complex identity of Austrian Jews.

When Jews stepped in to help the refugees—and they did so eagerly and generously, at least at first—they understood their work both as an act of traditional Jewish charity and an expression of Austrian patriotism. After all, the refugees were Austrian citizens who had fled from Austria's enemy. Any help to them necessarily supported the Austrian war effort and affirmed the viability of the multinational Habsburg state. At the same time, since the primary focus of Jewish patriotic war work became assistance for fellow Jews, such work strengthened notions of Jewish solidarity. Jews felt comfortable doing refugee work because it allowed them to work simultaneously for the benefit of Austria and the Jewish people. Anti-Semitic attacks on the refugees in the last years of the war also alerted Jews to the depth of anti-Jewish hostility in the various national camps and contributed to a greater sense among Jews in the Austrian half of the Monarchy that they shared a common fate.

When the Russian army invaded Galicia and Bukovina in August 1914, hundreds of thousands of people—Jews and non-Jews alike—fled to Hungary, Bohemia, Moravia, and Vienna. The exact number of refugees is difficult to ascertain, because it fluctuated as people returned home or fled again as the front shifted. At the end of 1915, the Austrian Ministry of Interior estimated that there were 385,645 refugees in Austria, of whom 157,630, or 41%, were Jews. Such a high percentage of Jews in the refugee pool reflects the fact that Jews, who formed 10% of the population of Galicia and Bukovina, had special reasons to fear the Russian advance. Most of the refugees fled to Vienna or to the Czech lands. In 1915, Vienna contained 77,090 Jewish refugees, about 56% of the total in the city; Bohemia housed 57,159 Jewish refugees, and Moravia 18,429, 59% and 32% of the refugee pools in those provinces, respectively. In addition, about 30,000 refugees fled to Hungary.[57]

Many refugees, especially those from West Galicia, returned home after the liberation of the province in the summer of 1915, but the Brusilov Offensive in the summer of 1916 impelled another stream of refugees, mostly from East Galicia and Bukovina, to flee westward. In 1917, the *Israelitische Allianz,* an organization that devoted itself to refugee aid during the war, estimated that there were about 200,000 Jewish refugees, 72,000 in Bohemia, 36,000 in Moravia, 40,000 in Vienna, 10,000 in Upper Austria, 4000 in Styria, and 20,000 in Hungary.[58] Some of the refugees could support themselves, but the government estimated in late 1917 that there were 152,160 Jewish refugees "without means," of which 49,730 were in Bohemia, 23,515 in Moravia, and 41,113 in Vienna, forming the majority of the destitute refugee population in the Czech lands and 86% in the capital.[59] Even though many returned home in 1917 and 1918, at the end of the war there were still large numbers of Jewish refugees in Vienna, Bohemia, and Moravia, most of whom found it impossible to return home because their towns had been destroyed by the fighting or because they feared the pogroms that were raging. In September 1918, Austria provided state aid to 326,261 refugees, including 68,286 Jews. In Vienna, 17,000 of the 20,000 refugees receiving government aid were Jewish.[60]

The experiences of the Galician and Bukovinian refugees varied widely. The Austrian authorities directed many refugees to hastily constructed refugee camps in Nikolsburg, Pohrlitz, Gaya, and Deutschbrod, all in Moravia, and in Bruck an der Leitha near the Hungarian border, where conditions were very primitive. The camps were overcrowded, filthy, and cold, providing no privacy but plenty of opportunity for diseases to spread.[61] The authorities also sent many refugees to small towns in Bohemia, Moravia, Upper and Lower Austria, and Styria, where they encountered both generosity and hostility, sometimes finding decent places to live but also suffering in horribly overcrowded, dirty, and wet barns, schools, or other facilities.[62] Many refugees simply went on their own to Prague or Vienna, hoping to find better opportunities in the cities. Some had the means to rent decent appartments or managed to live in relative comfort with friends or relatives, especially in Vienna, which had a sizeable Galician Jewish population before the war. Most, of course, were not so lucky, and experienced squalid urban conditions.

Middle-class and wealthy Galician and Bukovinian Jews who fled from their homes fearing Russian occupation usually suffered less than did the masses of poor refugees. Minna Lachs's family, for example, fled from Trembowla, Galicia, at the very beginning of the war. After a harrowing month-long journey by wagon over the Carpathians into Hungary, constantly afraid that they would be overtaken by "the Cossacks," "wild men with terrible, merciless eyes, long coats and high boots, swinging their gun stocks, attacking with their horses," they took the train to Vienna, "the most beautiful city in the world," where they were met by relatives. They suffered from bedbugs in the small hotel where they stayed the first night, but quickly found a decent apartment. Minna's father, who had been the Galician representative of an Austrian coal company, found employment in a refugee aid agency, and Minna happily attended school.[63] Manès Sperber's family fled Zablotow, Galicia, in 1914 because "we wanted to avoid even one day of Russian occupation."[64] They nevertheless returned home twice, becoming permanent refugees only in 1916. After a few months in a refugee camp in Moravia, the family moved to Vienna and began a rapid descent into poverty. Although the Sperbers experienced many hardships, including bedbugs in their rented rooms, they too fared better than those refugees who arrived in the city penniless.[65]

At the beginning of the war, as refugees began to flee westward, Jewish spokesmen assumed that these Austrian victims of Austria's war would be cared for primarily by the authorities.[66] Indeed, eager to encourage pan-Austrian solidarity, the Ministry of the Interior assumed responsiblity for the refugees and provided them with financial support. Although the Ministry spent over two billion crowns in refugee aid during the course of the war, state support proved inadequate, unable to cover the cost of rent and food during the inflationary war years.[67] To distribute the subsidies and handle the enormous refugee flood in Vienna, the Ministry of Interior and the Viennese municipality created the *Zentralstelle der Fürsorge für Flüchtlinge aus Galizien und der Bukovina,* later renamed the *Zentralstelle der Fürsorge für Kriegsflüchtlinge,* and appointed Dr. Rudolf Schwarz-Hiller, a liberal member of Vienna's city council and a Jew, to head the operation. Located on Zirkusgasse in Vienna's Leopoldstadt, Schwarz-Hiller's office worked diligently to distribute government aid to refugees and to provide them with food, shelter, medical and legal aid, and a host of other services.[68] The Jewish press lauded Schwarz-Hiller as "a genial, tireless [man] filled with the purest and most beautiful humanity."[69] Elsewhere, the Austrian authorities worked through local Jewish communities or other agencies to distribute state support. *Israelitische Kultusgemeinden,* Jewish organizations, and individuals all over Austria augmented this support, providing much needed money and aid to the Galician Jewish refugees.

Jewish organizations that had always tried to improve the lot of Jews in Galicia naturally offered their services to assist the refugees. The *Israelitische Allianz* provided the most significant financial assistance to Galician and Bukovinian Jewish refugees. It allocated large sums of money to local Jewish relief efforts all over the Monarchy, regarding these efforts both as a patriotic duty and as serving the interests of "our religious community" by providing "brotherly help" for suffering fellow Jews. Working closely with Austrian authorities, the *Allianz* provided blankets, pillows, straw sacks, and dishes for refugees in the refugee barracks in Nikolsburg. It also paid school fees for refugee children in Vienna, helped build and support schools in the refugee camps, and gave large sums of money to Jewish soup kitchens. The *Allianz* subsidized the Jewish refugee committees that sprang up everywhere, provided money to rabbis who helped refugees, and gave Schwarz-Hiller's office financial assistance. In 1915, it spent over half a million crowns on refugee aid, 200,000 in Vienna alone.[70] Between May 1916 and May 1917, it spent almost 3 million crowns on Galician and Bukovinian refugees. Financial constraints and the return home of many refugees reduced its outlay to only half a million crowns between May 1917 and May 1918.[71] The *Allianz* obtained much of its money from American Jews, especially from the American Jewish Joint Distribution Committee, and thus it suffered a major financial crisis when America entered the war.[72]

While the *Allianz* subsidized refugee relief, the Society to Help the Suffering Jewish Population in Galicia, an organization devoted to modernizing the Jews of Galicia, established schools for vocational training and workshops to provide employment for refugees. In September 1914, it established sewing rooms in Vienna for refugee women and girls. Using sewing machines provided by Bnai Brith women, refugee women produced linens for other refugees and for the military.[73] By the end of 1917, the Society had established 31 workshops and also offered needlework courses for women and girls in many cities.[74] After the liberation of Galicia, the *Hilfsverein* ran courses in Vienna to prepare Galician Jewish refugees to become chicken and egg farmers when they returned home.[75]

Israelitische Kultusgemeinden, especially in Bohemia and Moravia, often took the lead in coordinating local relief efforts. In Brünn, Moravia, home to about 6000 Jewish refugees, the *IKG* provided food at the railroad station for newly arrived refugees. In December 1914, it established a special committee, composed of eight men and eight women, to raise money and help refugees in Brünn and in the nearby camps. The committee hired refugees to staff its office, which dispersed the state refugee allotments and additional monies that the committee provided. It also provided subventions to the local Jewish soup kitchens, distributed clothing, linens, and blankets, provided entrance fees to the public baths, vaccinated the refugees against small pox and cholera, and gave new mothers extra money for food. In conjunction with the city employment office, the committee found jobs for refugees in factories and shops. A separate women's committee established a sewing workshop to employ refugees and produce linens for the refugee community.[76] Concerned about the religious and cultural needs of the refugees, the Brünn IKG also provided space to refugees for religious services. It arranged for matzah, offered free weddings and funerals, and provided civil legitimation to those Galician refugees who had only been married under religious auspices. For the educational needs of the refugees, the IKG created a kindergarten, arranged for older children to attend the public schools, founded a special elementary school with Polish-language instruction for those who did not want to attend German schools, and opened a reading room for Hebrew, Yiddish, and Polish books and newspapers.[77]

Other Jewish communities in Bohemia and Moravia conducted themselves in a similar manner. In Reichenberg, Bohemia, the IKG worked with city authorities to dispense bedding, clothing, and money to refugees, and it distributed books for refugee children attending the local public schools.[78] The Jewish community of Budweis, which numbered only 3000, established a refugee aid committee that gave financial assistance to 5000 refugees in southern Bohemia.[79] Even the tiny Jewish community of Linz extended itself generously to help 10,000 Jewish refugees sent to Upper Austria in 1916.[80]

As the largest Jewish community in the Czech lands, the Jews of Prague engaged in a major effort to help Jewish refugees. In September 1914, the Prague *Israelitische Kultusgemeinde* organized an independent refugee aid committee. Although several members of the IKG board opposed a Jewish committee for fear that sectarian aid would reduce government assistance, the majority of board members understood both their religious obligation to help fellow Jews and the practical need to provide them with kosher food.[81] The newly formed *Hilfskomitee für die jüdische Flüchtlinge aus Galizien und der Bukowina* enabled several Jewish humanitarian organizations, including the *Chevra Kadisha* and the "Bohemia" and "Praga" chapters of Bnai Brith, the Zionists, and the IKGs of Prague and its suburbs to work together to help Jewish refugees.[82] Although technically an independent agency, the *Hilfskomitee* was dominated by the *Kultusgemeinde,* which served as the conduit for the state support paid out to each refugee and regularly advanced the committee money to pay its bills.[83]

A Prague IKG report to the police on the activities of the *Hilfskomitee* from October 1914 to October 1915 reveals the extent of its activities. In addition to paying out over two and a half million crowns in state support, the committee distributed a half million crowns in rent subsidies as well as clothing, linens, shoes, straw sacks, and blankets. It also spent about 25,000 crowns catering to the religious needs of the refugees: renting spaces for their synagogues, providing kosher food and matzah during Passover, subsidizing access to the ritual bath, and supporting special schools for refugee children. Finally, the Committee spent about 50,000 crowns providing free food to needy refugees.[84] In February 1915, the Committee aided approximately 13,000 refugees,[85] a number that declined in late 1915 when many refugees returned home.

Unfortunately, Prague's Galician *Hilfskomitee* suffered from fiscal mismanagement and large deficits in mid-1916 when a new wave of refugees arrived. At that point, it reorganized under the auspices of the Vienna-based *Israelitische Allianz,* which provided it with 15,000 crowns a month and insisted that it extend its operations beyond the immediate suburbs. The Prague IKG continued to handle its accounts, but only had to contribute 5000 crowns a month to support its work.[86] The renamed *Zentralkomitee für jüdische Flüchtlinge in Prag* continued to do the same work as its predecessor but on a more modest scale.[87]

Because the government paid out state subventions directly in Vienna, the *Israelitische Kultusgemeinde* there did not have to create the same kind of refugee apparatus established by the Jews of Prague or Brünn. Instead, it subsidized Jewish relief organizations and provided grants or special services to individuals who begged the community for assistance. Most importantly, the IKG provided monthly subventions to the various soup kitchens that fed refugees and increased those subventions as the war progressed.[88] In addition, recognizing that many refugees would not want to send their children to the regular public schools, in October 1914, it opened a special elementary school with German language instruction for 400 refugee children.[89] That year, together with *Weibliche Fürsorge,* it prepared special Chanukah celebrations for hundreds of refugee children,[90] and in 1915, it offered free matzah to refugees in Vienna, Lower Austria, and Bohemia.[91] The IKG was not always as generous as it might have been, but it did spend a significant amount on refugee aid.

Although they received subsidies from the *Kultusgemeinden,* private Jewish charities did most of the work assisting refugees from Galicia and Bukovina. Humanitarian organizations like the Bnai Brith distributed clothing, food, and money to refugees and established sewing workshops for them.[92] Orthodox Jewish organizations like *Machzike Hadath* provided kosher food to refugees and religious education to their children.[93] Traditional charities opened or expanded already existing soup kitchens to give refugees free or inexpensive kosher food.[94] The Viennese Society for the Establishment of Kosher Soup Kitchens served refugees over six and a half million portions by December 1916, over one million of them free.[95] Uprooted Galician Jewish organizations relocated and mobilized to help refugees. The Orthodox Agudas Yisroel of Galicia, headquartered in Vienna during the war, established Hebrew schools, a kosher children's home, and a school to provide vocational training to refugee girls in Vienna, and distributed funds to help people celebrate the Jewish holidays properly.[96]

All over Austria, individual Jews banded together to provide food and shelter to needy refugees.[97] Rabbis were often prominent on these Galician refugee committees. Rabbi Moritz Lewin in Nikolsburg, for example, worked tirelessly throughout the war to assist refugees in Moravia. In 1915, he composed a registry of all Jewish refugees, so Galician and Bukovinian Jews could locate relatives scattered all over western Austria.[98] Supported by the *Allianz,* the Baron Hirsch Fund, the German Orthodox Agudas Yisroel, and by private donations, he dispensed money and clothing and tended to the religious needs of refugees in Moravia. He also interceded with the authorities to help refugees get their state support and to exhume and rebury the bodies of Jewish refugees accidentally buried in Catholic cemeteries. Rabbi Lewin devoted most of his effort to refugee children, helping to establish schools and providing Jewish books for schools in the refugee camps and elsewhere in Moravia.[99] Many refugees wrote to thank him for his efforts, and their letters reveal the terrible suffering they endured.[100]

Zionists likewise took it for granted that they had to help the Galician and Bukovinian Jewish refugees. For them, in particular, such assistance was more than an act of Austrian patriotism and humanitarianism; it was a strong statement of Jewish national solidarity. At the beginning of the war, Zionist youth groups like *Blau-Weiss* in Prague did railroad station duty, providing food and information to the thousands of refugees who arrived daily, and adult Zionist groups worked with the IKG to provide shelter and work for the refugees.[101] Members of *Blau-Weiss* also collected clothing for distribution in Prague and in the refugee camps in Moravia.[102] In the spring of 1915, Prague Zionists established a special school for refugee children that inculcated Jewish nationalism and provided Hebrew language instruction along with a modern secular education.[103] Headed by Dr. Alfred Engel, and supported by both Zionists and non-Zionists, the school had 1200 students in its regular classes and many others in its vocational classes. Engel also supervised similar schools elsewhere in Bohemia.[104] During 1914–1915, most Zionist groups in Bohemia and Moravia reported that all of their effort had been devoted to helping refugees.[105]

In Vienna as well, Zionists engaged energetically in refugee work, raising money, helping newly arrived refugees at the railroad station, distributing food and clothing, providing free legal advice, and opening a clinic to provide free medical care to needy refugees.[106] This clinic treated 45,000 refugees by November 1915.[107] Zionists took it upon themselves to intercede with the authorities and in 1917 asked parliament to correct abuses in the refugee camps in Moravia.[108] The Zionists also acted as intermediaries between the refugees and their relatives in America, channeling money and letters through the Copenhagen office of the World Zionist Organization.[109] In the first year of the war, like their colleagues in Prague, Viennese Zionists devoted themselves entirely to refugee work.[110] Indeed, Viennese Zionists claimed that their strong commitment to Jewish solidarity made them the dominant force in the refugee aid effort,[111] but there is no evidence that Zionists were more active in refugee work than other Jews. Moreover, later in the war, partially as a result of World Zionist Organization (WZO) scolding that they spent too much time on refugees and not enough on Palestine,[112] the Austrian Zionist establishment devoted less attention to the refugees.

By far the most active group on behalf of refugees were Austrian Jewish women. Indeed, work on behalf of refugees became the patriotic war work *par excellence* of middle-class Jewish women in Vienna, Bohemia, and Moravia during World War I. Helping the refugees was a natural activity for Jewish women. Like men involved in such work, they could demonstrate their patriotism, humanitarianism, and Jewish solidarity all at the same time. Moreover, the very fact that the recipients of their largesse were overwhelmingly women, children, and the elderly[113] made such work an obvious extension of their traditional roles as mothers and nurturers. Comfortable with a clientele of suffering Jewish women and children, and proud to help fellow Austrians and fellow Jews as their contribution to the war effort, liberal, religious, and Zionist Jewish women provided most of the labor and dominated the effort to assist the Galician refugees.

All reports of aid to refugees highlight the fact that individual women, ad hoc women's committees, or women's philanthropic organizations did most of the work for refugees in villages in Bohemia or Moravia, in the refugee camps, and in Vienna and Prague.[114] In Vienna, *Weibliche Fürsorge,* headed by Regine Ulmann, Sofie Grünfeld, Clotilde Benedikt, and Rosa Schur, devoted most of its effort during the war to refugees, beginning with a clothing drive to provide winter clothing for the refugees who had fled in the summer of 1914 expecting a short war. This umbrella organization also established day-care centers for children and provided them with kosher food.[115] Regine Ulmann organized a course to teach typing, clerical work, and sewing and embroidery to adolescent refugee girls with secondary education, presumably so these middle-class girls could earn a living.[116] A special committee headed by Sofie Grünfeld opened a soup kitchen for the refugees in Brigittenau.[117] Margarethe Grunwald led a major campain to provide refugees with potatoes for Passover when *Weibliche Fürsorge* realized the difficulties providing matzah.[118]

Women's committees sprang up all over Austria to help refugees. They held Chanukah parties in 1914 at which they distributed clothing, food, and toys to refugee children,[119] and they organized seders for refugees the following spring.[120] Jewish women's organizations dispensed clothing and household articles to poor refugees and held benefits to collect money for those in the refugee camps.[121] Zionist women's groups proved equally concerned with the plight of the refugees. In Prague, the Club of Jewish Women and Girls distributed clothing and household goods to refugees at the beginning of the war.[122] Members of the club taught at the refugee school, tutored refugee children, collected Yiddish books to distribute to refugees, and established a day-care center. They arranged courses in modern languages, stenography, calligraphy, and needlework for refugee girls.[123] Like their colleagues in Prague, Viennese Zionist women organized clothing, blanket, and potato distributions.[124]

Austrian Jews understood all this effort on behalf of refugees as women's contribution to the war effort, and they therefore frequently used military images to describe it. One reporter declared that the director of Sofie Grünfeld's soup kitchen "commanded" like a field marshal her female "auxiliary troops."[125] Similarly, a description of a home for refugee girls praised "the fighters against need and misery."[126] Even while using military language, however, everyone understood that these women still behaved as proper bourgeois women who served a traditional clientele for female philanthropy. They did "true women's work" in the words of Anitta Müller, one of the leading organizers of refugee aid.[127]

Of all Austrian Jews involved in refugee aid, the young Viennese Zionist Anitta Müller was by far the most important. Targeting refugee women and children as her clientele, Müller established a series of institutions to help them. When the refugees first started to pour into Vienna in the fall of 1914, Müller's first priority was pregnant women, new mothers, and their babies. Working closely with the government's refugee aid office, she established a lying-in hospital and a home where new mothers could spend a week or two before returning to their dismal quarters. She also opened a baby-care center, which dispensed medical care and advice, hygiene and modern child-rearing lessons, and free milk to nursing mothers. Equally worried about children in the filthy conditions in which many refugees were forced to live, Müller opened several day-care centers. In the course of 1914–1915, Müller opened a "tea and soup institute," that sold tea, coffee, and soup at nominal prices to about 3000 people a day, providing refugees with a pleasant space to eat, read newspapers, and socialize. Convinced that she had to teach refugee girls to earn a living, she opened a trade school that taught needlework to 950 women and girls during its first year.[128]

Supported by the government's refugee aid office, the *Allianz,* and wealthy Jewish individuals,[129] Müller's umbrella organization, the *Verein sociale Hilfsgemeinschaft Anitta Müller,* spent 250,000 crowns in 1914–1915, about half a million in 1915–1916 and 1916–1917, and 800,000 in 1917–1918. By the end of the war, the organization had assisted thousands of needy Galician and Bukovinian Jewish women and children.[130] Müller's institutions, staffed largely by Viennese Zionist women and female refugees, were instrumental in the professionalization of Jewish social work in Austria.[131]

Indefatigable, Müller became the guardian angel of the refugees, universally admired by Zionists and non-Zionists alike. The Jewish press repeatedly praised Müller for her efforts on behalf of the refugees. The *Österreichische Wochenschrift* called her a "tireless organizer" whose work was "colossal," an organizational genius with the ability to recognize problems and find solutions.[132] Proud of the sheer extent and success of her efforts and, even more, the sense of Jewish solidarity that motivated her, the paper extolled her as "a model for Jewish women in our time."[133] At the end of the war, the *Jüdische Korrespondenz* called her "the most popular Jewish woman in Vienna," and the president of the Austrian Bnai Brith declared that her work would go down in history and be remembered forever.[134] Refugees admired her as well. Minna Lachs recalled the words of a fellow refugee, who called Müller "the best woman that we have met in Vienna."[135]

That work on behalf of Galician Jewish refugees became the highest priority for Austrian Jews during the war, male and female alike, can be seen in their allocations of money for patriotic war work. In the first two years of the war, about half of the Viennese Jews who made personal contributions to the IKG for war work earmarked them for general purposes. In the last two years of the war, however, almost none earmarked their contributions for general war charity, preferring instead to specify either Jewish soldiers, Galician Jewish refugees, or Jews who returned to Galicia.[136] This shift in emphasis derived from many factors, not only the practical demands of helping the refugees themselves. The increased focus on the refugees also reflected the decline in Jewish interest in the fighting war when Austria no longer faced the Russian enemy after 1916, and the simultaneous rise in nationalist agitation and anti-Semitism that made Jews worry about the plight of fellow Jews from the east.

The Jews who helped the Galician refugees were motivated by three factors: humanitarianism, Austrian patriotism, and Jewish solidarity. In their propaganda, naturally, Jews emphasized the first two factors, but Jewish solidarity certainly played just as important a role, not only in the eyes of Zionists. At the beginning of the war, Jews insisted that they worked tirelessly on behalf of the refugees as an act of pure humanity for people who had suffered because of their patriotic attachment to Austria.[137] Like so many others, Dr. Heinrich Rosenbaum of the Prague IKG called such work "a commandment of humanity."[138] At a fundraiser in Karlsbad in November 1914, spokesmen emphasized not only that it was their human duty to help refugees, but also the hope that such efforts would erase all political, economic, and national differences in Austria.[139] Zionists as well emphasized the humanitarian imperative to help refugees in 1914.[140] At the same time, Jews considered such humanitarianism well deserved, since the Galician Jews had fled from the Russians because of their Austrian patriotism.[141] As J. Grobtuch, a Viennese Jew originally from Galicia, noted in the *Österreichische Wochenschrift,* "The refugees are Austrians who have sacrificed everything for this state and who can therefore claim their rights."[142] Similarly, Heinrich Schreiber reiterated in 1917 that "better and truer Austrians than they simply do not exist."[143]

Naturally, a desire to help fellow Jews and official requests for such help also played a large role in motivating Jewish beneficence. It was, as Markus Fischer of the Prague IKG noted, "the fulfillment of a religious duty."[144] Jews were delighted, however, that their religious obligation coincided with the obligation of the Austrian government to help war victims. Jewish charity supplemented state support to the refugees, therefore allowing Jews to feel that Jewish charity bolstered Austria. Aid to refugees was therefore patriotic war work,[145] and Jewish support to fellow Jews gained legitimacy by being part of a larger patriotic effort.

Yet, Jews also acknowledged that their behavior resulted from and contributed to a sense of Jewish solidarity. In a December 1914 lecture to the Bnai Brith chapter in Pilsen, Friedrich Eidlitz announced that Jewish aid to refugees derived from "a solidarity thousands of years old that binds the fate of all Jews in the world."[146] In 1917, the *Österreichische Wochenschrift* asserted that the Jewish women who helped the refugees did so both out of Austrian loyalty and compassion for suffering members of the Jewish people. In language amazing for a liberal paper, it insisted that "blood, race, and ethnic kinship . . . create not compassion, but something greater and more noble: the consciousness that they have a duty to help here."[147] Zionists were quick to point out that help for the refugees derived from their desire to help "members of our people who have been ripped and uprooted from their accustomed life."[148]

Attitudes Toward Galician Jews

German-speaking Jews in western Austria certainly extended themselves to help their fellow Jews from the east, but alongside their sympathy often lay more complex and sometimes negative attitudes. These ranged from a sense of social and religious distance, to feelings of superiority, condescension, and a desire to remake the Galician Jews over in the image of Germanized, westernized Jewry, to the hope that the refugees would soon return home and relieve them of their burden. Nowhere, however, was there genuine hostility or use of anti-Semitic slogans. Unlike the Jews in Germany, who often displayed extremely hostile attitudes to Eastern European Jews in their midst,[149] Austrian Jews accepted the Galician and Bukovinian Jews as a matter of course. They did so largely because their own propaganda contained the truth. That is, the refugees were indeed Austrian citizens who suffered as a result of Austria's war, a fact that the state itself recognized by providing them with financial support. Moreover, western Austrian Jews, especially in Vienna, had always had contact with Galician Jews, who formed the majority of Austrian Jewry, and thus seemed less foreign than Russian or Polish Jews in Germany.

Interestingly, Jews in Vienna seemed much more receptive to the Galician Jewish refugees than were the Jews in Prague or elsewhere in Bohemia. The Jewish press in Prague and Brünn published many articles dealing with the character of Galician Jewish refugees, some of them negative, and debated how best to cope with the problems posed by the presence of such Jews in Bohemia and Moravia. The Viennese Jewish press, on the other hand, seemed untroubled by Galician refugees and published no articles debating their character or any negative articles at all.[150] The greater receptivity of Viennese Jews likely derived from the large contingent of Galician Jewish residents in the city, many of them already acculturated, who could sympathize with their refugee relatives. Moreover, the large prewar influx of Galician Jews into the capital made them and their traditional costumes less unusual in Vienna than they were in Prague or Brünn, or the smaller towns and cities of Bohemia and Moravia.

There were other reasons for the Jewish press in Vienna to remain silent on the issue. The leading Jewish newspaper, the *Österreichische Wochenschrift*, was edited by Josef Samuel Bloch, a Galician Jew who would not have countenanced attacks on Galician Jewish culture. The Zionist paper, *Jüdische Zeitung*, the organ of the Austrian Zionist federation, did not generally reflect on issues as did the more-intellectual *Selbstwehr*, the Zionist newspaper in Prague. Moreover, a very large percentage of Zionists in Vienna were themselves born in Galicia and Bukovina, and, even if they had rejected much of traditional Jewish culture, they were not as troubled by it as were Zionists in Bohemia.

In general, the *Österreichische Wochenschrift* presented a positive picture of Galician Jews. In an article describing High Holiday services organized by Galician refugees in 1914, J. Grobtuch, a Galician Jewish activist long resident in Vienna, asserted that such services were "proof of the spiritual greatness of Galician Jewry," a Jewry utterly loyal both to God and to the Kaiser.[151] Writers for the paper usually praised the Galician Jews for their honest piety. Ida Barber painted an entirely sympathetic picture of the refugees in Marienbad in 1916, emphasizing their fervent belief in God.[152] Even at the end of the war, when the anti-Semites engaged in a frenzy of antirefugee agitation, the *Österreichische Wochenschrift* praised the Galician refugees for their faith and religious devotion.[153] For their part, Viennese Zionists applauded the presence of Galician Jews in Vienna because it helped unify Austrian Jewry and augment Zionist ranks.[154]

Such positive sentiments did not mean that Viennese Jews perceived no differences between themselves and the Galician and Bukovinian Jews, many of whom were religious, Yiddish-speaking, and poor. A report about the 1915 seder for refugees at Sofie Grünfeld's soup kitchen reveals some of the distance that separated prosperous Viennese Jews from the refugees. In her speech to the refugees, Grünfeld, who had lost a son and son-in-law in the war, admitted honestly:

> You were foreign to us, and your culture did not appear to be like ours. You had other customs, and we approached you not with the kind of love that brothers should bring their brothers in distress. But our contact with you has brought us closer, and the bearing and dignity with which you bear your tragedy fills us with sincere admiration.[155]

Similarly, the author of the 1915 pamphlet describing Anitta Müller's efforts noted that the refugees came from "a peculiar cultural area," one that was foreign to Viennese Jews. The author hoped that the two groups would build spiritual bridges to each other.[156]

Some Viennese Jews may have found the Galician refugees a minor annoyance. Private letters to the Jewish community complained about noisy refugee prayer-rooms,[157] but in public, a Viennese reporter for the Brünn-based *Jüdische Volksstimme* noted that Galician Jews abided by western customs in Viennese synagogues, which they attended in large numbers.[158] The Vienna *Israelitische Kultusgemeinde* treated the Galician refugees respectfully, if not always generously.[159] Complaints by refugees reveal that volunteers at soup kitchens sometimes treated them brusquely and served inadequate portions—grievances taken seriously and acted on by the IKG.[160]

In Bohemia and Moravia, Jews extended themselves to help refugees, but they do not appear to have accepted them as naturally or as graciously as Viennese Jews did. Although many leaders of the Prague IKG—especially its president Arnold Rosenbacher and its vice president, Robert von Fuchs—seemed genuinely committed to help Galician refugees, many members of the board displayed coldness and an overriding concern for the financial bottom line. Indeed, one member of the board even reminded the others that, according to its statutes, the Prague IKG was responsible only for its own members and therefore had "no religious or ritual responsibilities for the Galician refugees."[161] And unlike the Vienna *Kultusgemeinde,* which helped refugees outside the capital, the IKG of Prague would not help Jewish refugees in rural Bohemia.[162] The Prague Jewish community did distribute matzah to the refugees, albeit grudgingly because of the cost,[163] and it provided nice space for refugee high holiday services in 1915, but refused to do so the following year because of a "bad experience."[164] In addition, even as many Jews contributed time and effort to refugee aid, some of them seemed impatient with that effort, eager to see it end as quickly as possible. As early as November 1914, the IKG of suburban Smichow announced in a letter to the IKG of Prague that by contributing 1500 crowns to refugee aid, it had fulfilled its obligations toward the refugees.[165] In late 1915 and early 1916, as refugees returned home, many contributors to Prague's Galician *Hilfskomitee* seemed eager to suspend payments, even though several thousand refugees still resided in Prague and its suburbs.[166] Contributions increased during the second refugee influx, but the total number of contributors was far lower in the second half of the war than in its early months.[167]

The process employed for clothing and blanket distribution by Prague's Galician *Hilfskomitee* illustrates a distinct lack of sympathy for those in need. The committee sent postcards to refugees, written in German, not Yiddish or Polish, which entitled them to receive clothing at the distribution center, but only if they arrived with these cards at the exact time specified and accompanied by all the people whose names were indicated and none others. Refugees who did not arrive on time lost their right to clothing or blankets.[168] In all likelihood, the middle-class German-speaking Jews on the committee felt culturally superior to those they assisted. Indeed, a 1916 letter from the Prague IKG to the Bohemian governor declared that taking care of the refugees was a burden "because they mostly have to be treated like illiterates."[169]

At the beginning of the refugee stream, many Bohemian and Moravian Jews had to remind themselves to set aside their traditional prejudice against Galician

Jews.[170] For many, the influx of refugees provided their first real contacts with East European Jewry.[171] Some were horrified at what they saw. One memoirist from Brüx, Bohemia, summarized these attitudes. The Galician Jewish refugees

> found little sympathy in the eyes of the Jews. These people were not exactly presentable (*salonfähig*) in their strange clothes, with their gibberish (*Kauder-welsch* . . . Yes, even in spiritual and religious matters there were deep differences; they screamed their prayers . . . They quarreled and bargained with God as if they were equals.[172]

Bohemian Jews regularly complained about the cultural backwardness of Galician Jewry and condescendingly hoped that their exposure to western culture as refugees would somehow lead to the improvement and modernization of Galician Jewry. Speaking to the Prague chapter of Bnai Brith, Moritz Hammerschlag spoke glowingly of the opportunity to help the poor refugees at the same time as he attacked Hasidism as a "rigid, barbarous [attempt to] hold on to old forms and customs."[173] In a lecture to the Pilsen branch of Bnai Brith in December 1914, Friedrich Eidlitz arrogantly declared that since Galician Jews were living in the west, western Jews should decide what was worth conserving and what should be discarded in Galician Jewish culture.[174] Even when Jewish spokesmen spoke positively about the suffering refugees, they expressed their cultural superiority and their hopes that the refugees would become more like themselves.[175]

Zionists in Bohemia and Moravia shared these sentiments. Although they felt compelled to praise Galician Jews for their truly Jewish souls, which they assumed could be useful in the development of Jewish nationalism,[176] they too worried about the traditional appearance of Galician Jews. Bohemian and Moravian Zionists regularly expressed the hope that the war would lead to increased solidarity of eastern and western Jewry to the mutual benefit of both. Yet they assumed that such solidarity would lead to the westernization of their fellow Jews from the east, who would naturally rid themselves of their more unpleasant customs.[177]

The debate in the summer of 1915 in the pages of *Selbstwehr* over "peyos and caftan," the sidelocks and long coats worn by Galician Hasidic men, provides important insight into the attitudes of Bohemian Jews toward the refugees. Apparently, a group of Prague Jews, worried about the rise of anti-Semitism in the face of such obvious Jewish markers, had appealed to refugees to cut off their sidelocks. The debate commenced when Abraham Steigler, a Viennese member of the Marxist-Zionist organization, Poale Zion, charged those who made the appeal with wanting to corrupt Galician Jewry.[178] In response, some contributors defended the right of Galician Jewish men to wear peyos and caftan and praised the true religiosity of Galician Jewry,[179] while others attacked the custom as an example of the obscurantism and fanaticism of Galician Jewry.[180] Virtually all hoped that somehow the peyos and caftan would disappear as a result of the refugees' contact with western culture. One spokesman, for example, hoped that Galician Jews would learn from the "superior humanity" of Jews in the west.[181] Prague rabbi Emanuel Schwarz hoped that when the Galician Jews returned home, their sidelocks and caftans would disappear as the Russians soldiers had.[182] Similarly, Rabbi Leo Bertisch of Deutschbrod, Bohemia urged western Jews to regard the peyos and caftan as the national costume of Galician Jewry, even as he expressed the hope that progress and European culture would lead to its demise.[183]

Bohemian Jews regarded their efforts to educate the refugees as an integral part of their program to improve and remake them in the image of western Jewry. Describing an exhibit of school work done by Galician Jewish children in Prague, a writer for Selbstwehr acclaimed the beautiful results of Galician Jewish contact with western culture.[184] In a 1917 article, Alfred Engel insisted that his schools for refugees would lay the foundation for a reinvigorated, modernized Jewry in Galicia.[185] Similarly, a report about the refugee schools in Prague in the Jüdische Volksstimme declared that the one good result of the war was the opportunity to create a modern Galician Jewry.[186]

Some Bohemian and Moravian Jews treated the refugees with outright contempt. Jakob Federmann, the chair of a Jewish sickness benefits society in Boskowitz, Moravia, called the refugees "a Polish pestilence."[187] An article in February 1915 in the Brünn Zionist paper, Jüdische Volksstimme, noted that the Jews of Bohemia viewed the Galician refugees as inferior human beings and did not want their children to sit next to them in school.[188] Galician Jews complained in 1917 that the Brünn Jewish refugee aid committee treated the refugees in a high-handed manner, conducting cleanliness inspections at 5 A.M., pulling straw sacks out from beneath sleeping women, forcing people into the street to see if they needed disinfection, and marching them to the public baths.[189]

Yet, despite these exhibitions of superiority, Bohemian and Moravian Jews—indeed all western Austrian Jews—did their utmost to help Jewish refugees and felt genuine sympathy for their plight. In the summer of 1916, the Prague IKG wrote a heartwrenching, compassionate letter to the Viennese Jewish community, describing the inhuman conditions the new refugees had to suffer in the small towns in Bohemia, complaining about the indifference of the bureaucrats with whom they had already intervened to improve the situation, and urging joint action.[190] The Prague IKG received letters from Jewish communities in Bohemia seeking its assistance for the suffering refugees in their midst and expressing sympathy for their plight.[191] The Jewish community of Bischofteinitz, for example, wrote a heartfelt letter to Prague in August 1916 expressing its dismay that the authorities provided utterly unwearable wooden shoes to refugees who would perforce have to go barefoot in winter.[192]

One thing all Austrian Jews agreed on was that the anti-Semitic agitation against the refugees was grossly unfair. Anti-Semites blamed the refugees for food and housing shortages, black market profiteering, and all of the problems that the long war imposed. Especially in the last two years of the war, as the food situation became catastrophic, anti-Semites engaged in hate mongering against the refugees, demanded their expulsion, and implored local authorities to curtail their public activities.[193] In the early years of the war, the Burgfrieden compelled Austrian Jews to maintain a public silence on this animosity, although there were occasional hints in the press about mistreatment of the refugees.[194] In the last two years of the war, the Jewish press regularly reported high levels of local hostility to refugees, including acts of petty violence.[195] Jewish leaders were quick to denounce the anti-Semitic agitation and to intervene with the authorities to prevent the wholesale expulsion of refugees or infringements on their civil rights.

One incident in particular upset Jews greatly: the Prague municipal order in early 1917 barring Galician and Bukovinian refugees from using the streetcars or railroads. The Prague authorities barred the Jewish refugees without special permits from public transportation, ostensibly for fear that refugees spread spotted typhus. The prohibition led to many anti-Semitic incidents in which Prague Jews were thrown off streetcars. Jews in Prague and Vienna, quick to point out that there were no cases of typhus among the refugees, intervened with the authorities and got the order rescinded, but its promulgation revealed the high level of antipathy toward the refugees and the widespread belief that they were bearers of destructive contagion, a common anti-Semitic myth.[196]

In general, Jewish spokesmen responded to the charges leveled at the refugees by defending them as suffering Austrian patriots. When the Viennese police raided two coffeehouses in September 1917 to round up Galician refugees and determine if they were draft dodgers, Viennese Zionists denounced such behavior, questioning how the authorities could possibly chase patriotic Austrian citizens, the fathers of soldiers dying for Austria, like dogs.[197] Similarly, when the Christian Socialists blamed the refugees for the food and housing shortages and demanded the expulsion of Galician "foreigners," the Viennese Zionist press repeated that the refugees were Austrian citizens who had fled from Austria's enemy.[198]

Just as they differed in their attitudes to the Galician refugees, so too did the Jews of Vienna and the Czech lands diverge in their response to repeated calls for the expulsion of the refugees at end of the war. Faced with mounting demands for the immediate departure of the refugees in 1917 and 1918, Jewish spokesmen of all political persuasions in Vienna insisted that wartime devastation and anti-Jewish violence in Galicia made such return at least temporarily impossible. They also reiterated that the refugees were not foreigners but were loyal Austrian citizens who had fled to Vienna in the first place because of the behavior of Austria's enemies.[199] When the refugees became instant foreigners at the end of the war, Viennese Jews continued to lobby against their expulsion, largely on practical or humanitarian grounds. Aware that antirefugee sentiment grew in proportion to increasing food shortages, in December 1918, Viennese Zionists begged the World Zionist Organization to intervene with the Entente Powers for more food.[200]

In Prague, however, as anti-Semitic attacks on the refugees mounted at the end of the war, even the leaders of Prague Jewry who had worked most tirelessly on behalf of the refugees joined the chorus demanding the immediate departure of the Galician Jews. Fearful that the anti-Semitic slander endangered Prague Jewry, refugee advocate Robert von Fuchs proposed in October 1918 that the Prague IKG request the governor of Bohemia to "expel the 1300 refugees of Prague."[201] Although the IKG board was divided on how to proceed, a memo of agreement between it and the Jewish National Council in November stated that their first priority should be "the evacuation (*Abtransport*) of the refugees."[202] The Prague Jewish community probably never actually asked the government to expel the refugees, but the discussion reveals their deep anxiety in the face of anti-Semitic hysteria.

In contrast to the behavior of the Jewish liberals, Zionists in Prague, aided by the Zionists of Vienna, worked assiduously to prevent the expulsion of the refugees, which the Czechoslovak government scheduled for December 15, 1918. Genuinely afraid that refugees who returned to Galicia could lose their lives in pogroms, the World Zionist Organization urged Prague Zionists to intervene with the authorities to prevent the expulsion. At the same time, Zionists in Vienna urged the World Zionist Organization to lobby with the Entente Powers and the new Czechoslovak government to prevent the expulsion. Zionist intervention led to the indefinite postponement of the expulsion edict.[203]

The extent of anti-refugee anti-Semitism in the last years of the war served to remind Jews that only the supranational state could protect them. The fact that they could always appeal to the central authorities, and that the authorities behaved properly and correctly toward the refugees,[204] reaffirmed the traditional Jewish commitment to Habsburg Austria. Running like a leitmotif through all of the reports of wartime anti-Semitism was the conviction that the authorities would overturn any local anti-Semitic measures because they recognized that the refugees were loyal Austrian citizens. The Jewish press was filled with descriptions of good behavior on the part of the central government and its agents.[205] Private correspondence and discussions more honestly admitted the hostility of some local authorities, even local branches of the central authorities, but at the same time indicated the belief that the central offices of the Monarchy would be just and fair. The IKG of Prague, for example, complained bitterly to the IKG of Vienna in July 1916 about the indifference of local authorities, some of whom made the situation of refugees even worse. It asked Vienna to intervene with the Ministry of the Interior, presumably expecting help from that quarter.[206] The fact that Jewish refugee advocates could turn to Rudolf Schwarz-Hiller, the head of the refugee-aid office in Vienna, to intervene on their behalf, no doubt reinforced Jewish convictions about the central government. Schwarz-Hiller denounced anti-Semitic hate-mongers and affirmed the Austrian patriotism of the refugees.[207] No wonder Jews sought the continuity of the multinational empire; only it could be trusted to treat all Jews fairly.

Work on behalf of Galician Jewish refugees also served to remind Austrian Jews of their interconnectedness. Many Jewish communities turned to Vienna for leadership and guidance during these years, and Vienna willingly and generously accepted this responsibility. While helping poor Galician refugees may not have unified the west Austrians and the Galicians, it augmented a Jewish sense of solidarity within Austria. The fact that they all faced common problems—especially refugee aid and escalating anti-Semitism—also reminded them of their common fate.

Patriotic war work of every kind thus reinforced the identity of Austrian Jews. Contributing to the Red Cross or buying war bonds allowed Jews to express their devotion to the fatherland. They could give their *Gut und Blut* to ensure the victory of the Habsburg Monarchy. Yet the fact that circumstances compelled them to direct most of their charitable effort to fellow Jews made them acutely conscious of their loyalty to the Jewish people. Attending to the religious needs of Jewish soldiers and providing assistance to suffering Galician Jewish refugees reinforced Jewish solidarity. Both efforts allowed Jews to work for a Jewish cause as they served Austria, thus convincing them that they could best flourish in a supranational state. Patriotic war work may not have lessened anti-Semitism as they had hoped at first, but the very intensity of war-time anti-Semitism made them ever more loyal to a state they regarded as their best protection from attack. Serving on the home front enhanced their commitment to the survival of Habsburg Austria and reminded Jews that they were indeed a community of fate.

4

The Experience of Jewish Soldiers

Over 300,000 Jewish men served as soldiers in the Austro-Hungarian armed forces during World War I.[1] About 25,000 educated, middle-class Jews held commissions as reserve officers.[2] Jewish men fought alongside Polish, Ruthenian, German, Czech, Hungarian, Slovak, and other Habsburg soldiers against Austria's enemies, and Jewish officers commanded units of all nationalities. Jews served loyally and courageously, receiving large numbers of military decorations for valor in a long, bloody war, and the Jewish communities of Austria basked, however briefly, in the reflected glory of Jewish bravery. Like other Austrian Jews, Jewish soldiers justified their sacrifices by claiming to fight a just war against an evil enemy and to do their duty for their emperor and fatherland. They took satisfaction in the fact that they contributed as Jews to the defense of Austria.

The military experience of Jewish officers and men raises important questions about Jewish integration into the society of Austria-Hungary and about the impact of the war on Jewish identity. In theory, Jewish participation in the army should have led to increased integration of Jews. The much-vaunted camaraderie of the trenches and the conditions of mortal danger should have led Jews and non-Jews to greater social interaction and understanding. Fighting on the Eastern Front or in Italy, Jews and non-Jews, perhaps for the first time, would have had an opportunity to befriend each other. Yet, although the army, an institution that prided itself on its openness to ethnic, national, and religious diversity, did not tolerate overt anti-Semitism, and most Jewish soldiers insisted that they did not encounter any anti-Semitism in the service, the army experience did not lead to the further integration of Jews in Austrian society.

Although the army may not have provided opportunities for intimate interaction with non-Jews, it did serve as an important vehicle for the modernization of Jews who had not yet begun to modernize. In the army, large numbers of traditional Jews from Galicia, Bukovina, and Hungary became acquainted with non-

Jews, and perhaps more importantly, with modern acculturated Jews, those who had already adopted German, Czech, or Polish culture and who had acquired a western education. Not only did these modern Jews serve with the religious ones, but they often functioned as their officers. Moreover, Jewish chaplains— virtually all of them modern rabbis—also introduced many deeply religious Jews to modern Judaism. Forced by military necessity to violate Jewish laws about Sabbath rest or kosher food, attending modern Sabbath and holiday services run by Jewish chaplains, cut off from their families, many of whom were refugees, many Galician Jews encountered modernity while serving in the Austro-Hungarian army between 1914 and 1918. It is no wonder that the ranks of the modern Jews grew so quickly in the interwar period.

Above all, service in the Habsburg army during the First World War enhanced the Jewish identity of Jewish soldiers and their loyalty to Austria. Satisfaction with their military performance gave Jewish soldiers a heightened sense of Jewish pride and honor. Moreover, they assumed that their valor contributed to the continuity of the Austrian state to which they remained devoted. Yet Jews fought the war with a different agenda than did most of their fellow soldiers. Like all Habsburg Jews, they focused on the war with Russia, the enemy of Austria and the Jewish people. This focus enabled them to make sense of the war both as Austrians and as Jews and augmented their sense of themselves as one of the peoples of the multinational Austrian state. Their war experience thus strengthened the prewar identity of Habsburg Jewish soldiers.

Crafting a Sustaining Ideology

Our understanding of soldiers' experience in World War I has been shaped almost entirely by literary representations and scholarly analyses of the carnage on the Western Front.[3] Trench warfare there guaranteed that millions of soldiers died, mowed down by artillery and machine-gun fire every time they attempted an offensive action. British and French soldiers endured the mud and rats and dead bodies in hundreds of miles of trenches located only meters from the German soldiers who suffered similarly on the other side of the barbed wire. Weary soldiers on both sides of the line hid in the earth, powerless in the face of constant shelling. Although many soldiers had romantically imagined war as an escape from industrialized, bourgeois society into a manly community, in fact the war proved to be monstrously industrial, robbing men of their ability to act and of their belief in human potency. An air of unreality pervaded this war: Soldiers endured an endless barrage of noise, but could see almost nothing; they lived in a labyrinth of trenches amid a bombed-out cratered landscape filled with the dead and the dying; they ate the enemy's food when they took his trenches; they received mail and newspapers from home very quickly. The chasm between the mud and death of the trenches and the lives of those at home made many soldiers feel that they lived in a separate universe, the world of war.

Because World War I involved so much carnage, and because so many millions of soldiers died in its endless and futile battles, while death seemed virtually certain and the bloodletting pointless, observers and scholars have long debated why the soldiers nevertheless continued to fight. Writing of his own experience as a French soldier in the First World War, the historian Marc Bloch noted: "I believe that few soldiers, except for the most noble or intelligent, think of their country while conducting themselves bravely; they are much more guided by a sense of personal honor, which is very strong when it is reinforced by the group."[4] World War I novels stressed that camaraderie far more than patriotic ideology motivated soldiers in the endless slaughter.[5] Many scholars have emphasized the role of duty, pride, and comradeship in explaining the determination of soldiers to fight on. Yet, as George Mosse and others have shown so effectively, soldiers also had a need to make sense of the slaughter, to infuse their sacrifice on the battlefield with meaning and significance. Thus, while camaraderie, honor, pride, and duty played important roles in soldiers' lives, so too did ideologies stressing that soldiers fought for a just cause, for their fatherland, and for God.[6]

Even when soldiers rejected the jingoist patriotism of wartime propaganda, when they fervently wished for peace and hated the endless, meaningless war, they assumed that their side was right and the other evil. Stéphane Audoin-Rouzeau has shown that despite their hatred of the war and indifference to politics, French soldiers in the trenches persevered because their "republican patriotism" convinced them that France, the land of liberty and justice, would surely win, and they felt morally obligated to defend her against Germany. Comradeship, Audoin-Rouzeau argues, was less significant than veterans' groups asserted. Rather, national feeling inoculated ordinary French soldiers against depression and made it impossible for them not to persevere.[7] Similarly, Bill Gammage has emphasized the role of national pride and imperial necessity among Australian soldiers in the trenches. They may have volunteered out of a romantic urge for manly glory and adventure as well as a desire to do their bit to protect the empire that secured them against Asia. As the war progressed, however, they persisted not only from a sense of duty to themselves and their mates, but because their pride as Australians contributing as equal partners in the defense of empire impelled them to do so. Never doubting the justice of their cause, they viewed the Germans as evil aggressors who had to be defeated for the good of mankind.[8]

The soldiers of Austria-Hungary fought a different war than the soldiers in the trenches on the Western Front. Habsburg troops fought against the Russians in Galicia, Bukovina, and Russian Poland; against the Serbs and Romanians in the Balkans; and against the Italians in the Isonzo River valley and in the Trentino region of South Tyrol. While enormous numbers of soldiers died there in 1914 and 1916, the Eastern Front was a mobile one, without the senselessness and futility of trench warfare. By the summer of 1915, Habsburg troops—with indispensable aid from the German army—had defeated the Russians in Galicia, and even Russia's successful Brusilov Offensive in 1916 did not significantly alter the fact that the Central Powers had won the war in the East and occupied much of Poland and other areas of western Russia(see Map 2).[9] The war with Italy was a stalemate, but it never degenerated into utter carnage, and losses there were not as catastrophic as elsewhere.[10] Thus although the Habsburg army sustained extremely heavy casualties in World War I—about one million soldiers were killed and millions of others were wounded, taken prisoner, or suffered from illness[11]—Austrian soldiers fought a more conventional war than did the soldiers on the Western Front.

Nevertheless, Austrian soldiers suffered greatly. Not only did they sustain high casualties, but during the last two years of the war they had very little to eat and utterly inadequate uniforms. By 1917, as the army itself recognized, most soldiers regarded the endless war "as a senseless slaughter of men."[12] Yet they too persevered and soldiered on and did so without the same kind of national feeling that motivated the French or Germans. Habsburg authorities endlessly worried that Serb, Ruthenian, or Czech soldiers would prove unreliable against their fellow Slavs.[13] The incidents of desertions or wholesale surrenders by Czech or other Slavic soldiers—like the frequently mentioned surrender of the Czech 28th Infantry Regiment—only confirmed the suspicions of military leaders. Historian Norman Stone has argued that the unreliability of Czech and Ruthenian troops seriously handicapped the Habsburg Army on the Eastern Front, but even he notes that the lack of enthusiasm for the war on the part of many Czechs and Ruthenians had less to do with pan-Slavism than with poor leadership, bad treatment, and difficult conditions.[14] Virtually all other historians agree that Habsburg troops of all nationalities fought tenaciously against Russia and especially in Italy, where even Italian-speaking troops fought loyally for the Dual Monarchy.[15] While they may have needed German assistance for any successful offensive, most troops did their duty and fought with determination, some of them holding on in Italy after the state they were defending had fallen apart.

Despite well-documented devotion, the popular perception of Habsburg soldiers has been dominated by Jaroslav Hašek's novel *The Good Soldier Švejk,* in which the hero, a hapless, overly loquacious buffoon, regularly outwits his incompetent, pompous, and stupid superiors. Hašek, an anti-Habsburg Czech Communist, presented the Habsburg army as a confusing babble, and its soldiers as utterly indifferent to Habsburg patriotism, men who spent all their time trying to avoid service.[16] Similarly, S. Grübel's much less-famous play, *K. und k. Landsturm: Erinnerungen an den Doppeladler,* also presents the Habsburg army as a collection of stupid officers and men, unmoved by patriotic appeals, seeking to avoid frontline service and make some money on the side. Indeed, the unit depicted is a rag-tag collection of old, sick, and frail Galician peasants and Jews, all of whom are far too incompetent to fight.[17]

Naturally we must not take these satirical treatments too literally. Bureaucratic stupidity typifies all armies, and novels or plays that hold the army up for ridicule do not prove that soldiers, many of whom may have detested military officiousness, did not also share a sustaining ideology that allowed them to fight on. The Habsburg army may have come in for more than its share of ridicule after World War I because it was an easy target. After all, it so obviously depended on superior German troops to win any victories. Moreover, it was a vast array of men of very different backgrounds, speaking many languages, and using a German language of command of less than 100 words. The peacetime army had handled the linguistic problem by requiring all officers to speak German as well as the language(s) of the regiments in which they served. A large proportion of career officers, however, were killed in August 1914, and they were replaced by reserve officers, many of whom did not speak German particularly well and did not know the languages of the men they commanded at all. The linguistic abyss between officers and men, and even between fellow officers, did not lend itself to effective fighting.[18] Memoirists often commented on the linguistic babble in the army, a situation not conducive to any sense of common purpose.[19] Finally, nationalist politicians in the interwar successor states had a vested interest in emphasizing Czech, Hungarian, Serb, or Italian disloyalty to the Habsburgs, and citizens of these new states found it impolitic to discuss wartime Habsburg loyalty. Still the fact remains that the vast majority of Habsburg soldiers of all nationalities did remain loyal to the state for which they fought, did fight determinedly in an endless, brutal war, and did possess an ideology that rendered their suffering meaningful. Modern war, with its citizens' armies, requires no less.

Unlike the soldiers on the Western Front, little is known about Habsburg soldiers during World War I and what motivated and sustained them.[20] In his memoir about the Eastern Front, violinist Fritz Kreisler never explains what motivated Austrian soldiers, even at the very beginning of the war. Published in 1915, presumably for propaganda purposes, Kreisler's account just emphasized the brotherhood of Austrian soldiers under arms, the benevolence and wisdom of their officers, and their valor against the numerically superior Russians, whom they did not hate.[21] Scholars insist that all Habsburg soldiers, indeed all citizens of Austria-Hungary, united in their eagerness to fight Italy. An ally of the Central Powers, Italy had nevertheless declared war on Austria-Hungary in May 1915, encouraged by England and France, in order to gain territory—South Tyrol, Trieste and Istria, Gorizia and Gradisca, and northern Dalmatia—at Austrian expense. Thus Italy was a clear aggressor and all Austrians, especially the South Slavs, united in defense of the fatherland from Italian designs on its territory.[22] One Jewish memoirist, Arnold Höllriegel from Prague, recognized the significance of Italy to ordinary Austrian soldiers when he observed that "if Austria's war had any meaning at all it was to keep Trieste Austrian."[23] Surely some Habsburg subjects justified the war with Russia in terms of the need to combat aggression and invasion, and many Austrians regarded the war with Serbia as just because of Serbia's designs on Habsburg territory and her involvement in the plot to kill Franz Ferdinand.[24] In addition, loyalty to the old Emperor, Franz Joseph, and to the supranational dynastic state that he symbolized, must have compelled many Austrian soldiers to persevere in the war. We simply do not know the extent to which such old-fashioned dynastic or territorial concerns motivated ordinary Habsburg soldiers. Surely, though, many of them endured for the sake of their comrades, their regiments, their honor and pride—and because military discipline meant that they had no alternative.

Jewish soldiers, however, crafted a sustaining ideology that served their own needs and differed from that of other Habsburg soldiers. For them, as for Jews generally, the war with Russia provided a coherent justification for fighting and dying in battle. Unlike other soldiers, whose support for the war with Italy inspired them to fight determinedly, Jewish soldiers seemed unconcerned with the war in Italy, even though they fought there loyally. The war with Italy was not a Jewish war, and it did not represent the identity of Austrian and Jewish war aims as did the war with Russia. To the extent that they talked at all about their motivations in the war, Jewish soldiers only mentioned the significance of the war with Russia, the traditional enemy of the Jews, which had invaded Austria and forced Jews to flee in terror. Fighting Russia therefore had meaning to Jewish soldiers, and not only those from Galicia itself. Indeed, modern, German-speaking Jewish soldiers from Vienna, Bohemia, Moravia, and Bukovina shared this war ideology, which helped sustain them through the long years of war. Jews had no quarrel with Italy, and seemed unconcerned with Italy's designs on Austrian territory, in which few Jews lived. Yet Jewish soldiers did fight and die in large numbers in Italy. They did so undoubtedly because they had no choice, but also because they had a vested interest in preserving the supranational Austrian state itself.

Soldiers' letters, published during the war in the newspapers or in special volumes, emphasized that some soldiers perceived the war as a *Rache für Kishinev*, revenge for Russian pogroms.[25] These letters also reveal that Galician soldiers in particular had special reasons for caring more about the war with Russia than the one with Italy. After all, they worried terribly about the fate of their families, many of whom had fled from the invading Russian army and from whom they had not heard.[26] Soldiers' letters published during the war might not necessarily provide insight into how soldiers actually felt. Newspaper or book editors might have chosen to print certain letters because they supported the themes of wartime propaganda. Yet just because published letters conformed to the official propaganda line did not make them untrue. Surely, Galician Jewish soldiers were motivated by their genuine worry about their families under Russian occupation. In his (unpublished) letter to his parents from the Isonzo Front in April 1917, Moritz Pollack, a soldier from Prossnitz, Moravia, described the anguish of Galician Jewish soldiers who had not heard from their families.[27] Such worry could easily motivate these soldiers to fight Russia valiantly, while the struggle against Italy would seem less personally significant. Jewish soldiers from elsewhere in Austria agreed. None of the published letters from Jewish soldiers on the Italian front mentioned the Italians, an omission that must certainly indicate less interest in the war with Italy on the part of all Austrian Jews.

Unfortunately, very few unpublished letters or diaries of Jewish soldiers exist. Those that are available mostly describe day-to-day experience—fighting, being wounded and sick, living in the trenches—but rarely pause to reflect on the larger issues of the war. Nevertheless, diaries of German-speaking Jewish soldiers reveal a greater concern for the war with Russia than the one with Italy. Teofil Reiss, an army medic from Vienna stationed on the Eastern Front for most of the war, began his diary on January 1, 1915 with the motto, "With God for fatherland and Kaiser," but he rarely reflected on political issues in almost four years of nearly daily entries.[28] His diary reflects, however, his fundamental devotion to Austria and his support for the war against Russia. Reiss complained regularly about mud, cold, lice, poor food, and filthy hospitals, but he was obviously proud of his military service, his work with the wounded, and especially the various medals for bravery he received.[29] While he ironically commented that people at home who think all soldiers are enthusiastic fighters have never been at the front,[30] he nevertheless delighted in the fact that Austrian soldiers were "hunting [the Russians] like dogs" in Russian Poland.[31] Moreover, whenever he spent time behind the lines because of illness or wounds, he was very eager to get back to the front, describing it in November 1915 as "much nicer" than behind the lines,[32] presumably because he had more interesting work, and, as a medic for an artillery unit, he was safer than if he were in the infantry.[33] Indeed, in the fall of 1917, he was upset with all the shirkers who hid behind the lines, and he yearned to return to the front, even as a regular gunner if necessary.[34] When Emperor Franz Joseph died in November 1916, Reiss noted that it was especially the Jews who mourned, and he was appalled by the Ukrainians and Czechs who would remain loyal to the new Emperor only if he granted them independence. "I don't want to know or hear anything about that. The Czechs and Ukrainians are very disloyal (*falsch*)" he concluded.[35]

Reiss' pride, his desire to serve at the front, and his delight with Russian defeat all reveal that he viewed the war with Russia as something meaningful to him personally. He does not wax eloquent, like the propagandists, about a just war between the forces of light and the forces of darkness, because he knows the filth and suffering of war. Moreover, from the large number of spelling and grammatical mistakes in his German, it is obvious that Reiss was not a well-educated man, equipped with the tools of refined analysis. Yet his very moving diary is a testament to the views of ordinary Viennese Jews who felt compelled to fight Russia but had no interest in the war with Italy. Indeed, in April 1918, Reiss was sent to fight in South Tyrol, and his attitude there stands in stark contrast to his earlier views. When he fought against Russia, he was always eager to serve at the front, but in Italy his only desire was to remain behind the lines. After recuperating from wounds in the summer, he was ordered to return to the front, and, he noted in his diary, "naturally I reported sick."[36] Many factors explain Reiss' change in attitude. He had married in February 1918 and wanted to live to enjoy married life; he feared the much greater brutality of the fighting in Tyrol compared with that on the Eastern Front, and by the summer of 1918 he may have become weary of war. One suspects, however, that Reiss simply had no interest in fighting the Italians, whom he does not even label as the enemy, while the struggle against Russia, "the enemy," was filled with meaning for him.

Similarly, Bernhard Bardach's war diary reveals a much greater interest in the war with Russia than with the war with Italy. Bardach, a career army doctor born in Lemberg in 1866, held no romantic illusions about the war. At the very beginning, he understood that even if Austria won, the war would lead to "mass murder and the annihilation of innumerable souls."[37] Most of his diary details the difficult and chaotic conditions on the Eastern Front, the repeated decimation of his regiment, and the horrors of marching in the rain and mud. Yet in the spring of 1915 his depression was replaced with elation over the German-Austrian victories against the Russians in Galicia. He noted on April 5, 1915: "Our joyful mood was indescribable." On May 2, after the great offensive began, he described the surrender and flight of Russian soldiers as "a magnificent sight."[38] Throughout May and June he recorded his own glee and the "colossal, general jubilation" of all the soldiers over the German-Austrian victories and the Russian retreat.[39]

Bardach, who spent most of the war in the east, also expressed his pleasure over Austrian success on the Italian front.[40] Nevertheless, his satisfaction with military gains in Italy pales in comparison with his absolute joy over trouncing the Russian enemy.

Memoirs of Jews from Vienna, Bohemia, Moravia, or Bukovina who served as soldiers in World War I also reveal the importance of the war with Russia, but not the war with Italy. Few were as bellicose as Wolfgang von Weisl, a militant Zionist medical student from Vienna, who noted in his memoirs that "a war against Jew-murdering czarism was holy for me."[41] Hans Kohn and his Zionist colleague Robert Weltsch joined a Prague regiment in 1914 to defend their fatherland "which we believed to be in danger." The Czechs in the regiment, Kohn noted, were not enthusiastic about the war, but ostensibly Kohn, Weltsch, and other "German" Jews were.[42] Fritz Lieben, a Viennese reserve officer stationed in Galicia, recalled that when he reported for service on August 1, 1914, "military service now seemed something meaningful."[43] The reconquest of Lemberg impressed him deeply and he naively hoped that it would lead to a rapid end of the war.[44]

When the war broke out, seventeen-year-old Adolf Mechner of Czernowitz, gripped by enthusiasm, wanted to volunteer, but his mother refused her consent.[45] Mechner was drafted a year later as a "one year volunteer," a special status for those with Gymnasium education, which qualified them for reserve officer training. By this time, his war enthusiasm, dampened by his family's flight from Bukovina in fear of the invading Russian army, had revived in the wake of Austrian successes in the East. He wrote:

> We believed at that time everything that the newspapers brought, that Austria-Hungary and Germany were attacked in a treacherous way by the enemies and that we acted in self-defense. The young people, all of them, were proud to wear the uniform and to contribute to the defense of the fatherland.[46]

Mechner disobeyed a direct order by his superior to surrender during the Russian offensive in the summer of 1916 because he could not bear the idea of becoming a Russian prisoner.[47] Unlike other Jewish memoirists, Mechner seemed eager to fight on the Isonzo front during the last year of the war. He (unsuccessfully) begged to participate in the spring 1918 offensive after receiving a wound in his hand, and he was very proud of the medals he received in Italy; yet he did not view his service in Italy in patriotic terms, observing that by the summer of 1918, "my patriotism was long gone, or at a low point." Obviously uncomfortable with his eagerness to serve on the Italian front, he argued that he preferred to be there only because "I was protected there from the chicanerie (sic) of officers" and from military drill.[48]

Not all Jewish soldiers were quite so eager to fight. Some Jews opposed war, or understood that war, even a justifiable war was not a romantic adventure but rather an occasion for suffering and death. Religious Jews surely also feared having to violate religious law while serving in the military. Further, some Czech Jews may have shared lack of enthusiasm for the war with some of their Czech nationalist compatriots. Prague-born Hella Roubicek Mautner insisted that her cousins, who identified as Czechs and had been educated in Czech schools, served in the army "but they were not out to die for the Habsburgs," and that her brother was "also an unwilling soldier."[49] Arnold Hindls, an engineer from Moravia, remembered in his memoirs the "unpleasant" feeling he had when he realized that as a reserve officer, he would surely be called to active service in the summer of 1914. Hindls and his family considered themselves members of the German cultural community in Brünn, so his negative feelings were not caused by Czech antipathy to an Austrian war. He simply did not want to fight. His memoir movingly describes the horrors of the Eastern Front, where he served until captured by the Russians in December 1914.[50] Other young Jews opposed war and tried to avoid it. Joseph Floch claimed that when World War I broke out, he immediately recognized it as "the greatest crime," which would only lead to slaughter and annihilation, and he became depressed in the face of the enthusiasm for war that he witnessed in his native Vienna. When he was examined by his draft board, according to his wife, he allowed his cross-eyes, which he could normally control, to float freely and thus was declared unfit for service. By 1916, wise to such tricks, the board drafted him, but he somehow managed to get himself assigned first to office work and then as a portrait painter for his regiment's officers.[51]

Some Jews tried to evade military service. Despite their desire for revenge against Russia, some Galician Hasidim mutilated themselves so that the army would declare them unfit for service.[52] Other Jews, drafted into the army, tried to obtain relatively safe assignments. George Clare of Vienna noted in his memoirs that after his father was drafted in November 1914 "strings were pulled" so that he could serve as a clerk in the service corps.[53] Otto Friedman of Salzburg admitted that he volunteered for the army, not out of "enthusiasm," but to get into a unit of his choice, an artillery unit with his brother-in-law.[54] Ulrich Furst's father, an officer in an engineering battalion in Vienna, feared being sent to the front, presumably in Italy, and did not forward his papers for promotion to his major.[55]

Jews, of course, were not the only soldiers to evade difficult military assignments. In a wonderfully comic scene in Grübel's play *K.u.k. Landsturm,* all the soldiers—Jews and non-Jews alike—who are scheduled to leave for the front put powder in their eyes so that they cannot go, and then they bribe the sergeant with cigarettes to avoid punishment[56]. Jews may have served at the front in numbers slightly lower than their proportion in the population, but they did so because they often knew German and had more education than regular recruits and thus were frequently assigned to the artillery, the medical corps, and to military administration.[57] The large number of medals won by Jewish soldiers attests to the fact that they also fought bravely at the front.[58]

Although some Jews may have tried to avoid onerous military duty, others regarded their military service as a point of honor. David Neumann, for example, a sergeant from the Burgenland (then in Hungary), who grew up in Vienna, recalled in a 1988 interview that he would have been sick if he had been declared unfit when he was drafted in 1914.[59] Rudolph Pick from Vienna, who entered the army in March 1918, described his incredible joy when he became a lieutenant at a time when most people were exhausted from the war: "Back in Vienna, no one could believe that I was already an officer. Mother was happy, my girl friends admiring, and I received another extra uniform. At that time I loved being in the army."[60] Yet even he was pleased that his family had pulled some strings so that he could serve in Vienna and sleep at home.[61]

Many Jewish soldiers felt that their military service served the useful purpose of giving the lie to anti-Semitic canards about Jewish cowardice. They were proud that their behavior could serve as proof of Jewish honor and military skill and would win all Jews more respect. Indeed, the desire to demonstrate Jewish honor served as an important element in the sustaining ideology of many Jewish soldiers during World War I. David Neumann, from Vienna, who served in a Hungarian regiment with few Jews, observed "that I, as a Jew, had to prove that I was a good soldier."[62] When Eric Fischer was drafted as a "one year volunteer" in 1916 after he graduated from the Wasagymnasium in Vienna, he refused to tell the draft board about his heart condition because "I considered it my duty not to contribute to the often heard taunt of the Jews as cowards."[63] Responding to a letter congratulating him for winning the silver medal for valor, Corporal Josef Fischer wrote to the Jewish community of Vienna in April 1917 that "it has always been my constant aspiration here in the field to excel as a Jew in order to prove that we Jews also do our best in the service of the fatherland."[64] In late 1917, Corporal Alfred Ellinger and "one year volunteer" Konrad Heim asserted in a letter to the *Österreichische Wochenschrift* that they fought for Kaiser, fatherland, and "the honor of Jewry."[65] The desire to demonstrate Jewish honor and refute anti-Semitic charges also served an important role in the war ideology of Jewish soldiers in Germany.[66]

Comradeship, however, did not play a large role in motivating Jewish soldiers to persevere during the war. Austrian Jews who fought loyally against Russia or Italy almost never argued that they did so because of their obligation to comrades, living or dead. Indeed, comradeship as a motivating force for any soldiers has probably been greatly exaggerated. Not only did class divisions between officers and men persist, but the high casualty rate meant that decimated units were constantly filled with new soldiers who had very little opportunity for establishing bonds.[67] Linguistic and national differences would have made comradeship in the Habsburg army even more difficult than in other armies.

For Jews in particular, other factors also mitigated against forming close relations with non-Jewish soldiers. The sheer number of Jews, and their concentration in certain regionally based regiments, created a situation in which Jews could befriend other Jews in their regiments without any need to socialize with Gentiles. Most Jews in the army, like the vast majority of Austro-Hungarian Jewry, were deeply religious, Yiddish-speaking Jews from Galicia, Bukovina, or Hungary. In the army, as at home, they could be separated from non-Jews by walls of cultural, linguistic, and religious difference. In any Galician regiment, there would surely be sufficient numbers of other traditional Jews to make it unnecessary to socialize with Polish or Ruthenian peasants, with whom many could not converse in any case. But even the Germanized, modern Jews of Austria did not generally experience greater social interaction with non-Jews in the army. Viennese Jews often had to serve in regiments from the regions from which their families had emigrated and whose languages and cultures they did not share. Bohemian and Moravian Jews might find themselves isolated as German speakers in Czech regiments. In such circumstances, it was natural for Jews to seek out the companionship of fellow Jews, whose numbers made it easy to do so. Jews and Gentiles might companionably march to battle together, but they would not necessarily become friends or even comrades.

Jewish diaries and memoirs sometimes describe warm companionship, but not anything close to the deep comradeship depicted in war literature. Teofil Reiss from Vienna, for example, mourned his comrades who fell in battle,[68] and he noted how happy everyone was whenever he returned to his unit after illness, wounds, or furloughs.[69] While behind the lines, he shared festive meals and "drank to brother-hood" with his fellow soldiers, yet at the same time he felt utterly alone, even not-ing in November 1916 that there was no one "with whom I can really talk."[70] Many memoirists remember good soldierly relationships. Ulrich Furst's father "had become good friends during the war years" with a "small and congenial group" of fellow officers, especially with two fellow Jews,[71] and Lt. Rudolph Pick warmly recalled talking and playing cards with the sergeant with whom he had "a nice, free, relationship."[72] Other memoirists indicate the limits of such compan-ionship. Reserve officer Fritz Lieben from Vienna felt that he enjoyed generally good relations with his fellow soldiers, but that it was somewhat problematic to live with people with whom one would not have chosen to live, alluding, certainly, to the fact that he was not really friends with the others. Moreover, in a telling aside, he also expressed his aversion to the drunkenness he encountered in the service.[73] Most Jewish memoirists do not mention friends or comrades at all, even when they describe their military service in great detail.

Although comradeship did not play a major role in the war experience of Jewish soldiers, those who wrote memoirs were quick to point out that they encountered no anti-Semitism in the army. Eric Fischer related that his experi-ence as a schoolboy in Vienna had prepared him to expect anti-Semitism in the army, but he encountered none. Fischer correctly attributed the absence of anti-Semitism to two Habsburg realities: The army itself had a positive attitude toward the Jews and the fact that so many of his officers were fellow Jews.[74] Similarly David Neumann insisted that while anti-Semitism had been ubiquitous in civil-ian life in prewar Vienna, "in the army there was no anti-Semitism in any shape or form."[75] He mentioned only one minor anti-Semitic incident that he experi-enced, and that was the exception that proved the rule. There was probably more anti-Semitism in the army than these two memoirists would have us believe. In his diary Teofil Reiss reported several incidents that revealed that his command-ing officer held conventional anti-Jewish views. The officer praised Reiss for his courage under fire, wished that all Jews were equally brave, and warned him not to "make business" when he went to Cracow to receive his medals.[76] Yet this same captain disapproved when a lieutenant put Reiss on report as "an insolent Jew," and he arranged to send the lieutenant to the front.[77] In her memoirs, Lil-lian Bader, from Vienna, related a 1917 incident in which her future husband rep-rimanded Tyrolese soldiers for saying "Damn the Jews" in his presence.[78]

It stands to reason, given the prevalence of anti-Semitic animosity in the population at large, that Jews encountered anti-Semitic insult in the army. Indeed, to some extent at least, the absence of comradeship may reflect the tense relationship between Jewish and non-Jewish soldiers. Censorship or self-censorship prevented Jewish newspapers from reporting anti-Semitic incidents in the army during the war, but there are hints in the press that such incidents occurred. The voluminous files of the *Israelitische Kultusgemeinde* in Vienna contain a small number of complaints about anti-Semitic incidents in the army during four years of war. In one case, in 1917, a Jewish doctor from Brünn described an artillery captain who abused his Jewish soldiers using language that shocks post-Holocaust sensibilities. Punishing a Jewish soldier for no apparent reason, he publicly attacked all Jewish soldiers, viciously declaring: "International Jewish rabble, I want to annihilate all of you; I want to shoot all of you and throw your flesh to the dogs to eat even if I have to die for it."[79] The files of the *Jüdisches Kriegsarchiv* also contain a small number of complaints of anti-Semitism in the army, including reports of Galician peasants mouthing anti-Semitic canards.[80] One 1917 report by the president of the Jewish community of Sambor, Galicia, complained that when he protested that Catholic priests blessed all the soldiers, including Orthodox Jews, before battle, the commander of the tenth army corps responded: "Summa summarum, the Russians have not been here long enough."[81]

These incidents could easily alarm Jews, but the small number of such complaints indicates that they were also rare. Jews probably took ordinary insults in their stride. Moreover, they undoubtedly were confident that the army itself, an institution famous for its toleration of national and religious difference, would not allow discrimination. Their confidence was definitely well placed. The Austrian army had always allowed large numbers of educated Jews the privilege of serving as reserve officers. In 1897, almost 19% of all Habsburg reserve officers were Jews, and that percentage applied during the war as well. Both the German and the Habsburg armies permitted Gymnasium graduates to avoid their regular military obligation by serving instead as one year volunteers, who would undergo officer training and then be eligible for a reserve officer's commission. In contrast to the German army, which allowed no Jews at all to serve as reserve officers, the Habsburg army had permitted large number of Jews to do so. The Habsburg army even contained some Jewish career officers, although their numbers were small, and they did not generally serve in the most prestigious regiments.[82] Individual officers, especially non-Jewish reserve officers, might harbor anti-Semitic views, but the army as an institution considered itself above national and confessional strife, valuing loyalty to the fatherland and the dynasty above all else.[83]

As a result of this attitude, the army refused to investigate anti-Semitic charges that Jews shirked military responsibility. The army had always considered the Jews loyal,[84] and the military establishment saw no reason to do anything about anti-Semitic complaints that Jews avoided front-line duty. In laconic official style, the k.k. Minister for Defense of the Fatherland wrote in September 1917: "I do not think it is opportune to issue any general orders in the matter of decreasing the Jewish element behind the lines."[85] Even when Jewish spokesmen themselves asked the army for data on Jews at the front, presumably so they could refute anti-Semitic charges, the army would not comply. In November 1916, Jewish army chaplain Samuel Funk requested statistical information on Jewish officers and men in Infantry Regiment #4. The army not only refused his request, but Minister of War Baron Alexander Krobatin and army Chief of Staff Baron Franz Conrad sent letters to all units noting that "it does not seem appropriate to draw up statistics on the basis of religious distribution."[86] Jewish soldiers knew that they would suffer no discrimination in such an army, and they felt that it deserved their loyalty.

Their experience stands in sharp contrast to the experience of German soldiers in World War I. In the German army, anti-Semitism flourished among the officers, especially the reserve officers, and Jewish soldiers experienced both insult and rejection. Growing anti-Semitism during the war led to the increased estrangement of Jewish and non-Jewish soldiers in the trenches.[87] More importantly, despite their support for the German war effort and their very significant losses in the field, German Jews felt betrayed by the German army, which did indeed conduct a military census in 1916. The German army insisted that it surveyed the religious distribution of soldiers on the front and behind the lines to give the lie to anti-Semitic charges that Jews shirked military responsiblity, but the so-called "Jewish census" humiliated Jewish soldiers, alienated them from their fellow soldiers, and made them feel that their sacrifices for the fatherland had been in vain. Moreover, all German Jews regarded the census, the results of which were never published, as a victory for anti-Semitism and a sign that the government legitimized it.[88] Austrian Jewish soldiers—indeed Austrian Jews generally—could feel genuine relief that their army appreciated them and would not acquiesce to anti-Semitism. Such relief surely served to augment the profound loyalty of Jews for the multinational Habsburg state.

The Issue of Identity

Serving in the army strengthened the Austrian identity of Austrian Jews, but it did not necessarily integrate them into Austrian society. Jewish soldiers fought for Austria, but they did not fully share the unifying war ideology of other Habsburg subjects. They felt themselves an integral part of the Austrian war effort, yet worried about anti-Semitism even as they expressed gratitude that the institutions of the supranational state protected them from it. They got along with their fellow soldiers, but even in the trenches they did not bridge the social distance between themselves and non-Jews.

Fighting for Austria seems to have deepened the Jewish identity of many Jewish soldiers. Observing Jewish religious rituals in the field, especially Passover seders and High Holiday services, provided Jewish soldiers with a welcome respite from battle, a source of comfort, a taste of home, and a proud symbol of Jewish solidarity. Large numbers of soldiers were observant traditional Jews, and all Jews took pride in the fact that such religious Jews could serve as valiant soldiers. Those Jews who had already modernized also took pleasure in the fact that large numbers of Jews in the military could gather to celebrate Jewish holidays.

They did not become more observant because of their military experience, but their joint celebrations reminded them that Jews as a group were making a major contribution to the Austrian war effort and were bound together as Jews. Jewish soldiers in Germany also took pleasure in Jewish celebration in the field,[89] but the larger number of Austrian Jewish soldiers provided greater visibility and a more concrete sense of Jewish solidarity. Moreover, heightened Jewish identity in Austria was not based, as it was in Germany, on a reaction to anti-Semitism or on the encounter with Eastern European Jews.[90] Anti-Semitism, as we have seen, presented little obstacle to Jewish soldiers, and Austrian Jews were familiar with Jews from the east. The sheer number and visibility of Jewish soldiers, especially at holiday celebrations, augmented their already well-established Jewish identity. Religious ritual thus reinforced ethnic separateness for those Jews who participated.

One moving example of the role of Jewish celebration in both the Austrian and Jewish identities of Jewish soldiers can be found in Teofil Reiss' diary. In the spring of 1916, Reiss, then behind the lines in Hungary, serving as cook as well as medic, took it on himself to prepare a seder and kosher food for the Jews in his unit. With the *Menagegeld*, the army's per diem allocation for soldiers' food, Reiss went off to Vienna to obtain the necessary supplies, "so that Jewish soldiers should know that one can also eat kosher in the military." He obtained matzah and wine from local Hungarian Jewish communities. At the seder itself, he asked all those assembled to rise and swear their blood to defend Kaiser and fatherland. "It was so festive," Reiss exclaims, "that everyone present cried."[91]

Similarly moving is an April 9, 1917 letter from Moritz Pollack, a junior reserve officer (*Zugsführer*) on the Isonzo front, to his parents in Prossnitz, Moravia, describing the seder he attended. Pollack was struck by the fact that the Germans, Poles, Hungarians, Czechs, Russians, and Romanians at the seder were "all of them Jews." The army chaplain gave a talk, first in German and then in Yiddish, while many of those present wept. The food was plentiful and good—soup with two dumplings (made from groats, since matzah was not available), meat, and prunes—and eaten in far more comfortable conditions than most of them had enjoyed for a long time. At the end of the seder they sang out "Next year in Jerusalem" with great feeling, and sang *bimhero,* (i.e., *Adir Hu,* a song about the speedy arrival of the messianic age) with a melancholy laugh. After the seder, they all sat for a long time, talking companionably together.[92] The actual meaning that Jewish soldiers ascribed to the phrase "Next year in Jerusalem" varied. Many understood the phrase in its traditional messianic or modern Zionist sense, while others understood it symbolically, as an expression of their desire to be home with their children or of their longing for peace.[93] In any case, Pollack and the other soldiers surely came away from the evening with an enhanced sense of Jewish solidarity.

Letters from soldiers published in the Jewish press were often more overt, probably selected in the first place to prove the significance of religious celebration for Jewish identity. One Jewish soldier on the Isonzo front, describing High Holiday services there in 1916, remarked on how amazing it was that a place that had never before heard Jewish prayer now contained "such a magnificent Jewish congregation, filled with the spirit of religious fervor, devotion to God, and fraternal solidarity," generated by physical danger and the spirit of the High Holidays.[94] Some Jewish soldiers felt that services in the field or in POW camps were far more meaningful than services had ever been at home,[95] and many reports of those services mention that the soldiers wept, so moved were they by the significance and spirit of the day.[96] Jewish chaplains concurred. Samuel Lemberger, who had arranged High Holiday services on the Romanian front in 1916, wrote that the soldiers who attended them "felt the living Jewish spirit that filled the gathering." They possessed "a sense of belonging and loyalty and love for the faith of our fathers."[97] Jewish soldiers who used the small-format prayer book for soldiers prepared by the Jewish community of Vienna must also have felt connected to other Habsburg Jews as they prayed.[98]

A sense of Jewish solidarity in the army was expressed as well in a nearly mythic story repeated in many Jewish newspapers, "*Kaddish* in the Trenches." While serving on the Eastern Front, Dr. Oskar Faludi was approached by another soldier to join a *minyan,* the quorum of ten needed for prayer, to say *kaddish,* the prayer for the dead, for his father. The five Jews in Faludi's unit went to say *kaddish,* lit a candle in the trench, and had "the most unforgettable experience" of their lives. While they were saying *kaddish,* which they said not just for Faludi's father but for all Jews who had fallen in battle, an officer approached, wanting to use the candle to light his cigarette. When they explained that he could not use a memorial candle for his cigarette, he told them that he too was a Jew, and he joined them in prayer.[99]

This story might imply that Jewish soldiers had a hard time finding each other, but in fact, most Jews, especially those in Galician, Hungarian, and even Viennese units, served together with large numbers of fellow Jewish soldiers. The sheer numbers of Jewish soldiers who attended Passover seders or High Holiday services indicates that it was not at all hard in the Austrian army to find fellow Jews to perform Jewish rituals. Joachim Schoenfeld, from Sniatyn, Galicia, recalled in his memoirs how he had been unable to leave the Isonzo front to attend his father's funeral in a Galician refugee camp in 1917. Nevertheless, because there were so many Jews in his regimental headquarters, "putting together a Minyan" so he could say *kaddish* for his father, "was no problem."[100] When army chaplain Samuel Nagelberg thanked Red Cross chaplain Béla Fischer for 25 copies of the scroll of Esther, he wondered, "How should I even begin [to distribute them] when in my unit there are almost 2,000 Jewish soldiers?"[101] Such numbers reinforced both Jewish comfort in the Habsburg army and the sense that Jews formed a separate group within it.

The fact that the army itself facilitated Passover seders and High Holiday services encouraged Jewish soldiers in their loyalty to the Dual Monarchy and the Jewish people. Each year, the army ordered that Jewish soldiers receive kosher food for all eight days of Passover. Where Jews were stationed near Jewish communities, those communities made the necessary arrangements with the local military authorities, receiving the *Menagegeld* for all soldiers involved. Where there were no Jewish communities—primarily on the Italian front—Jewish soldiers themselves set up kosher field kitchens with new utensils, slaughtered kosher meat, and obtained matzah, potatoes, and beets.[102] The army also regularly gave Jewish soldiers behind the lines leave to attend Passover seders and High Holiday services,[103] and Jewish army chaplains, or even ordinary, energetic soldiers, organized the services.[104] In 1916, the army went one step further, ordering that Jewish soldiers behind the lines could have separate kosher kitchens if at least 100 men in a given unit wanted kosher food.[105] Jewish soldiers were delighted,[106] but it is not clear if kosher field kitchens ever operated on a regular basis. In December 1916, the Austrian Minister for Defense of the Fatherland told the representatives of the Viennese Jewish commnity that he did not want to hear their complaints about non-compliance. After all, he noted, Jewish soldiers had served in the army for decades and had never had kosher food before.[107]

That many Jewish soldiers felt obligated to keep kosher even while serving in the army should come as no surprise given the fact that so many of them were deeply religious Jews from Galicia and Hungary. Many memoirists recall how they, or others in their units, simply subsisted on bread, marmalade, coffee, and perhaps some cheese during their years in the service. Joachim Schoenfeld, from Galicia, remembered that on the train taking him to the front, Jews traded the allocated sausages for butter, "trying to avoid eating *trayfe* (nonkosher food) for as long as possible," and some Jews "never ate any meat from the army kitchens during their entire war years."[108] Letters and cards sent to the IKG of Vienna by religious soldiers from Galicia also reveal their devotion to keeping kosher under very difficult conditions. Many soldiers, especially those stationed where there were no local Jews to help them, plaintively appealed for matzah at Passover, implying that they would starve without it. Hermann Olesker, for example, wrote to the Vienna IKG from Styria in February 1915, explaining that the 400 Jewish soldiers in his unit normally "live on dry bread and water" and obviously needed matzah on Passover.[109] A group of soldiers in his unit simultaneously appealed to the *Israelitische Allianz* for potatoes and matzah, because they would "rather fast for the eight days [of Passover] than eat leavened bread."[110] Religious Jews from western Austria also tried to avoid nonkosher food. David Neumann from Vienna remembered that he had "only eaten artificial honey, bread, and similar things for almost a whole year" before he ate the regular mess.[111]

The large number of Jews who kept kosher and observed traditional Jewish rituals played an important role in the self-perception of all Habsburg Jewish soldiers. They could all take pride that even deeply pious Jews served the fatherland. Moreover, the public nature of keeping kosher in the army made it clear that the Jews formed a separate, identifiable group in Austria. Interestingly, this obvious separation from other soldiers did not embarrass Austrian Jews, even highly acculturated Jews from Vienna or Prague. Contemporary accounts praised the Galicians and Hungarians for their piety, and memoirs written later simply took it for granted.

In January 1915, for example, Chief Rabbi Moritz Güdemann of Vienna wrote to the IKG board, reminding them that in the army there were thousands and thousands of Jewish soldiers, "especially Galician religious Jews, who would under no circumstances eat *chomez* during Passover."[112] The board was sensitive to this issue, understanding that most Jewish soldiers "belonged to the strictly religious circles of the Jewish population."[113] Jewish chaplains especially took pride in the fact that most soldiers observed kashrut strictly. In April 1915, Chaplain Majer Tauber described to the readers of the *Österreichische Wochenschrift* how most of the Jewish soldiers in his unit, "very religious" Jews from east Galicia and northern Hungary, "suffered great privations to observe the Jewish dietary laws," eating the regular solider's mess only when they were utterly debilitated. He, a modern rabbi from Lemberg, comforted them and told them that God would forgive them, especially since they fought a holy war against Russia.[114]

Austrian Jews took pride in the fact that most Jewish soldiers observed other Jewish rituals as well. Orthodox soldiers appealed to the Viennese Jewish community for prayer books, prayer shawls, ritual fringes, phylacteries, Torah scrolls, printed Bibles, scrolls of the book of Esther, collections of psalms, and other necessities for personal and communal religious life. Their field postcards, usually written in German, but often reflecting a Yiddish original, offer moving testimony to the profound piety of large numbers of Habsburg soldiers,[115] a piety that Vienna's Jewish notables very much respected.[116] In December 1915, for example, one year volunteer Raves Salsmann requested prayer books for himself and his friends because they were "now fighting against our enemies and would like to address a few words every day to the Almighty." Soldiers requested full-length prayer books without German translation, not just the abbreviated soldiers' prayer book prepared by Vienna.[117] In the fall of 1915, a group of 300 soldiers in their forties wrote to Rabbi Moritz Güdemann in Vienna asking him to intervene with the appropriate authorities so that they would not have to shave, an act prohibited by religious law.[118] Many requests reflected the fact that soldiers belonged to one or another Hasidic sect. Chaim Kleinmann, stationed in Dorna Watra, requested a pair of phylacteries "if possible from a Galician *sofer*" (scribe) and three prayer books "nusach Sefardim," that is, according to the custom of the Hasidim.[119]

The army experience may have heightened the identity of Jewish soldiers, but their Jewish identity did not necessarily remain static. Religious Jews held fast to Jewish religious law, but their experience in the military acquainted them, in many cases for the first time, with the larger world of secular culture and modern Judaism. Even if they did not befriend non-Jews, they still came into contact with them and got to know them. More importantly, they became acquainted with modern, secularized Jews. Even in Galician regiments with large numbers of pious Galician Jews, there were modern Jews from the cities and Viennese Jews who had been born in Galicia or Bukovina. Moreover, Jewish army chaplains, who played a major role in helping all Jews observe Jewish rituals and feel connected to the larger Jewish community, also introduced traditional Jews to modernized Jewish religious worship and customs.

At the beginning of the war, the Habsburg army contained only ten Jewish chaplains, all captains in the reserve.[120] As the number of Jews in the army swelled, the army commissioned many more Jewish chaplains as captains in the reserve, some of them only for the duration of the war. By 1917, there were 43 Jewish chaplains and 76 by 1918.[121] In addition, ordinary rabbis volunteered as "subsidiary" chaplains. They visited the Jewish wounded and catered to the religious needs of Jewish soldiers stationed in their vicinities.[122] Even if they came from traditional backgrounds, most of the chaplains were modern rabbis, university educated and trained in modern religious seminaries, often possessing Ph.D. degrees. Sixty percent of the chaplains in 1914 had Ph.D.'s, 28% in 1917, and 36% in 1918.[123] Twelve of the sixteen rabbis who served as chaplains with the Isonzo army at the end of 1917 had Ph.D.'s.[124] Orthodox Jews in Hungary may have requested that traditional rabbis serve as chaplains as well, but modern Jews parried this attempt, insisting that chaplains show evidence of a modern education, possessing at least the *Matura,* the certification of a completed Gymnasium education.[125]

Chaplains in the army tended to the religious needs of the soldiers in their charge. They arranged and led religious services, organized kosher food and Passover seders, and provided soldiers with prayer books and other religious articles. They also wrote to the relatives of wounded and fallen soldiers and distributed small sums of money as well as packets of food, cigarettes, and knitted goods at Chanukah that paralleled the Christmas presents distributed to all soldiers. They blessed troops departing for the front, performed marriages ceremonies, visited the sick, and helped bury the dead.[126] Chaplains regularly appealed to Austria's Jewish communities for assistance in these tasks. In August 1914, for example, Chaplain Dr. Josef Sagher asked the Vienna IKG for Torahs, Torah ark curtains, prayer books, a large white silk Tallit with blue and gold borders, presumably to cover the table on which the Torah would rest, a fancy skullcap for himself, and other necessities for communal prayer.[127] Most chaplains displayed sensitivity to the religious needs of their men. While serving in Galicia at the beginning of the war, Chaplain Majer Tauber of Lemberg, a graduate of the Vienna Rabbinical Seminary with a Ph.D., conducted Passover services "in the Hasidic style, with much singing."[128] Chaplain Dr. Leo Bertisch, from Deutschbrod, Bohemia, expressed his respect for the rabbinic knowledge of the Jewish soldiers in his unit. Unlike the members of his congregation at home, who were only interested in a good sermon, his Galician, Bukovinian, and Hungarian soldiers wanted to "hear Torah."[129]

Soldiers complained, however, that the chaplains did not always do their job, that they did not provide matzah for Passover or arrange services for the holidays.[130] Many Jewish soldiers never came into contact with Jewish chaplains at all.[131] Such complaints, though very real, probably reflected the fact that there were simply too few chaplains to attend to the religious needs of all the Jewish soldiers. Chaplain Bernard Hausner, who served on the Isonzo front, reported in 1916 that he arranged services in eight different locations but could only personally participate in four of them.[132] A letter by a soldier describing High Holiday services arranged by Chaplain Majer Tauber on the Isonzo in 1916 complained that there were simply not enough rabbis for all the Jewish soldiers there. An ensign from Pressburg led services in his area.[133] Moreover, the sheer difficulty of obtaining matzah when wheat was in short supply and the problems of coordinating a large effort with recalcitrant and often stingy Jewish communities made the task of the chaplains very difficult.[134] Naturally, the exigencies of the fighting war itself meant that most soldiers did not have the luxury of attending religious services even if chaplains were able to arrange them. Teofil Reiss ruefully noted while at the Eastern Front in October 1916: "Today is Yom Kippur. God will have to delay [his judgement]; [I] can't go pray."[135]

Not all chaplains were equally devoted. Some chaplains may have preferred to sit in regimental headquarters and write reports, as some of their Catholic colleagues charged;[136] others may have become mired in bureaucratic wrangling and territorial disputes;[137] and some may have been difficult men, insensitive to the needs of their charges. But most of them undoubtedly tried as hard as they could to satisfy an extremely diverse and needy clientele. Rabbi Adolf Altmann, for example, the rabbi of Meran, Tyrol, volunteered his services as a subsidiary chaplain in 1915 and became a regular Jewish chaplain in December 1916. Born in Hungary, the recipient of both a traditional Jewish and a modern university education, Altmann had served as rabbi in Salzburg for eight years before he arrived in Meran in early 1914. During the war, he worked exceedingly hard, attending to his own community as well as to the Jewish soldiers in Tyrol. At the time of his appointment as a regular chaplain, he received the golden service cross for his services. His son Manfred recalled that this enormous workload gave his father added moral strength because "he was very conscious of the significance of his activities."[138]

Sensitive though they usually were to the piety of the soldiers, chaplains also served as agents of Jewish modernization. In the first place, most of them conducted modern-style worship services, traditional in content but modern in aesthetic sensibility. Religious services conducted by the chaplains probably resembled services in the synagogues of Vienna, Prague, and other Habsburg cities that used the so-called "Vienna Rite," that is, the traditional liturgy conducted in a modern style, with order, decorum, and an edifying, vernacular sermon.[139] Rabbi Arnold Frankfurter, the Jewish chaplain for the Vienna garrison, arranged three types of religious services for the High Holidays, one for "German" soldiers (for those who spoke German), one for Hungarian soldiers, and one "according to the Galician rite," but all three services contained a sermon, a sign of modern religious worship.[140] Similarly, Bernard Templer conducted services "with sermon" for the soldiers behind the lines in Moravia, Silesia, and western Galicia.[141] When Samuel Link, a rabbi from Pilsen, Bohemia, arrived in South Tyrol, he discovered that religious services there were led by a Polish cantor in a very traditional, noisy manner. Sharing the negative assessment of Galician Jews common to Bohemian Jewry, and therefore determined to educate his mostly Galician flock in the ways of modernity, he instituted services in which the cantor might still "evoke the sad melancholy of the old songs," but the soldiers would pray softly and even feel guilty if they allowed their voices to rise above the rest. Although the pious Jews mistrusted him at first, he related, they came to realize that he was as good a Jew as the loudest of them.[142]

Secondly, chaplains functioned as pastors, not as traditional rabbis. The very office of chaplain exposed Jews in the army to the modern rabbi and his new role. The traditional rabbi, a figure familiar to the large number of pious Habsburg Jewish soldiers, was a student of the Talmud who rendered judgments in cases of Jewish law. Hasidim also revered another type of Jewish religious leader, the *rebbe,* whose mystical functions included intercession with God and advising his flock. Jewish chaplains, however, provided neither the legal judgments of the traditional rabbi nor the intercessionary powers of the Hasidic *rebbe*, but rather the pastoral functions of the modern rabbi. In his very role, the Jewish chaplain personified the modern rabbi and thus acquainted large numbers of traditional Jews with this new type of Jewish religious leader.[143]

Chaplains may have tried to familiarize traditional Jews with the world of Jewish modernity, but they, and indeed all Austrian Jews, took pride in the fact that so many Jewish soldiers adhered strictly to Jewish religious law while serving as valiant soldiers. When army chaplain Geza Fischer wrote to Rabbi Béla Fischer, a Red Cross chaplain, requesting prayer books for his "very many very religious and very brave Jewish soldiers,"[144] he voiced an Austrian Jewish truism. Rabbi Leo Bertisch did so as well when he described a seder on the Italian front in 1917, attended by "Galician Jews with full beards, most of them totally Orthodox, many decorated with medals for their bravery."[145] Jewish newspapers during the war were filled with stories about how Jewish religious objects—especially *tfillin,* small leather boxes containing Biblical verses on parchment that are bound by leather straps to the head and forearm during morning prayers—saved the lives of Jewish soldiers. One Jewish soldier described the Austrian attack on Tarnow, Galicia, the signal for which came just after some men in his company had finished morning prayers. A young yeshiva student stormed forth wearing his *tfillin,* which saved his life when a bullet lodged within it.[146] Another letter reported how *tfillin* in a soldier's backpack saved his life by preventing a bullet from entering his lungs.[147] The *Jüdische Volksstimme* in Brünn reported with pride that in the reconquest of Lemberg, Galician Jews went forth to battle wearing their *tfillin* and reciting the *shma,* the central prayer of the Jewish liturgy affirming the belief in one God.[148]

These stories obviously fulfilled an important need among Jewish soldiers to see Judaism and Jewish solidarity as sustaining them during the war.[149] They also provided a specifically Jewish set of symbols that helped Jewish soldiers make sense of their sacrifices in the war. George Mosse has convincingly argued that German soldiers relied very heavily on Christian symbols to help them cope with the horror of trench warfare. They developed the myth of the fallen soldier cradled in the arms of Christ and drew liberally from the rich Christian tradition about death and resurrection to transcend death at the front, overcome the fear of death, and invest the slaughter with some meaning. The dead had not died in vain, but had been sacrificed for the sake of the nation, and both they and the nation for which they had died would find eternal life. Christmas thus assumed enormous significance at the front as a celebration of Christian hope.[150] Most older studies of World War I soldiers ignored or denied the importance of Christian symbols, but more recently, scholars have admitted the role of religious symbolism among soldiers in the trenches. John Horne has argued that Catholicism provided French soldiers in World War I as well with a ready-made vehicle for understanding the war in terms of sacrifice and redemption.[151] Most recently, Jay Winter's study of grief and mourning during and after the war has emphasized the significance of traditional symbols—classical, romantic, and religious—

in helping ordinary Europeans cope with their losses. He notes that Christian religious symbols, in particular the crucifixion, the pietà, or New Testament scenes,
provided the possibility of resurrection, redemption, and transcendence.[152] No
studies of Austrian soldiers exist, but presumably they too found comfort in traditional Catholic attitudes toward death and resurrection.

Such a Christianization of the war experience posed obvious problems for Jewish soldiers who did not and could not share Christian symbols. Mosse has claimed
that in Germany, Jewish soldiers accepted the "structures of Christian mythology,"
not their specific religious content,[153] but he has neither explained nor proven his
point. Indeed, the evidence from Austria, and probably from Germany as well, points
exactly in the opposite direction. Jewish soldiers, and the larger Jewish community
of which they were a part, ignored the Christianization of the war experience, and
chose instead to view their sacrifice in Jewish terms. They understood their deaths in
terms of contemporary Jewish needs: to refute anti-Semitism and bring honor to
the Jews, to make a Jewish contribution to the war effort, to fight for a Jewish cause,
to express their Austrian and Jewish identities, and to revel in Jewish solidarity.

Interestingly, they did not turn to Jewish traditions of sacrifice, such as the
story of the binding of Isaac in Genesis, or to medieval Jewish martyrdom.
Rather, they drew on ancient traditions of Jewish valor. They were not martyrs at
all, but rather Maccabees, valiant heroes defending the Jewish right to live as
Jews, in whatever manner they chose. Jewish chaplains never lost an opportunity
to remind their charges that they fought in the tradition of the Jewish heroes of
antiquity.[154] Chanukah and Passover, festivals that celebrate Jewish national freedom, and the Jewish High Holidays, with their focus on divine judgment, provided Jewish soldiers with Jewish symbols that sustained them in war. Even when
they did not observe Jewish ritual, Jewish soldiers found comfort in Jewish religious tradition and in Jewish solidarity.[155] The prevalence of Christian symbols
probably only underscored their sense of separation from non-Jews, and their
conviction that Jews formed a separate group in society.

The issue of burying soldiers in common graves, especially popular in the
early, euphoric days of the war, forced Jews to come to grips with whether they
could share war symbols with their fellow citizens. Mosse argues that German
Jewish willingess to bury their dead sons in common soldiers' graves, marked
with crosses, proves that German Jews shared the Christian symbolism of the cult
of the fallen soldier.[156] The issue is, of course, far more complex, intertwined as
it is with concerns about patriotism and brotherhood. German Jews may have
agreed to such graves because they wanted to demonstrate that they belonged to
the German nation, and they may have tolerated the cross as a necessary part of
that effort. In Austria, Jews also longed to assert their devotion to the fatherland
and their brotherhood with all other Austrians, although not with any particular
nation. They also agreed to common graves, at least at the beginning of the war
and in places like Vienna where they had assimilated at least to some extent. But,
Austrian Jews never accepted the Christian symbolism that was attached to those
graves, and they very quickly created their own graves and memorials to provide
Jewish symbols with which to mourn the Jewish dead.

In September 1914, Richard Weisskirchner, the Christian Social mayor of Vienna, informed the Jewish community that the Viennese city council had decided to bury all Viennese who had died for the fatherland, or at least those who died of their wounds in Viennese hospitals, together in a common grave "without any distinction of nationality or religious confession."[157] The IKG carefully replied that it fully agreed in principle with this noble decision, but, if the city did indeed indicate the religion of buried soldiers, then the Hebrew acronym for "let his soul go to eternal rest," the traditional inscription on Jewish graves, should be inscribed next to Jewish names.[158] In fact, the IKG had further stipulations and objections. In the first place, it would not bury any Jewish soldier in a common grave if either he or his family objected, presumably for religious reasons. Secondly, it wanted IKG officials to wash and prepare the bodies of Jewish soldiers, since Jewish law required that only Jews touch the Jewish dead, and it wanted a rabbi to officiate at the burial of Jewish soldiers. Finally, and most important, the IKG reserved the right to refuse to participate in a common burial if the memorial contained any religious symbols.[159] IKG secretary Dr. Theodor Lieben met with Mayor Weisskirchner to voice these concerns. While the mayor readily agreed to most of these stipulations, he hedged on the important issue, saying that no decision had yet been reached about it.[160] Apparently the IKG did agree to a common grave, which probably did have a cross, and, at least in 1914, refused a request to establish a special grave for Jewish soldiers in the Jewish section of the central cemetery.[161]

Yet many Viennese Jews, despite their loyalty to the fatherland, chose to bury their fallen sons in Jewish graves. They appealed to the IKG of Vienna to exempt their sons, husbands, and cousins from the common grave and to bury them instead in the Jewish section of the cemetery.[162] Indeed, between September 1914 and March 1915, only 15 Jews were buried in the common soldiers' grave in Vienna.[163] Of course, most Viennese fallen in this period were buried in regular military cemeteries in Serbia or Galicia, not in Vienna, but even so, this low number reflects the fact that no matter how loyal, Jews, even modern Viennese Jews, preferred Jewish burial. Orthodox Jews in Vienna protested the common grave, voicing their opposition to burying beneath a cross, arguing that a common grave was "not a sign of patriotism, but rather a sign of religious degeneration."[164]

Statistics on the burial of Jewish soldiers during the war simply do not exist. Most Jewish soldiers must have been buried in military cemeteries near the fronts. At the beginning of the war, all graves were marked by simple crosses, which noted if the soldier was a Jew. Later the custom arose of engraving a Jewish star on the cross that marked Jewish graves. By 1916, the army stopped putting crosses on Jewish graves altogether, marking them instead with a wooden tablet twenty centimeters by seventy centimeters, inscribed with a Jewish star and the Ten Commandments.[165] In some cases, Jewish war dead were buried in Jewish cemeteries. In late 1915, Chaplain Adolf Altmann requested that fallen Jewish soldiers in the Tyrol be prepared for burial by the Jewish community of Meran and buried in the Jewish cemetery there unless families requested burial elsewhere.[166] Similarly, many Jews who died in Galicia were buried in Jewish cemeteries there, sometimes after their bodies were exhumed from general military cemeteries.[167] Frequently, exhumation was not possible because ordinary soldiers had been buried in common, not individual graves.

Although the sense of brotherhood and common national purpose motivated some Jews to agree to common graves at the beginning of the war, within a short time the desire surfaced to honor the Jewish dead with special memorials. To some extent this desire derived from the need to counter anti-Semitic charges of Jewish cowardice. Jewish memorials also bolstered Jewish pride by reminding the Jews that they had fought and died for the fatherland as Jews. Finally, separate Jewish memorials provided Jews with a private Jewish place in which to mourn. On September 3, 1914, Vienna's chief rabbi Moritz Güdemann wrote to the IKG, suggesting that the Jews of Vienna establish a memorial plaque, as the Jews of Breslau had done, to honor fallen Jewish soldiers "as a protection against possible later anti-Semitic denials that Jews had paid their tax in blood (*Blutsteuer*)" during the war.[168] In January 1915, Hermann Stern published a letter in the *Österreichische Wochenschrift* praising Vienna for its noble desire to bury all sons of the fatherland in a common grave. At the same time, he urged the Jewish community to bury some Jewish soldiers in the Jewish section of the cemetery and establish a memorial to fallen Jewish soldiers, so that a future generation might not wonder if the Jews had not fought in 1914.[169] In response to such requests, the IKG of Vienna did establish a special tomb for fallen Jewish officers and men in the Jewish section of the cemetery.[170] Similarly, the Jewish burial society in Nikolsburg, Moravia, set aside a place in the Jewish cemetery as a grave for Jewish soldiers in 1915.[171]

After the war, in 1929, the Jewish community of Vienna erected an impressive memorial to "our sons who fell in the World War 1914–1918" to provide an appropriate Jewish symbol and location for mourning. The small monument of grey stone, octagonal in plan, approximately fifteen feet high and open to the sky, evokes the ancient Israelite temple in Jerusalem. Inside, at the top of the entranceway, is a Jewish star, and the structure is encircled by a crenellation of rounded stones, alternating single ones, resembling tombstones, and double ones, reminiscent of the two tablets of the law, the usual artistic rendition of the Ten Commandments. The names of Viennese Jews who died in the war, officers and men, are inscribed on stone slabs on the inside surfaces of the walls, and benches face the slabs so visiters can sit and reflect on the dead and on the prominent inscription in Hebrew and German, from Isaiah 2:4: "Nation shall not lift up sword against nation; neither shall they learn war anymore."

This monument certainly does not glorify war and manly heroism. Instead, it is like a grave, a place to remember the dead and the horror of war. It offers hope through its pacifist, prophetic message. The enclosedness of the memorial provides comfort, protection, and a separate Jewish space in which to mourn. Near the memorial are the graves of Jewish soldiers, mostly officers who died in Galicia, presumably those whose families could afford to have their bodies moved or exhumed. These simple headstones list name, rank, details of deaths, military decorations, and sometimes sentimental words about the individual—"he was our happiness, the sun of our life," for example, on the grave of Lt. Eugen Knebel—or attempts to articulate the meaning of death, such as "he fell . . . in loyal fulfillment of his duty for his Kaiser, his fatherland, and the Jewish people" on the grave of Cadet Heinz Koch.[172] In 1934, the Association of Jewish Front Soldiers erected two low stones in the same areas, inscribed in Hebrew and German, honoring fallen Viennese Jews buried there and elsewhere.[173] This monument, with its collection of graves and the two memorial stones, does not share the symbolism—Christian, Germanic, classical, or modern—common to World War I memorials elsewhere.[174] The symbols are Jewish ones, appropriate for a Jewish place of mourning.

The experience of war in the Habsburg army thus solidified both the Austrian and the Jewish identities of Jewish soldiers. Fighting and dying for Austria, they felt that the army and the state they served supported and appreciated them, and they renewed their commitment to its continuity as the best protector against the anti-Semitism that raged in the last two years of the war among the civilian population. Serving alongside so many fellow Jews, especially religious Jews from Galicia, Bukovina, and Hungary, also reminded all Jews of the vigor of Jewish culture and the value of a separate Jewish identity. These commitments would guide all Austrian Jews in 1917 and 1918 as the various nationalities more actively pursued their political agendas and anti-Semitism flourished. Austrian Jews, who retained a staunch commitment to the supranational state, now found themselves in a difficult dilemma, one that tried their patience and challenged their cherished tripartite identity.

5

Clinging to the Old Identity, 1916–1918

When the old Emperor Franz Joseph died on November 21, 1916 at the age of 86, Manès Sperber's father sobbed while saying his morning prayers. He declared to his son that "Austria has died with him. He was a good emperor for us. Now everything will be uncertain! It is a great misfortune for us Jews!"[1] At the turn of the century, many had predicted that the Monarchy would dissolve when Franz Joseph died. Eric Fischer, for example, recalled that when he was a child everyone would say, "as long as the old gentleman . . . is alive, the Monarchy will keep together; then it will break up immediately."[2] The Habsburg Monarchy did not collapse when Franz Joseph died in the middle of World War I, but its future, and the future of the Jews within it, were "uncertain," as Herr Sperber said.

Uncertain about the future of the country and their role in it, the Jews of the Austria desperately clung to their old identities. They remained devoted to the preservation of the Austrian *Gesamtstaat,* the inclusive state, the supranational, multinational Austria, because they were convinced that only it protected them from anti-Semitism and accorded them the freedom to develop their Jewish identities however they chose. All types of Jews and Jews from all regions of the Monarchy insisted on their loyalty to the state and their desire to preserve it. They developed plans to reconfigure the state to conform to twentieth century demands for greater democracy and national self-determination, but most of them remained fundamentally committed to the continuity of the multinational state. This intense commitment endured to the very last moments of the Monarchy and even beyond.

In addition to clinging to their Austrian identities, Jews experienced a deepening of their Jewish identities in the last two years of the war. Not only did rising anti-Semitism make them more conscious of their Jewishness, but so did political uncertainty about the Monarchy. Jews—in particular the German-speaking Jews who lived in Bohemia, Moravia, Bukovina, and Vienna—felt that they needed to find a place for themselves as Jews in an Austria destined for profound political transformation. They tried to unite, albeit unsuccessfully, to form Austria-wide organizations to represent Jewish interests in public discussion of how to reconstitute the state. Moreover, some Jews responded to growing separatist nationalism by insisting ever more strongly on a Jewish national identity within Austria. Even Jews who eschewed Jewish nationalism felt Jewish ethnic attachments more strongly in these years.

In the last two years of the war, Austrian Jews continued to espouse the tripartite identity they had developed in the nineteenth century. They insisted that they were Austrian politically; German, Czech, or Polish culturally; and Jewish in a religio-ethnic sense. The success of nationalist politicians placed a lot of pressure on Jews to rethink their national identities, but this pressure only made the Jews ever more loyal to the Dual Monarchy that had allowed them lots of freedom to develop their identities as they pleased. Widespread anti-Semitism among the nationalist activists only deepened Jewish commitment to the old Austria.

Kaiser Franz Joseph's death provided Jewish spokesmen with the perfect opportunity to reiterate their loyalty to Austria. Jewish spokesmen wrote articles, and Jewish communities all over the Monarchy held special services to honor the dead emperor and repeat all the principles of the cult of Franz Joseph. He had liberated the Jews from the fetters of the Middle Ages. The champion of freedom and equality, he always extended his protection to the Jews.[3] Rabbi Adolf Altmann of Meran, Tyrol, delivered a sermon praising Franz Joseph as a virtuous, just, holy man, a loyal and good father to all his peoples. The Jews had loved their emperor and would continue to love him for all eternity.[4] Similarly, Max Grunwald, the rabbi of the Leopoldstadt temple in Vienna, asserted in a speech to the Austrian Israelite Union, that "we depart from the shades of our divinely blessed Kaiser Franz Joseph I in sorrowful memory of the profound benevolence that he extended so often to our fathers and to us. We and our children will preserve in our hearts a gratitude that will be inextinguishable."[5] A large delegation of Jewish communal leaders, Zionist activists, and Galician Orthodox rabbis, many of them refugees in Vienna and presumably dressed in Hasidic fashion, attended the funeral in St. Stephan's Cathedral.[6]

Jews genuinely mourned the old emperor. Rabbi Moritz Güdemann of Vienna noted in his diary on November 22, 1916, that Franz Joseph had been "a true *tzaddik* (righteous man)," and he hoped, in traditional Jewish fashion, that his memory would be for a blessing.[7] Joachim Schoenfeld remembered that his fellow Jewish officers "sincerely mourned the death of the humane monarch."[8] At the official Jewish service of mourning in Vienna, mourners intoned the *kaddish* and the *el moleh rachamim*, traditional prayers for Jewish dead, in honor of the emperor.[9] In his sermon at a memorial service for Franz Joseph in Graz, David Herzog expressed the terrible pain of the Jews at the death of "our dearly beloved emperor," not only because he was "the best and most noble monarch," or because he was the "ideal embodiment of our Monarchy," but also because he did not live to see the peace for which he longed.[10] Austrian Zionists labeled Franz Joseph's death a "misfortune," and declared that "we Jews stand on the bier of our old, beloved Kaiser with hearts deeply disturbed."[11] One spokesmen noted that he would remain "the standard and the model . . . of how one can be a good and true Austrian."[12]

Naturally, Jews paid homage to the new Emperor Karl, but their statements of loyalty betrayed their nervousness, not about him personally, but about the future of the Monarchy and their place in it. At a special meeting of the *Israelitische Kultusgemeinde* of Prague, for example, vice president Robert von Fuchs expressed his hope that Karl would win peace for his peoples and ensure "justice and equality" for the Jews.[13] Fuchs' language highlighted the fact that Karl would have to deal with the national aspirations of his peoples. More important, Fuchs clearly worried that Jewish legal rights, guaranteed under Austrian law since 1867, might be threatened under new political arrangements. Similarly, Alfred Stern, the president of the Vienna IKG, who on December 11 led a deputation of nineteen Jews from all over Austria to the new emperor, urged Karl to protect the "legal equality" that the Jews had long enjoyed.[14] The new Kaiser graciously praised the Jews for their loyalty and their sacrifices during the war and assured them that there would be no dimunition in the legal rights of any citizen in his realm.[15] Jewish organizations, liberal as well as Zionist, also sent greetings to the new emperor emphasizing their loyalty and their hope that he would uphold the "constitutional freedoms" and "legal equality" of all his subjects.[16]

Jews in Austria had good reason to worry about their status. The new emperor faced many problems. War weariness had become widespread. Although the military situation looked promising at the end of 1916—after all, Russia had been effectively eliminated as a protagonist in the conflict, and the Central Powers had almost completed the task of defeating both Romania and Serbia—still the war showed no signs of ending. Tied to the German alliance, and thus compelled to remain in the war as long as Germany continued to fight on the Western Front, unwilling, furthermore, to concede territory to the Italians, Austria continued to wage war despite the fact that most of its people yearned for an end to the bloodshed.[17] Their war weariness was greatly exacerbated by terrible food shortages at home, shortages made worse by a disorganized system of food distribution. Especially in the big cities, it became very difficult to obtain bread and other necessities. Women regularly went to the countryside to "hamster," to buy or otherwise obtain food from the peasants. But hamstering was illegal, and these women faced serious punishment if caught.[18] As the government continued to wage war, soldiers continued to die, and people at home went hungry and were punished for trying to feed their families, many Austrians began to distrust the central government. Worried about the potential for revolution, the government ruthlessly quashed massive strikes by workers in January 1918, an action that did not endear it to the dissatisfied public.[19]

Widespread dissatisfaction allowed for the proliferation of anti-Semitism. As the *Burgfrieden*, the internal truce at the beginning of the war, began to disintegrate, anti-Semitic agitators felt increasingly free to make heinous charges against the Jews. In addition to the usual litany, anti-Semites now insisted that the Jews were all war profiteers, price gougers, and black marketeers, making money from the terrible suffering of starving Austrians. Jews, they argued, had shirked their military responsibility to enrich themselves at the expense of other Austrians. In Vienna and the Czech lands, the presence of Galician refugees enraged the anti-Semites, who declared that refugees profited from the misery of the local populations. In Galicia, anti-Semites insisted that Jews cheated the peasants in the war-ravaged area.[20]

Nationalist enthusiasm, or rather the growing desire of the Poles, Czechs, and others for independence from supranational Austria, also led to increasing anti-Semitic agitation. In mixed-nationality areas like Galicia, Bukovina, Bohemia, Moravia, and Silesia, nationalists often inveighed against the Jews if they perceived them as belonging to another national camp or as supporting Austria itself. Anti-Semitic invective became more vocal after May 1917, when Kaiser Karl reopened parliament and encouraged public debate on the future of Austria. Anti-Semitic rhetoric gave way to anti-Jewish violence as the food situation and political order deteriorated sharply in 1918. In that year, pogroms against the Jews, which some observers labeled "hunger riots," but which everywhere had a nationalist dimension, broke out in Galicia, Bohemia, and Moravia.[21]

In the last two years of the war, nationalist politicians, especially those who had fled abroad, began more vigorously to demand not only autonomy but actual independence from Austria-Hungary. They were encouraged to make such demands by American President Woodrow Wilson's Fourteen Points, which called for the national self-determination of all peoples, even though Wilson was not yet committed to the break-up of the Monarchy and had left vague the issue of national self-determination for Austrian nationalities. Recognizing the need to assuage the aspirations of Austria's nationalities, especially given widespread dissatisfaction with the privations of an endless war, many groups, including the Social Democrats, proposed schemes to reorganize Austria along a variety of federalist lines. Some schemes proposed giving the Czechs, Poles, and South Slavs the same status Hungary had enjoyed under the dualist compromise. Other schemes sought to provide many of the nationalities with autonomy, whether determined by territory or by personal affiliation. None of the proposals to grant greater rights to the nationalities ever came close to realization, partly because Hungary opposed giving any other nationality parity within the Habsburg Monarchy, but mostly because the Entente began in 1918 to encourage nationalist activists— especially the Poles, Czechs, and South Slavs—to work for sovereignty. Once it became clear in the summer of 1918 that the Central Powers would lose the war, the desire for national independence and the creation of new nation-states at the expense of Austria-Hungary became so strong that Emperor Karl's October 1918 attempt to give the nationalities a large measure of autonomy within a federally reorganized Monarchy simply fell on deaf ears.[22]

German-speaking Jews responded to the political and social crises besetting Austria, and to the anti-Semitism that those crises engendered, by fervently seeking the continuity of multinational Austria. They assumed that only it could or would protect them from the threat posed by anti-Semitism, especially the anti-Semitism rampant in the ranks of the nationalist agitators. Jews feared that if the Austrian imperial bureaucracy no longer administered day-to-day affairs in the provinces, they would be placed at the mercy of radical nationalists, who might persecute them, deprive them of their legal equality, and force them to adopt a new identity. That new identity—as Germans, or Czechs, or Poles—would be difficult to acquire, not least of all because radical Germans, Czechs, and Poles refused to accept the Jews as bona fide members of their national communities. Facing such potential difficulties, it was no wonder that the overwhelming majority of Austrian Jews preferred to maintain the old Austria.

The Issue of Galicia

The struggle over the future of Galicia provided the Jews with an opportunity to articulate their desire for Austrian continuity. Austrian Jews universally sought to keep Galicia within the multinational Austrian *Gesamtstaat*. They assumed that any Austrian administration would treat the Jews more equitably and more justly than any Polish administration. Although in theory they supported the nationalist aspirations of the Poles, Jewish spokesmen continued to urge Austria to retain control over Galicia long after most people assumed that Galicia would become part of an independent Poland. This commitment to an Austrian Galicia did not derive from anti-Polish animosity but from the fear that Polish nationalists, once in full control, would persecute the Jews. Pogroms in Galicia in 1918 convinced them that Jews would suffer without Austrian protection. Concern for the physical safety of Galician Jewry, combined with their traditional loyalty to Austria, galvanized the Jews in defense of the *Gesamtstaat*.

The status of Galicia became a contested issue after the Central Powers drove the Russians out of the province and conquered Russian Poland in 1915. German and Austrian troops divided Russian Poland into two zones of occupation, and German and Austrian statesmen repeatedly renegotiated the future status of Poland.[23] Austria wanted to attach Poland to Austria in some fashion. Not willing to annex Poland outright, and hoping to ensure Austrian devotion to the German alliance, Germany sometimes supported the "Austro-Polish solution," as long it included guarantees for German economic domination of Poland. At other times, Germany opposed the Austrian solution, partially out of fear of the further Slavicization of Austria-Hungary, but mostly because it wanted to keep Poland more firmly in the German sphere of influence and guarantee its own economic domination. Austria compromised, and on November 5, 1916, the Central Powers announced the creation of an "independent" Kingdom of Poland, allied to the Central Powers, which would control Polish foreign relations and military affairs. Galicia was not included in this "kingdom." Austrian authorities decreed a "special status" for Galicia within Austria, guaranteeing even more autonomy to the local Polish elites than had hitherto been the case.

In late 1917, Austria once again insisted on attaching Poland to the Monarchy, this time with Galicia as a part of Poland, but German military and political leaders opposed this effort, insisting on their right to dominate Poland. After conceding to German economic demands, Austria agreed in August 1918 to create a Polish kingdom—which would include Galicia—within the Habsburg Monarchy, with this kingdom enjoying the same kind of rights as Hungary had enjoyed since 1867. In 1918, however, Polish nationalist politicians wanted real independence for Poland, including Galicia, and the Entente supported their cause. Indeed, the independence of Poland became the central feature of Wilson's Fourteen Points. Wilson did not specify whether Galicia would be a part of Poland, but Polish nationalists, especially those from Russian Poland, assumed that it would be. Ruthenian nationalists, on the other hand, fearing Polish domination, wanted Ruthenian East Galicia to form a separate crownland in Austria, and after February 1918, a part of independent Ukraine.

Jews wanted to keep Galicia Austrian. Even before the Central Powers liberated Galicia from Russian occupation, one spokesmen for the *Österreichische Wochenschrift* argued in March 1915 that only the state could oversee the reconstruction of Galicia in a fair manner, because only the state would conduct itself for the benefit of "all its peoples (*Stämme*) and religions."[24] After most of Galicia was restored to Austria in the summer of 1915, Jewish spokesmen, Zionist and non-Zionist alike, articulated their firm commitment to continued Austrian rule over Galicia because only the central authorities would deal equitably with all the inhabitants of the province.[25] Worried about Polish anti-Semitism in the province, Austrian Zionists insisted that the rebuilding of Galicia and Bukovina should be "an all Austrian matter, an imperial matter." After all, only if the central government rather than local authorities took charge would there be assurance that the rebuilding would be justly administered.[26]

In November 1916, when Austria and Germany announced the creation of the Kingdom of Poland, Austrian Jews worried about the impact on the Jews of local Polish control of an autonomous Galicia. They thus reiterated their commitment to maximum Austrian control of the province. The editor of Vienna's *Österreichische Wochenschrift*, Galician-born Josef Samuel Bloch, warmly greeted Polish freedom but at the same time expressed his hope that now that they were no longer oppressed by the Russians, the Poles would not oppress the Jews.[27] A pessimistic article in January 1917 expressed much anxiety about how the Poles would treat the minorities in Galicia—the Ruthenians and the Jews—whom they despised.[28] Alone among the Jews, Orthodox spokesmen expressed their support for the special status of Galicia and the extension of Galician self-administration, but they too assumed Galicia would remain an Austrian province.[29]

Zionists and Jewish nationalists especially expressed their anxieties about Galician autonomy. While wishing the Poles best wishes in their new (theoretical) state, the Zionist organization admitted in the press that it was "not joyful" about the new arrangements. It reminded its readers of the "unfriendly relations" between Poles and Jews, and it urged the Austrian authorities to protect all three national groups in Galicia—Poles, Ruthenians, and Jews.[30] Prague Zionists likewise saluted the Poles for realizing their dream of an independent Poland but reiterated their commitment to a unified Austrian state, which by definition did not put the interests of one nation over the interests of any other. Austrian control would serve as the best protection for all the nations in Galicia, including the Jews. The editors of *Selbstwehr* feared that greater autonomy for Galicia would prove very dangerous for the Jews (and Ruthenians), who would be delivered over to the Poles. Moreover, they understood that without Galician Jewry it would be harder for them to press for Jewish national rights in Austria.[31] The un-

certainty of politics in the province and their fear of a Polish administration persecuting the Jews without fear of intervention by the central government
prompted the Zionists to repeat their demand for the recognition of the Jews as
a nation and the establishment of a Jewish voting curia in Galicia.[32]

One of the most forceful spokesmen for Jewish national rights in an Austrian
Galicia was Max Rosenfeld, a member of the Socialist Zionist Poale Zion from
Galicia. In a series of books and pamphlets in 1917 and 1918, Rosenfeld reiterated
his opposition to extending autonomy in Galicia because he feared that the
Poles, who harbored the notion that they were a master-nation (*Herrennation* or
Herrenvolk), would oppress both the Ruthenians and the Jews. He utterly opposed "Polish imperialism," the desire to include in a new Polish state all the former territory of the Polish crown, since that would violate the national rights of
the nationalities residing there. The 1917 proposal to give Galicia a special status
in a Poland attached to Austria disturbed him, because the Poles refused to recognize any national rights for the Jews there. Thus he called for national autonomy
for all the nationalities in Galicia: Poles, Ruthenians, and Jews. Only if Poland accorded rights to its minorities would it avoid the fate of "the classical land of nationality conflict: Austria."[33]

Throughout 1916, 1917, and 1918, German-speaking Austrian Jews acted as if
the status quo would prevail, that is, as if Galicia would remain part of Austria.
Jews in Vienna, Bohemia, and Moravia mobilized their resources to help Galician
Jews restore their homes and livelihoods devastated by the war. The Bnai Brith,
for example, focused on helping the large numbers of children in Galicia who
had been orphaned by the war and considered opening new chapters in Galicia
to cultivate the Jewish masses there.[34] Similarly, the *Israelitische Allianz* spent
much money feeding and clothing the Jews who suffered in war-torn Galicia.[35]
Showing an unusual degree of unity, representatives of the Bnai Brith, the
Allianz, *Weibliche Fürsorge*, the Zionists, and the institutions created by refugee activist Anitta Müller joined forces in the Society to Save the Abandoned Jewish
Children of Galicia and Bukovina. It couched its appeals for money in patriotic
terms, arguing that helping orphans, whose fathers had died as heroes, would re-
dound to the glory of the fatherland.[36] Jews also lobbied to protect the rights of
Jews in Galicia and in the Austrian zone of occupation in Russian Poland, although on this issue Jewish liberals worked through the Central Committee for
the Protection of the Citizen Interests of the Jewish Population in the Northern
Theater of War,[37] and the Zionists lobbied on their own.[38]

Jews worried endlessly about anti-Semitic incidents in Galicia, especially about
unfair treatment of Jews by Polish officials. Censorship prevented them from complaining in the press before 1918, but they nevertheless recorded such incidents privately.[39] In March 1918, Benno Straucher, a Jewish nationalist who represented a
district in Bukovina, complained in parliament about the behavior of Galician
Poles who, angry that Austria had ceded some Polish territory to Ukraine in the
treaty of Brest-Litovsk, the recently signed peace treaty with Russia, had called for
the expulsion of the Jews from Galicia and had rioted against the Jews in several
places while the local authorities did nothing.[40] Jews became extremely alarmed
in April 1918 when a full-scale pogrom erupted in Cracow, during which some

Polish legionnaires and policemen joined the mob while most of the Polish police stood by. The army had to intervene to put down the rioting.[41] This alarm grew when similar pogroms occurred elsewhere in the province.[42] Although some Jews recognized that severe food shortages played a major role in causing the riots,[43] most blamed Polish anti-Semitism. Only the Orthodox press did not attack the Poles for their behavior, presumably because the Orthodox traditionally supported Polish interests in Galicia (and in Poland generally) to receive Polish support on issues of concern to the Orthodox community.[44]

Whatever the cause of the riots, Jews worried that disintegrating Austrian control of Galicia would lead to widespread attacks on the Jews. In 1917 and 1918, Jews wanted to keep Galicia Austrian to protect their fellow Jews from physical harm.[45] They thus opposed the desire of Polish nationalists to separate the province from Austria.[46] At the same time, Galician Zionists realistically began to think about working with Zionists in Poland itself.[47]

Attempts at Unity

The issue of Galicia, or rather the need to defend the rights of Jews there, served as a catalyst for several attempts to unify all Austrian Jews into one umbrella organization. During the last three years of the war, Jewish liberals, the Orthodox, and the Zionists all tried to create Austria-wide organizations to represent Jewish interests. All these attempts failed, largely because Jews with different ideological agendas found it impossible to agree on program or organizational structure. Morover, each group wanted to dominate the proposed umbrella organization, and the others refused to succumb. Nevertheless, the repeated attempts to create an Austria-wide Jewish organization reflected the profound commitment of Austria's Jews to the continuity of multinational Austria.

As early as the end of 1914, the president of the Jewish community of Vienna, Alfred Stern, had urged the creation of a unified organization of Austrian Jews to combat the anti-Semitism that he feared would rage when the war ended.[48] After the liberation of Galicia such calls became more frequent. In the summer of 1915 one writer in the *Österreichische Wochenschrift* suggested that Jews create an organization to represent all of Austrian Jewry, both to help the Jews of Galicia and Bukovina and to counter the anti-Jewish animosity that existed despite Jewish loyalty and heroism.[49] At the same time, a member of the Austrian Israelite Union called for a unified organization of all Jewish communities in Austria. Drawing on the greater sense of Jewish unity generated by the war, such an organization would not only help Galician or other Jews in need, but "extended over the entire Reich, it should serve as the glue for a strong, enduring union" of Jewish communities and Jews.[50] Later that year, Rabbi Gedalje Schmelkes of Przemysl, Galicia, a refugee in Vienna, also called for an Austria-wide Jewish organization to represent Jewish interests and help the suffering Jews of Galicia.[51] Throughout 1916 and 1917, many spokesmen called for Austrian Jewish unity, registering their dismay that a unified organization had not yet taken shape. Most insisted that Austrian Jews needed unity to ensure their legal position in an increasingly hostile atmosphere.[52]

Prewar attempts to create a federation of Jewish communities had foundered, largely because traditionalist religious leaders in Galicia had refused to join with liberal communal leaders in "western" Austria (that is, Vienna, Bohemia, and Moravia) out of fear the latter might try to dictate religious affairs. During the war, however, many Jewish liberals hoped that Galician rabbis would now be willing to work with them. The very presence of those rabbis and other Galician Jewish leaders in Vienna as refugees, combined with the acute problems faced by Galician Jewry, encouraged Jewish communal leaders in western Austria to think that their quest for Jewish unity could now succeed. In July of 1916, the Jewish community of Vienna took the lead and gained preliminary governmental approval to create a unified organization of all Austrian Jewry. The Vienna IKG called for a federation of all *Israelitische Kultusgemeinden* at the provincial and countrywide levels. Such a federation would be governed by a board consisting of IKG representatives and rabbis from Austria's largest Jewish communities.[53] While many supporters of the proposals had criticisms of specific issues, like the number of representatives from Galicia or Bohemia,[54] they nevertheless emphasized that such a federation would give Jews a more forceful voice with which to lobby on behalf of Jewish rights.

The Jewish liberals who sought Jewish unity in 1916 tried to reassure the Galician Orthodox that they had nothing to fear from the new proposal, since the federation would not interfere in the internal affairs of any community.[55] Yet fears that Galician Jews would themselves want to dictate religious policy in more-liberal Jewish communities in the west motivated Prague's Jewish notables to object to Vienna's proposal. This opposition, like their attitudes to the Galician Jewish refugees in their midst, reflected the fact that Jews in Bohemia harbored far more negative feelings about Galician Jews than did Viennese Jews. One Prague IKG board member even observed that the differences between western Austrian and Galician Jewish communities were so great that they "could never be bridged." Prague's IKG suggested instead that the Jews of western Austria form a federation. Vienna, however, remained utterly committed to the unity of all Austrian Jews, a commitment that Prague leaders assumed derived from the fact that war conditions effectively silenced the Galicians anyway. Vienna managed to obtain Prague's approval for the plan.[56]

It nevertheless proved impossible to form a federation of Jewish communities, although the proposal did not founder simply because of Galician Jewish intransigence. True, many Galician Jewish leaders did in fact object to the proposal because they feared that Jewish liberals from western Austria would impose their will on them. Yet others were willing to go along if Galician Jewry had more representatives.[57] The proposal foundered because of the same political uncertainties that led Vienna to suggest it in the first place. The joint German-Austrian announcement of the Kingdom of Poland and the "special status" of Galicia in November 1916 made many Galician Jewish leaders feel the need to proceed cautiously about joining an Austrian federation. Galician rabbis who were refugees in Vienna thought that in the new political situation they should just create a federation of Galician Jewish communities, which could, presumably, keep its options open.[58] Many Jews in western Austria thought as well that now it would be best to create a federation without the troublesome Galicians.[59] Mostly, the idea foundered because the exigencies of wartime made it impossible for the Jews of Galicia to focus on organizational matters when it took all their energy just to carry on.

The reopening of parliament in May 1917 and the potential that it created for a political transformation of Austria made Jews renew their call for an Austria-wide Jewish organization, which they hoped would represent Jewish interests in the public debate about constitutional change.[60] Such calls reflected Jewish fears about the impact of heightened anti-Semitism on their status, a fear that made them far more willing than ever before to step into the political arena as Jews. These calls also reflected a greater sense among Jewish liberals that the Jews formed a special group in Austria whose political interests had to be taken into account. After all, as one spokesmen noted in the *Österreichische Wochenschrift*, how could the government even consider changing the constitution without the participation of representatives of the Jews, a population one-and-a-half million strong.[61]

Zionists and Jewish nationalists pursued the goal of Austrian Jewish unity most aggressively. In the first place, Zionists from all over Austria coordinated their efforts more successfully during the war,[62] in large part because so many Galician and Bukovinian Zionists spent the war years as refugees in Vienna. More important, Zionists hoped to use a pan-Austrian Jewish organization as the vehicle through which they could assert their leadership of Jewry, a role they had long sought.[63] At regular intervals in 1915 and 1916, Zionist or Jewish nationalist spokesmen issued calls for a pan-Austrian Jewish organization to represent Jewish interests.[64] Jewish nationalist spokesman Hermann Kadisch, for example, wrote a series of articles in the Prague Zionist paper *Selbstwehr* urging Jews to prepare for a new Austrian constitution by creating an all-Austria organization to work for Jewish ethnic interests and Jewish national autonomy to ensure the national, religious, and social equality of the Jews in Austria, especially those in Galicia.[65] At first, Zionist and Jewish nationalist proposals for Austrian Jewish unity remained vague about the structure of such an organization. The Austrian Zionist leadership in Vienna even initially supported the proposal of Vienna's Jewish community for a federation of Jewish communities, arguing that any organization was better than none.[66] Some Prague Zionists, however, opposed Vienna's plan for a federation of IKGs because they feared it would be undemocratic, run by the same old men who ran communal affairs, and would not sufficiently take into account the needs of the Orthodox or the Zionists.[67] By the fall of 1916, Austrian Zionist leaders rejected a federation of Jewish communities, since it left no room for their goal of securing Jewish national rights.[68]

In late 1916, Prague Zionists proposed a different kind of organization to unite Jews: a democratically elected Jewish congress, modeled on the American Jewish congress movement. A congress, they reasoned, would be stronger than a federation of IKGs and therefore much better equipped to fight anti-Semitism and work for Jewish rights in Austria.[69] Undoubtedly they also assumed that the Zionists would control a democratically elected organization. In 1917, *Selbstwehr* invited prominent Zionists and anti-Zionists from all over Austria to debate the virtues of a Jewish congress in its pages. Zionists grew very enthusiastic about a congress.[70] For example, Benno Straucher, the Zionist parliamentary deputy from Czernowitz, Bukovina, argued that a Jewish congress would unite all Austrian Jews, speak authoritatively in their name, and work for the equality of the Jews as one of the nations of Austria with full national cultural autonomy.[71] Non-Zionists, including Robert von Fuchs of the Prague IKG, Alfred Stern and Rudolf Schwarz-Hiller of Vienna, and Theodor Sonnenschein of Troppau, Silesia, opposed the congress, presumbably because they feared Zionist domination and opposed Zionist goals, but officially because they worried that a congress would be an unwieldy instrument through which to protect Jewish rights. They preferred either a federation of Jewish communities or small committees of prominent individuals—traditional Jewish *shtadlanim*—to fight threats to Jewish rights.[72]

While this debate raged in the pages of *Selbstwehr*, the Austrian Zionist establishment in Vienna ignored it, issuing instead vague calls for a unified organization of all Austrian Jews to fight anti-Semitism and demand Jewish national rights in a politically transformed Austria.[73] The reopening of parliament in May 1917, and the opportunities it provided both for anti-Semitic agitation and the realization of national self-determination, made these Zionist leaders long for Jewish unity. Yet they opposed a Jewish congress unless they could guarantee in advance that it would demand Jewish national autonomy in Austria. Despite their advocacy of democracy in Jewish affairs, they nevertheless wanted to control the congress.

In 1917–1918, Arthur Hantke, of the World Zionist Executive in Berlin, and the deputy he sent to Vienna, Prague Zionist Sigmund Katznelson, worked assiduously to convince Austrian Zionist leaders—essentially those from Vienna, Galicia, and Bukovina—to create an Austrian Jewish congress. The Austrian Zionist leaders resented the Prague Zionists for proposing the congress without even consulting them, and Hantke had to mollify them and insist that they not punish the Prague circle.[74] It was not just territoriality, however, that made the Zionist establishment oppose the congress. Both Robert Stricker and Rudolf Taussig, the two most important Viennese Zionists, opposed a congress because they feared that a democratically elected congress would not support their program of Jewish national rights. Although most Austrian Zionists supported a congress, Stricker and Taussig opposed it because they did not want to demonstrate to the world that the Zionists in fact formed a minority among Austrian Jews.[75]

At a July 15, 1917 meeting, Zionists from all over Austria debated the issue of the congress. Adolf Stand, a parliamentary deputy from Galicia, passionately insisted that a congress would help Zionists build bridges to other groups, allow Jews to make claims at the postwar peace conference, contribute to the rebuilding of Jewish life in Galicia and Bukovina, and represent Jewish interests in the public discussion about Austrian constitutional change. As expected, Viennese Zionist leader Robert Stricker opposed the congress, largely because Austrian Jews did not all support the recognition of Jews as a nation. Eschewing the idea of working with Jews with different ideologies, he called instead for a congress of Jewish nationalists, one that would support his own nationalist agenda. More optimistic than Stricker, Max Brod, the writer and literary critic from Prague who would play a leading role in Jewish nationalist affairs after the war, felt that a democratically elected Jewish congress would possess a Jewish national orientation. Austrian Zionists compromised. They decided to support a congress but did not use the strong nationalist rhetoric that Stricker advocated. Instead, they declared that a democratic Austrian Jewish congress would work for the recognition of the Jewish people (*Volk*) and the protection of their rights in a reorganized Austria. It would also strive to improve Jewish life in war-ravaged areas and fight anti-Semitism.[76]

By August, Prague Zionists feared that Stricker had undermined this compromise. He packed the preliminary conference committee with his people and used more strident rhetoric—calling for the recognition of the Jews as a nation—in his propaganda on behalf of a congress. Such rhetoric, they feared, would only make non-Zionists, the majority of Jews in western Austria (Bohemia, Moravia, and Vienna) refuse to participate in a congress, which they would correctly regard as a tool of the Zionist organization. Prague Zionists preferred to tread softly, to convene a democratic organization that could in fact speak in the name of all Jews and then be used to spread the Zionist message.[77] The Zionist Executive in Berlin agreed. Hantke wrote to Stricker and Taussig in September to convince them to follow the model set by the American Jewish congress movement, which put its Zionist agenda on the back burner to forge a united Jewish organization.[78]

Stricker continued to oppose the congress and to resent the interference of Prague Zionists in what he considered his turf,[79] preferring instead to call a congress of Jewish nationalists that could articulate forcefully the Jewish nationalist position.[80] Katznelson worried about Stricker. He reminded Hantke in November that he did not think that it was realistic to expect that the Jews of Austria, especially the Jews of Bohemia, would support the recognition of the Jews as a nation. Given the controversial nature of Jewish nationalism, it made sense not to include nationalist demands, even in the Bohemian Zionist platform, much less in a call for an Austria-wide Jewish congress. He feared that any efforts on behalf of a congress would founder on Stricker's intransigence on this issue.[81] Surely Katznelson was aware that non-Zionists who supported the congress, like the leaders of the Austrian Israelite Union, would refuse to participate if Stricker got his way and restricted the congress to Jewish nationalists.[82] Katznelson worked hard in Vienna to generate support for the congress, but he continued to find it very difficult to work with Stricker, who, he assumed, was working behind his back to undermine the more broadly based congress that he and the WZO preferred.[83] When he returned to Prague in May 1918, Katznelson felt depressed, not only about the future of the congress, but about Austrian Zionism in general with Stricker as its leader.[84]

Zionists were no more successful than Jewish communal leaders in creating a unified Jewish organization to represent the Jews. No Austrian Jewish congress ever came into existence. Personality clashes and ideological divisions between different groups of Zionists and Jewish nationalists, not to mention between

Zionists and non-Zionists, made the creation of a democratic mass organization impossible, especially during the war. The failure of the congress movement, however, was not caused by a lack of commitment to a unified Austrian Jewry within a unified, multinational Austria. Even when most Jews realistically realized that Galicia would probably not remain part of the Monarchy, they continued to hope that the rest of Austrian Jewry and Austria itself would remain united. The issue was really one of control: which ideological trend would represent a united Austrian Jewry. Each group made its own bid for such control, and the others refused to follow.

In 1918, the orthodox also made an attempt to create an Austria-wide Jewish organization to represent their interests in the political arena. Fearful that the Zionists were gaining ground in their bid to represent Austrian Jewry, orthodox spokesmen laid their own claim to leadership.[85] At a preliminary conference in February, in which orthodox Jewish representatives from Bohemia, Moravia, Galicia, and Vienna participated, orthodox spokesmen made it clear that they felt it was their responsibility to unite all Jews to serve the interest of "unfalsified Judaism" and to make sure that the needs of observant Jews were secured in public life.[86] This conference ostensibly sought to organize orthodox Jews only in western Austria, presumably because by February many Jews realized that Galicia might not form part of Austria. Nevertheless, several Galician rabbis participated in the conference, along with representatives of the Galician branch of the orthodox Agudas Yisroel, probably because most Jews in Austria still naturally included Galicia in their plans for all Austria. Orthodox leaders met several times during the spring of 1918, but they too proved incapable of uniting Austrian Jewry.

Depite their inability to unite, throughout 1917 and 1918, Austrian Jews acted as if they still belonged together. Prague Jewish leaders often turned for advice and assistance to the Vienna IKG or Vienna-based organizations like the Austrian Israelite Union.[87] In April 1918, in a conscious gesture of commitment to Austrian Jewish unity, the Prague IKG sent a representative to work with Austria's orthodox Jews.[88] Other Jewish communities turned to Vienna for help against anti-Semitism.[89] Zionists in Bohemia, Moravia, and Vienna, including Galician and Bukovinian Zionists living as refugees in Vienna, also worked together, even though they mistrusted each other and held different ideological views. They wrote for each others' newspapers and reported on each others' activities. True, on occasion, Galician Zionists thought it might be politically wise to build bridges to Poland and Polish Zionists,[90] but they mostly worked side by side with their Austrian colleagues. Motivated by the desire to strengthen their position in the discussion of Austrian political reform, the Austrian Zionist establishment tried in April 1918 to convert the Galician Zionist party from an autonomous body into a part of a truly all-Austrian Zionist organization. They understood that the presence in Vienna of Galician Zionist leaders facilitated this effort.[91] Moreover, as late as October 1918, Zionists planned an all-Austria conference.[92] Jewish youth felt the need to unite on an Austria-wide basis as well. On May 18–20, 1918, 2000 young Jews from all over Austria held a youth congress in Vienna, dedicated to uniting eastern and western Jews on the basis of cultural Zionism.[93]

Rising anti-Semitism in the spring and summer of 1918 again impelled Jews to call for unity to deal with the threat more effectively.[94] The German People's Congress, held in Vienna on June 16, 1918, especially angered Jews and galvanized them into action. At the congress, Austrian Germans had declared themselves the "foundation pillars" of the Monarchy, which they vowed themselves to save, and had used the opportunity to vilify the Jews and call for violence against them.[95] In response, Jews became more vocal in their condemnation of anti-Semitism and more willing to fight it than ever before. As one spokesman in the *Österreichische Wochenschrift* put it: "We Jews of Austria-Hungary . . . are not defenseless Russian ghetto-Jews, who allow themselves to be plundered or slaughtered." Having fought at the front and suffered as refugees, he warned, Austrian Jews were ready to face down those who threatened pogroms.[96]

At the end of July, the Jewish community of Vienna mobilized all the Jewish communities of Austria to protest anti-Semitism. Alfred Stern, the octogenarian president of Vienna's Jewish community, gave an impassioned speech condemning the anti-Semitic frenzy and serving notice that Jews had reached the absolute limits of their patience in the face of such attacks. Stern called on the Jews to assemble to organize self-defense against anti-Semitism, justifying such action in terms of the terrible losses the Jews had suffered in the war. The Jewish community of Vienna issued a resolution on July 26 in the name of all Austrian Jews, reiterating Jewish loyalty to Austria, expressing dissatisfaction with official tolerance for anti-Semitic agitation, and asserting that anti-Semitism posed a grave danger to the state. While the IKG had never taken a public political position before, it now used very strong language to pledge the Jews "to organize for the protection of their own existence and for defense against the danger that threatens them."[97]

Although most Jewish communities in Austria supported this resolution, the Prague IKG refused to support it because it feared that its strong language would antagonize the government.[98] Prague's unwillingness to follow Vienna's lead in the summer of 1918 did not derive from opposition to an all-Austria effort or from the desire for Czech Jewish independence from Vienna but rather from ordinary disagreement with the new aggressive posture pursued by Vienna's Jews. Similarly, work on a union of Bohemian Jewish communities in early 1918 did not prefigure any independent posture of Bohemian Jewry but simply represented preliminary steps for a future all-Austria union.[99] Even if Austrian Jewry could not overcome its traditional differences to unite, it remained committed to Austrian continuity.

On Behalf of Austrian Continuity

However unsuccessful, attempts at Austrian Jewish unity and anxiety about the future of Galicia reflected the profound attachment of Austrian Jews to the continuity of supranational Austria. Austrian Jews from all regions and of all ideological inclinations remained committed to the Austrian *Gesamtstaat* throughout the last years of the war. Endless statements of loyalty to Austria in the German-language Jewish press did not result from a cynical strategy to impress the authorities by repeating official government propaganda. Instead, they reflected a real hope that multinational Austria would continue, thus providing the Jews with protection from anti-Semitism in society at large and within the national camps. Moreover, Jews sought Austrian continuity because the multinational state provided Jews with much freedom to develop their Jewish identities—traditional, modern, Jewish national, secular, socialist, assimilated—however they pleased. For the Zionists and Jewish nationalists in particular, only the multinational Austrian *Gesamtstaat* allowed them to claim that the Jews were a nation deserving autonomy. Surely, in any real nation-state, Jews would have a much more difficult time demanding the national rights Zionists sought.

Jewish insistence on Austrian continuity reflected considerable nervousness about Austria's future. In a letter to the new Minister President von Körber at the end of 1916, the Austrian Israelite Union mentioned the "deep social cleavages" that existed in Austria and hoped that "our old Austria" had the energy to overcome them.[100] At the beginning of 1917, the editors of the *Österreichische Wochenschrift* expressed their confidence that the Central Powers would surely win the war after their recent successes against the Russians in Galicia and especially against Romania. At the same time, the uncertain status of Galicia and the growing threat of anti-Semitism made them worry about Austria itself.[101] Orthodox Jews appeared more optimistic, but they too fretted over the impact of plans for transforming Austria. They urged the Jews, "the state-upholding element par excellence," to work with moderate, loyal elements to renew and consolidate the Monarchy.[102]

The reopening of parliament in May 1917 compounded Jewish nervousness. The editors of the *Österreichische Wochenschrift* feared that nationalist politicians did not possess a fundamental commitment to the "concept of Austria" and would undermine it. Indeed, they worried that the Jews might be the only group still committed to Austrian continuity. They observed that "in fact, the Jews are not only the most loyal supporters of the Monarchy; they are the only unconditional Austrians in this state (*Staatsverband*)."[103] Angry that anti-Semites had gone on the offensive despite Jewish sacrifices in the war, Heinrich Schreiber insisted in June 1917 that "we [Jews] stand by this state," which had an obligation to treat Jews as the brave and worthy citizens which they had proven themselves to be.[104] Schreiber's concern for Austrian continuity did not preclude fundamental changes in Austria's constitution. Indeed, he welcomed the chance to reform Austria and give its peoples greater freedom.[105] Jewish spokesmen supported calls for democratization, even though democracy might give anti-Semites greater voice.[106] At the same time, they declared that Jews possessed an "inviolable state loyalty" that made them a "state-upholding element of proven trustworthiness."[107]

Jewish nervousness mounted in 1918, impelling many liberal Jewish spokesmen to reiterate both Jewish loyalty to Austria and their desire for Austrian continuity. In May 1918, one writer in the *Österreichische Wochenschrift* expressed his hope that the longed-for peace would find Austria united and not hounded to death by inner conflict. He yearned to see the nationality conflict resolved by compromise so that all the inhabitants of the state could enjoy cultural and eco-

nomic progress.[108] By the summer, Jews worried about the disastrous consequences of anti-Semitism. Shocked at the viciousness of the German nationalist
congress in June, the paper once again insisted that the Jews were "the only Austrians loyal to the state left in the Monarchy."[109] Later that summer, the newspaper worried that anti-Semitic agitation would lead to generalized national strife
that the government would prove unable to contain.[110]

Jewish communal leaders also agonized about the impact of anti-Semitism
and responded by insisting on the profound loyalty of the Jews to Austria. In its
August 1918 resolution against anti-Semitism, the Jewish community of Vienna
declared that "the Jews were and are a state-upholding element of unconditional
loyalty, and have the right to demand to be treated as such."[111] Ever optimistic,
Orthodox Jewish spokesmen also insisted on their everlasting loyalty to the emperor and the Monarchy.[112] One vigorous statement of Jewish support for
multinational Austria came from the pen of Nathan Birnbaum, who had created
the first Jewish nationalist organization in Vienna in 1882, but who had later rejected Zionism in favor of Yiddishism and religious orthodoxy. In a 1915 pamphlet, Birnbaum argued that the Jews of Galicia and Bukovina were "practically
predestined to affirm and love Austria. In fact Austrian (Galician-Bukovinian)
Ostjuden display a thoroughly positive, unshakable, and passionate devotion to
Austria."[113] It was a devotion they shared with German-speaking Jews in Bohemia, Moravia, and Vienna.

Zionists and Jewish nationalists insisted even more forcefully on the need for
Austrian continuity and on undying Jewish loyalty to the multinational state. Pleas
for the "inviolability of the whole Monarchy," coupled with affirmations of undying Jewish attachments to it, became a litany in the Zionist press.[114] Zionist parliamentary deputy from Bukovina Benno Straucher asserted in mid-1917 that the
Jews were "a state-upholding element . . . whose patriotism is not broken by
any provincialism . . . We Austrian Jews declare ourselves unconditionally and
without any reservations for Austria."[115] Viennese Zionist Robert Stricker argued,
with some hyperbole, in a speech in Prague in November 1917 that "We nation-
ally-conscious Jews want a strong Austria. Only it can provide a home to its nations. We believe that an Austria must exist. If there were no Austria, it would be a
misfortune for the entire world."[116] Throughout 1918, Austrian Zionists insisted
that a multinational Austria must exist because only it could provide "a peaceful
union of nations, a prototype, so to speak, of a future world federation." After all,
"the idea of the Austrian state is an indubitable necessity."[117]

For the Zionists, Austrian continuity provided the necessary precondition for
the fulfillment of their political agenda. Zionists wanted the state to recognize
the Jews as one of the nations of an Austria transformed into a federation of autonomous nationalities. Zionists and Jewish nationalists had agreed on this goal in
their Cracow program of 1906. Like the Social Democrats, who also sought to
transform Austria into a federation of nationalities, Zionists wanted membership
in any nationality, including the Jewish one, to be based on personal choice, not
on territory.[118] The political developments of the last two years of the war encouraged the Zionists to press ever harder for their goals. Not only had Kaiser
Karl invited proposals for constitutional change, but the nationalities had begun

to work for "national self-determination." Given Jewish geographic and cultural dispersion, Jews could only hope for such national self-determination in a multi-national federation. Although many Zionists thought that concern for national autonomy in the diaspora deflected energy from the ultimate goal of creating a Jewish state in Palestine,[119] Austrian Zionists relentlessly lobbied for Jewish national rights in Austria.

The man who most vigorously campaigned for Jewish autonomy in an Austrian federation of autonomous nationalities was the Jewish nationalist publicist Hermann Kadisch. In scores of articles in all the Zionist newspapers, and in many pamphlets, Kadisch articulated his program for Jewish national rights in a transformed but unified Austria. Kadisch rejected the notion that nationalist aspirations could only be satisfied by the creation of independent nation-states. Indeed, he felt that the war had proven that Austrians of different nationalities could work together for a common goal. What they did deserve, however, was national autonomy and national equality, which would create a strong, unified, harmonious Austria in which no nation exercised hegemony over the others, but in which a strong central government continued to function.[120] In this new Austria, in which nationality would be determined on a personal, not a territorial basis, Jews would be recognized as one of the autonomous nationalities.[121] Such demands, he repeatedly averred, were based on unconditional loyalty to Austria. Indeed, he believed that Jewish nationalism would strengthen the Austrian state.[122] Kadisch recognized that the Jews, scattered as they were in several crownlands, had a vested interest in Austrian unity. He utterly opposed any attempts at destroying that unity or in expanding provincial autonomy unless minority groups like the Jews could be guaranteed proportional representation in all official bodies.[123]

Kadisch responded to the reopening of parliament in 1917 with a renewal of his call for the transformation of Austria into a democratic state with a strong central government and autonomy for all the nationalities, including the Jews.[124] In an important pamphlet, *Jews and Austrian Constitutional Reform*, Kadisch decried national chauvinists who sought to create nation-states at the expense of the national minorities in their midst, and called for constitutional reform that would guarantee Austrian unity while allowing the free national cultural development of all peoples. In short, he proposed what he had long sought: the reorganization of Austria as a federation of equal, autonomous nationalities, organized by personal preference, not territory. He criticized Jews who joined "foreign nationalities" and called for the recognition of the Jews as a nation. While he noted the practical value of German as the language of communication between all peoples of the Monarchy and understood that Jews valued German culture, he insisted that Jews not engage in German politics but instead to work to reduce intergroup tensions. He remained confident that Jewish nationalism would serve as "a strong bulwark of the idea of the Austrian state."[125]

In 1918, Kadisch continued to make the same demands. In April, he argued that Austria needed to replace dualism with "a great-Austrian federal state of independent peoples" who would eschew national chauvinism. In particular, he warned the Czechs not to oppress the Germans in Bohemia.[126] In September

1918, he still optimistically assumed that transforming Austria into a federation of equal nationalities with a strong central government would preserve Austrian unity and contribute to social, economic, and cultural progress. He opposed Austro-German inclinations to hand over Galicia to Poland, and he rejected territorial autonomy.[127]

Kadisch was not alone in his demands. The Jewish National Association, to which he belonged, advocated reorganizing Austria as a federation of autonomous nationalities and recognizing the Jews as one of those nationalities.[128] This association, organized in the late nineteenth century, united Zionists and diaspora Jewish nationalists from Vienna, Galicia, and Bukovina. During the war, Viennese Zionist Robert Stricker served as chair. The presence of Galician and Bukovinian board members in Vienna as refugees during the war surely facilitated its political activity.[129] After the Austrian parliament reopened in 1917, Salomon Kassner, the Bukovinian cochair of the association, insisted that Austria must allow Jews national self-determination. Opposed to including the Jews in either the German or Polish nation within Austria, he demanded that Jewish national rights apply not only in the east, in Galicia and Bukovina, but in western Austria as well.[130] Jewish nationalists worried that those planning constitutional changes would ignore their concerns, and they urged the government to include Jewish nationalists on all relevant committees.[131]

Zionists not associated with Stricker's Jewish National Association also took up the call for Jewish national autonomy in a reorganized Austria. Benno Straucher, a member of parliament from Bukovina, regularly demanded Jewish national rights. In a speech in parliament on June 16, 1917, Straucher called for national cultural autonomy and proportional representation for the Jews along with their absolute equality as citizens in a new, democratic state.[132] Similarly, Max Rosenfeld, a socialist Poale Zionist from Galicia, lobbied for Jewish national autonomy in an Austrian federation of nationalities. Fearful of the impact on Jews if Austria were to dissolve into nation-states, Rosenfeld wanted a strong Austrian state to continue to stand above the various national camps and handle issues of common concern. He called on local Jewish religious communities to transform themselves into Jewish national communities and to serve as the first level of Jewish national self-government, handling cultural, educational, economic, and political affairs on a democratic basis. Since Rosenfeld believed that Judaism had preserved Jewish nationalism for millenia, he argued that all Jews who had not converted to Christianity should constitute the Jewish nation.[133]

Other Zionist spokesmen also regularly called for national autonomy.[134] In early 1918, a delegation of Jewish nationalists and Zionists presented the government with a set of demands, chief among them that the Jews be recognized as a nation with the right to proportional representation in all elected bodies based on the creation of Jewish voting curias. In such a system the Jews (along with the other nations) would have a predetermined number of parliamentary representatives based on their proportion in the population and for whom only the Jews could vote. Thus Jews (and other nations) could elect delegates to represent their national interests in parliament. The delegation also demanded Jewish schools supported by public funds, special government offices to deal with Jewish matters, and the establishment of an all-Austria, democratically elected, representative body to run Jewish national affairs.[135] By April, Zionists in western Austria (Bohemia, Moravia, and Vienna) had tempered their demands, presumably in deference to the opposition of the more realistic Bohemian Zionists. At that point, they called for the right of Austrian Jews to affirm their membership in the Jewish nation and for the protection of national minority rights in areas of mass Jewish settlement, that is, in Galicia and Bukovina.[136] In August, Galician Zionists insisted that national autonomy was "the only way out of the chaos of the endless nationality conflict and the ever more critical political crisis" and called for the self-determination of the Jewish nation in Austria.[137] Zionists and Jewish nationalists in Bukovina also sought national autonomy for the Jews in a unified Austria in which Bukovina formed a part. Insisting that Bukovinian Jews were the "preeminent bearers of the Austrian state-idea,"[138] they demanded the recognition of the Jewish nation.[139] Although socialist Zionists worried that those who called for Jewish national autonomy were not sufficiently committed to full democracy or the Yiddish language, they too demanded Jewish national autonomy in a new Austrian nationalities-state.[140]

Bohemian and Moravian Zionists faced a more complex situation. Effusive pro-Austrian rhetoric could prove problematic in a region where Czech nationalist politicians increasingly sought far more than national or provincial autonomy. Czech leaders who had fled abroad, like Thomas Masaryk, worked for complete Czech independence, supported by the Entente Powers. Czech politicians at home had to proceed more cautiously, but they too wanted more than the Austrian authorities were willing to offer. After the reopening of parliament in mid-1917 and Kaiser Karl's amnesty of Czech political prisoners, support for Czech (or Czechoslovak) sovereignty grew.[141] In this atmosphere, it behooved Jews not to speak too loudly about how much they supported the Austrian *Gesamtstaat*. Indeed, many of the affirmations of Jewish loyalty to Austria found in the pages of the Zionist press in Bohemia and Moravia in 1917 and 1918 were articles written by Hermann Kadisch, who was from Vienna, or reprinted speeches of Straucher from Bukovina or Stricker from Vienna. Zionists in Bohemia and Moravia publicly supported Austria, but they displayed political sagacity and restraint by not expressing that support too boldly.[142]

If a Czech state was indeed to be created, it behooved the Jews not to appear to oppose it. Yet there are no hints in the Zionist press of Prague or Brünn of support for Czech independence. Indeed, the opposite is the case; the German-speaking Zionist establishment in these provinces regularly criticized the "Czech Jews," those who supported Jewish affiliation with the Czech nationalist cause, arguing that it was false nationalism to work for the destructive tendencies of a nation to which one did not belong.[143] Moreover, Prague Zionists felt no sympathy for the Czech Jews when they suffered from Czech nationalist anti-Semitism.[144]

Bohemian and Moravian Zionists certainly shared the Zionist commitment to the recognition of the Jews as a nation. Jewish national identity solved the problem the Jews faced. By belonging to the Jewish nation, Jews could remain neutral in the Czech-German conflict.[145] If they were Jews, Czechs would not hate them as Germans and Germans would not resent them for changing sides and joining the Czechs. In the context of Austrian politics in 1918, however, maintaining such neutrality proved complicated. Proposals and counterproposals to create separate Czech and German crownlands in Bohemia and Moravia confused the situation. In February 1918, Prague Zionists warned Jews "not to allow themselves to be misused for the goals and ambitions of other nationalities" but to work instead for national conciliation and justice. Jews, of course, could not throw off their German culture and become Czechs but should act as "a part of the newly-arising Jewish people."[146] Anti-Semitic agitation by German and Czech nationalists[147] only deepened Zionist commitment to the neutrality offered by a Jewish national posture. Prague Zionists condemned the anti-Semitism in both camps but took special care not to offend the Czechs.[148]

Zionists in the Czech lands joined their colleagues elsewhere in calling for national rights and Jewish autonomy.[149] These calls assumed the continuity of multinational Austria, even as they reflected worry about its future. Like other Zionists, they wanted to reorganize Austria to accord the peoples national self-determination and equality.[150] In their calls for Jewish national rights, however, Bohemian and Moravian Zionists proved more moderate than their colleagues in Galicia, Bukovina, or Vienna. The editors of the Brünn-based socialist Zionist *Jüdische Volksstimme*, for example, only sought official recognition of the Yiddish language and the establishment of Yiddish-language schools, presumably in Galicia.[151] At a meeting in November 1917, Prague Zionist Ludwig Singer called for cultural autonomy for Jews, but this cultural autonomy included only the reconstitution of the Jewish religious community as a *Volk*-community and concern for Jewish education.[152] In August 1918, the editors of *Selbstwehr* called for Jewish national autonomy, especially in Galicia and Bukovina, but only to control schools and other cultural institutions. They pointedly did not demand the proportional representation, voting curias, and official Jewish delegates on governmental bodies that Stricker, Straucher, and Rosenfeld advocated.[153] Their greater moderation surely reflected that Bohemian and Moravian Zionists were far more realistic than their colleagues elsewhere. They undoubtedly realized that neither the Austrian government nor the government of a potential Czechoslovak state would accede to demands for full-fledged Jewish autonomy. It would therefore be a waste of Zionist energy to fight too vigorously for Jewish national rights, especially since the majority of Jews in Bohemia and Moravia—indeed the majority of all German-speaking Jews—opposed national autonomy for the Jews.

Throughout 1918, Prague Zionists felt increasingly frustrated with the Vienna Zionist establishment, especially with Robert Stricker's insistence on full national autonomy. To some extent, Prague Zionists simply resented that Stricker and his cronies in Vienna made representations to the government without consulting them.[154] But Prague Zionists also disagreed with Stricker's agenda. Robert Weltsch, in Vienna that year, complained bitterly to his friend Leo Herrmann about how hard it was to try to get Stricker to work on "real Zionism" instead of the goals of the Jewish National Association.[155] This animosity would build in October 1918 as the Monarchy disintegrated.

Although the Zionist establishment in Vienna, Galicia, and Bukovina remained wedded to the concept of Jewish national autonomy, it is hard to gauge the popularity of Jewish autonomy among Austrian Jews at large. Liberal Jews were certainly hostile to the idea. At a speech at Bnai Brith's May 1918 convention, president S. Ehrmann categorically rejected the idea that Jews should constitute a nation with their own voting cadastre. Jewish autonomy, he asserted, would mean "the annihilation of Judaism in western Austria." Although national rights might be necessary in the east, he conceded, they must not be extended to Jews in the west.[156] In the ensuing discussion, a Bnai Brith member from Moravia agreed with Ehrmann that national rights would prove dangerous to the Jews.[157] Orthodox Jews as well, despite loyalty to traditional views of Jewish peoplehood that combined ethnicity and religion, also rejected the Zionist demand for Jewish national rights in Austria. They resented the Zionists, who did not view religion as central to Jewish nationhood, for claiming to speak in the name of all Jews. Moreover, they felt that the uncertainty about Galicia, where autonomy might be viable, meant that it was premature to talk about Jewish national rights.[158] Recognizing the danger to the Jews of siding with either side in any of the national conflicts, especially the one between Poles and Ruthenians in Galicia, the orthodox hoped that Jews could simply be loyal to the state in which they lived.[159]

The ideology crafted by Austrian Jews in August 1914 remained intact throughout the war. The events of 1916–1918 vindicated their faith in their own ideology. Having gone to war to defeat the Russians, the enemy of Austria and the Jewish people, they naturally delighted in Russian defeat. They greeted the Russian Revolutions, which ended czarism and emancipated the Jews, with great joy, hailing the liberation of their Russian brethren from czarist oppression.[160] They were equally delighted with the defeat of Romania and the liberation of Romanian Jewry.[161] After the Bolshevik government of Russia requested peace talks, Austrian Jews had a sense that the war was virtually over and peace was imminent.[162] They applauded the March 1918 peace treaty of Brest-Litovsk as a sign that God had punished Russia for persecuting the Jews.[163] The *Jüdische Korrespondenz* announced that the date the treaty was signed, March 3, 1918, was a day of salvation for the Jewish people because "the bloody martyrs of Kishinev and Zitomir, Homel and Odessa, Siedlice and Bialystok had been avenged."[164] Jews also praised Austrian efforts to ensure Jewish rights in Romania in the May 1918 treaty with that country.[165] Zionists hailed the creation by the Central Powers of an independent Ukraine in February 1918, because the new Ukrainian state promptly recognized the Jews as a nation and granted them autonomy.[166] The treaties with Russia, Romania, and Ukraine made Austrian Jews feel that they and Austria had accomplished their goals of defeating evil and liberating East European Jewry.

By the spring of 1918, therefore, most Austrian Jews—except presumably those still fighting in Italy and their families—felt that Austria had won the war. Since the war with Italy had never held any special significance to them as Jews, they had always ignored it. Naturally they hoped for Austrian victory against Italy, and praised the troops who fought there "for the honor and security of the fatherland,"[167] but their occasional references to the fighting in Italy contained no particular interest or enthusiasm. For them, the war was over, and they yearned for peace.[168] They focused their attention now on combating anti-Semitism and reorganizing Austria to guarantee Jewish rights.

During the last two years of the war, Austrian Jews confidently maintained the identity they had constructed in the late nineteenth century. They remained deeply loyal to the Austrian *Gesamtstaat* because they realized that only it guaranteed their civil and political equality while permitting them the luxury of their traditional tripartite identity. Only in a multinational Austria could they be loyal Austrian patriots; adherents of German, Czech, or Polish culture; and part of a Jewish ethnic community all at the same time. Only in Austria could they be Austrian in a political sense; German, Czech, or Polish in a cultural sense; and members of the Jewish people. By the fall of 1918, Jews had a sense that they were the only loyal Austrians left in Austria, but they still hoped that Austria would survive.

At the same time, most Jews felt that Jewish identity had deepened during the war. One writer for the *Österreichische Wochenschrift* acknowledged in February 1918 that "Jewishness," that is, concern for Jewish culture, the Jewish people, and Jewish issues, had grown during the war.[169] Edmund Kohn, another writer for this non-Zionist paper, even implied in September 1918 that the Jews were one of the nations of Austria.[170] Jewish nationalists, of course, regularly asserted that the war had made "the Jewish sense of belonging together and Jewish pride deeper and stronger" at the same time as it had led to greater support for the Zionist movement.[171]

Jews clung to this Austrian-Jewish identity ever more forcefully in the last months of the war because they understood that rising anti-Semitism and the growing strength of separatist nationalism threatened this tripartite identity. New nation-states might not be nearly so tolerant of Jewish claims to separate the political, cultural, and ethnic strands of their identity. They might demand that Jews join the national political community even while denying them the possibility of ever doing so. The crisis that beset Austria-Hungary in October 1918 and the ultimate dissolution of the Habsburg Monarchy that followed presented the Jews with a terrible dilemma, a dilemma that threatened their deeply held convictions and forced them to construct a new identity in an atmosphere of hostility and uncertainty.

6

The Dissolution of the Monarchy and the Crisis of Jewish Identity, October 1918–June 1919

When World War I ended and the Habsburg Monarchy collapsed, Erna Segal, a young Viennese woman born in Galicia, was "deeply shocked." As she remembered:

> We were raised with deep reverence for the imperial family, we loved Austria and its rulers and now with one blow everything had come to an end. What now? I asked myself.[1]

Although her father hoped that the end of the bloodletting might be a blessing for humanity, he feared that disaster would result from the "dismemberment" (*Zerstückelung*) of Austria.[2] Similarly, Minna Lachs, a schoolgirl in Vienna whose family had fled there from Galicia in 1914, remembered that she felt a sense of impending catastrophe in October 1918. When her father returned from the army in November, her mother, relieved to have her husband home, assumed that everything would get better, but her husband feared that everything "would first get worse."[3]

Both Segal and Lachs expressed the anxieties that many Austrian Jews felt with the collapse of the Habsburg Monarchy in October–November 1918. While other Austrians—Czechs, Poles, South Slavs—rejoiced in their newly declared national sovereignty and freedom from Habsburg domination, many Jews felt uncertain about the future and what it held for them.[4] Fearful of the anti-Jewish violence that erupted in most of the successor states and worried about their status in those new states, most Jews sincerely mourned the passing of Austria-Hungary.[5] Austria, after all, had not only protected them from nationalist anti-Semitism but had also allowed them their comfortable tripartite identity. Only in supranational Austria could they be Austrians in a political sense; German, Czech, or Polish by culture; and Jewish by ethnic affiliation. With the demise of the multinational state, Jews confronted nation-states generally unwilling to allow them to divide their identities so neatly. These nation-states demanded that they adhere to the dominant national community at the same time as anti-Semitic national leaders were declaring them unfit for membership. Moreover, the well-known Jewish allegiance to old Austria rendered the Jews suspect in the new states.

The Jews of the former Habsburg Monarchy thus faced a grave crisis right after World War I. They now had to craft new national identities to fit the new states in which they lived: German-Austria, Czechoslovakia, Hungary, Poland, Romania, and Yugoslavia (see Map 3). In Hungary, which was now a true Magyar nation-state, Jews had no trouble doing so because they had already adopted Magyar identity. But Jews elsewhere found constructing new identities very difficult. The easiest part was political. Jews understood that it would do them no good to go into permanent mourning for Habsburg Austria, and they realistically declared their loyalties to the new states in which they lived. What was difficult was adopting the national identities of the new states. Most Jews who had embraced German, Czech, or Polish culture still could not think of themselves as members of those national communities, those *Völker*. They continued to think of themselves as adherents of German, or Czech, or Polish culture, but not as Germans, Czechs, or Poles. Indeed, although the old supranational state no longer existed, Jews hoped still to separate national and political identity. They saw themselves as loyal citizens of the states in which they lived and participants in those states' dominant culture, but they could not identify as members of the dominant nation, at least not in the same way as Germans, Czechs, or Poles could. Moreover, widespread anti-Semitic violence complicated the possibilities of adopting a new national identity. Most Jews either hoped or pretended that the new successor states would resemble the old Austria and not force them to adopt a new national identity.

The crisis of identity precipitated by the collapse of the Habsburg Monarchy induced many Jews, far more than before the war, to assert a Jewish ethnic identity or even a Jewish national one. In all the successor states, Zionists formed Jewish national councils to demand the recognition of the Jews as a nation and the extension to them of national minority rights. Even when these councils failed, they represented a significant attempt at contructing a new Jewish identity, especially in Poland and Czechoslovakia, where a Jewish national identity made the most sense, given the presence of several national minority groups. Most German-speaking Jews did not embrace Jewish nationalism, but the postwar crisis made many of them espouse Jewish ethnic solidarity far more vigorously than before. In a period of profound uncertainty, they groped for an identity that would work for them as comfortably as did the old.

This chapter will focus on the Jews of German-Austria, now essentially the Jewish community of Vienna,[6] and on the German-speaking Jews of Czechoslovakia. It was they who experienced the crisis of the collapse of Habsburg Austria most acutely.

Mourning the End of Habsburg Austria

Although Austria-Hungary had long suffered from conflict among her nationalities and other political, economic, and social problems, few suspected that the

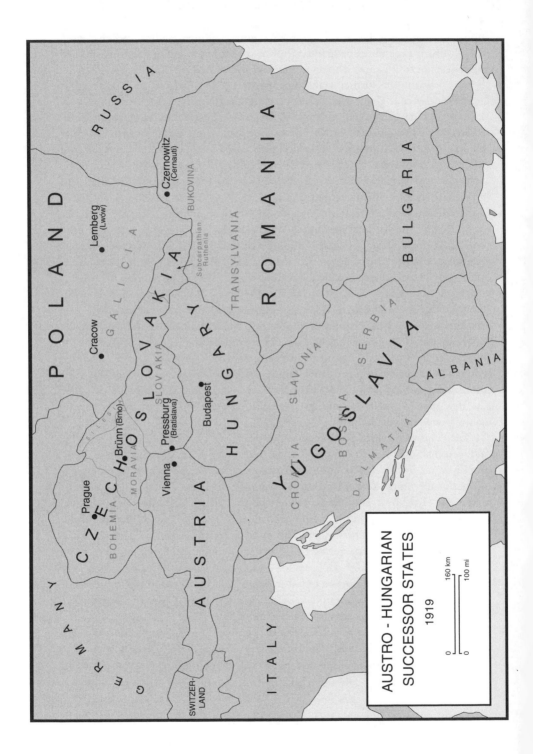

RUSSIA

POLAND

GERMANY

CZECH

Prague

BOHEMIA

Brünn (Brno)

MORAVIA

SILESIA

Cracow

GALICIA

Lemberg
(Lwów)

Czernowitz
(Cernauti)

BUKOVINA

Subcarpathian
Ruthenia

SLOVAKIA

SLOVAKIA

Pressburg
(Bratislava)

Budapest

HUNGARY

TRANSYLVANIA

ROMANIA

BULGARIA

ALBANIA

SERBIA

SLAVONIA

YUGOSLAVIA

BOSNIA

CROATIA

DALMATIA

Vienna

AUSTRIA

SWITZER-
LAND

ITALY

AUSTRO - HUNGARIAN
SUCCESSOR STATES

1919

160 km

100 mi

0

0

Monarchy would collapse or that many of the nationalities would declare their independence at the end of the war. Few nationalist politicians even proposed actual independence until the final months of the war. Moreover, the dissolution of the Monarchy was not one of the war aims of the Entente until the summer or early fall of 1918. Point 10 of American President Woodrow Wilson's Fourteen Points issued in January 1918 assumed the continuity of Austria-Hungary, even though, in the spirit of national self-determination, it called for greater autonomy for Austria's nationalities. Only in the summer of 1918, when the German spring offensive failed and it became obvious that the Central Powers would lose the war, did the Entente begin actively to encourage nationalist politicians who wanted independence from Austria-Hungary. Thus France, England, and the United States supported the efforts of Czech politicians Thomas Masaryk and Edward Beneš, who had formed a Czech National Council in Paris, in their quest for an independent state of Czechs and Slovaks, enabling them to wrest the mantle of leadership of the Czech national movement away from more cautious politicians at home. They also supported the Yugoslavs as well as the Poles, who sought a united Polish state. At the same time, the specter of defeat, apparent only in the summer of 1918, also emboldened radical nationalists to demand independence.[7]

Events moved very rapidly after October 4, when Germany and Austria requested an armistice on the basis of Wilson's Fourteen Points. To satisfy Point 10, Kaiser Karl issued his October 16 manifesto, calling for the reorganization of Austria into a federation of national states. Leaving Hungary's status intact and assuming that the Poles and Italians would be part of Poland and Italy, respectively, Karl proposed the creation of German, Czech, South Slav, and Ukrainian federal states within Austria. By this time, however, nationalist leaders wanted more than autonomy, and they ignored the manifesto, which succeeded only in generating more support for independence. Moreover, the Entente itself had nullified Point 10 by its promises to support Czech independence, and even the Kaiser realized that he could not keep the Czech lands in the Monarchy.

By the end of October 1918, various national committees declared their independence from Austria. These declarations reflected the tension between the principle of national self-determination and the desire for territory deemed to belong historically to a particular nation despite the presence in it of other national groups. On October 21, the Czech National Council in Paris declared Czech independence; on October 28, politicians in Prague declared a Czechoslovak Republic; and on October 30, the Slovak National Council announced that Slovakia, long part of Hungary, would now become part of Czechoslovakia. At the same time, the Germans of Bohemia and Moravia opposed their inclusion in Czechoslovakia and wanted to belong to "German-Austria," and the Magyars of Slovakia expressed their dismay when Czech troops entered Slovakia in November. Similarly, Galician Poles made it clear to Vienna at the end of October that Galicia was now part of independent Poland, even though the Ukrainians (formerly Ruthenians) in East Galicia objected vigorously, and a war between Poles and Ukrainians ensued. Bukovina was also a contested region: Initially, a Ukrainian group took charge, but on October 27, the Bukovinian Romanians declared

Bukovina to be part of Romania, a declaration converted into fact on November 11 when the Romanian army occupied Bukovina. In the chaos of October/November, Hungary too became a separate entity, shorn of much of her non-Magyar territory, since Croatia-Slavonia and the Vojvodina (as well as Austrian Dalmatia and Slovenia) joined the new South-Slav state, while Romania took Transylvania, and Slovakia and Sub-Carpathian Ruthenia joined Czechoslovakia (see Map 3).

As the imperial government and state disintegrated, its Germans remained uncertain about their future. The Social Democrats continued to favor federalism or, if necessary, merger with Germany. Both courses of action, they felt, complied with the principle of self-determination. The Christian Socials, on the other hand, hoped that the Monarchy could persist. On October 21, the German deputies in parliament established themselves as the provisional national assembly of a new Austrian state composed of the German-language areas of old Austria, which included the German-speaking areas of the Czech lands. On October 30, they declared this state, "German-Austria," to be an integral part of a German Republic. The old state was now on its deathbed. By October 27, Austria had asked for a separate peace, and on November 3, Austria and Italy agreed to an armistice. Austria surrendered on November 4. By that time, most Habsburg soldiers were simply going home. Kaiser Karl never formally abdicated, but on November 11, he did renounce all participation in Austrian state business. The following day, November 12, German-Austria declared itself a republic and expressed its desire for *Anschluss*, union with Germany, a merger that the Allies refused to allow.

It is a truism of Central European history that the nationalities of the old Austria rejoiced in their new-found independence, glad to be free of Habsburg domination. Yet it is also true that in October 1918, most Habsburg subjects were far too weary of war, and far too hungry, to be as concerned about nationalism, political sovereignty, and the collapse of the Monarchy as the nationalist politicians and propagandists.[8] Moreover, most of the new states contained sizeable numbers of national minorities, many of whom were unhappy to find themselves included in states dominated by other nations, and some of whom appealed to conationals elsewhere to come to their aid. Several of the new states, including Austria, Czechoslovakia, and Yugoslavia, faced the difficult task of forging a national identity. Austria, or German-Austria as it was first known, consisted almost entirely of Germans, but the Allies would not allow it to join Germany, so the German-Austrians needed to create a new Austrian identity, a difficult task in the interwar years. Czechoslovakia contained Czechs, Slovaks, Germans, Magyars, Ruthenians, and Jews, and creating a Czechoslovak identity proved elusive. Now including Bukovina with its Ruthenians and Germans, and Transylvania with a sizeable population of Hungarians and Germans, as well as Bessarabia with its population of Ukrainians and Russians, Romania faced the challenge of assimilating these other nationalities into a fiercely Romanian nation-state.[9] In addition, many old Austrians did not know where they belonged. Members of the old Habsburg elite—high-level bureaucrats and army officers—felt utterly homeless. So too did many Jews.

In his play *November 3, 1918*, the Viennese playwright Franz Theodor Csokor movingly described the dilemma of many Habsburg subjects at the moment the Monarchy collapsed. Written in 1936 against the backdrop of the Nazi threat, the play depicts how a group of convalescent soldiers, representing some of the national groups in the Monarchy, react to the news. As a Polish cavalry officer prepares to hurry home to his people, a colonel, the perfect example of the supranational Habsburg army officer, appeals to his men to honor the tolerance and brotherhood of the Monarchy and its army. When they respond by making plans to join their nations, he commits suicide. Unlike his men, he has no home to which he can return. At his funeral, the men, some of whom are preparing to take up arms against each other, place earth on his grave in the names of their respective homelands, once part of Austria but now sovereign states. The Jewish doctor is in a dilemma. Like the colonel, he belongs to none of the nations, and so he places earth on the grave in the name of Habsburg Austria.[10] Although not central to the dramatic tension of the play, the position of the Jew reflects the popular notion that Jews mourned the old Austria and would have a hard time in the new successor states. The reality was far more complex.

Jewish responses to the collapse of Habsburg Austria varied considerably by region and by political or religious orientation. Although a sense of anxiety about the future typified all Jewish response, many Jews, especially in the new Czechoslovak Republic, greeted the new order warmly and proceeded to craft a place in it for themselves, even if that place was not as members of the dominant nation in the new state. Others felt the sense of loss and the dilemma of identity more acutely and, unable to construct a new identity, continued to assert the old identity, even if it no longer made sense. Zionists and Jewish nationalists responded exuberantly to the opportunity to assert Jewish national identity and to stake their claim to leadership of the Jewish people. Other Jews rejected Jewish nationalism but groped for some kind of new Jewish identity that would sustain them in the new political situation. Like other Habsburg subjects, most Jews simply adjusted to the new situation without much reflection. They were far too tired of war and its losses, too hungry and poor, and too upset by anti-Jewish violence to do anything but simply cope.

Jews in Vienna, both those long resident and the Galician refugees stranded there, felt the loss of Habsburg Austria most acutely. In the first weeks of October 1918, writers for the *Österreichische Wochenschrift* continued to hope that Austria would remain united and expressed their dismay over the possibility of a new political order that would divide Habsburg Jewry. In particular, they worried about the fate of Jews in the Czech lands, and especially about Galician Jews, who would suffer at the hands of the Poles.[11] Orthodox Jews expressed their desire for the continuity of the Monarchy even more forcefully, blaming disintegration on the desire of Austria's enemies to dismember her and insisting that all citizens, and certainly the Jews, would benefit from a united Austria–Hungary.[12] Most Jewish spokesmen understood that they had to adjust to the principle of national self-determination, but they did not yet have a clear idea of how it would affect them. Jewish liberals like Rudolf Schwarz-Hiller, the municipal councillor who headed the government's refugee aid office, called for Jewish unity to ensure Jewish rights in a reconfigured Austria.[13]

Viennese Zionists also yearned in October 1918 for Austrian continuity. Willing to concede that the government had stifled legitimate nationalist aspirations, they nevertheless hoped that the Jews could help keep Austria united.[14] Moreover, they felt that the growing pressure for national self-determination would allow them to press more effectively for Jewish national rights. Thus they were pleased that the Kaiser met with the new Viennese chief rabbi Hirsch Perez Chajes, a committed Zionist, who impressed Karl with the need for Jewish national rights.[15] At a mass meeting on October 14, Zionists demanded Jewish autonomy and pledged their support in the task of reconstructing Habsburg Austria.[16] Not surprisingly, Zionists viewed Kaiser Karl's call to reorganize Austria as a federation of autonomous nations with great excitement because they hoped it would provide them with the opportunity finally to win Jewish national rights. To prepare for Jewish autonomy within a reformulated Austrian *Völkerstaat*, the Zionists held an Austria-wide conference on October 20.[17]

Most Jews in Vienna genuinely mourned the dissolution of the Monarchy at the end of October. When the German deputies in the Austrian parliament declared a German-Austrian state on October 21, Heinrich Schreiber expressed the anguish of liberal Viennese Jews, wondering "if this day would become for us Jews another, new ninth of Av," the traditional day for mourning catastrophes in Jewish history. He reiterated the traditional Jewish loyalty to Habsburg Austria, declaring:

> We acknowledge openly and honestly the deep pain in our hearts about the gloomy and painful transformation and upheaval. It is with . . . deep sadness . . . that we bid farewell to the united fatherland, and we stand shocked before the grave of old, familiar, honorable memories and feelings . . . that a day of calamity has dashed into ruins. Our only comfort is the thought that we Jews are not guilty for it.[18]

Worried about anti-Semitism, Schreiber hoped that German-Austria would guarantee equality to all its citizens, irrespective of background. In late 1918, the Jewish press regularly repeated this plea.[19]

The orthodox press even more clearly expressed the fear that small, nationalist states would discriminate against the Jews. Orthodox spokesmen argued that while the strong central state had checked intolerance and hatred, the new states, infused by nationalist anti-Semitism and unhindered by higher authority, would make the situation of the Jews unbearable.[20] Among the Jews, only the Zionists treated the dissolution of the Monarchy in a matter-of-fact manner, even criticizing former government policies for hampering the nationalities.[21]

In mid-November, after German-Austria became a republic, the *Österreichische Wochenschrift* reiterated its sense of loss at the demise of the Monarchy, albeit more obliquely than a few weeks earlier. Paying formal respects to the new republic and wishing it well, the editors did not wax eloquent or hail it in glowing terms as a symbol of the victory of democracy and national rights. Instead, they blamed the collapse of the Monarchy on the machinations of Austria's enemies and sadly described Karl's letter of farewell to his peoples. More important, their plaintive requests for justice and equality reflected their anxiety that the new nation-state might deprive them of their citizenship rights.[22] They were certainly willing to offer their fealty to the new state, but they felt deep and genuine sadness about the passing of the old one.

In hindsight, Jewish memoirists from Vienna also expressed their deep regrets over the demise of the supranational state. David Neumann, who had served as a sergeant in the army, recalled that during his trip back to Vienna "I cried for my fatherland." After all, the fact "that Austria-Hungary was destroyed was, in my opinion, one of the worst catastrophes of the twentieth century."[23] In less dramatic language, Vinca Safar, a doctor in Vienna, admitted that she later missed the Monarchy and felt that if Austria-Hungary had become a federal state, perhaps the Second World War would never have occurred. At the time, she knew only that the future was uncertain.[24] Chemist Fritz Lieben shared that sense of uncertainty, reflecting later in his memoirs that "I believe that the destruction of the Danubian Monarchy was a misfortune, even though at the time, perhaps, it could no longer be sustained." Like others, Lieben felt that the existence of the Monarchy could have spared Europe the horrors of World War II.[25] Economist Toni Stolper, as well, who had always believed that Austria could not survive, nevertheless felt she had lost her country at the end of the war. Describing the collapse as "the catastrophic downfall," she linked Hitler's later success to the problems of Austria's Germans.[26] Contemporaries had no idea about the path the future would take, but they thought that the collapse of the multinational state would have negative consequences. Army doctor Bernhard Bardoch noted in his diary in late October 1918 that the nations of Austria, following their "traitorous" leaders and egged on by the Entente, had "lost their heads."[27]

There were certainly Viennese Jews who greeted the republic warmly on political grounds because it promised greater democracy than the Monarchy, yet their memoirs reflected their unease. Olly Schwarz, an activist in the women's movement, liked the Republic because it extended the franchise to women and allowed her a political career. Yet, in her memoirs, she records how stunned everyone was when the Monarchy collapsed and how fearful she became when parliament disintegrated into chaos just after it declared the Republic on November 12.[28] Ernst Saxonhouse thought that justice prevailed with the collapse of the Monarchy, yet he also mentioned that his father was in shock, unable to speak for days.[29] Strikingly absent was any joy about the new government. Unlike Jews in Weimar Germany, who welcomed their new democratic republic, Jews in German-Austria simply felt uneasy about the political transformation and worried about their status in the new nation-state.

The situation of the Galician Jewish refugees living in Vienna typified the dilemma that Jews faced with the dissolution of the Monarchy. Indeed, the refugees, threatened with expulsion everywhere, now suffered as foreigners in the lands to which they had fled during the war as citizens. They were truly homeless. Manès Sperber, whose family had fled to Vienna from Galicia in 1916, described that feeling movingly. His family chose to remain in Vienna because "our old homeland would become foreign." At the same time, they feared for their situation in Vienna and wondered what they would do "if the new homeland remained foreign for us?"[30] Although her family had sensed that Austria would lose the war, Minna Lachs felt enormous loss in November 1918 when she had to rip out the picture of the Kaiser from her schoolbooks without anything to put in its place.[31] She worried about her family's future in the small new German-Austria, which could not even feed itself. When other refugees returned to Galicia, Minna realized that she no longer felt that Galicia was home. Her family desired to stay in Vienna, and, unlike most Galician refugees, they succeeded in obtaining Austrian citizenship.[32] Although not a refugee, Bernhard Bardach, who was born in Sambor, Galicia, experienced the same sense of loss at the end of the war. A career army doctor, he identified as an Austrian and felt utterly alienated from the Polish nation. Although he recognized that German-Austrians also harbored anti-Jewish animosity, for lack of any viable alternative, he cast his lot with the rump Austrian state.[33]

Many refugees wanted nothing more than to return to their homes, and of course large numbers did return, especially to western Galicia where the political situation had stabilized.[34] Others could not return home, however, either because their homes had been destroyed during four years of war or because the Polish-Ukrainian war made return impossible or because they realistically feared pogrom violence. Yet they could not stay in Vienna either. Not only did the anti-Semites lobby vigorously for the expulsion of the refugees, but most Viennese agreed that the refugees did not belong in German-Austria and had to leave as soon as possible.[35] Thus, the refugees felt truly homeless: they could not go home, and no one wanted them to stay.

Galician or Bukovinian Jews who did return home often felt that they did not belong in Poland or Romania and preferred instead to return to Vienna, the capital of their former—or true—homeland. Joachim Schoenfeld, who had served in the army in Italy, tried to return to East Galicia in November 1918, but the fighting that raged between Poles and Ukrainians and pogroms against the Jews induced him to return to Vienna, where he enrolled in the university.[36] When the war ended, Adolf Mechner felt lucky that he was home on furlough in Czernowitz, Bukovina. Very quickly, however, he felt uncomfortable living in Romania. His once beautiful, cultured city became delapidated and corrupt; Romanian had replaced German as the dominant language and "it took a long time till people learned to speak it." Perhaps more important, "anti-Semitism could be noticed everywhere." Discontent, Mechner went to Vienna, enrolled as a medical student at the university, and later opted for Austrian citizenship.[37]

At the end of 1918, Galician refugees had a sense of not belonging anywhere. Jews in Galicia and Bukovina were probably too busy coping with poverty, hunger, destruction, political chaos, and violence to worry about where they did or did not belong. All Jews, however, could regard the political turmoil and anti-Jewish violence that erupted in 1918–1919 in all the successor states, especially in Poland, as proof that Austria's collapse was a calamity. They watched in dismay as, in Joachim Schoenfeld's words, "the birth of Poland was accompanied by rivers of Jewish blood."[38]

Having lost its independence at the end of the eighteenth century when Russia, Prussia, and Austria partitioned it, Poland became an independent state once again in November 1918. The independence of Poland had been a central feature of Wilson's Fourteen Points, and the victorious Allies were eager to see the reborn Poland take its place in the community of nations. The struggle over the borders of the new state, however, reflected the tension between the principle of self-determination and the desire for historical territory. Many Poles wanted the borders of Poland to extend as far as those of the former Polish commonwealth and thus to include large parts of the Ukraine, Lithuania, White Russia, and, of course, all of Austrian Galicia. Ukrainian nationalists in eastern Galicia resisted Polish hegemony. During the war, most Ukrainians in Galicia (formerly known as Ruthenians) had remained loyal to the Habsburgs and had urged the government to convert eastern Galicia into a separate crownland free of Polish control. In the fall of 1918, Ruthenian leaders found themselves at cross-purposes with the various factions battling for control of the short-lived Ukrainian National Republic, which had declared its independence in Dnieper Ukraine after the Russian Revolution. Despite the obvious appeal of joining a Ukrainian nation-state, on November 1, Ruthenians—now called Ukrainians—declared an independent Western Ukrainian National Republic. In the months that followed, they engaged in a bitter war with the Poles for control of Galicia, a struggle that the Poles won in July 1919 when they incorporated all of Galicia into Poland. Independent Poland also included Volhynia and parts of White Russia and Lithuania.[39]

In the context of the Polish-Ukrainian struggle for control of Galicia and of the conflicts between various factions in Dnieper Ukraine, violent pogroms erupted that claimed large numbers of Jewish lives. It is difficult to ascertain the exact number of the dead, but probably 100,000 Jews were killed in Poland and Ukraine—mostly in Ukraine—between the end of World War I and 1920, when the Poles (in Galicia) and the Russian Bolsheviks (in Dnieper Ukraine) imposed their firm control.[40] In Galicia, the Jews asserted their neutrality in the conflict between Poles and Ukrainians (Ruthenians),[41] but Polish mobs, often led by Polish legionnaires, nevertheless attacked the Jews for their alleged support of Ukrainian independence. The largest pogrom occured in Lemberg. Polish soldiers led an attack on the Jewish quarter of the city on November 21–23, 1918 that claimed 73 Jewish lives. Such anti-Jewish violence, launched not just by peasants or starving city dwellers but by Polish soldiers, seemed to offer proof to the Jews of the dangers of life in independent Poland, of the problems inherent in nation-states, and of the calamity caused by the collapse of the Habsburg Monarchy.

Jewish newspapers all over old Austria reported the pogroms in Galicia in horrific, often exaggerated, detail. They universally blamed the Poles, especially Polish soldiers, for either leading the pogroms or for standing by while they raged, and they praised the Ukrainians, who despite launching pogroms elsewhere in Ukraine promised to guarantee Jewish national rights in their republic. One article in the *Österreichische Wochenschrift* in early December 1918, for example, insisted that prewar pogroms paled compared with the truly frightful events in Lemberg in late November when the Poles retook the city from the Ukrainians. The author laid the blame for the pogroms squarely on the soldiers of the Polish Legion, who, he asserted, used alleged Jewish sympathies for the Ukrainians as an excuse to attack, killing hundreds and plundering thousands.[42] The paper's editors claimed larger fatalities, between 1000 and 3000 dead, but also went further, accusing the politicians of the Polish Liquidation Commmission, in charge of the transfer of Galicia from Austria to Poland, with instigating the soldiers' attack on Jews even as they claimed that "bandits" or "army deserters" had started the pogroms.[43] Other writers used far more hostile language, branding the Poles brutal, barbaric, hypocritical cowards who should be punished by the Allies for their despicable behavior.[44] The orthodox press, which had refrained from anti-Polish rhetoric during the war, also blamed the Polish authorities for the atrocities in Lemberg, wondering what "evil spirit" had taken hold of the Poles to spill so much Jewish blood and besmirch the honor of the reborn Poland. Using less-incendiary language, and not exaggerating the actual damage, Vienna's orthodox newspaper called on the Polish government to condemn the pogroms and end the violence.[45]

The Zionist press likewise lambasted the Polish Legion for its role in the pogroms in Galicia, declaring the Poles not mature enough to have their own state if their first action was to assault Jews and lie about it in public.[46] The reports of Viennese Zionists about pogroms in Galicia drew an explicit connection between the fall of the Monarchy and anti-Jewish violence, regarding it as "the first catastrophic consequence" of the new political situation.[47] Zionists insisted that they had always supported Polish independence, but they now anguished over the consequences for Jews and other minorities in Poland.[48] In his book about the pogrom, Galician Zionist Joseph Tenenbaum provided extensive evidence for the role of the Polish military, asserting that they wanted "nothing less than the complete annihilation of the Lemberg Jewish community" and the elimination of the Jews from Poland. Horrified that in the age of Wilsonian principles the Poles responded to their freedom by killing Jews, he hoped that the Allies at Versailles would punish the new state.[49]

As pogroms erupted elsewhere in Galicia in the following months,[50] the Jewish press became even more hostile to the Poles. The *Österreichische Wochenschrift*, for example, declared that Polish soldiers and the right-wing National Democratic party had embarked on "a truly pharaonic frenzy of destruction and annihilation" against the Jews of Galicia in the name of Christianity and national chauvinism, thereby revealing their unworthiness for national independence. The paper urged the civilized world to take action against Polish barbarism.[51] Indeed, the pogroms in Cracow and elsewhere in the spring of 1919 made Jewish spokesmen of all political and religious orientations demand that the Versailles Peace Conference take strong measures to guarantee Jewish rights in Poland.[52] Zionists, for example, railed against the Poles "who hurl themselves in a wild, barbaric, bloody, and systematic way against the Jewish minority," and implored the Paris Peace Conference to extend to them national autonomy and thus prevent the "war of annihilation" that the Poles were waging against Jews and other national minorities.[53] With Jews of Galicia facing so much violence, it was natural for Jews everywhere to mourn the passing of the Habsburg Monarchy.

In the new Czechoslovakia, where Czechs rejoiced in their new-found independence,[54] such mourning would have branded the Jews as traitors. It would have been politically stupid to mourn Austria amidst the nationalist euphoria of the Czechs in late 1918. Thus, unlike the Jews in Vienna, Jews in the Czech lands did not publicly express their sadness at the collapse of the Monarchy. Jews who before the war had identified with the Czech national struggle of course supported the new order enthusiastically.[55] German-speaking Jews reacted cautiously, expressing their loyalty to the new state, but they were initially anxious about their place within it. They became more confident when they realized that the new Czechoslovakia, like Austria before it, was a multinational state, filled with Czechs, Slovaks, Germans, Magyars, Ruthenians, and Jews, whose leaders, especially President Thomas Masaryk, would pursue a policy of tolerance for national diversity. In an odd way, Jews came to regard Czechoslovakia as a smaller scale, improved version of the old Monarchy and Masaryk as a stand-in for the beloved Franz Joseph.

In late October 1918, before the formal declaration of Czechoslovak independence, but when it was already obvious that such a state would come into existence, the leaders of the Prague Jewish community held a series of confidential meetings to discuss the "serious situation" in which they found themselves. Upset about escalating anti-Semitism, most of them supported a formal request to expel the Galician refugees, the main target of anti-Semitic agitation. They worried about the popularity of anti-Semitism among Czech nationalists, even as they reassured themselves that many Czech leaders harbored no anti-Semitic animus, and that anti-Jewish hostility derived in part from the traditional pro-Austrian posture of the Jews. Anxiety about anti-Semitism, fear that Czech leaders might not be able to control the anti-Semites, and their sense that they had to adjust to new political realities impelled Prague's Jewish leaders to attempt to impress the new authorities with their loyalty. Expressions of loyalty did not reflect, at least at this point, any heartfelt excitement about a Czech nation-state. An oddly formal quality, a flatness, a sense of obligation characterized the discussions of loyalty, not enthusiasm. As board member N.L. Kohner argued, the Czechs had to know "that the Jews were always patriotic and will also be patriotic to the Bohemian state. The religious scriptures of the Jews require them to be patriotic."[56] Prague's Jewish notables voted unanimously on October 27 to send the Czech authorities a formal declaration of Jewish loyalty that they hoped would induce Czech leaders to guarantee freedom and equality to the Jews.[57] The deputation that brought this statement to the Národní Výbor (the Czech National Council) wisely included not only the German-speaking notables of Prague but also Czech-speaking Jewish leaders from Prague's suburbs.[58]

In the weeks that followed, Prague's Jewish leaders adjusted to the new situation with the air of resignation touched with continued worry about their relationship to the new state. When the leaders of the Czech Jewish movement demanded that the Jewish community conduct its business and religious services in Czech, IKG president Alois Koserak noted "that in light of political conditions changes must be undertaken." No discussion followed, and subsequent minutes were in German, although the IKG did publish its loyalty statement in both Czech and German.[59] Responding to rumors that the Národní Výbor had received the Jewish deputation in an unfriendly manner and had reproached them for their conduct during the war, Koserak insisted that Dr. Rasin had treated them well, requesting only that the Jews have the same feelings for the new state as they had for old Austria,[60] a statement that reflected the Czech leaders' concern about Jewish loyalty.

Some Jews in the Czech lands embraced the new state. At the end of the war, Arnold Hindls from Leipnik, Moravia was a prisoner of war in Russia who desperately wanted to return to his homeland. Upon his arrival there in June 1920, he felt that he was "finally a free citizen of a free state."[61] Initially unable to find work, he tried his luck in Vienna, where he had studied to be an engineer before the war and where he, like many Moravian Jews, also had close relatives, but he returned to Brünn because "I . . . preferred to work in the newly established Czechoslovakia."[62] Hella Roubicek Mautner also made the transition from Austria to Czechoslovakia without discomfort. She recalled that

> Our family had no problem after the fall of the empire because we were bilingual. But for many Jews who had no ties to the Czech population, the change was very hard. I enjoyed it.[63]

Mautner's family adjusted easily because they already identified with the Czech community.

Other Jews found the need to shift loyalties from Habsburg Austria to Czechoslovakia far more difficult. Bertha Allerhand Landre, who lived in Austrian Silesia, felt an enormous rupture in her life when her region became part of Czechoslovakia. She did not share in the Czech celebration of independence, although she did grudgingly admit that Czechoslovakia's status as a victorious nation allowed for better economic conditions than prevailed in German-Austria or Germany. Like many other Jews, she went off to Vienna to study.[64] Prague Zionist Hans Kohn, a prisoner of war in Siberia, expressed his disappointment with Czechoslovakia when he returned in the spring of 1920. He thought that the new government "was building on faulty foundations. It identified the new state with a single ethnic, linguistic group, at the expense of the other groups living in what was now the new Czech state." Unhappy with chauvinistic nationalism in Central Europe, Kohn abandoned Prague and ultimately left Europe altogether.[65] Max Brod was so busy with his Zionist activity at the time that he barely noticed the end of Habsburg Austria. Later, however, from the perspective of hindsight, he remarked that "today, I consider it a European misfortune that people allowed Austria to perish."[66] The whole world, he insisted, would have been better off if Austria had been reorganized as a federation of free peoples, which would have served as a bulwark against both Russian and German aggression.[67]

Despite Brod's later misgivings, the Zionists in fact greeted Czechoslovakia with great enthusiasm, recognizing immediately the potential opportunities for Jewish national rights that the new state afforded. Although they worried about Czech anti-Semitism, they had faith that the new state would respect the national rights of its Germans, Slovaks, Magyars, Ruthenians, and Jews and would become a true multinational state that would grant Jews autonomy. In the heady days of late 1918 and early 1919, the Zionists could imagine Czechoslovakia as an improved version of Austria, a state that allowed its nations, including the Jews, to control their own destinies. This state had wise leaders able to guarantee such toleration, and it even incorporated a hinterland in the East with large numbers of traditional Jews who could be tapped for the Zionist cause. Thus the Zionists of Czechoslovakia had an easier time adjusting to the collapse of the Habsburg Monarchy than any other German-speaking Jewish group in old Austria. Despite their long history of loyalty to the Habsburg Monarchy, these Zionists barely noticed that the war had ended and the Monarchy had collapsed, so eager were they to become players in the new order.

In mid-October 1918, Prague Zionists watched events in a state of breathless anticipation, excited about the implications of the victory of the principle of national self-determination. At this point they still spoke in public about their desire for national autonomy within an Austrian federation,[68] but in private they expressed their openness to either an Austrian federation or a new Czech polity. Indeed, they no longer considered it necessary to deal with the central government or to work to save it, but thought it politically wise to establish contacts with the "majority nation."[69] By the end of October, although still talking about an Austrian federation, they recognized that the Czechs were on the verge of "the fulfillment of all their aspirations," and they expressed their faith that the "worthy" Czechs would treat the other peoples of their new state with justice. The Zionists also hoped that Czech leaders would disavow anti-Semitism, recognize the Jews as a nation, and grant them autonomy and minority rights.[70]

Although Zionists expressed boundless enthusiasm for the new order, their concern for justice, legal rights, and the end of anti-Semitism reflected profound nervousness as well. This nervousness persisted despite repeated affirmations of confidence in the Czech leaders. Taking pride, for example, that American Zionist Louis Brandeis must have influenced Wilson to support Czech national aspirations, the editors of *Selbstwehr* bravely insisted that it was "sheer nonsense to believe that the young Czechoslovakian state will imitate the methods of czarist Russia."[71]

Most Bohemian Zionists did not engage in anti-Habsburg oratory in November 1918. The one exception, albeit an important once, was Ludwig Singer, the head of the newly formed Jewish National Council. In a speech delivered to a mass meeting on November 10, Singer declared:

> On the ruins of an Austria based on big lies, free nation-states arise. We Jews have no cause to shed any tears for Austria, which was governed in an antisemitic-clerical way and exploited the Jews.[72]

Singer, who had been an activist in the Czech-Jewish movement before he became a Zionist,[73] shared Czech antipathy toward the Habsburgs, but on this issue he remained an isolated voice. The Prague Zionist *Selbstwehr* never engaged in anti-Austrian polemics, presumably because the editors did not hate the old Monarchy. More typical than Austria-bashing were affirmations of faith in the new Czechoslovakia and expressions of hope that it would allow the Zionists to implement their own agenda. The Jewish National Council in Brünn, for example, resolved on November 5 that "we can correctly hope that in the Czechoslovakian state all of our goals will be realized."[74]

Whatever their initial feelings, most Jews in Czechoslovakia developed a positive attitude toward the new state. In particular, they revered President Thomas Masaryk and credited him with ensuring that Czechoslovakia did not oppress any of its national groups. Masaryk had long enjoyed Jewish esteem. In the late 1890s he had defended Leopold Hilsner, who had been charged with ritual murder in the infamous Polna Affair.[75] Zionists especially revered Masaryk because he supported their cause, and they proudly displayed his picture next to Herzl's at their meetings.[76] Jews thus placed a great deal of faith in Masaryk and expected that he and his colleagues would halt the anti-Semitic agitation raging in Bohemia, Moravia, and Slovakia.

Full-fledged pogroms did erupt in many places in Bohemia and Moravia in the months after the end of World War I, and these pogroms shocked the Jews who always assumed that anti-Jewish violence only occurred in Russia, the Ukraine, and Poland. The riots rarely resulted in fatalities, but rioters did beat up Jews, plunder their stores, and destroy their property.[77] The rioters blamed the Jews for wartime food shortages and attacked the Jews for their traditional loyalty to Austria and German culture. In sharp contrast to the Jewish press coverage of pogroms in Galicia, which held Polish soldiers and the Polish authorities responsible, virtually all reports of Czech pogroms blamed the hungry, ignorant mobs and insisted that the Czech authorities would certainly squelch such violence. The Jewish press thus contrasted bad Poland and good Czechoslovakia.

In an editorial on December 6, 1918, the Prague Zionist newspaper *Selbstwehr* responded to anti-Jewish riots in the capital by insisting that the Czech government "has always had the limitless, enduring will to tolerate absolutely no disturbances and to protect the life and property of all citizens." Aware of anti-Semitic agitation in the Czech press, but wishing to exonerate the Czechs, the newspaper argued that Czech rioters had been provoked by German nationalists.[78] Such propagandistic statements, of course, covered a more complex reality. The Zionists worried, at least at first, about the ability of the government to protect Jews from violence and about widespread anti-Semitism in the Czech population.[79] In the wake of the pogrom in Holleschau, Moravia, for example, the Jewish National Council of Czechoslovakia met with Minister President Kramář to inform him of Jewish fears, to request Czech military intervention, and to demand punishment for the rioters. Anxious about anti-Semitic agitation in the Czech press, these Zionists hoped that the government of the "free Czechoslovakian Republic would do everything to provide sufficient protection to its Jewish citizens."[80] Zionists blamed the pogroms on the Czech population, sometimes even on Czech soldiers, and understood that local Czech authorities often stood by without responding. At the same time, Zionists felt that the Czechs were not as bad as the Poles and hoped that the government would quickly put an end to the violence for the good of the fledgling state.[81] Non-Zionists agreed.[82] The outbreak of anti-Jewish violence in Slovakia in the spring of 1919 did not shake this faith in the ability of Czech leaders, especially Masaryk, to control the situation.[83]

The Zionists, who had rejoiced in November 1918 when Masaryk made a public declaration of support for the Jewish national movement,[84] counted on him to forge a decent Czech state and end anti-Semitism.[85] When he arrived in

Prague in December 1918, *Selbstwehr* praised him as the great leader who would lead his people "out of the Austrian morass into freedom." Reminding readers of his history of opposition to anti-Semitism, the editors hoped that "in the face of his calm and unbiased judgement barbarous antisemitism will finally give way to a more sensible, just, and honorable situation for the Czechs themselves" and full equality for the Jews.[86] The Brünn Zionist newspaper, *Jüdische Volksstimme*, echoed this sentiment in March 1919:

> The 68-year-old ruler of the new state, who takes hold of the reigns of government with youthful courage and determination, has promised repeatedly to secure full protection and security for Jewish citizens and will know how to make his words come to pass.[87]

How nicely philosophy professor Masaryk fit into Emperor Franz Joseph's shoes!

Faith in Masaryk's ability to quell anti-Semitism and guarantee Czechoslovak tolerance for the Jews also appears in the memoirs of Jews from Bohemia and Moravia. Bertha Landre did not greet the new state with joy but nevertheless recalled that her mother felt confident that "men like Masaryk" would ensure good relations between the nationalities of Czechoslovakia.[88] Nina Lieberman, who spent her childhood in the 1920s in Tachov, Bohemia, felt that

> Czechoslovakia, with its German-, Czech-, and Slovak-speaking populations had to practice co-existence, and it was fortunate to have, in Thomas Masaryk, a leader of outstanding ability and proven moral fiber.[89]

Reconstructing Identity in Czechoslovakia

All Jews in the former Habsburg Monarchy faced a crisis in late 1918 and early 1919. Not only did they need to craft a new political loyalty, which they did with varying degrees of success, but they had to construct a new national identity as well. The task was easiest for the Zionists of Bohemia and Moravia, committed as they were to a definition of the Jews as a nation and living as they did in a multinational state. These Jewish nationalists simply asserted that Jews formed a nation, one of the nations of Czechoslovakia. Thus they could simply transfer their old tripartite identity to the new state. Now they could be Czechoslovaks politically, German or Czech culturally, and members of the Jewish nation. They felt that their construction of Jewish identity worked perfectly for the new circumstances.

Energized by the creation of Czechoslovakia, which they viewed as a tolerant multinational state with pro-Zionist leaders, Zionists felt confident that they would now finally win Jewish national rights. Zionists reveled in the fact that increasing numbers of Jews joined their cause. As the antagonism intensified between Czechs and Germans in Bohemia and Moravia and between Slovaks and Magyars in Slovakia, growing numbers of Jews, especially in Moravia, Silesia, and Slovakia, came to agree with the Zionists that Jews should identify as Jews and assert their neutrality in the raging nationality conflicts. Zionists felt that they were on the verge of triumph, all the more because demography now favored them. After all, Czechoslovakia included Slovakia, historically part of Hungary, where a large reservoir of traditional Jews could be tapped for the Zionist cause.

Finally, the Prague circle was delighted to be free of the control of Viennese Zionists like Robert Stricker, with whom they had long disagreed.[90]

By end of October 1918, Zionists in Prague established a Jewish National Council (*Jüdischer Nationalrat,*) headed by Ludwig Singer, Karl Fischel, and Max Brod, to work for the recognition of the Jewish nation and national minority rights in Czechoslovakia.[91] In line with their previous policy, and realistic about the limits of what they could achieve, these Prague Zionists did not seek the apparatus of full-blown national autonomy—Jewish voting curias and Jewish delegations in the government—long desired by Galician, Bukovinian, and Viennese Zionists, but simply "minority rights in the national/cultural sphere."[92] The Council sent a detailed memorandum to the Národní Výbor on October 28 demanding the recognition of the Jews as a nationality and the right of Jews to declare themselves members of the Jewish nation. They also insisted on full civic equality and on national minority rights, that is the right to administer Jewish cultural affairs, including education, social welfare, and relations with the Jewish national home in Palestine. The Jewish National Council sought modern Jewish elementary and secondary schools, state support for Jewish cultural and educational institutions, and democratically elected Jewish religious communities. Local parents' associations would decide the language of the Jewish national schools, which would teach Jewish history and culture. The memorandum expressed the Zionists' desire for good relations with the Czechs, but warned them that democracy and humanity required an end to anti-Semitic excesses.[93] Max Brod, who worked "feverishly" on behalf of the Council, expressed his excitement and optimism in a letter to his friend Leo Herrmann, then in the Zionist office in Berlin. Brod felt that the Czechs were very sympathetic to the Council's goals and might allow the Zionists to create Jewish national schools. The Zionists had trounced the "assimilationists," Brod proudly informed Herrmann.[94]

In the weeks and months that followed, Brod's optimism grew. He felt that Zionism and its version of Jewish identity had triumphed. In a letter on November 4 to Herrmann, Brod boldly declared:

> We have experienced here a complete victory of the Jewish national idea over assimilationism and are in the middle of a movement whose grandeur we never anticipated.[95]

Brod remained confident that the new government would recognize Jewish nationality. So too did his colleagues on the Jewish National Council, who reported to the World Zionist Organization in late December that the German "assimilationists," that is, the leaders of the Prague Jewish community, did not understand that only Jewish national politics would work in the Czech state. Zionists felt confident that they had real influence on the government, most of whose members sympathized with the Jewish national position.[96] After their audiences with President Masaryk on December 31, 1918 and March 22, 1919, the Jewish National Council believed that he would recognize the Jewish nation in Czechoslovakia.[97]

The Zionist sense of triumph grew as support for Jewish nationalism mushroomed in the months following the end of the war, especially among Jews in Moravia and Silesia. In early November 1918, "Sinai," the organization of orthodox Jews in Prague, joined the Zionist body, a step that *Selbstwehr* hailed as a sign of the "victory of the national idea in Jewry."[98] By February 1919, Brod could report that the Jewish National Council in Prague enjoyed very good relations with the orthodox.[99] Even more significantly, Jewish National Committees (usually called *Jüdische Volksräte*) sprang up in many cities in Moravia and Silesia and affiliated with the Prague-based Jewish National Council for Czechoslovakia. Moreover, in Moravia and Silesia even the *Kultusgemeinden*, traditionally opposed to Jewish nationalism, declared their support for it. As early as October 30, the Federation of Moravian IKGs adopted a resolution recognizing the Jews as a nation, and on November 10, a similar federation in Silesia voted to support the Jewish national program.[100] The *Jüdischer Volksrat* in Brünn, established on November 5, sent a deputation jointly with the federation of Moravian IKGs to the local Národní Výbor requesting political and civil equality as well as national minority rights, including representation in all political, economic, and cultural bodies in the state. The *Volksrat* also wanted the authorities to recognize the Jewish National Council as the sole representative of the Jewish people. It felt confident that "in the Czecho-Slovak state all our goals will be realized."[101] In January 1919, the council urged the Jews of Brünn to indicate on the local census that they belonged to the Jewish nation, and over half of the Jews in the city did so.[102] By the spring, Jewish nationalists in Moravia had organized a provincial national council and had begun to plan the establishment of Jewish national schools with Czech language instruction.[103]

Zionists also welcomed the opportunity to tap the traditional Jews of Slovakia for the cause of Jewish nationalism. In December, the Jewish National Council sent an orthodox Jew, M. Ungar, to Slovakia to mobilize the Jews there,[104] and it also supported local attempts to spread Jewish nationalism.[105] The Zionist press painted a positive picture of the orthodox Jews of Slovakia, those in the orbit of the Pressburg yeshiva, and the Hasidim of Eastern Slovakia.[106] In an open letter to all "national Jews" in January 1919, the Prague Zionist establishment expressed its delight that so many delegates from Slovakia had attended the first National Congress of Czechoslovak Jews held that month. Such participation revealed, they declared, "that in the large, Jewishly-conscious Jewry of the new province of the Czechoslovak state we have found a reservoir of vitality for our people."[107] The congress, attended by over 300 delegates, confirmed the Zionist conviction that most Jews supported Jewish nationalism and welcomed the Zionists as their leaders.[108]

As self-appointed leaders of the Jewish people, the Zionists felt responsible for all Jews in Czechoslovakia. Accordingly, the *Jüdischer Nationalrat* intervened regularly with the government, sometimes at the request of the World Zionist Organization, to protest pogroms wherever they occurred[109] and to petition the authorities to postpone or cancel threatened expulsions of Galician refugees.[110] The Council also engaged in relief activities for the estimated 18,000 Galician Jewish refugees in Czechoslovakia, who as foreigners no longer received state subsidies.[111]

The Jewish National Council also sought to take over the Jewish religious communities and convert them into democratic *Volksgemeinden*, a goal of Zionist politics since 1898. As early as November 4, 1918, the *Jüdischer Nationalrat* in Prague asked the IKG there to form a joint commission to reformulate the voting rules for the Jewish community on the basis of universal suffrage. Although members of the Jewish community board expressed their annoyance at Zionist interference in communal affairs, they nevertheless agreed to discuss joint political action with the Zionists.[112] The memorandum of agreement worked out by the *Jüdischer Nationalrat* and the IKG, by a committee chaired by Max Brod, greatly exaggerated the danger of internal divisions within the Jewish community and the need to avoid communal war. Insisting that neither side had to compromise its convictions to work together on common problems, the memorandum demanded parity for both groups in all matters. The memorandum proposed creating a commission, composed of representatives of the *Jüdischer Nationalrat*, the Prague IKG, the provincial federations of Jewish communities, and other large Jewish organizations, to work for "all common Jewish interests" and especially "for the departure of the refugees."[113]

Chafing at the challenge to their previously undisputed authority in Jewish affairs and uncertain about the political future, the Prague IKG board nevertheless agreed in principle on November 18 to create the proposed Jewish commission.[114] What is most remarkable is the relative ease with which the Zionists engineered this cooperation. The Prague Jewish notables undoubtedly agreed so quickly because in mid-November they feared anti-Semitic violence against the refugees and because the political situation convinced them of the wisdom of cooperating with the Zionists, especially in light of growing Zionist strength and pro-Zionist attitudes among government leaders.

Such cooperation did not last long. By the following week, the members of the Prague IKG became angry with the Zionists for wanting more than their fair share of delegates. They adhered to the conservative notion that people who paid more taxes should have more power and resented that the Jewish nationalists were dictating the terms of democratizing the IKG.[115] On December 5, the *Jüdischer Nationalrat* demanded the resignation of IKG president Alois Koserak, but the board responded by expressing its firm confidence in Koserak's leadership and refusing to allow him to resign.[116] At the same time, the IKG publicly announced that the Jewish National Council did not represent the interests of Czechoslovak Jewry, much to the dismay of *Nationalrat* leaders.[117] Although the IKG took some modest steps to broaden the franchise in communal elections and to ensure the inclusion of Czech-speaking Jews, the IKG remained a largely unreformed institution in the following decades.[118] Jewish nationalists in Prague, unlike their colleagues in Moravia and Silesia, did not succeed in taking over the Jewish communal establishment. Jewish communual leaders undoubtedly felt that circumstances did not require them to surrender to their ideological opponents.

Despite this failure, the Jewish National Council felt that its ideology provided the most viable identity for Jews in Czechoslovakia. After all, Jewish national identity rendered the Jews neutral in the nationality conflict between Czechs and Germans or Slovaks and Magyars and enabled them to be patriotic citizens of the state, speakers of whatever language they preferred, and at the same time members of the Jewish nation. Max Brod, the writer and literary critic who served as vice president of the *Jüdischer Nationalrat* of Czechoslovakia, explained Jewish national identity most eloquently. Brod described himself as a friend of all things German, but "not a member of the German *Volk*," instead, a man related by culture, but not by blood, to the Germans. After all, "language, education, reading material, culture have made me a thankful friend of the German people, but not a German." Passionately attached to German culture, he wanted to preserve German cultural institutions in Prague. Although he spoke Czech fluently and loved Czech folk customs, music, and landscape, Czech culture remained foreign to him. Brod felt that Jewish nationalism, especially when it eschewed chauvinism and worked for humanity and justice, provided him with an identity that accurately reflected his views.[119]

The Zionist press regularly made the case that a Jewish national identity best suited the Jews in Czechoslovakia. In an appeal of November 15, 1918, for example, *Selbstwehr* reassured readers that they could be loyal citizens of Czechoslovakia, staunch adherents of Czech or German culture, and also work for the interests of the entire Jewish people through the Jewish National Council.[120] The *Jüdische Volksstimme* in Brünn insisted a week later that "only a strong, honorable, manly national politics can actually protect the interests of all Jewry."[121] Appealing to the Jews to declare themselves on the census to be members of the Jewish nation, the *Jüdischer Volksrat* in Brünn warned Jews against becoming the slaves of either the Germans or the Czechs. Professing membership in the Jewish nation, the paper averred, allowed Jews to avoid the nationality conflict and assert their loyalty to the new state.[122] Zionist leaders assumed that anti-Semitic violence resulted from Jewish involvement in "the camps of foreign nations" or that many people regarded the Jews as "representatives of the old Austrian spirit." Only a Jewish national identity would cause anti-Semitism to subside and overcome Czech resentment.[123] Although by the spring of 1919 many Bohemian Zionists worried that diaspora politics deflected their attention from the true aim of Zionism, the establishment of a Jewish state in Palestine, the majority agreed that the quest for Jewish national rights in Czechoslovakia served Zionism and the Jews in the new republic.[124]

Many non-Zionist Jews, especially in Moravia and Silesia, agreed with the Zionist assessment. In December 1918, Dr. Theodor Sonnenschein, the president of the IKG of Troppau, Silesia and a prominent member of Bnai Brith, wrote an article, "Religion or Nation?" in the *Österreichische Wochenschrift* explaining why a Jewish national identity was necessary in Czechoslovakia. Sonnenschein reminded his readers that Jews were not merely a religious group. Religion, after all, hardly united a Jewish university professor with the Belzer rebbe! "What binds us is not religion," he insisted, "but many thousands of years of common history, of persecution and oppression endured together." Conceding that Jews did not form a nation by conventional standards, he argued that Jews nevertheless formed a special people. Whereas in nationally unified states Jews had to identify with the dominant nation, in mixed-language countries Jews had to declare themselves a separate nation "if they did not want to suffer the same fate as the Jews in Lemberg or Slovakia." In Moravian cities, where battles between Czechs and Germans raged, asserting either traditional German loyalty or a new-found Czech identity would surely lead to the "annihilation" of the Jews. The situation was even worse in trilingual Silesia. Here it was "a commandment of self-preservation" for the Silesian Jewish communities to support a Jewish national identity.[125]

Although Sonnenschein defended Jewish nationalism on pragmatic rather than on ideological grounds, he nevertheless regarded it as the only correct path for Jews in Czechoslovakia. So too did Max Beer, an orthodox spokesman from Mährisch Ostrau, Moravia. He urged all observant Jews to support Jewish nationalism because it would prevent apostasy and encourage Jews to return to the fold. Once Jews realized that they were not Germans or Czechs, but rather Jews, members of the Jewish nation, then they could be reeducated in the ways of Torah.[126] Aware of such non-Zionist support for their program, the Jewish national committees in Moravia and Silesia emphasized that they were not arms of the Zionist movement but merely concerned with Jewish national identity in the new state.[127]

Committed to a national program for Jews, the Jewish National Council in Czechoslovakia lobbied at the Paris Peace Conference for national minority rights for Jews in Czechoslovakia, Poland, and elsewhere in Eastern Europe.[128] The Council's delegates, Hugo Bergmann and Norbert Adler, joined the effort launched by the World Zionist Organization, the American Jewish Congress, and Jewish national councils from Eastern Europe to guarantee not only civil rights but also national rights for Jews in the successor states. The Peace Conference, horrified by the pogroms in Poland, did force the Poles to agree to some minimal minority rights for Jews, including state support for Jewish schools, but the Allies did not include national minority rights for Jews in the treaty with Czechoslovakia, which they assumed would treat its minorities fairly.[129] Jewish nationalists were disappointed that Versailles failed to guarantee them national rights,[130] but in February 1920, they delighted when the Czechoslovak government recognized the Jews as one of the nations of the new state.[131]

Although the Jewish National Councils of Czechoslovakia had not demanded Jewish voting curias, in the municipal council elections of June 15, 1919, they nevertheless campaigned vigorously for candidates pledged to represent Jewish interests. Warning the Jews to remain neutral in the nationality conflicts, Zionist propagandists urged Jewish men and women to participate as Jews in public life.[132] They castigated Jewish liberals for siding with the Germans, whose numbers included anti-Semites, and argued that for Jews to vote for Jewish candidates instead of German ones was an assertion of Jewish identity, not an act of treason toward German culture.[133] Indeed, the *Jüdische Volksstimme* in Brünn reminded the voters: "We are Jews! Not Czechs, not Germans! As Jews we want to represent Jewish interests," not simply strengthen the Germans.[134]

In both Prague and Brünn, the bourgeois Zionists and the Socialist Poale Zion entered separate electoral slates, largely because the latter wanted to protect the interests of Jewish workers. Interestingly, all the "Jewish" slates included several women, a reflection of the new reality of female suffrage and the need to attract female voters.[135] The Zionists considered the municipal elections a great success, even though only a few Zionists actually won mandates. In Prague, Jewish lists attracted about 5000 votes, sending three Zionists and one Poale Zionist to represent Jewish interests in the city council, and one of them, Ludwig Singer, to sit on the smaller *Stadtrat*. In Brünn two Jews received mandates to represent Jewish interests, and similar small numbers of "Jewish" delegates won elections to city councils in many other cities in Bohemia and Moravia.[136]

The Jewish nationalists in Czechoslovakia felt that their version of Jewish identity solved the dilemma of Jews in the new state, and they convinced themselves that they had become the dominant voice in Jewish affairs, especially since Czech leaders like Thomas Masaryk and Edward Beneš sympathized with Zionism. Yet it is not at all clear how most Jews resolved the crisis of identity that they faced. There is no question that growing numbers of Jews, especially in Moravia, Silesia, and Slovakia, began to assert a Jewish national identity. It is also true that this identity grew at the expense of the old German identity, at least as measured by the census. But Jews who identified with the Jewish nation did not necessarily abandon their German cultural identity. A Jewish national identity enabled them to convert their old Austrian tripartite identity into a new Czechoslovakian one, espousing loyalty to the multinational state and its benevolent old ruler, adherence to German, Czech, or Magyar language and culture, and at the same time to Jewish ethnic identity. Just as in the old Austria the Jews were jokingly referred to as the only Austrians in Austria, now Jews would be the only Czechoslovakians in Czechoslovakia. But not all Jews wanted to profess membership in the Jewish nation. The Czech Jews, those who had long identified with the Czech national movement, hoped for a growth in Czech identity among the Jews. Yet, although Jews increasingly learned Czech, the number of Jews who identified as members of the Czech nation did not grow significantly in the interwar period.[137]

German-speaking Jews who found it impossible to assume a Jewish national identity, even in the new political context, faced the most severe dilemma, especially in Bohemia. They thought of themselves as members of the German cultural community and as Jews, but not in the Zionist sense. Unfortunately, they did not leave behind much evidence of the nature of their crisis and how they resolved it. Bohemian non-Zionist Jews did not publish a newspaper in which they debated the issue. In the spring of 1919, the Viennese Jewish newspaper *Österreichische Wochenschrift* reported that a group of Jews in Reichenberg, Bohemia had published a declaration in their local German-language newspaper affirming that they were "German citizens of the Jewish confession" whose Jewishness consisted in belonging to the Jewish religious community but whose nationality was German. "By virtue of our mother tongue and language of daily speech, our education and upbringing, and all our thoughts and feelings we belong to the German *Volk*."[138] Such statements of membership in the German *Volk* were quite rare for Jews, and in the absence of other evidence, it is hard to determine how typical it was. Nina Lieberman, the daughter of a Galician rabbi who spent her childhood in Tachov, Bohemia, remembered that the Jews of Tachov "clung to German culture" in the 1920s and that the president of the Jewish community, a "staunch representative of German 'Kultur' had a portrait of Bismarck hanging over his desk!"[139] Undoubtedly, most Jews in Bohemia persisted in their German identities, which they understood in cultural terms. Like the Zionists, they hoped that Czechoslovakia would function like the old Austria, allowing them the luxury of a Czechoslovakian political identity, a German cultural identity, and a Jewish ethnic one. Although they never would have announced their Jewish ethnic affiliation as boldly as the Zionists or the Jews in Eastern Europe, they nevertheless understood that Jews formed a separate religio-ethnic group, a community of fate, which, to borrow Fredrik Barth's terminology, maintained clear ethnic borders.

Reconstructing Identity in German-Austria

In the rump state of German-Austria, the situation was radically different and far more problematic. Unlike Czechoslovakia, *Deutschösterreich* was a nation-state in which the overwhelming majority of inhabitants considered themselves members of the German nation. Indeed, in the spirit of national self-determination, many of them sought *Anschluss* with Germany.[140] In such a nation-state, it would be difficult for Jews to insist that they did not belong to the dominant nation, especially since they spoke its language and identified with its culture. The creation of a German-Austria presented the Jews who lived there, essentially the Jews of Vienna, with a grave crisis. They had liked the old Austrian identity because it had afforded them so much latitude for Jewish ethnicity, but such ethnicity would be more problematic in a nation-state that demanded the political, cultural, and ethnic/national loyalty of its citizens. The Jews in German-Austria certainly professed their loyalty to the new state as well as their affiliation with German language and culture, but they could not bring themselves to adopt a German national identity that had the same meaning for them as it did for the Germans. The virulence of anti-Semitism in the new state did not make their task of adopting a German-Austrian national identity any easier. Although they generally did not view the new state as a reincarnation of old Austria, they nevertheless hoped that they could continue the old Austrian tripartite identity: loyal to the state and its culture yet also functioning as a separate ethnic group. Indeed, although the new political logic might have dictated embracing a German national identity, in fact more Jews turned to Jewish ethnicity and also to full-blown Jewish nationalism than ever before.

Zionists and Jewish nationalists reacted to the creation of the new Austria by assuming, without actual evidence, that the new German-Austrian nation-state would practice the same kind of tolerance for national minorities as did the old multinational Austria. Under the leadership of Robert Stricker, they tirelessly lobbied for the state to recognize the Jews as a nation and grant them national rights. Such rights were never even remotely possible, but Stricker and the Austrian Zionist establishment persisted nevertheless. Such persistence, lasting through the 1930s, reflected the inability of these men to come to grips with the new political reality. They dealt with the crisis by acting as if it simply did not exist. They had developed an ideology of Jewish nationalism suited to the situation of the Jews in the Habsburg Monarchy, and they continued to cling to it, unable to change. Nevertheless, despite the fact that Jewish national rights were not viable in Austria, increasing numbers of Jews affiliated with Zionism because it offered them an identity that enabled them to cope with escalating anti-Semitism.

As in Czechoslovakia, the Zionists in Austria created a Jewish National Council to demand national rights for Jews in the new state. The Council, originally created on October 20 for all-Austria, reconstituted as the Jewish National Council of German-Austria on November 4, 1918, declaring the loyalty of "the citizens of Jewish nationality" to the *Volksstaat Deutschösterreich*. Decrying the old Austria for oppressing so many national groups, the Jewish National Council demanded that the new state recognize the Jews as a nation and accord them civil and political equality as well as minority rights, namely the right to control Jewish cultural affairs, including education, and Jewish representation in all elected bodies and relevant government agencies. The Council also demanded the reconstitution of Jewish communities as democratic *Volksgemeinden*.[141]

Such demands for full national autonomy came despite the opposition of Robert Weltsch, a Prague Zionist sent to Vienna in 1918 by the World Zionist Organization. In October 1918, Weltsch had watched events unfold, sharing his apprehension with fellow Prague Zionist Leo Herrmann, then in Berlin. Weltsch had long regarded the Vienna Zionists with disdain, but in the confusion of events that autumn, he became convinced that they were not only incompetent but also misguided. On October 28, he lamented that the Viennese Zionists still did not have a realistic program, focused as they were on such outdated slogans as national autonomy and national minority rights. In particular, he complained that Robert Stricker refused to accept the fact that Galicia and Bukovina no longer belonged to Austria and that the territorial basis for his program no longer existed. Weltsch certainly considered the Jews a nation and wanted the Jewish National Council to represent Jews to the government, but he felt that the old politics were "highly destructive" and feared the impact of even modest requests for cultural autonomy on the civil status of the Jews.[142] Herrmann agreed that it was no longer realistic for the Zionists to work for Jewish national autonomy in Austria.[143]

Even Stricker must have realized that the government would never grant Jewish voting curias or full national autonomy, because under his leadership, the *Jüdischer Nationalrat* did not lobby actively for such traditional Jewish nationalist goals. The Council insisted that the Jews formed a nation and that the Austrian government should recognize them as such, but it did not spell out exactly what such recognition might entail. Even Stricker himself, in the *Wiener Morgenzeitung*, the daily newspaper he began publishing in January 1919, never called for full autonomy, although he regularly repeated the initial position of the Jewish National Council, calling for "national/cultural self-administration" and Jewish delegates on all representative bodies.[144] The Council propagandized for Jewish national identity, tried to elect Jewish nationalists to the new parliament, and sought the mantle of leadership in the Jewish community. It did not succeed to the extent that it hoped, but it did offer an attractive identity for some Jews in Austria.

Immediately after its formation, the Jewish National Council entered into negotiations with the *Israelitische Kultusgemeinde* ostensibly to formulate a joint program but also to force the Jewish community to democratize its electoral rules, paving the way, the Zionists surely hoped, for them to take over the community.

The negotiations broke down immediately and the Zionists demanded the resignation of octogenarian president Alfred Stern, whom they regarded as the embodiment of the assimilationism they opposed. In an angry speech to the board of the IKG on November 5, Stern insisted that the Zionist desire for separate Jewish voting cadastres would be a "death blow" to the Jews, guaranteeing that the state would treat them as foreigners. He urged the IKG to avoid contact with the *Jüdischer Nationalrat*, but the board, fearing violence, voted instead to accept his resignation and to form a joint commission with the Council to formulate new voting rules.[145] Despite this apparent success, the Jewish National Council did not take over the Jewish community or even significantly change its voting rules.[146]

The Jewish National Council nevertheless viewed itself as the leader of the Jewish people, not just in German-Austria, but all over the former Habsburg Monarchy as well. Thus it intervened with the authorities on behalf of Galician refugees in both Vienna and Czechoslovakia, urging the postponement of expulsion orders. It also worked on behalf of pogrom victims everywhere. In November 1918, it presented formal protests to the Polish Liquidation Commission in Cracow and to Poland's representatives in Vienna. It organized protest meetings in Vienna, helped provide charitable assistance to pogrom victims, and urged the World Zionist Organization to use its influence with the Allied governments to put pressure on Poland and Czechoslovakia to end the violence.[147] In the months that followed, it continued these tasks.[148] In July 1919, for example, it urged World Zionist Organization leaders to intervene with the Czech leaders in Versailles to end the pogroms then raging in Slovakia.[149] Exaggerating its role, the Jewish National Council argued that this work entitled it to assume the mantle of leadership in the Jewish world.[150]

In Vienna itself, the Council became involved in welfare work on behalf of starving Jewish children.[151] It also made plans to create Jewish national schools whose curriculum would include Hebrew, Jewish history, and literature.[152] The *Jüdischer Nationalrat* was especially proud that it organized demobilized Jewish soldiers into a Jewish unit within the Vienna city guard to protect the Jews, especially in heavily Jewish Leopoldstadt and Brigittenau, from anti-Semitic violence.[153] Despite their hostility to the Jewish National Council, Jewish notables in Vienna supported the Council's paramilitary group. In February 1919, the IKG provided a subvention of 30,000 crowns to the group, and in May 1919 gave it an additional 3000 crowns.[154]

The issue of citizenship in German-Austria presented the Jewish National Council with its most significant ideological challenge. Regarding nation and state as one, German nationalists in the new state wanted to predicate citizenship on membership in the German nation. The *Jüdischer Nationalrat* had a different view of the state, one in which citizenship was predicated not on national identity, but on political loyalty. They regarded themselves as loyal citizens of the Austrian Republic and opposed any attempt to limit citizenship to "Germans," especially since they regarded themselves as members of the Jewish nation, not the German one. Aware of the anti-Semitic subtext of the attempt to limit citizenship, the Council intervened with the government and obtained President

Karl Renner's promise that the law would not adversely affect the Jews.[155]
Hence Austrian law did not restrict citizenship to "Germans," but it did exclude
former Austrians from Galicia who migrated after August 1, 1914—that is, the
refugees.[156]

The Jewish National Council fervently hoped that the new Austria would not
function as a German nation-state. Indeed, the Hebrew title for the Jewish
National Council for German-Austria, *Moetzet Leumit L'yehudei Austria Ha'ashkenazit,* purposefully used the medieval Hebrew word for German (*ashkenazit*),
with its vague territorial references, rather than the modern Hebrew word (*ger-
manit*) with its obvious connection to modern German nationalism, to distance
itself from the notion that the new Austria in fact was a German nation-state.[157]
Jewish nationalists hoped that like the old Austria, the Austrian Republic would
simply be a state, albeit one that adhered to the principle of self-determination
and allowed them to affirm a Jewish national identity.[158] At the same time, they
insisted that "we German-speaking national Jews" are "friends of German culture and the German people, in whose language we think and feel."[159] As one
spokesmen for Zionist youth noted: "We know that we are not Germans of the
Mosaic religion, but rather Jews of German speech."[160] Naturally, Zionists proclaimed their absolute loyalty to the state. One February 1919 article in Stricker's
Wiener Morgenzeitung argued that Jews in German-Austria were "members of the
Jewish people whose center is in Palestine" and citizens of the state "in whose
flourishing they take an active interest." Not only was there no conflict between
these two concerns, but the fact that Jews had no territorial interests elsewhere in
Europe and no unique language rendered them the most loyal citizens.[161]

Zionist spokesmen engaged in a polemical battle in late 1918–1919 to convince Jews in German-Austria that only a Jewish national position served their
interests. They attacked the traditional leaders of the Jewish community as traitors and extravagantly enjoined "all right-minded Jews" to wage "a war of annihilation" against them.[162] Robert Stricker remained convinced that only a
vigorous Jewish nationalist posture would deflate anti-Semitism and persuade
Gentiles to respect the Jews.[163] A staunch political Zionist, who later became a
member of the Revisionists and then the Jewish State Party, Stricker remained
committed to his diaspora nationalism throughout the interwar period.[164] Other
Zionists emphasized the need for education to inculcate Jewish nationalist ideology among the Jews. Anitta Müller, for example, felt that Jewish women would
be the prime bearers of the Jewish national idea if only they received a proper
education.[165]

The National Assembly elections of February 16, 1919 provided the Jewish
nationalists with the opportunity to propagandize for their cause. They focused
their efforts on the area of Vienna with the highest concentration of Jews, the
voting district "Vienna North-East," which included the heavily Jewish Leopoldstadt and Brigittenau. The nationalists urged Jews there to vote for the Jewish nationalist list headed by Robert Stricker, Leopold Plaschkes, and Erna Patak.
Stricker, they vowed, would represent the Jews as a Jew in the new national assembly.[166] Convinced that only a nationalist posture would end anti-Semitism,
Zionist spokesmen railed against candidates who, while Jewish, did not represent

Jewish national interests, especially against left-liberal Julius Ofner.[167] Since women could now vote for the first time, the Zionist press made specific appeals to women to vote for the Jewish nationalist list. Stricker's *Wiener Morgenzeitung* contained a regular feature, "Women's Rights and Women's Work," edited by Anitta Müller, which insisted that women, while not yet politically mature, nevertheless were the bearers of the Jewish national idea.[168]

Jewish nationalists rejoiced when Robert Stricker won a mandate in the constituent national assembly. In a system of proportional voting, the real victors were the Social Democrats and Christian Socials; Jewish nationalists received slightly less than 5% of the votes in Vienna North-East, an area at least 25% Jewish. They nevertheless insisted that Stricker's election revealed "the death of assimilationism," the success of Jewish nationalism, and the end of anti-Semitism. They glorified Stricker as the man who would now not only represent Jewish interests effectively, but also (despite only having one vote) win for the Jews the national rights they deserved.[169] Stricker shared this assessment. He introduced himself to the national assembly by declaring, "I am a Jew,"[170] and he spent his short time there inveighing against anti-Semitism.[171]

Jewish nationalists also fielded candidates in the Vienna municipal elections and the Lower Austria provincial elections in May 1919. Arguing the need for Jewish national representatives to deal with the problem of refugees and anti-Semitism in public life and to work for the establishment of Jewish schools, the Jewish nationalists presented lists in all of the districts in Vienna where sizeable numbers of Jews resided. The lists contained the usual Zionist stalwarts as well as the names of several woman, including Anitta Müller and Erna Patak.[172] Once again, the Zionists hailed their meager victory—Jakob Ehrlich, Leopold Plaschkes, and Bruno Pollak-Parnau were elected to the Vienna city council—as a sign that Jewish nationalism had won the hearts and minds of all Austrian Jews.[173] In his maiden speech at the Vienna City Council on May 22, Jakob Ehrlich announced that Jewish nationalists would never infringe on the German character of the city. They only wanted to develop Jewish culture and guarantee Jewish equality.[174]

Although the Zionists had not lobbied for autonomy during the electoral campaigns, they did hope that the Paris Peace Conference would see fit to grant the Jews national minority rights in all the successor states, including German-Austria. As early as January 1919, the Jewish National Council asked the World Zionist Organization to see to it that the Allies require Austria to recognize the Jews as a nation, to grant them the right to administer their own cultural institutions, including schools and charities, and to allow Jewish representation on all governmental bodies.[175] All spring, Viennese Zionists insisted that minority rights were the only way to protect Jewish rights in the new, anti-Semitic nation-states.[176] The Zionists must have been disappointed that the treaty with Austria protected Jewish civil rights but contained no provisions for Jewish minority rights of any sort.

The events of the first half of 1919 caused many Zionists to take stock of their relationship both to the old Austria and to the new. During the course of the elections, they expressed a genuine pleasure in the fact that they now lived in a democratic republic. Comfortable with the new form of government, they began to criticize repressive policies of Habsburg Austria.[177] Moroeover, they resented the Allies for regarding German-Austria as the continuation of old Austria and punishing it at Versailles.[178] Yet their vision of the new Austria did not resemble that of other citizens. In the first place, most Zionists felt uncomfortable with the possiblity of *Anschluss* with Germany, even if they deemed it a matter for the "Germans" to decide and declared their formal neutrality on the issue.[179] Indeed, Stricker voted against *Anschluss* at the national assembly.[180] In addition, Zionists hoped Austria would not be a real nation-state, and they acted as if it would allow them the status of a separate nation. Finally, they behaved as if Habsburg Austria still existed functionally, faithfully reporting in the press on Jews in Bohemia, Moravia, Galicia, and Bukovina. Stricker himself yearned for some new form of Danubian unity to replace the old, beloved Habsburg Monarchy. In a signed editorial in the *Wiener Morgenzeitung* in late June 1919, Stricker expressed his frustration with East Central Europe, a collection of disorganized, militaristic, despotic, chauvinistic states that could easily lead Europe into endless, bloody war. Although he did not seek to revive the Monarchy, Stricker argued that "the only possible solution" to the problems that beset the region lay in "the unification of the peoples of Austria-Hungary in a federation of states."[181] Obviously, such a federation fit his agenda far better than the nation-state in which he lived.

It seems that the Jewish nationalists did not really succeed at any of their endeavors in the months after the Monarchy's collapse. Their call for elections for a permanent Jewish National Council fell on deaf ears as insufficient numbers of Jews registered to vote.[182] Their commitment to Jewish national rights could not succeed given the political realities. They lived in a nation-state that would never accord such rights, and they had lost the territorial basis for Jewish nationalism, the hinterland in Galicia and Bukovina. Diaspora nationalism had a better chance of success in Eastern Europe than in Austria. In Poland or Lithuania, where anti-Semitism raged, Jews were one of several national minorities, and masses of traditional, Yiddish-speaking Jews formed the basis of a separate Jewish society.[183] Yet although the Jewish National Council in Vienna did not take over the IKG or elect more than a tiny number of representatives, all of whom lost their seats in the next round of elections, the Jewish nationalists did succeed in making themselves important players in Austrian Jewish politics. They also challenged the other Jews of Austria, those that did not espouse Jewish nationalism, to rethink the meaning of Jewish identity in the new state.

The dissolution of the Habsburg Monarchy and the creation of German-Austria called into question all the fundamental assumptions on which the identity of the majority of Vienna's Jews rested. They no longer lived in the capital of a large, multinational empire that was not obsessed with its German identity, but in a city that seemed too big for the small German nation-state over which it presided. They would no longer enjoy the comfort of their old Habsburg tripartite identity that allowed them to be Austrian by political loyalty, German by culture, and ethnically Jewish. German-Austria now required them to be Germans, not just Austrians, but they could not bring themselves to adopt a German national identity. They had no trouble declaring loyalty to the new state, and they confidently asserted their attachment to German culture, but they found it hard to accept that cultural affiliation would no longer be enough. In the months that followed the end of World War I, therefore, the ordinary Jews of Vienna faced the most complicated identity crisis of all the former Habsburg Jews.

That identity crisis was complicated by the threat of anti-Semitism and the challenge of Zionism. No pogroms erupted in German-Austria in the aftermath of the war as they did in most of the other Habsburg successor states, but anti-Semitic agitation in a population exhausted by the war and its aftermath nevertheless made the Jews very nervous. Moreover, many Jews feared that the attempt to make Austria German could easily lead to discrimination against them, even to loss of citizenship rights, especially since radical German nationalists denied to Jews membership in the German nation. Adopting a new German-Austrian identity in this context would prove very difficult. At the same time, the relative success of Zionism all over former Habsburg Austria, not to mention its success internationally in obtaining the Balfour Declaration, by which the British government pledged itself to develop a Jewish homeland in Palestine, forced Jews to come to grips with the nature of Jewish identity in the nation-state.

Vienna's non-Zionist Jewish majority responded to the crisis by engaging in a serious debate about Jewish identity. An endless stream of articles in the liberal and orthodox press reflected the turmoil and conflict that accompanied the Jewish quest to reconstruct an identity that would fit changed political realities. Insisting that the Zionists did not represent all Jews, and that the Jews did not form a nation at all, Jewish spokesmen nevertheless declared that the Jews were not Germans either, at least not in the way that German nationalists understood the term. Instead, the Jews were Jews, members of the Jewish people and not just adherents of the Jewish faith. Jews could be loyal citizens of German-Austria, connected to the Austrian soil on which they lived, and committed to German culture, but also proud Jews. Thus, like the Zionists whom they detested, liberal and orthodox Jewish leaders hoped that the new nation-state would allow them the luxury of separating their political, cultural, and national identities, of being simultaneously Austrians and Jews. Although they eschewed Jewish nationalism, and would never become militant about Jewish ethnicity, they too retreated to the comfort of a Jewish ethnic identity, hopeful that despite anti-Semitism the new state would tolerate their inability to become part of the German *Volk,* although they embraced German culture.

From the pages of the Jewish press to the halls of the *Israelitische Kultusgemeinde,* non-Zionists in German-Austria rejected the Zionist bid for leadership and insisted that the Jewish National Councils did not represent the Jews. In mid-October 1918, one writer for the *Österreichische Wochenschrift* heatedly decried Jewish nationalist solutions to the Jewish problem. Although he willingly conceded that national minority rights might be necessary for the persecuted Jews in Eastern Europe, such rights, he insisted, would be "impossible," "unbearable," and "disastrous" for western Jews.[184] Repeated articles in the months that followed insisted that Jews did not form a nation and expressed hostility to the notion of Jewish national rights.[185] Jewish liberals and the orthodox asserted that the Jewish National Council did not represent all Jews and they issued regular calls for Jewish unity, presumably assuming that they would determine the agenda of a unified Jewry.[186]

Those who rejected Jewish national rights feared that anti-Semites would use such minority rights as an excuse to deprive the Jews of their civil rights. In its November 5 appeal to the Jews of Vienna, the IKG argued that the demands of the *Jüdischer Nationalrat* could have dangerous consequences for the full equality of the Jews in the new state.[187] Jewish spokesmen expressed their anxiety that if the Jews formed a nation, they would return to the ghetto.[188] The orthodox worried that Jewish national rights would facilitate an anti-Semitic boycott of the Jews and encourage anti-Semites to regard them as a "state within the state," a group deserving oppression.[189] During the national assembly elections in early 1919, liberal politician Julius Ofner charged that Zionist demands would only encourage anti-Jewish hatred and render the Jews foreigners in their own homeland.[190]

From the moment German-Austria came into existence, Jews struggled with the issue of their identity in the new state. In the same article of late October 1918, in which he had lamented the demise of Habsburg Austria, Heinrich Schreiber sensitively described the dilemma faced by most Jews. Rejecting the notion that Jews formed a nation, he insisted that Jews should feel and think themselves Jewish and should want to be known as Jews. At the same time, Jews were loyal citizens of the political community "in which our ancestors lived and worked, in which they died, in whose culture and economic and political improvement they participated, . . . for which we ourselves live and die, often rewarded with ingratitude and hatred." Loyal to the new state, he could not bring himself to say he was a German in a national sense. Indeed, for him "Germanness" remained cultural and Jewish identity primary. He concluded, "We are Jews, we are Austrians, and when that is too little we are German-Austrians, by birth and customs, education and culture, attitude and feeling."[191] Others expressed similar views. "L.W.," a woman speaking in the name of many other women, transferred her traditional loyalty from Habsburg Austria to the new state. She argued:

> Yes, we have a fatherland, a homeland! For it we sacrificed our husbands, sons, and grandsons without complaint, . . . for this beloved, poor, and now dismembered fatherland, for German-Austria, we live and die. This land, whose language we speak and understand, where we have our families, our lives, and our dear graves, is and remains our homeland.[192]

Thus for "L.W.," apparently, political identity was mostly a matter of attachment to place, the place where her relatives were buried.

None of the Jews who tried in late 1918 to come to grips in the press with Jewish identity asserted a German national identity. All of them continued to understand their "German-ness" purely in cultural terms. In early December, a group of Jewish notables, including officers of the Austrian Israelite Union, the Bnai Brith, and Jewish communities outside Vienna, published an appeal in the *Österreichische Wochenschrift* asserting that Jews were citizens of German-Austria and German "through *Heimat*, language, and education."[193] Though these men feared that anti-Semites might deprive them of rights if they did not consider themselves German,[194] they nevertheless did not feel comfortable with a German national identity.

Their attitude to *Anschluss* with Germany reflected the unwillingness of Jews to see themselves as German in a national sense. Although there was no debate on the issue in the liberal or orthodox press, memoirs—admittedly written after the Holocaust and therefore potentially biased against *Anschluss*—do attest to the reluctance of Jews to be part of greater Germany. Lilian Bader, for example, noted that Vienna "had everything to lose and nothing to gain by being incorporated into greater Germany."[195] Similarly, Erna Segal remembered that most people had no interest in *Anschluss*.[196] Although Toni Stolper and her husband Gustav did support union with Germany, and even moved there in 1924,[197] most Jews did not want to be part of a greater Germany.

Indeed, there is ample evidence that Austrian Jews continued to behave as if Habsburg Austria still existed, at least in an abstract sense. Not only did the Jewish press continue to cover events in the Habsburg successor states in great detail, but also Jews mobilized their now-meager resources to help pogrom victims in Galicia, Bohemia, and Moravia and to intercede on their behalf.[198] The *Österreichische Wochenschrift* reminded its readers that the Galician refugees in Vienna were Austrian citizens, and victims of the war and the collapse of Austria-Hungary, even though German-Austria had refused citizenship to them.[199] Jewish organizations found it both difficult and sad to break up into new national units.[200] Viennese Jewish newspapers circulated beyond the borders of the new Austria.

In the months after World War I, the old debate about the essence of Jewish identity raged once more, spurred on by the Zionist challenge, the escalation of anti-Semitism, and the new political context. Some Jewish notables, repeating the liberal formula developed in the nineteenth century, insisted that Jewish identity was based solely on the Jewish religion.[201] Other Jewish notables disagreed. They too rejected the Zionist definition of the Jews as a nation, but they felt that Jewishness encompassed far more than religious faith. Rabbi David Feuchtwang, for example, wrote an impassioned article in the *Österreichische Wochenschrift* in late December arguing that it was false and unhistorical to label the Jews only a religious group. All Jews, Feuchtwang insisted, agreed with Herzl that the Jews formed "a people, one people." Jews were a nation, but unlike other nations, whose essence was the state or the *Volk*, the essence of Jewish nationhood was the religious idea. Thus, like earlier Viennese rabbis, Feuchtwang concluded that the Jews formed a religio-ethnic group, a *Religionsvolk*.[202] Similarly, in an open letter to Vienna's Zionist chief rabbi Hirsch Perez Chajes, S. Ortony found both religious or national definitions of Jewish identity unsatisfying. He declared that Jews were people who possessed a Jewish heart, respect for the religion of their ancestors, a sense of family, concern for suffering Jews everywhere, and the honor not to abandon Judaism.[203]

Dr. A. Schwadron articulated the meaning of Jewish identity most clearly in his article, "The Jewish Problem in German-Austria," published in late January

1919 in the *Österreichische Wochenschrift*. Lamenting the orgy of national chauvinism that had balkanized Europe and led to a decline in human civilization, Schwadron mourned the demise of nationally tolerant Habsburg Austria. He admitted that most Jews in Austria had assimilated into German culture, but he insisted that Jews were German, not in a *völkish* sense, but in a cultural one. Jews did not form either a separate nation or even a religious group, since most of them no longer practiced Jewish ritual. Rather, Schwadron insisted, Jews were ethnically Jewish because they felt that they belonged to the Jewish people. He concluded that Jews formed a "national-religious" group.[204] S. Krauss made a similar point in his article, "The Crisis of Viennese Jewry," in the journal of the Bnai Brith early in 1919. Although Krauss thought that most Jews in Vienna considered themselves Jews of German nationality for whom religion formed the essence of Jewish identity, he nevertheless argued that a strong sense of belonging to the Jewish people prevented the Jews from assimilating into the nations in whose midst they lived. He concluded:

> We acknowledge that by dint of our excellent religion we [belong] to the Jewish people. . . . We are a nation of those who profess the eternal ideas of Judaism . . . united by common descent, common history, [and] persecution suffered together . . . a nation of priests of the God of Israel, not more and not less.[205]

It seems that most Jews acknowledged that Jewish identity possessed both ethnic and religious dimensions. Such was certainly the view of Josef Samuel Bloch, the feisty editor of the *Österreichische Wochenschrift*, who wrote a series of articles in the summer of 1919 entitled "The Central Jewish Problem." Bloch argued that Jews possessed the "ethnological isolation, uniqueness, and exclusivity" of a race as well as a firm sense of belonging to an "ethnic community" (*Stammesgemeinschaft*). At the same time, Jews formed "a metaphysical-ethical God-community."[206] Perhaps the strongest assertion of Jewish ethnicity came from a spokesman for the Austrian Israelite Union that Bloch had helped form many decades earlier. An article in the Union's journal in the spring of 1919 argued that the Jews were not primarily a *Volk*, but rather a religious community whose members shared the same ethnicity (*Stamm*) and blood.[207]

Orthodox Jews participated in the debate as well. Orthodox spokesmen reiterated their traditional position defining Jewishness similarly as a combination of ethnic and religious elements. An article in early December 1918 in the *Jüdische Korrespondenz* ridiculed nonreligious Jews who said that Jewish identity was based on religion as well as utterly assimilated Jews who felt that the Jews formed a nation. The author insisted that no good Jew could possibly deny the *Volkscharakter* of the Jews, although at the same time he observed that the most important element in Jewish national identity was religion.[208] Led by the Adas Yisroel Schiffschul, Vienna's orthodox synagogues and organizations issued a resolution on December 5 declaring that "through our origins, through our thousands of years of history, and especially through our holy religion we Jews are . . . a closed national community (*Volksgemeinschaft*)."[209]

Although Austrian Jews had long articulated most of these views of Jewish identity, it seems that the experience of war, the dissolution of the Monarchy, and the challenges posed by anti-Semitism, Zionism, and life in a nation-state deepened the Jewish identity of many Austrian Jews. Spokesmen for the Bnai Brith and the Austrian Israelite Union as well as writers in the Jewish press now used much stronger language for Jewish ethnic identity than they had before. Rabbi Adolf Altmann, who left his position in Meran, Tyrol, for Salzburg in the summer of 1919, felt bitter disappointment at the collapse of Habsburg Austria and the rise of anti-Semitism despite so much Jewish sacrifice. He decided, his son Manfred recalled, to focus his attention on the development of Jewish volk-identity and on making the Jewish community a *Volksgemeinde*.[210]

Some Jews became Zionists as a result of their experience during the war and its aftermath and not only because they were moved by the terrible plight of Jews in Eastern Europe. Eric Fischer, for example, remembered that toward the end of the war he became "more and more sympathetic to Zionism," but he did not initially join the movement because Austrian politics had made him "permanently allergic to any nationalistic talk or action." Nevertheless, he did become a Zionist, ostensibly because his wife's family were Zionists, but presumably also because it offered him a coherent identity.[211] At the end of the war, Minna Lachs came to feel that Jews had to have their own land, a land in which they belonged, like the Germans in Germany or the English in England.[212]

It appears that the months after the war witnessed an outburst of Jewish ethnicity all over former Habsburg Austria. Jews responded to the collapse of the Monarchy and the creation of nation-states, not by constructing new national identities, but instead by hoping that they could transfer their old identities to the new political situations. Jews in Czechoslovakia and in German-Austria declared their loyalty to the new states, but they did not embrace either a Czech or a German national identity. Instead, they persisted in the tripartite identity they had developed in Habsburg Austria that allowed them to join the dominant nation only in a cultural sense while they continued to belong to the Jewish people.

Indeed, increased Jewish ethnic feeling was a direct response to the situation in which the Jews found themselves. Unable to join the Czech or German nation in as full a way as Czech or German nationalists demanded, they retreated to the comfort of Jewish ethnicity, joining the Zionist movement in ever-larger numbers or simply asserting their Jewishness. Vicious anti-Semitism—ubiquitous in this period—did not cause this greater ethnicity, but it certainly enhanced it, making many Jews realize that they could not join the Czech or German nation even if they wanted to. In Germany as well, the postwar surge in anti-Semitism encouraged a greater assertion of Jewish ethnic identity, an identity complicated by the fact that Jews considered themselves part of the German nation.[213] The absence of that sense of belonging allowed Jewish ethnicity to flourish in former Habsburg lands.

The German-speaking Jews of former Habsburg Austria persisted in the identity they had developed during the Monarchy because they felt comfortable with it even if it was not appropriate in the new political situation. They responded to the collapse of the Monarchy with the hope that somehow the new states would allow them to adhere to their old identities. Czechoslovakia did give the Jews the opportunity to recreate a new tripartite identity, and most Jews there asserted their loyalty to Czechoslovakia, adherence to German or Czech culture, and membership in the Jewish people, indeed, even in the Jewish nation. Austria proved less hospitable, but the interwar period was so chaotic and crisis-ridden that Jews simply adhered to their old identity even if it did not fit the situation in the new nation-state. They too asserted political loyalty to Austria, German cultural affinity, and Jewish ethnic identity. Such identity may have been more suited to a multinational or multiethnic society than to the nation-state of the First Austrian Republic, but Austrian Jews clung to it because it best conformed to their deeply held convictions.

Epilogue

World War I and, in its wake, the demise of the Habsburg Monarchy and the emergence of nation-states in East Central Europe created a situation that challenged the carefully crafted identity of the Jews. In Habsburg Austria, Jews had long been accustomed to a comfortable tripartite identity that enabled them to assert patriotic loyalty to the state, to share the culture of one or another of the Monarchy's nationalities, and still to feel themselves to be part of the Jewish people. Jewish identity could range from the traditional religious position, that the Jews were a nation in exile awaiting redemption; to a liberal one, which argued in public that Jewish identity was just religious, even while acknowledging privately the significant ethnic dimension in Jewishness; to a Zionist or diaspora nationalist identity, with its insistence that the Jews should form a modern secular nation. This tripartite identity, however, depended on the existence of the supranational, multinational state that did not promote its own ethnic national identity, but insisted rather on old-fashioned dynastic and territorial loyalty. In such a state, Jews had been able easily to become Austrian state patriots while adopting German, Czech, or Polish culture and remaining free to assert any kind of Jewish identity they chose.

World War I enhanced the tripartite identity of the Jews and made them even greater supporters of the supranational state that allowed them this comfortable identity. Jews shared the patriotic enthusiasm of August 1914 and gave their *Gut und Blut* for the fatherland throughout the war. They did so largely because they understood the war not just as a great patriotic effort, but because it was for them a Jewish holy war to liberate the Jews of Galicia and Eastern Europe from Russian oppression. Jews embraced the war effort because they could fight for Austria and the Jewish people at the same time. They also hoped that their sacrifices on the battlefield and their tireless work on the home front would dispel anti-Semitic myths about Jewish cowardice and foster the brotherhood of Austria's peoples. Their experience in the army convinced them that their loyalty to Austria was well placed. Even as anti-Semitism flourished, the Habsburg army refused to allow any discrimination against Jewish soldiers. Moreover, success on the Eastern Front pleased the Jews, for their country had achieved its military goals and had saved the Jewish people of Eastern Europe from czarist domination. At the same time, the experience of war deepened the Jewish identity of soldiers and those who served on the home front. In particular, work on behalf of the hundreds of thousands of Galician Jewish refugees who fled to Bohemia, Moravia, and Vienna in 1914 and 1916, and the anti-Semitic hostility that greeted them, enhanced Jewish solidarity and reminded all Habsburg Jews that they formed a community of fate.

In the last two years of the war, anti-Semitism proliferated in an atmosphere of widespread war weariness, acute food shortages, and rising nationalist agitation, and Jews clung ever more tightly to their attachment to the supranational state. They sought to preserve multinational Austria because they viewed it as their best defense against the anti-Semitism so widespread in the nationalist camps. Only the central government, they felt, could administer the provinces justly. Thus Jews desperately hoped that Galicia would remain in Austria because they feared that Polish nationalists would deprive Jews of their rights. When Galicia erupted in an orgy of anti-Semitic violence in 1918, Jews truly understood the consequences of Habsburg collapse. They wanted to preserve supranational Austria, however, not only because it protected them from pogroms: The multinational state also allowed them the freedom to adopt the culture of one of the Monarchy's peoples while remaining as Jewish as they chose.

When the Habsburg Monarchy disintegrated in October–November 1918 and new nation-states emerged, Jews not only mourned the old Austria but also faced a grave crisis of identity. The new nation-states defined the national community in ethno-national terms and demanded a kind of loyalty that proved difficult for Jews. Jews might have already adopted German, Czech, or Polish culture, but they did not feel themselves to be members of the German, Czech, or Polish nations because the nationalists often defined membership in biological or racial terms. Moreover, widespread anti-Semitism meant that Jews could not join those nations even if they wanted to. Jews responded to the crisis by clinging to their old tripartite identity, even if it no longer really suited the new political context. Thus, for example, the Jews in German-Austria asserted their loyalty to the Austrian Republic and their adherence to German culture, but they did not affirm their membership in the German *Volk*. Instead, they retreated to the comfort of a Jewish ethnic identity, and some to a Jewish nationalist one, hoping that the German-Austrian nation-state would somehow allow them to do so. In Czechoslovakia, the Jews imagined the new state as an improved version of the old, multinational Austria. They affirmed their loyalty to the state and continued to adhere to whatever culture they had already adopted, but increasingly they asserted a Jewish national identity. In Poland and Romania, most Jews, traditionally religious and Zionists alike, identified themselves simply as Jews.

The 1920s and 1930s proved difficult for the Jews of East Central Europe. In Poland and Romania, Jews suffered from widespread anti-Semitic hostility and official discrimination. Poland considered itself a Polish nation-state, despite the fact that it had incorporated areas of historic Poland that contained non-Poles. About a third of all citizens of interwar Poland were ethnic minorities, including Ukrainians (14%), Lithuanians (0.3%), White Russians (4%), Germans (4%), and Jews (10%). The Poles, who dominated the state politically and culturally, resented the protections of minority rights that Versailles had stipulated and ignored the provisions of the Polish Minorities Treaty. For their part, the ethnic minorities disliked Polish hegemony and attempts at forced assimilation. Beset by political, social, and economic problems, and by setbacks in foreign policy, in the mid-1930s Poland's authoritarian regime imposed anti-Jewish measures long demanded by the anti-Semites, including many intended to drive Jews from the economy.[1] Most Poles regarded the Jews as an inferior, foreign group, not as Poles, no matter how Polonized they were. In the interwar period, the right-wing National Democratic Party, under the leadership of Roman Dmowski, led the anti-Semitic charge, declaring that the solution to all of Poland's problems was to get rid of the Jews. The Catholic Church as well, long-regarded as the embodiment of the Polish national spirit, inveighed against the Jews as the epitome of moral corruption and Bolshevism and urged good Poles to boycott the Jews and avoid their evil influence. Frequently, Jews encountered anti-Semitic violence, especially at the universities, which physically segregated Jews in the classroom by mandating a special "Jewish bench" in 1937. The government responded to this agitation by looking for ways to encourage mass emigration of the Jews.[2]

The Jews of interwar Poland, numbering over three million, identified themselves mostly as Jews, not Poles. In the 1921 census, 74% of the Jews in the new state declared themselves Jews by nationality, and in the 1931 census, based on mother tongue, not nationality, 80% of Jews declared Yiddish their mother tongue, and 8% Hebrew. Many of those who affirmed Jewish nationality were deeply religious Jews who continued to hold fast to traditional notions of Jewish identity. In Galicia, which had the largest percentage of Polonized Jews in Poland, the percentage of Jews affirming a Jewish national identity was somewhat lower than the national average but still a substantial majority of about 60%. Whether traditional or modern, the overwhelming majority of Polish Jews, including those of former Austrian Galicia, belonged to a separate Jewish society within Poland. They did not consider themselves Poles in a national sense even if they felt that they were loyal citizens of the Polish Republic.[3] As a result, they formed many Jewish political parties to represent divergent Jewish interests—Zionist, Socialist, orthodox, bourgeois Jewish nationalist—in parliament and city councils. These parties may not have succeeded in alleviating Jewish distress, but they and their youth movements did sustain a separate Jewish society in Poland, one with a vibrant cultural life in Yiddish, Hebrew, and Polish.[4]

The situation of the Jews in Romania was worse. At the end of World War I, Romania, an independent state since 1878, gained several territories that contained ethnic Romanians, including former Austrian Bukovina, Hungarian Transylvania, and Russian Bessarabia. All of these territories also contained large numbers of non-Romanians, including Hungarians and Germans in Transylva-

nia, Germans and Ruthenians in Bukovina, Ukrainians and Russians in Bessarabia, and Jews throughout. The government sought to strengthen the Romanian
nation-state by displacing the "foreigners" with an expanded Romanian elite. In
Bukovina, Romanian authorities suppressed Ruthenian language, schools, and
institutions and sought to disenfranchise the Ruthenian minority. The group
most hurt by Romanian efforts at national integration was the Jews. Indeed, the
government used anti-Semitism as a tool in its campaign to nationalize the country, labeling Jews as foreigners, blaming them for Romania's problems, and seeking to eliminate them from schools, cultural institutions, and the economy.[5]
Although the Jews were citizens of Romania, they suffered much official discrimination and popular violence. Not surprisingly, Jews in Romania overwhelmingly identified as Jews by nationality. In the census of 1930, 92,492 of the
93,101 Jews in the province of Bukovina declared themselves members of the
Jewish nation. Surely not all of the deeply religious, Yiddish-speaking Jews or
the modern, German-speaking Jews of Bukovina considered themselves Zionists, but a Romanian identity was simply not an option for them.[6]

Hungary also suffered from anti-Semitic excess in the interwar period, but the
Jews who lived there firmly identified as Magyars by culture and nationality.
Such identification was already widespread in late nineteenth century Hungary,
which had long since fashioned itself a nation-state, and thus the Jews of interwar Hungary continued an old tradition. After World War I, Hungary lost much
of its historical territory, including Slovakia and Sub-Carpathian Ruthenia to
Czechoslovakia, Transylvania to Romania, and Croatia-Slavonia and Vojvodina to
Yugoslavia. Unlike the former Kingdom of Hungary, Trianon Hungary, so-called
for the treaty that legalized its new borders, was now in fact a Magyar nation-
state. Yet it deeply resented its territorial losses and the fact that many Magyars
lived in other countries. Conservative Hungarian ruling elites maintained their
old privileges and hoped to reassert control over the lost territory. In the 1920s
and 1930s, Hungary increasingly came under the influence of the radical right,
ultimately allying itself with Nazi Germany and regaining some of its former
land. Although the Jews, numbering 444,567 in 1930 and forming 5% of the
population, identified themselves firmly as Hungarian patriots and Magyar nationalists, they nevertheless suffered from anti-Semitic hostility and discrimination. Indeed, anti-Semites claimed that the Jews were alien and inferior, not
Magyar. No longer needed to bolster the number of Magyars in the country, resented for their prominent role in industry, commerce, and the professions, and
blamed for the abortive Béla Kun Communist regime of 1919 because of the
large number of Jews in its ranks, Jews became useful as a scapegoat for Hungarian problems. Legislation during and after 1938 narrowed the ability of Jews to
obtain higher education and participate in economic and public life.[7]

Hungarian Jews responded to this new attack by clinging more desperately to
their Magyar identity. Trianon Hungary no longer contained the large reservoirs
of orthodox Jews, most of whom lived in Slovakia, Ruthenia, and Transylvania.
Most of the Jews in interwar Hungary were modern, religiously liberal, and
committed to the Magyar nation. Thus, unlike the situation in most of the other
Habsburg successor states, no Zionist or Jewish nationalist movement of any

consequence developed in Hungary, even when anti-Semitic discrimination became more pronounced.[8] Indeed, some Jews responded to anti-Semitism by converting to Christianity and thus more fully embracing a Magyar identity.[9]

Czechoslovakia presented the Jews with the greatest opportunity. Unlike most of the states in East Central Europe, interwar Czechoslovakia possessed a viable democratic government that guaranteed civil rights and political equality to all her citizens, including the Jews. Jews here experienced no official or officially tolerated anti-Semitic discrimination. Yet the new state suffered from nationality conflicts that may not have paralyzed it but did pose serious threats. In the first place, despite the fact that the state called itself Czechoslovakia, no real Czechoslovak national identity ever emerged. In fact, Czechoslovakia was a Czech nation-state, dominated politically, culturally, and economically by the Czechs, who imposed their national history, symbols, and heroes on increasingly resentful Slovaks, Germans, Magyars, Ruthenians, and Poles. The state created the fiction of a Czechoslovak identity by counting Czech and Slovak as one language and lumping the two groups together on the census. Even so, only two thirds of the population of interwar Czechoslovakia, which numbered about fourteen million, were "Czechoslovak," as measured by mother tongue. About 25% of the population spoke German, 5% Magyar, and 4% Ruthenian. Moreover, the new state never created a Czechoslovak political identity that would unite all its national groups.[10]

Despite their inclusion in the dominant nation, Slovaks felt patronized and colonized by the Czechs, who replaced the former Hungarian bureaucracy of Slovakia with a Czech one and opened Slovak schools that taught Czech culture and national loyalty. Slovakia had formed a part of Hungary for centuries, and its inhabitants, still largely rural, poor, and undereducated, felt relief that they no longer had to deal with pervasive pressure to Magyarize. They also benefited from land reform that hurt Hungarian landlords. Nevertheless, they disliked Czech centralism and sought autonomy within Czechoslovakia. Increasingly, they supported separatist populist movements, and during the depression they turned to fascism.

The Germans—who numbered over three million and accounted for a quarter of the population of the new state—felt especially aggrieved that their right to national self-determination had been sacrificed to Czech desire for the historic territory of the Bohemian crown. As part of its agreements with all minorities, the new state did allow the Germans extensive language rights, including German schools and the right to use German in dealing with the government, where they formed 20% of the population, but they nevertheless deeply resented their minority status. By the mid-1920s, apparently because their economic situation was far better in Czechoslovakia than if they lived in Germany or Austria, the Germans seemed to make peace with the state, and German political parties, especially the agrarians, liberal democrats, and Christian Socials, joined government coalitions, while the Social Democrats acted as a loyal opposition. Unfortunately, the Germans of Bohemia and Moravia suffered disproportionately during the depression and increasingly supported Konrad Henlein's radical German nationalist *Sudetendeutsche Partei*, which became a virtual arm of the Nazi Party in Germany. In the elections of May 1935, Henlein's party received most of the German vote and thus 15% of all the seats in parliament. By 1938, all the German bourgeois parties joined forces with it, and in the May/June 1938 municipal elections, the Sudeten German Party received over 90% of the German vote.[11] Such developments did not augur well for the Jews.

The Jews of interwar Czechoslovakia, who numbered 354, 342 in 1921, enjoyed full legal equality and never doubted the ability and commitment of the government to protect them. Nevertheless, with the exception of the Jews who had long identified as Czechs, they did not belong to the dominant nation in the state in which they lived. The 1920 constitution, concerned with individual rights, allowed Jews to choose Jewish national minority status if they felt they belonged to the Jewish nation. No matter what their mother tongue, Jews had the right to designate on the census that they belonged to the Jewish nation.[12] Many Jews did so, indeed 51% countrywide in 1921. In that year, only 22% of the Jews of Czechoslovakia indicated that they were members of the Czechoslovak nation, while 19% declared themselves German by nationality, 12% Magyar, and 4% Ruthenian.[13]

Naturally there were significant regional variations. In Sub-Carpathian Ruthenia and Slovakia (formerly Hungarian territory) the masses of traditional Jews still affirmed a primary identity as Jews. Those who had modernized, however, had adopted a Magyar identity, a natural choice before the war when Hungary controlled Slovakia, but one that proved most unpopular in postwar Czechoslovakia. Unlike other Magyars in Slovakia, who yearned for a return of Hungarian control, the Jews, aware of anti-Jewish legislation in Trianon Hungary, felt comfortable in Czechoslovakia. They adopted a Czechoslovakian political identity, even as they still affirmed loyalty to Magyar culture and membership in the Jewish people. Thus for the first time they now followed the old Habsburg tripartite pattern, adjusted to new political realities. They undoubtedly hoped that such a tripartite identity would save them from Slovak anti-Semites, who had viewed the Jews as Magyar oppressors. Moreover, the majority of the 137,000 Jews in Slovakia, 54% in the census of 1921, identified themselves as Jews by nationality. Such an identity would surely be more acceptable to the Czech authorities than their old Magyar one. Indeed, only 15% of the Jews in the province declared themselves Magyars, and 22% indicated a "Czechoslovak" identity. Whether they identified as Jews, Magyars, or Czechoslovaks, however, Slovak anti-Semites resented the Jews for their loyalty to Czechoslovakia, which they interpreted as support for the Czechs.[14]

As we have seen, Jews in Bohemia and Moravia—who in 1921 numbered 79,777 and 45,306, respectively—warmly supported the new state and its democratic institutions. Many also affirmed a Jewish national identity, especially in Moravia. A careful examination of the census statistics makes it clear that Jews continued to adhere to the tripartite identity they had developed in Habsburg times, transferred to the new state. Thus, although they undoubtedly possessed a Czechoslovak political identity and loyalty and could speak Czech fluently, Jews did not come to embrace a Czech national identity. Indeed, the percentage of Jews in both Bohemia and Moravia who identified as Czechs had remained remarkably stable since the late nineteenth century. In the censuses of both 1920

and 1930, 47% of Bohemian Jews declared themselves Czech, 3% fewer than in
1910. Similarly in Moravia, where 14% of Jews identified as Czech in 1910, only
16% did so in 1920 and 18% in 1930.[15] Many historians argue that the old German identity declined as Jews increasingly embraced a Jewish national identity.[16]
While statistically true—after all, Jewish national identity had not been counted
in the old Austrian census—the evidence indicates that Jews in the Czech lands
continued to adhere to a German cultural identity even if many of them now
announced loyalty to the Jewish nation. The old German identity had always
been cultural, not necessarily a national identity, and many Jews, especially in
Moravia, identified themselves as Jews, once given the opportunity. Thus, in 1921,
48% of Moravian Jews declared themselves members of the Jewish nation, and,
in 1930, 52% did so. In Bohemia, where Jewish nationalism was far weaker, only
14% of the Jews in 1920 and 21% in 1930 declared a Jewish nationality. In both
provinces, though, the percentage of those who identified as German remained
stable in the interwar period. In Bohemia, 33% of the Jews declared themselves
German in 1921 and 31% in 1930. In Moravia, the figures were 35% and 29%.[17]
Even in Bohemia, where 60% of Jewish children attended Czech-language elementary schools in the interwar period, 60% of Jews in *Gymnasium* attended
German ones.[18] Moreover, most Jewish cultural institutions continued to function in German. Thus at least German-speaking Jews could possess a tripartite
identity. They could be Czechoslovakians politically, Germans culturally, and also
Jews. The government's commitment to protect Jewish rights allowed such an
identity to flourish. Only growing anti-Semitism among the Germans and Slovaks in response to events in the 1930s threatened Jewish security.

Jews in the Austrian Republic may also have yearned for the old tripartite identity, but such an identity proved harder to legitimate in interwar Austria. The republic was a German nation-state that demanded full German loyalty from all its
inhabitants. Jews certainly asserted their loyalty to the republic and shared its dominant culture, but they did not think they were members of the German *Volk,* and
most Germans agreed. To make matters more complicated, interwar Austrians did
not develop a new Austrian identity. They were Germans, and most of them
yearned for union with Germany. Hence they did not construct a viable identity
specifically for Austrian Germans. Moreover, anti-Semitism raged in the new republic, especially in the ranks of the Christian Social Party, which dominated politics throughout the 1920s and 1930s, and in parties further to the right, including
the Austrian Nazis. Even the Socialists used anti-Semitic rhetoric in their newspapers and electoral campaigns. Parliamentary democracy itself came to an end, and
in 1934, Austria reorganized itself as a corporatist, authoritarian regime under the
Fatherland Front, which regarded Austria as a German Christian state. Neither the
Christian Socials nor the Fatherland Front actively discriminated against the Jews,
and they did not share radical German nationalist and Nazi racial views of the Jewish question. They did, however, regard the Jews as the source of all the ills of
modernity, as a foreign group, indeed a separate nationality, that threatened good
Germans and whose influence had to be curtailed.[19] In March 1938, the Austrian
and German Nazis who orchestrated the *Anschluss,* the union of Austria with Germany, threatened the very existence of the Jews in Austria.

The Jews of interwar Austria consisted of two different communities: the Jews of Vienna, who numbered 201,513 in 1923, and about 30,000 Jews in the Burgenland, an area of western Hungary given to Austria in 1920 that contained several communities of German-speaking orthodox Jews.[20] These Jews tried to cope with escalating anti-Semitic animosity, but none of their strategies proved effective. Liberal, Zionist, and orthodox Jews all urged unity but found themselves unable to unite to meet the challenges posed by anti-Semitism and the political and economic crises of interwar Austria, which simply overwhelmed the Jews.[21]

Although some Jews responded to the difficult situation in Austria by embracing Socialism and abandoning formal Jewish affiliation, many Jews retreated to the comfort of the Jewish community and Jewish identity. Austria did not allow Jews to declare themselves on the census as members of the Jewish nation, but the interwar period did witness rising support for Zionism and Jewish nationalism. By 1932, Zionists had won a majority of seats on the board of the Viennese *Israelitische Kultusgemeinde.* Still led by Robert Stricker, Austrian Zionists persisted in their old policy of urging the state to recognize the Jews as one of the nations of Austria, even though the state categorically refused to do so. Despite the fact that Austria was now a homogeneous nation-state, Stricker and his supporters continued to behave as if the old multinational Habsburg Austria still existed and that it might be persuaded to accord them national minority status. The Zionists also ran candidates for local and national elections, despite the fact that most Jews did not vote for Jewish nationalist candidates, realistically recognizing that their only hope against anti-Semitism lay in voting for the Social Democrats. By 1930–1931, the Austrian Zionist Federation abandoned its policy of running candidates, much to the chagrin of Stricker and his circle.[22]

Even if Zionist politics proved ineffective in Austria, Jews increasingly identified as Jews. Religiously observant Jews could find comfort from anti-Semitic hostility in Jewish religious tradition.[23] Even Jews who had long abandoned Jewish religious observance considered themselves Jews and associated mostly with other Jews. They were loyal to the state in which they lived, despite its disdain for them, and completely comfortable in German culture, yet they were not Germans but Jews. Indeed, the very nature of the new state made them nostalgic for the old Austria, which had made it easier for them to be culturally German and ethnically Jewish. Members of the Association of Jewish War Veterans expressed this sentiment quite bluntly in an article in their newspaper in July 1933, noting that "we Jews, who pursue neither a German nor a Slavic national identity, especially we Austrian Jews," fondly remembered the Monarchy, with its openness to all peoples.[24] The creation of a German nation-state in Austria meant that the Jews could no longer uphold their old tripartite identity, but it was one they liked and wanted to have despite the fact that the political circumstances had changed.

The new political reality discouraged ethnic diversity in Austria, and yet the Jews nevertheless persisted in feeling that they were an ethnically distinct group. The opposite was the case for other minority groups in Austria. Many descendants of Czech or other Slavic immigrants responded to the reality of a German nation-state not only by changing their names and trying to submerge themselves in the dominant nation, but often by becoming fanatical German national-ists and Nazis.[25] Rampant anti-Semitism prevented Jews from pursuing this op-tion. Of course, some Jews did convert to Christianity to escape the stigma of Jewish identity, and others embraced Socialism in the hope that it would create a better world. Most Jews, however, understood that they could never become German as long as Germans defined their identity in ethnic or racial terms. In fact, most Jews had no desire to become part of the German *Volk* because they felt they belonged to the Jewish people.

The experiences of the Jews in the Habsburg Monarchy and in its successor states place in sharp relief both the dilemma of the Jews as a religious and ethnic minority and the more fundamental problem of constructing ethnic and national identity. Jews formed a classic ethno-religious minority in Europe. They per-ceived themselves to be a community of descent with a rich historical culture, but in fact, most modern Jews no longer lived their lives immersed in that cul-ture, and they no longer followed most of the rules of Jewish religious tradition. In the course of the nineteenth century they had adopted German, Czech, Hun-garian, or Polish culture, but residual Jewish loyalties and behavior patterns per-sisted. Jews associated primarily with other Jews, and they understood that they formed a community of fate with their fellow Jews. In short, following Fredrik Barth's definition of ethnicity, they behaved like an ethnic group, whose borders were clear to Jews and Gentiles alike. Jews continued to function as an ethnic group even though they had exchanged traditional Jewish culture for the cultures of the people in whose midst they lived. They were an ethnic group even if they eschewed overt ethnic assertiveness and, like the Jewish liberals, insisted that Jew-ish identity was based solely on the religion they no longer fully observed. To be sure, anti-Jewish prejudice played an important role in the persistence of Jewish ethnicity, encouraging many Jews to socialize with other Jews and to affirm Jew-ish solidarity. Yet Jews behaved as a viable ethnic group not only in response to widespread anti-Semitism but also because they found value in maintaining some form of Jewish culture and identity.

The attachment of the Jews to their own ethnic group made it particularly difficult for them to adopt fully any of the national identities that surrounded them in Habsburg Austria or its successor states. Scholars are correct to insist that national identities are constructed or "imagined," yet just because they are con-structed does not mean that they are easy to adopt, especially in Central and Eastern Europe where the ethno-cultural version of national identity is so preva-lent. Indeed, if Anthony Smith is right and nationalism derives its power from the loyalty of people to preexisting ethnic groups, then the fact that the Jews possessed a vigorous ethnic identity made it hard for them to become full-fledged members of other nations, in particular those that, like the Germans, Czechs, or Poles, viewed themselves as ethno-cultural communities of descent. They could join the nation if it were defined in cultural terms, but they could not join the *Volk*. Moreover, since Jewish ethnicity was intimately bound up with the Jewish religion, for Jews to merge fully into another ethnically defined nation, they had to convert to Christianity. Although some Jews did undergo baptism for the sake of full acceptance, most were not willing to go that far. Thus it was not only prejudice against the Jews that prevented them from fully joining other ethno-national communities. It was also that Jews formed an old, well-established ethnic group whose identity was sanctioned by religious tradition and who possessed a long history as a separate entity in society.

Interestingly, the Jews themselves shared the general Central and Eastern European conviction that nations were communities of descent. Although one could become a Jew by religious conversion, most Jews were the descendants of other Jews. Zionism, which sought to make Jews over into a political nation with their own state, perceived Jewish national identity in romantic, ethnic terms. The Jewish state that most Zionists envisioned would be a nation-state in which the nation would consist of the Jewish people.

Even if Jews shared an ethno-cultural definition of the nation, most Jews understood that as a minority group they flourished best in countries in which national identity did not depend on ethnic descent but rather on political loyalty. They knew that Jews—indeed all minority groups—enjoy a more secure status in nations that define themselves as polities of citizens rather than as mythic, ethnic communities. True, nations based on citizenship, like France, seek to assimilate all inhabitants of the country into one uniform culture, but assimilation there is into the nation as cultural and political community, not as biological kinship group. Such assimilation is relatively easy, especially for the Jews. Ethnic and religious minorities function best in countries whose national identity is fundamentally political, especially if those countries allow for ethnic and cultural diversity. Only in such places do they have the opportunity to develop their own identities freely.

Habsburg Austria was not a nation-state at all, and its government, at least in theory, was supranational. That it did not develop an overarching national identity based on a community of citizens presented the state with grave problems in an era that glorified the right of the nation to self-determination. Nevertheless, the Jews of Habsburg Austria appreciated that the state did not develop its own ethno-national identity but rather remained an old-fashioned territorial state to which they could be loyal without having to adopt a foreign national identity or renounce their Jewish ethnic identity. Some Jews certainly might have preferred greater democracy or another kind of state altogether, one based not on loyalty to the Monarch, but on the polity of equal citizens. In the context of East Central Europe, however, supranational Habsburg Austria offered them the best opportunity to be loyal citizens of the state while remaining free to be as Jewish as they chose.

Such was not the case in the nation-states of East Central Europe in the interwar years. Most of these states were not ethnically homogenous, but they often tried to impose the national culture of the dominant group on the other national groups. None of them managed to create an overarching political identity that would have united all of the nationalities into a larger, political nation. Even Czechoslovakia, which alone in the region maintained a viable democracy, and which practiced a fair measure of toleration toward its national minorities, did not create a Czechoslovakian identity with which Czechs, Slovaks, Germans, and

Hungarians felt comfortable. Indeed, in interwar Czechoslovakia, the Jews were the only Czechoslovakians.

In this context, the situation of the Jews deteriorated rapidly. Increasingly isolated, victims of unofficial (and in many countries official) persecution, the Jews suffered greatly. They were left an easy target during World War II, when the Nazis, who considered the Jews an evil and inferior race, earmarked them for annihilation. Jewish prosperity and creativity—indeed that of all minority groups—depended on the creation of a political nation, one based not on ethnicity but on citizenship, which could win the loyalty of all its citizens. Such political nations failed to appear in Central Europe after the demise of the Habsburg Monarchy, which, while surely flawed, at least had the advantage of not viewing itself in exclusive, nationalistic terms.

Notes

INTRODUCTION

1. Anthony D. Smith, *Theories of Nationalism* (New York, 1971), p. 171. See also Smith, *Nationalism and Modernism* (London, 1998).

2. Hans Kohn, *Nationalism: Its Meaning and History* (Princeton, 1955, 1965), p. 9; Kohn, *The Idea of Nationalism: A Study in Its Origins and Background* (New York, 1944), pp. 10, 15–16, 18–19. Writing against the backdrop of the Nazi concept of the nation as blood community, Kohn took great pains to emphasize that nationalism is solely a political idea.

3. Ernst Renan, "What Is a Nation," trans. by Martin Thom, in Homi K. Bhabha, ed., *Nation and Narration* (London, 1990), pp. 19–20.

4. Ibid., p. 19. The whole essay is found on pp. 8–22.

5. Benedict Anderson, *Imagined Communities: Reflections on the Origins and Spread of Nationalism,* rev. ed. (London, 1991; orig. 1983), p. 6.

6. Ibid., pp. 133–134, 145–146.

7. See especially Anthony D. Smith, *The Ethnic Origins of Nations* (Oxford, 1986), pp. 17–18; Smith, *Nationalism and Modernism*; and John Armstrong, *Nations before Nationalism* (Chapel Hill, NC, 1982).

8. Smith, *Theories of Nationalism,* p. 176.

9. Ibid., pp. 178–180, 186–189.

10. Ernest Gellner, *Nations and Nationalism* (Ithaca, NY, 1983), p. 1. Gellner argues that nationalism developed because modern industrial society required a large class of educated people and therefore also a state to marshall the resources necessary for a large educational infrastructure. In general, Gellner is too simplistic and deterministic.

11. Smith, *Ethnic Origins of Nations,* pp. 135–150; Kohn, *Nationalism: Its Meaning and History,* pp. 15–71; E. J. Hobsbawm, *Nations and Nationalism since 1780: Programme, Myth, Reality,* 2d ed. (Cambridge, 1992; orig. 1990).

12. Rogers Brubaker, *Citizenship and Nationhood in France and Germany* (Cambridge, MA, 1992). Brubaker's analysis proceeds from his desire to explain why France today has a liberal citizenship law that extends French citizenship automatically to the children of im-

migrants raised in France, while Germany grants citizenship only to the descendants of Germans, and thus not to people resident in Germany for generations.

13. Smith, *Nationalism and Modernism,* p. 126, does well to remind us that even French civic nationalism contained ethnic elements, just as German nationalism possessed a civic dimension.

14. Smith, *Ethnic Origins of Nations,* pp. 24–30; Armstrong, pp. 241–282.

15. Smith, *Ethnic Origins of Nations,* pp. 67–68, 114, 119, 124; Armstrong, pp. 203–213, 238–240.

16. Armstrong, p. 240.

17. Fredrik Barth, "Introduction," in Fredrik Barth, ed., *Ethnic Groups and Boundaries: The Social Organization of Cultural Difference* (Boston, 1969), pp. 9–38.

18. For further detail, see chapter 1.

19. Because Hungary fashioned itself a nation state, the situation of the Jews there more closely resembled the situation of the Jews in Germany. For more details on the complex identities of Habsburg Jews, see chapter 1.

20. Ezra Mendelsohn, *The Jews of East Central Europe between the World Wars* (Bloomington, IN, 1983), ch. 1 and 4.

CHAPTER I

1. *Ungarisches statistisches Jahrbuch,* vol. 19 (1911), pp. 18–19; Erno Laszlo, "Hungarian Jewry: Settlement and Demography, 1735–38 to 1910," in Randolph L. Braham, ed. *Hungarian-Jewish Studies* (New York, 1966), p. 68.

2. *Österreichische Statistik,* N.F., 1:1 (1912), pp. 54*, 94–95.

3. Ibid., pp. 94–95.

4. Ibid.

5. Marsha L. Rozenblit, *The Jews of Vienna, 1867–1914: Assimilation and Identity* (Albany, NY, 1983), p. 17; *Österreichische Statistik,* N.F., 1:1 (1912), pp. 3, 38–39.

6. Rozenblit, *Jews of Vienna,* pp. 13–45.

7. The best comprehensive books on the history of the Habsburg Monarchy in English are C. A. Macartney, *The Habsburg Empire 1790–1918* (New York, 1969); A. J. P. Taylor, *The Habsburg Monarchy, 1809–1918* (Chicago, 1948, 1976); Robert A. Kann, *A History of the Habsburg Empire, 1526–1918* (Berkeley, CA, 1974); and Alan Sked, *The Decline and Fall of the Habsburg Empire 1815-1918* (New York, 1989). In German, see the multi-volume *Die Habsburgermonarchie 1848–1918,* edited by Adam Wandruszka and Peter Urbanitsch, and published by the Österreichische Akademie der Wissenschaften.

8. See *Die Habsburgermonarchie 1848–1918,* vol. 3, "Die Völker des Reiches" (Vienna, 1980); Robert A. Kann, *The Multinational Empire: Nationalism and National Reform in the Habsburg Monarchy, 1848–1918,* 2 vols. (New York, 1950); Oscar Jászi, *The Dissolution of the Habsburg Monarchy* (Chicago, 1929, 1961).

9. Henryk Batowski, "Die Polen," in *Die Habsburgermonarchie 1848–1918,* vol. 3, "Die Völker des Reiches," pp. 522–554; Kann, *Multinational Empire,* vol. 1, pp. 221–232; Piotr S. Wandycz, *The Lands of Partitioned Poland, 1795–1918* (Seattle, 1974); Wandycz, "The Poles in the Habsburg Monarchy," in *Nationbuilding and the Politics of Nationalism: Essays on Austrian Galicia,* Andrei S. Markovits and Frank E. Sysyn, eds. (Cambridge, MA, 1982), pp. 68–93.

10. Jiří Kořalka, *Tschechen im Habsburgerreich und in Europa 1815–1914* (Vienna, 1991); Jiří Kořalka and R. J. Crampton, "Die Tschechen," in *Die Habsburgermonarchie 1848–1918,* vol. 3, "Die Völker des Reiches," pp. 489–521; Jan Havránek, "The Development of Czech Nationalism," *Austrian History Yearbook* 3 (1967), pt. 2, pp. 223–260; Kann, *Multinational Empire,* vol. 1, pp. 151–219.

11. On the Germans of Austria, see Berthold Sutter, "Die politische und rechtliche Stellung der Deutschen in Österreich 1848 bis 1918," in *Die Habsburgermonarchie 1848–1918,* vol. 3, "Die Völker des Reiches," pp. 154–339; Kann, *Multinational Empire,* vol. 1, pp. 51–107; and two extremely interesting articles by Pieter M. Judson, "'Whether Race or Conviction Should Be the Standard': National Identity and Liberal Politics in Nineteenth-Century Austria," *Austrian History Yearbook* 22 (1991), pp. 76–95; and "'Not Another Square Foot!' German Liberalism and the Rhetoric of National Ownership in Nineteenth-Century Austria," *Austrian History Yearbook* 26 (1995), pp. 83–97. See also Andrew Whiteside, "The Germans as an Integrative Force in Imperial Austria: The Dilemma of Dominance," *Austrian History Yearbook* 3 (1967), pt. 1, pp. 157–200; and Erich Zöllner, "The Germans as an Integrating and Disintegrating Force," *Austrian History Yearbook* 3 (1967), pt. 1, pp. 201–233.

12. István Deák, *Beyond Nationalism: A Social and Political History of the Habsburg Officer Corps, 1848–1918* (New York, 1990). For a literary portrayal of the Austrian identity of the bureaucrats see Joseph Roth, *Radetzky March* (New York, 1933). Contrary to this view, see Solomon Wank, "The Habsburg Empire," in *After Empire: Multiethnic Societies and Nation-Building,* Karen Barkey and Mark von Hagen, eds. (Boulder, CO, 1997), pp. 45–57, who argues that the Habsburg elites were "in some irreducible sense German" (p. 51), but even he acknowledges that their Germanness was cultural.

13. For this distinction, see Brubaker.

14. Gerald Stourzh, "Die Gleichberechtigung der Volksstämme als Verfassungsprinzip 1848–1918," *Die Habsburgermonarchie 1848–1918,* vol. 3, "Die Völker des Reiches," pt. 2, pp. 975–1206.

15. László Katus, "Die Magyaren," in pt. 1, pp. 410–488; Ludwig Gogolák, "Ungarns Nationalitätengesetze und das Problem des Magyarischen National- und Zentralstaates," in *Die Habsburgermonarchie 1848–1918,* vol. 3, "Die Völker des Reiches," pt. 2, pp. 1207–1303; Kann, *Multinational Empire,* vol. 1, pp. 22–24, 130–139.

16. Peter Urbanitsch, "Die Deutschen in Österreich. Statistisch-deskriptiver Überblick," in *Die Habsburgermonarchie, 1848–1918,* vol. 3, "Die Völker des Reiches," pt. 1, Table 1, between pp. 38 and 39.

17. Ibid., Table 1, "Die Bevölkerung der Kronländer Cisleithaniens nach der Nationalität und nach der Umgangssprache 1851–1910."

18. Gary B. Cohen, *The Politics of Ethnic Survival: Germans in Prague, 1861–1914* (Princeton, 1981), ch. 1.

19. On problems of migrants, see Michael John, "'We Do Not Even Possess Our Selves': On Identity and Ethnicity in Austria, 1880–1937," *Austrian History Yearbook* 30 (1999), pp. 17–64.

20. Wolfdieter Bihl, "Die Juden," in *Die Habsburgermonarchie 1848–1918,* vol. 3, "Die Völker des Reiches," pt. 2, pp. 880–948, esp. p. 903; and Gerald Stourzh, "Galten die Juden als Nationalität Altösterreichs?" in Anna M. Drabek, Mordechai Eliav, Gerald Stourzh, eds., *Prag—Czernowitz—Jerusalem: Der österreichische Staat und die Juden vom Zeitalter des Absolutismus bis zum Ende der Monarchie. Studia Judaica Austriaca* 10 (1984), pp. 73–116.

21. Jacob Katz, *Tradition and Crisis: Jewish Society at the End of the Middle Ages* (New York, 1961); Salo W. Baron, *A Social and Religious History of the Jews,* 1st ed. (New York, 1937), vol. 2, pp. 87–163.

22. To use terms explained in Smith, *Ethnic Origins of Nations,* pp. 114–124.

23. On Jewish emancipation, see Reinhard Rürup, "The Tortuous and Thorny Path to Legal Equality: 'Jew Laws' and Emancipatory Legislation in Germany from the Late Eighteenth Century," *LBIYB* 31 (1986), pp. 3–33; Jacob Katz, *Out of the Ghetto: The Social Background of Jewish Emancipation, 1770–1870* (Cambridge, MA, 1973); Arthur Hertzberg, *The French Enlightenment and the Jews* (New York, 1968).

24. Paula E. Hyman, *The Emancipation of the Jews of Alsace: Acculturation and Tradition in the Nineteenth Century* (New Haven, 1991); Hyman, *From Dreyfus to Vichy: The Remaking of French Jewry, 1906–1939* (New York, 1979), pp. 1–62; Jay R. Berkovitz, *The Shaping of Jewish Identity in Nineteenth-Century France* (Detroit, 1989); David Sorkin, *The Transformation of German Jewry, 1780–1840* (New York, 1987); Marion R. Kaplan, *The Making of the Jewish Middle Class: Women, Family, and Identity in Imperial Germany* (New York, 1991); Steven M. Lowenstein, "The Pace of Modernisation of German Jewry in the Nineteenth Century," *LBIYB* 21 (1976), pp. 41–56; Michael A. Meyer, *Response to Modernity: A History of the Reform Movement in Judaism* (New York, 1988).

25. On anti-Semitism in France and Germany, see Peter Pulzer, *The Rise of Political Anti-Semitism in Germany and Austria,* rev. ed. (Cambridge, MA, 1988); George Mosse, *The Crisis of German Ideology* (New York, 1964); Mosse, *Toward the Final Solution: A History of European Racism* (New York, 1978); Jacob Katz, *From Prejudice to Destruction: Anti-Semitism, 1700–1933* (Cambridge, MA, 1980); Stephen Wilson, *Ideology and Experience: Anti-Semitism in France at the Time of the Dreyfus Affair* (Rutherford, NJ, 1982). On Jewish response to anti-Semitism in France and Germany, see Michael R. Marrus, *The Politics of Assimilation: A Study of the French Jewish Community at the Time of the Dreyfus Affair* (Oxford, 1971); Ismar Schorsch, *Jewish Reactions to German Anti-Semitism, 1870–1914* (New York, 1972); Jehuda Reinharz, *Fatherland or Promised Land: The Dilemma of the German Jew, 1893–1914* (Ann Arbor, MI, 1975). For an interesting exploration of the relationship of Jews to French and German nationalism, see George L. Mosse, *Confronting the Nation: Jewish and Western Nationalism* (Hanover, NH, 1993). Unfortunately, Mosse does not really address the question of the extent to which German Jews regarded themselves as members of the German *Volk*.

26. On anti-Semitism among Austria's Germans, see Pulzer, *The Rise of Political Anti-Semitism,* rev. ed., pp. 121–183; 195–213; Paul Molisch, *Geschichte der deutschnationalen Bewegung in Österreich* (Jena, 1926); Andrew G. Whiteside, *The Socialism of Fools: Georg Ritter von Schönerer and Austrian Pan-Germanism* (Berkeley, CA, 1975); John W. Boyer, *Political Radicalism in Late Imperial Vienna: Origins of the Christian Social Movement 1848–1897* (Chicago, 1981); and Bruce F. Pauley, *From Prejudice to Persecution: A History of Austrian Anti-Semitism* (Chapel Hill, NC, 1992).

27. William O. McCagg, Jr., *A History of Habsburg Jews, 1670–1918* (Bloomington, IN, 1989), p. 38.

28. This point is brilliantly made by Martin Broszat, "Von der Kulturnation zur Volksgruppe. Die nationale Stellung der Juden in der Bukowina im 19. und 20. Jahrhundert," *Historische Zeitschrift* 200 (1965), pp. 572–605, esp. 579–584. Cohen, *The Politics of Ethnic Survival,* pp. 13, 23–26, 42 makes a similar point about those Bohemians who adopted German culture in the first half of the nineteenth century.

29. Here I disagree fundamentally with Steven Beller, "Patriotism and the National Identity of Habsburg Jewry, 1860–1914," *LBIYB* 41 (1996), pp. 215–238, who argues that Austrian Jews who adopted German culture identified as members of the German nation. Some intellectuals did, to be sure, yet, even Beller acknowledges the primarily cultural basis of such identification.

30. Robert S. Wistrich, *The Jews of Vienna in the Age of Franz Joseph* (Oxford, 1989), pp. 30–31, 132–135; Wistrich, "Liberalism, *Deutschtum* and Assimilation," *The Jerusalem Quarterly* 42 (Spring 1987), pp. 100–102; Beller, pp. 219–220.

31. On the significance of *Bildung* for Jews in Germany, see David Sorkin, *Transformation of German Jewry*; Sorkin, "The Genesis of the Ideology of Emancipation: 1806–1840," *LBIYB* 32 (1987), pp. 11–40; George L. Mosse, *German Jews beyond Judaism* (Bloomington, IN, 1985); Mosse, *Confronting the Nation,* pp. 131–145; and Kaplan, pp. 8–10, 25–63. Joining

the middle class was a prominent feature of the Germanization of Bohemians in the first part of the nineteenth century as well; see Cohen, *Politics of Ethnic Survival*, pp. 13, 20, 24, who argues that the Germans of Prague only developed an ethnic identity in response to rising Czech nationalism.

32. Broszat, pp. 579–580, 583–584. Hillel J. Kieval, *The Making of Czech Jewry: National Conflict and Jewish Society in Bohemia, 1870–1918* (New York, 1988), p. 16, makes a similar point for Bohemian Jews. Again, I disagree with Beller, "Patriotism and National Identity," who makes the opposite point, that Jews supported Austria because they sought German (liberal) hegemony in the state.

33. Wistrich, *Jews of Vienna*, pp. 37, 114, 131–163; Wistrich, "Liberalism, *Deutschtum*, and Assimilation," pp. 103–107; Gary B. Cohen, "Jews in German Liberal Politics: Prague, 1880–1914," *Jewish History* 1, #1 (Spring 1986), pp. 55–74. The affiliation of nineteenth-century Central European Jews with liberalism was nearly universal. See Peter Pulzer, *Jews and the German State: The Political History of a Minority, 1848–1933* (Oxford, 1992) and Jacob Toury, *Die politische Orientierung der Juden in Deutschland; von Jena bis Weimar* (Tübingen, 1966).

34. This point is essentially the opposite of McCagg, who argues in his interesting if problematic *History of Habsburg Jews*, pp. 57–64, 100, that the inability of Austria to create a modern national identity in the nineteenth century facilitated the "national 'self'-denial" and the economic and cultural integration of the Jews because it did not place any demands on the Jews to adopt a particular national culture. I think, on the contrary, that the absence of an Austrian national identity facilitated the retention of Jewish ethnic identity even as it fostered economic and cultural integration and modernization.

35. Although not in the majority, many Austrian officials recognized Jewish ethnicity in the late nineteenth century. Stourzh, "Galten die Juden als Nationalität Altösterreichs?", pp. 86, 90. In his article on the Jews in Austria, Wolfdieter Bihl, p. 880, calls them "eine Gemeinschaft spezifischer Prägung—eine Abstammungsgemeinschaft mit der Jahwereligion als historischem Kern und geistigem Zusammenhalt." Austrian Jews of all political views would have agreed.

36. Alfred Pribram, *Urkunden und Akten zur Geschichte der Juden in Wien* (Vienna, 1918), vol. I, pp. 494–500. On the promulgation of the Edict, see Katz, *Out of the Ghetto*, pp. 161–164.

37. Raphael Mahler, *A History of Modern Jewry, 1780–1815* (New York, 1971), pp. 330–341; Mahler, *Hasidism and the Jewish Enlightenment: Their Confrontation in Galicia and Poland in the First Half of the Nineteenth Century* (Philadelphia, 1985); Michael Silber, "The Historical Experience of German Jewry and Its Impact on Haskalah and Reform in Hungary," in *Toward Modernity: The European Jewish Model,* Jacob Katz, ed. (New Brunswick, NJ, 1989), pp. 107–157, esp. 110–112.

38. Hillel J. Kieval, "Caution's Progress: The Modernization of Jewish Life in Prague, 1780–1830," in *Toward Modernity: The European Jewish Model*, pp. 71–105, especially 89–99; Ruth Kestenberg-Gladstein, *Neuere Geschichte der Juden in den böhmischen Ländern, Erster Teil: Das Zeitalter der Aufklärung, 1780-1830* (Tübingen, 1969), pp. 41–65.

39. Kieval, *Making of Czech Jewry*, p. 61; Gary B. Cohen, "Jews in German Society: Prague, 1860–1914," *Central European History* 10 (1977), p. 37; *Österreichische Statistik*, N.F., 1:2 (1914), pp. 54–55.

40. Kieval, *Making of Czech Jewry*, ch. 1–3.

41. Cohen, *Politics of Ethnic Survival,* pp. 76, 81–83, 101–102, 106–107, 176–182, 224–226; Cohen, "Jews in German Society," pp. 28–54. German nationalists were also anti-Semitic, but in Prague, Cohen explains, Germans eschewed anti-Semitism largely because they needed Jewish numbers. Traditional historiography also insisted on the German ori-

entation of Bohemian and Moravian Jewry. See Hans Kohn, "Before 1918 in the Historic Lands," and Ruth Kestenberg-Gladstein, "The Jews between Czechs and Germans in the Historic Lands, 1848–1918," in *The Jews of Czechoslovakia*, vol. I (Philadelphia, 1968), pp. 12–20 and 21–71.

42. Wilma A. Iggers, *Die Juden in Böhmen und Mähren: Ein historisches Lesebuch* (Munich, 1986) and Rudolf M. Wlaschek, *Juden in Böhmen: Beiträge zur Geschichte des europäischen Judentums im 19. und 20. Jahrhundert* (Munich, 1990).

43. Kieval, *Making of Czech Jewry*, pp. 36–40, 56–57; Cohen, "Jews in German Society," p. 38.

44. *Österreichische Statistik*, N.F. 1:2 (1914), pp. 54–55.

45. Exerpted in Iggers, *Die Juden in Böhmen*, p. 213. All translations from the German are my own.

46. Eric Fischer, "Memoirs and Reminiscences (1898–1985)," unpublished memoir, LBI, p. 30. Aunt Paula, Fischer adds, spoke "kitchen Czech" to the maid.

47. Friedrich Bill, "Kuriose Biographie; Von Franz Josephs und meiner Geburt bis zum Tode Mitteleuropas," unpublished memoir (1954), LBI, p. 8. See also Fischer, p. 30. For a similar situation in Leipnik, Moravia, see Arnold Hindls, "Erinnerungen aus meinem Leben" (1966), unpublished memoir, LBI, pp. 2–3, 15.

48. Arnold Höllriegel (Richard Arnold Bermann), "Die Fahrt auf dem Katarakt (Autobiographie ohne einen Helden)," unpublished memoir, LBI, pp. 4–6, 21–25.

49. Fritz Mauthner, *Prager Jugendjahre: Erinnerungen* (Frankfurt, 1969; orig. 1918), pp. 49–51. He too felt Bohemian (p. 130).

50. Else Bergmann, "Familiengeschichte," unpublished memoir, LBI, pp. 26–27.

51. Olly Schwarz, "Lebens-Erinnerungen," unpublished memoir, LBI, pp. 3, 12–14. Her family moved to Vienna in 1898.

52. As excerpted in Wilma Iggers, *Women of Prague: Ethnic Diversity and Social Change from the Eighteenth Century to the Present* (Providence, RI, 1995), p. 231.

53. As excerpted in Iggers, *Die Juden in Böhmen*, p. 216.

54. Hans Kohn, *Living in a World Revolution: My Encounters with History* (New York, 1964), pp. 35–36.

55. Joseph Wechsberg, *The Vienna I Knew: Memories of a European Childhood* (Garden City, NY, 1979), p. 148.

56. See, for example, Otto Ehrentheil, "Part of the Honors," unpublished memoir (1977/78), LBI, pp. 17, 19, 31; Fischer, p. 25; Hindls, p. 2.

57. As excerpted in Iggers, *Women of Prague*, p. 201.

58. *Hella*, transcription of taped reminiscences of Hella Roubicek Mautner, privately printed by her children, Nelly Urbach and Willy Mautner (Washington, 1996), pp. 22, 31, 39, 44. I thank Nelly Urbach for providing me with a copy of this book.

59. Joseph Wechsberg recalled in his memoirs, p. 202, that the Jews of Mährisch Ostrau "considered Vienna, not Prague, our spiritual capital." The Jews of Moravia deserve serious scholarly attention. Virtually all studies of Jews in the Czech lands focus on Bohemia. On Moravia, see only Hugo Gold, ed., *Die Juden und Judengemeinden Mährens in Vergangenheit und Gegenwart* (Brünn, 1929) and Theodor Haas, *Die Juden in Mähren: Darstellung der Rechtsgeschichte und Statistik unter besonderer Berücksichtigung des 19. Jahrhunderts* (Brünn, 1908).

60. Kohn, *Living in a World Revolution*, pp. 3, 67.

61. Ibid., pp. 11–18. Kohn would have liked Austria-Hungary to transform itself into a federation of nationalities.

62. Höllriegel, pp. 5–6.

63. Gertrude Hirsch, "Memories of My Childhood and Early Married Life," unpublished memoir, LBI, pp. 47–48.

64. Bertha Landre, "Durch's Sieb der Zeit gefallen; Jedes Menschenleben ist ein Roman," unpublished memoir, LBI, pp. 9–10.

65. *Hella*, p. 32.

66. Manès Sperber, *God's Water Carriers* (New York, 1987), p. 74.

67. See, for example, Joachim Schoenfeld, *Jewish Life in Galicia under the Austro-Hungarian Empire and in the Reborn Poland 1898–1919* (Hoboken, NJ, 1985), p. xix. On the cult of Franz Joseph among the Jews, see the excellent description by Wistrich, *Jews of Vienna*, pp. 175–181.

68. Schoenfeld, p. xx. Yossel is the Yiddish nickname for the Hebrew name Joseph; Froyim is a nickname for Ephraim, a Hebrew name in place of Franz. Froyim also sounds somewhat like the Yiddish *frum*, or "religious," a statement of admiration for the emperor's Catholic piety.

69. Minna Lachs, *Warum schaust du zurück. Erinnerungen 1907–1941* (Vienna, 1986), pp. 20, 22, 51.

70. On the nearly total separation and mutual hostility between Jews, Poles, and Ruthenians, see Norman Salsitz (as told to Richard Skolnik), *A Jewish Boyhood in Poland: Remembering Kolbuszowa* (Syracuse, NY, 1992); also Schoenfeld, pp. 11–13, 126; Sperber, pp. 12–13, 38; and virtually all sources on interwar Polish Jewry.

71. Ezra Mendelsohn, "Jewish Assimilation in L'viv: The Case of Wilhelm Feldman," in *Nationbuilding and the Politics of Nationalism*, pp. 94–110; Piotr Wróbel, "The Jews of Galicia under Austrian-Polish Rule, 1869–1918," *Austrian History Yearbook* 25 (1994), pp. 97–138, esp. 113–117. See also Schoenfeld, pp. 8, 49–51; Lachs, p. 10.

72. *Österreichische Statistik*, N.F., 1:2 (1914), pp. 54–55; Jacob Thon, *Die Juden in Oesterreich* (Berlin, 1908), pp. 108, 110; Arthur Ruppin, *The Jews of Today* (New York, 1913), pp. 113–114.

73. *Oesterreichisches statistiches Jahrbuch*, 1875, pt. V, pp. 32–43; *Österreichische Statistik*, 52:3, pp. 30–37.

74. Mendelsohn, *The Jews of East Central Europe between the World Wars*, pp. 18–19.

75. Jewish memoirs do not mention any Ruthenian identity, although they do insist that Jews got along with their Ruthenian neighbors and servants. According to the 1910 census, only 2% of Galician Jews listed Ruthenian as their *Umgangssprache* (*Österreichische Statistik*, N.F., 1:2 (1914), pp. 54–55). On Ruthenian anti-Semitism, see John-Paul Himka, "Ukrainian-Jewish Antagonism in the Galician Countryside During the Late Nineteenth Century," in *Ukrainian-Jewish Relations in Historical Perspective*, Howard Aster and Peter J. Potichnyj, eds., 2d ed. (Edmonton, 1990), pp. 111–158.

On the Ruthenians of Galicia, see Paul Robert Magocsi, *A History of Ukraine* (Seattle, 1966), pp. 383–457. Interestingly, Magocsi makes the same point about Ruthenians (whom he calls Ukrainians) as I do about Jews. That is, the multinational Austrian framework allowed them to be loyal Austrians and Ukrainian national patriots at the same time (p. 456).

76. Salsitz, pp. 51, 54–62. Manès Sperber, p. 62, on the other hand, admits that he did not enjoy learning Polish in school.

77. Helene Deutsch, *Confrontations with Myself* (New York, 1973), pp. 66–67, 196–197.

78. There is unfortunately not much scholarship in any language on the Jews and Jewish identity in turn-of-the-century Galicia. See McCagg, pp. 105-122, 182–187. The literature of interwar Poland indicates that most Galician Jews viewed themselves primarily as Jews. See Mendelsohn, *Jews of East Central Europe*, pp. 11–83, especially 18–19; Mendelsohm, *Zionism in Poland: The Formative Years, 1915-1926* (New Haven, 1981); Mendelsohn, "A Note on Jewish Assimilation in the Polish Lands," in *Jewish Assimilation in Modern Times*, Bela Vago, ed. (Boulder, CO, 1981), pp. 141–149; Celia S. Heller, *On the Edge of Destruction: Jews of Poland Between the Two World Wars* (New York, 1977); and Yisrael Gutman, Ezra

Mendelsohn, Jehuda Reinharz, and Chone Shmeruk, eds., *The Jews of Poland between Two World Wars* (Hanover, NH, 1989).

79. *Österreichische Statistik*, N.F., 1:2 (1914), pp. 54–55. On the Jews of Bukovina generally see McCagg, pp. 171–174; Broszat, pp. 572–605; N. M. Gelber, "Geschichte der Juden in der Bukowina, 1774–1914," in *Geschichte der Juden in der Bukowina*, Hugo Gold, ed. (Tel Aviv, 1958–1962); and Salomon Kassner, *Die Juden in der Bukowina*, 2nd ed. (Vienna, 1917). On Bukovina nationality politics generally, see Kann, *Multinational Empire*, vol. I, pp. 329–332.

80. Adolf Mechner, "My Family Biography," unpublished memoir (1978–1981), LBI, especially pp. 55–69.

81. Broszat, p. 579.

82. Ibid., pp. 585-95; Stourzh, "Galten die Juden als Nationalität Altösterreichs?", pp. 91–94; Kassner, pp. 46–49, 53–57; John Leslie, "Der Ausgleich in der Bukowina von 1910: Zur österreichischen Nationalitätenpolitik vor dem Ersten Weltkrieg," in *Geschichte zwischen Freiheit und Ordnung: Gerald Stourzh zum 60. Geburtstag*, Emil Brix, Thomas Fröschl, and Josef Leidenfrost, eds. (Graz, 1991), pp. 113–144.

83. McCagg, pp. 123–139, 187–195; Wolfgang Häusler, "Assimilation und Emanzipation des ungarischen Judentums um die Mitte des 19. Jahrhunderts," *Studia Judaica Austriaca* 3 (1976), pp. 33–79; George Barany, "Magyar Jew or Jewish Magyar," in *Jews and Non-Jews in Eastern Europe, 1918–1945*, Béla Vago and George L. Mosse, eds. (New York, 1974), pp. 51–98; Mendelsohn, *Jews of East Central Europe*, pp. 85–128, esp. 85–94; Robert Kann, "Hungarian Jewry During Austria-Hungary's Constitutional Period (1867–1914)," *Jewish Social Studies* 7 (1945), pp. 357–386; Michael K. Silber, "The Entrance of Jews into Hungarian Society in Vormärz: The Case of the Casinos," in *Assimilation and Community*, Jonathan Frankel and Steven Zipperstein, eds. (Cambridge, 1992), pp. 284–323; and most recently, Raphael Patai, *The Jews of Hungary: History, Culture, Psychology* (Detroit, 1996). Patai does a good job describing the Hungarian identity of Hungarian Jews, but incorrectly places the transformation in the first half of the nineteenth century when it took place in the second half. This book suffers from the absence of a scholarly apparatus.

84. Michael Silber, "The Historical Experience," in *Toward Modernity*, p. 127.

85. Bihl, "Die Juden," *Die Habsburgermonarchie*, vol. 3, pt. 2, p. 907; Silber, "The Historical Experience," p. 127; McCagg, p. 190.

86. Victor Karady, "Religious Divisions, Socio-Economic Stratification and the Modernization of Hungarian Jewry after the Emancipation," in *Jews in the Hungarian Economy 1760–1945*, Michael Silber, ed. (Jerusalem, 1992), p. 170 and Table 3 (p. 182).

87. Raphael Patai, *Apprentice in Budapest: Memories of a World That Is No More* (Salt Lake City, 1988), pp. 6–7.

88. Ibid., p. 80.

89. As quoted in Patai, *Jews of Hungary*, p. 344; original in *Egyenlöség*, July 10, 1904. On the general rejection of Zionism, pp. 328, 337–347.

90. Karady, p. 177, makes this point, a very welcome corrective to conventional wisdom that holds that all Hungarian Jews were intense Hungarian nationalists.

91. Charles Fenyvesi, *When the World Was Whole: Three Centuries of Memories* (New York, 1990), pp. 112–115.

92. Ibid., p. 109.

93. For the 1910 breakdown of Viennese population by place of origin (as measured by *Heimatrecht*, place of legal residence rights), see *Österreichische Statistik*, N.F. 2:1, pp. 33*, 2–27. On Czechs in Vienna, see Monika Glettler, *Die Wiener Tschechen um 1900: Strukturanalyse einer nationalen Minderheit in der Grossstadt* (Munich, 1972).

94. Sigmund Mayer, *Ein jüdischer Kaufmann 1831 bis 1911: Lebenserinnerungen* (Leipzig, 1911), p. 280.

95. Arnold Höllriegel, who grew up in Prague, but attended the last four years of *Gymnasium* in Vienna, was shocked by the vehemence of the German-Czech conflict in Prague when he returned to attend university there after his years in "care-free," "unfanatic" Vienna (Höllriegel, p. 22). Interestingly, although vicious anti-Semitism flourished in Vienna, it was less obsessed with the "German-ness" of the Jews than anti-Semitism elsewhere. See Boyer, pp. 41, 215; Carl Schorske, "Politics in a New Key: An Austrian Trio," *Fin-de-Siècle Vienna: Politics and Culture* (New York, 1980), pp. 136, 139; and Richard S. Geehr, *Karl Lueger: Mayor of Fin-de-Siècle Vienna* (Detroit, 1990). On the other hand, Michael John, "We Do Not Even Possess Our Selves," reminds us that the Germans dominated in Vienna, forceably assimilating Czech immigrants, some of whose descendants became fanatical German nationalists to overcompensate for their sense of inferiority in the German city. Of course, the fact that they could do so attests to a less rigid attitude to German identity than elsewhere.

96. Interestingly, in his brilliant study of the satirist Karl Krauss, Edward Timms seems to make the opposite point. He argues that "the Jewish population of Vienna experienced the crisis of Austrian identity in its most acute form." (*Karl Krauss: Apocalyptic Satirist: Culture and Catastrophe in Habsburg Vienna* (New Haven, 1986), p. 13). I would argue that the crisis, or rather the complexity, of Austrian identity made it easier for Jews to negotiate their Jewish identity, even if, like Kraus, they chose to negate that Jewish identity by conversion. It was precisely in Vienna that Kraus could be, as Timms notes, "a Jew by birth, an Austrian by nationality, a Viennese by residence, a German by language," even if Kraus the satirist rejected all those identities (p. 182).

97. For a detailed description, see Rozenblit, *Jews of Vienna*.

98. In his impressive study of Viennese Jewry, Wistrich, *Jews of Vienna*, correctly points out (p. x) that my book on the Jews of Vienna "did not really address in depth . . . such crucial questions as the nature of Jewish identity and self-definition." This book is my attempt to take up Wistrich's challenge and address in depth that very question. Wistrich and I agree that the Jews of Vienna were more ethnically Jewish than were the Jews in Germany. See his "The Modernization of Viennese Jewry," pp. 59, 63. While we also agree on the causes for this greater ethnicity—the immigrant nature of the community, the dynamics of national affiliation in Austria-Hungary, and anti-Semitism—Wistrich places far more weight on the response to anti-Semitism than I would. He also emphasizes the culture and politics of the elite, while I am concerned with the lives of ordinary Jews.

99. Stefan Zweig, *The World of Yesterday* (New York, 1943), p. v.

100. See for example, Toni Stolper, memoirs taped and transcribed by her grandson Alistair Campbell, unpublished memoirs, LBI, p. 1.

101. George Clare, *Last Waltz in Vienna: The Rise and Destruction of a Family, 1842–1942* (New York, 1980), pp. 15, 17, 31.

102. Erna Segal, "You Shall Never Forget," (German text), unpublished memoir, LBI, pp. 15, 21.

103. See, for example, Fritz Lieben, "Aus meinem Leben," unpublished memoir (1960), LBI, p. 3; Segal, p. 26.

104. Mayer, pp. 289, 350, 485.

105. Arthur Schnitzler, *My Youth in Vienna* (New York, 1970), p. 13.

106. Ehrentheil, p. 99.

107. Max Kriegsfield, "Escape into Fear. An Austrian Jew's Odyssy," unpublished memoir, LBI, preface.

108. Marsha L. Rozenblit, "Jewish Identity and the Modern Rabbi: The Cases of Isak Noa Mannheimer, Adolf Jellinek, and Moritz Güdemann in Nineteenth-Century Vienna," *LBIYB* 35 (1990), pp. 103–131.

109. Isak Noa Mannheimer, "Gutachten des Herrn Predigers Dr. Mannheimer in Wien," in *Rabbinische Gutachten über die Beschneidung,* Salomon Abraham Trier, ed. (Frankfurt, 1844), pp. 89–104, quotation on p. 91.

110. Adolf Jellinek, *Der jüdische Stamm: Ethnographische Studien* (Vienna, 1869), pp. 45, 47. For a similar analysis of Jellinek, see Wistrich, *Jews of Vienna,* pp. 114–120 and Robert S. Wistrich, "The Modernization of Viennese Jewry: The Impact of German Culture in a Multi-Ethnic State," in *Toward Modernity: The European Jewish Model,* p. 56.

111. Adolf Jellinek, "Die Israelitischen Allianzen," in *Aus der Zeit: Tagesfragen und Tagesbegebenheiten,* 2d series (Budapest, 1886), p. 131.

112. *Die Neuzeit,* 10 March 1893, p. 113.

113. Moritz Güdemann, *Jerusalem, die Opfer und die Orgel: Predigt, am Sabbath, 25. Adar 5631 (18. März 1871)* (Vienna, 1871).

114. Moritz Güdemann, *Nationaljudenthum* (Leipzig, 1897), pp. 13, 19.

115. Moritz Güdemann, *Sechs Predigten im Leopoldstädter Tempel zu Wien* (Vienna, 1867), esp. pp. 11–18.

116. Josef S. Bloch, *My Reminiscences* (Vienna, 1923), p. 182. Bloch translated his own memoirs into English and is thus responsible for any infelicitous phrasing in the quotation.

117. See, for example, *OW,* 14 August 1896, pp. 649–650; 11 August 1905, pp. 499–500.

118. Bloch, *Reminiscences,* p. 182. See also Josef S. Bloch, *Die nationale Zwist und die Juden in Oesterreich* (Vienna, 1886). Wistrich, *Jews of Vienna,* p. 194, describes the paper as espousing a "veritable cult of loyal pro-Habsburg Austrianism." For a good analysis of Bloch's position, see Wistrich, *Jews of Vienna,* pp. 194–198, 270–309, and Wistrich, "The Modernization of Viennese Jewry," pp. 60–63.

119. *OW,* 30 April 1886, pp. 193–195. See also *Mittheilungen der Österreichisch-israelitischen Union,* vol. 2, no. 12 (May 1890), pp. 2–3.

120. Bloch was instrumental in the creation of the Union even though he never assumed leadership of the organization. See his *Reminiscences,* pp. 182, 188–193; *OW,* 15 October 1884, pp. 1–3. On the Union generally see Rozenblit, *Jews of Vienna,* pp. 154–161; Wistrich, *Jews of Vienna,* pp. 193–202, 289–292, 310–343; Jacob Toury, "Troubled Beginnings: The Emergence of the Österreichisch-Israelitische Union, *LBIYB* 30 (1985), pp. 457–475.

121. Rozenblit, *Jews of Vienna,* pp. 161–174; Wistrich, *Jews of Vienna,* pp. 347–493; Adolf Gaisbauer, *Davidstern und Doppeladler: Zionismus und jüdischer Nationalismus in Österreich, 1882–1918* (Vienna, 1988); Adolf Böhm, *Die zionistische Bewegung,* 2 vols., 2d rev. ed. (Tel Aviv, 1935–1937), vol. I, pp. 135–137, 323–325, 332–347.

122. In general, the Zionist movement appealed largely to East European Jews. On Zionism in Galicia and Bukovina, see Gaisbauer, pp. 63–70, 194–244.

123. For an excellent analysis of Prague Zionism see Kieval, *The Making of Czech Jewry,* pp. 93–153, 200.

124. Max Brod, *Streitbares Leben, 1884-1968,* rev. ed. (Munich, 1969), pp. 52–53.

125. *OW,* 5 July 1907, pp. 440–441.

126. *Jüdisches Volksblatt,* 13 February 1903, pp. 1–2.

127. For the Jewish national program, see Hermann Kadisch, *Jung-Juden und Jung-Oesterreich* (Vienna, 1912); "Programm der Jüdischen Volkspartei," *Jüdisches Volksblatt,* 10 January 1902, p. 1; Gaisbauer, pp. 451–523; Böhm, vol. I, pp. 342–347. Jewish nationalists were clearly influenced by the 1899 Brünn Platform of the Austrian Social Democrats and by socialist thinkers Karl Renner and Otto Bauer, even though the latter never included the Jews as one of the nations of Austria in their own schemes for the national reorganization of Austria. See Karl Renner, *Der Kampf der österreichischen Nationen um den Staat* (Leipzig, 1903).

128. "Programm der zionistischen Partei der Juden in Oesterreich," CZA, Z2/433; "Thesen der Krakauer Partei-Congress," A 141/191, and "Programm der zionistischen Partei in Oesterreich," A196/17.

129. *JZ,* 20 June 1907; *Neue Nationalzeitung,* 10 October 1907, pp. 1–2; Böhm, I, pp. 343–344. In Vienna, the Zionist Isidor Schalit ran for parliament from the Leopoldstadt, but lost decisively (Rozenblit, *Jews of Vienna,* pp. 175–184).

130. Rozenblit, *Jews of Vienna,* pp. 185–193. Only in 1932 did the Zionists win a majority on the *Kultusgemeinde* board in Vienna. See Harriet Pass Freidenreich, *Jewish Politics in Vienna, 1918–1938* (Bloomington, 1991), pp. 48–83.

131. Thon, pp. 69–71, 75–81; Rozenblit, *Jews of Vienna,* pp. 132–146. Some recent works on Austrian Jews have chosen to count as Jews not only converts but anyone with some Jewish ancestry. See for example, McCagg, *History of Habsburg Jews,* and Steven Beller, *Vienna and the Jews 1867–1938: A Cultural History* (Cambridge, 1989). This study will not deal with such tenuous Jews but rather with people who considered themselves Jewish.

CHAPTER 2

1. For an excellent discussion of "the spirit of 1914," see Reinhard Rürup, "Der 'Geist von 1914' in Deutschland; Kriegsbegeisterung und Ideologisierung des Krieges im Ersten Weltkrieg," in *Ansichten vom Krieg. Vergleichende Studien zum Ersten Weltkrieg in Literatur und Gesellschaft,* Berndt Hüppauf, ed. (Königstein/Ts., 1984), pp. 1–30. For war enthusiasm among German women, see Ute Daniel, *Arbeiterfrauen in der Kriegsgesellschaft: Beruf, Familie und Politik im Ersten Weltkrieg* (Göttingen, 1989), pp. 24–25. Most recently, Niall Ferguson, *The Pity of War* (New York, 1999), pp. 174–210, argues that enthusiasm for war in August 1914 typified only the urban, middle-classes and not society as a whole. Evidence, however, indicates more broad-based support for the war effort even if many people understood the negative consequences of war.

2. On France, see Hyman, *From Dreyfus to Vichy* pp. 49–62; on Germany, Egmont Zechlin, *Die deutsche Politik und die Juden im ersten Weltkrieg* (Göttingen, 1969), pp. 10–16, 86–100; Eva G. Reichmann, "Der Bewusstseinswandel der deutschen Juden," in *Deutsches Judentum in Krieg und Revolution, 1916–1923,* Werner E. Mosse and Arnold Paucker, eds. (Tübingen, 1971), pp. 511–514, 548; Werner Jochmann, "Die Ausbreitung des Antisemitismus," in ibid., p. 409; and Stephen Magill, "Defense and Introspection: German Jewry, 1914," in *Jews and Germans from 1860 to 1933: The Problematic Symbiosis,* David Bronsen, ed. (Heidelberg, 1979) pp. 209–233.

3. Z. A. B. Zeman, *The Break-Up of the Habsburg Empire 1914–1918: A Study in National and Social Revolution* (London, 1961), pp. 42–62; Arthur J. May, *The Passing of the Hapsburg Monarchy, 1914–1918* (Philadelphia, 1966), pp. 6, 83, 86–88; 287–289; Macartney, pp. 810–813; Victor S. Mamatey, "The Czech War Time Dilemma: The Habsburgs or the Entente?" in *East Central European Society in World War I,* Béla Király and Nándor F. Dreisziger, eds. (Boulder, 1985), pp. 103–111; Richard B. Spence, "The Yugoslav Role in the Austro-Hungarian Army, 1914–1918," in ibid., pp. 354–365.

4. The literature on the origins of World War I is vast. In English, see Samuel Williamson, Jr., *Austria-Hungary and the Origins of World War I* (New York, 1991); Williamson, "Vienna and July 1914: The Origins of the Great War Once More," in *Essays on World War I: Origins and Prisoners of War,* Samuel R. Williamson, Jr. and Peter Pastor, eds. (New York, 1983), pp. 9–36; May, pp. 17–85; James Joll, *The Origins of the First World War* (London, 1984). Refocusing on Austo-Hungarian lust for war in 1914, Williamson takes issue with German historian Fritz Fischer who had placed the blame for starting World War I squarely on Germany. See Fritz Fischer, *Germany's Aims in the First World War* (New York, 1967).

5. Mechner, "My Family Biography," p. 72. See also Kohn, *Living in a World Revolution*, p. 82.

6. Schoenfeld, p. 129; Esti D. Freud, "Vignettes of My Life," unpublished memoir, LBI, pp. 12–13; Hindls, "Erinnerungen," p. 61; Höllriegel, "Die Fahrt auf dem Katarakt," p. 148; Regina Berger Lederer, "From Old World to New: Omi's Stories," unpublished memoir, LBI, p. 6.

7. Virtually all the memoirs that mention the assassination contrast it with the pleasures of the memoirists' vacations that summer. See, for example, Schoenfeld, p. 130; Höllriegel, p. 149; Kohn, p. 82; Zweig, p. 218; Landre, "Durch Sieb," p. 96.

8. Lillian Bader, "One Life is not Enough," unpublished memoir, LBI, p. 74. See also Zweig, p. 215; Freud, p. 13.

9. *OW*, 3 July 1914, pp. 461–462; 10 July 1914, pp. 481–482; 17 July 1914, pp. 497–498.

10. *JZ*, 3 July 1914, p. 1.

11. *Selbstwehr*, 3 July 1914, p. 1. Such views were also expressed by the Israelitische Kultusgemeinde of Vienna in its condolence letter to the Kaiser, CAHJP, AW 246/5; and by the IKG of Prague, JMP, IKG-Repräsentanz Prag, Sitzungs-Protokoll 1914, meeting 30 June 1914.

12. *JVS*, 1 July 1914, p. 1.

13. *JVS*, 1 July 1914, p. 1; *OW*, 10 July 1914, pp. 486–487; 17 July 1914.

14. Lachs, p. 25.

15. Sperber, p. 69.

16. Bader, pp. 75–76. See also Stolper, p. 49, who says she was "thunderstruck" at the beginning of the war.

17. See, for example, Höllriegel, pp. 151, 153; Mechner, p. 73; Landre, p. 97; Bader, p. 76; Lachs, p. 27; Egon Basch, "Wirken und Wandern: Lebenserinnerungen," unpublished memoir, LBI, p. 30; Jacob Katz, *With My Own Eyes: The Autobiography of an Historian* (Hanover, 1995), p. 19.

18. Lieben, p. 104.

19. Zweig, pp. 221–223, 228; quotations on p. 223.

20. Höllriegel, p. 152.

21. See, for example, Bader, p. 75; Lieben, p. 104; Zweig, p. 223. Some memoirists also remember that the Czechs were somewhat less enthusiastic. See Kohn, p. 86; Brod, *Streitbares Leben*, pp. 92–93.

22. Zweig, p. 226. See also Kohn, *Living in a World Revolution*, p. 86.

23. Sperber, pp. 69–70.

24. Landre, p. 97; Hindls, p.61.

25. Segal, "You Shall Never Forget," p. 14.

26. Landre, pp. 97, 99. For a theoretical discussion of men as "valiant warriors" and women as "beautiful souls" see Jean Bethke Elshtain, *Women and War* (New York, 1987), pp. 3–4, 47–52, 93, 147, 148.

27. Bader, p. 76.

28. Sperber, p. 70; Schoenfeld, p. 132, says everyone cried at the train station.

29. Joseph Floch, unpublished memoir, LBI, p. 21. The English is Floch's own. Other memoirists also feared the war would lead to disaster; see, for example, Stolper, p. 64.

30. Kohn, *Living in a World Revolution*, pp. 83, 59. See also Sperber, p. 70; Bader, pp. 76–77.

31. See, for example, Kohn, *Living in a World Revolution*, p. 85; Mechner, p. 73.

32. See, for example, Höllriegel, p. 152; Sperber, p. 71; Moritz Güdemann, "Aus meinem Leben," unpublished memoir (1899–1918), LBI, typescript version, p. 217; Wolf-

gang von Weisl, "Skizze zu einer Autobiographie," in *Die Juden in der Armee Österreich-Ungarns* (Tel Aviv, 1971), p. 35.

33. "An unsere Glaubensbrüder," 29 July 1914, CAHJP, AW 357/2, AW 356.

34. *OW*, 31 July 1914, p. 529; 4 September 1914, p. 609; 30 October 1914, p. 740. The Waidhofen pledge, a statement of racial anti-Semitism articulated by the dueling fraternities in Austria, declared that Jews were devoid of honor and incapable of rendering satisfaction in duels.

35. *MONOIU*, July–August 1914, pp. 1–2. See also November–December 1914, pp. 1–3.

36. *JZ*, 31 July 1914, p. 1. See also *JVS*, 19 August 1914, p. 1.

37. See, for example, memorandum, Zionist Central Committee for Western Austria, n.d., but probably August or September 1914, CZA, Z3/840; letter of Leo Herrmann, a Prague Zionist then serving as secretary of the World Zionist Executive, 23 April 1915, CZA, Z3/842.

38. On the anti-Russian theme in Austrian war propaganda, see May, pp. 297–301, 306. Socialists in both Germany and Austria also viewed the war as a struggle against Russian despotism (May, pp. 287–288). Socialists understood this struggle with Russia in abstract terms, but Jews personalized it. To them, Russia was evil not just because of a repressive government, but because it persecuted Jews.

39. *OW*, 7 August 1914, pp. 547–548; 14 August 1914, p. 561.

40. *Zweimonats-Bericht . . . der . . . Bnai Brith*, vol. 17, #4 (1914), p. 127; and editorial, pp. 129–130.

41. *Jung Juda*, 21 August 1914, p. 213.

42. *OW*, 11 September 1914, p. 630; see also pp. 627–628.

43. *OW*, 28 August 1914, p. 596. See also Eugen Tannenbaum, ed., *Kriegsbriefe deutscher und österreichischer Juden* (Berlin, 1915), pp. 177–181.

44. *OW*, 14 August 1914, pp. 562–563; 21 August 1914, pp. 577–579; 28 August 1914, pp. 593–595; 4 September 1914, pp. 610–611; 18 September 1914, pp. 640–643; 8 October 1914, pp. 681–683; 16 October 1914, pp. 697–699; 13 November 1914, pp. 773–775; 20 November 1914, pp. 793–795; 18 December 1914, pp. 873–874.

45. R. Färber, *Unser Kaiser, ein Sendbote Gottes; Predigten zum allerhöchsten Geburtstage Sr. Maj. des Kaisers Franz Joseph I. und aus anderen patriotischen Anlässen* (Mährisch Ostrau, 1915), pp. 23–30, quotation, p. 27.

46. "Zu Chanukah 5675 (1914)," in Ibid., pp. 30–34.

47. D. Herzog, "Das Gelöbnis der Treue," in his *Kriegspredigten* (Frankfurt, 1915), pp. 14–18. See also "Die Pflichten unserer Tage," pp. 25–34. For similar views, see speech at IKG Wien celebrating Franz Joseph's 84th birthday in 1914 in CAHJP, AW 305/10.

48. A. J. Hoover, *God, Germany, and Britain in the Great War: A Study in Clerical Nationalism* (New York, 1989), p. 56.

49. *Selbstwehr*, 27 August 1914, pp. 1–2, 6; 20 September 1914, p. 2. Of all the Zionist papers, *Selbstwehr* was by far the most intellectually engaging.

50. *JVS*, 19 August 1914, p. 2; 10 September 1914, p. 1.

51. Printed appeal, CAHJP, AW 357/1; reprinted in *OW*, 28 August 1914, p. 596. For a similar appeal by Galician Zionists, see *JVS*, 3 September 1914, p. 3.

52. See, for example, *OW*, 11 December 1914, p. 855; 25 December 1914, pp. 898, 908, 909; 15 January 1915, p. 48; 19 November 1915, p. 858; 24 December 1915, pp. 940, 949; *JZ*, 11 December 1914, p. 1; *Jung Juda*, 4 December 1914, p. 277.

53. *OW*, 24 December 1915, p. 940. Rabbinic sermons sounded the same note. See, for example, Emanuel Schwartz, *Der Krieg kommt, um das gebeugte u. gekränkte Recht herzustellen; Predigt gehalten bei der Chanukkafeier 1915* (Prague, 1915), p. 7.

54. *OW*, 24 December 1915, pp. 940, 949; Schwartz, *Der Krieg kommt*, p. 8; S. Guttmann, *Festrede anlässlich des 67. Jahrestages der Thronbesteigung unseres Allergnädigsten Kaisers und Königs Franz Joseph I. bei dem am 2. Dezember 1915 im Tempel zu Lemberg stattgehabten Festgottesdienste* (Lemberg, 1915), pp. 3–4.

55. *Jung Juda*, 26 March 1915, pp. 82–83.

56. See, for example, *OW*, 11 September 1914, pp. 625–626; 23 October 1914, pp. 721–722; 25 December 1914, p. 898; 21 May 1915, p. 381.

57. See, for example, Färber, *Unser Kaiser*, pp. 26, 38; Schwartz, *Wenn du in den Krieg ziehst . . .* (Prague, 1914), pp. 3–4; Herzog, *Kriegspredigten*, pp. 27, 30, 94; Isaak Hirsch, *Die Juden und der Krieg* (Wiznitz, 1915) p. 14; Guttmann, pp. 4, 6; articles by Rabbi W. Reich in *OW*, 28 August 1914, p. 593; 4 September 1914, pp. 610–611; 18 September 1914, p. 64; and letters by Jewish chaplains, *OW*, 16 April 1915, pp. 290, 293; 8 October 1915, pp. 737–738.

58. Färber, *Unser Kaiser*, p. 26; Reich in *OW*, 28 August 1914, p. 593.

59. *Jung Juda*, 21 August 1914, p. 213; 18 September 1914, p. 229; 9 October 1914, p. 245; 12 February 1915, p. 48; 26 March 1915, p. 94; 28 May 1915, p. 145. See also *OW*, 7 August 1914, p. 545; 23 October 1914, pp. 721–722.

60. *Jung Juda*, 26 March 1915, p. 94.

61. On German Jews, see Zechlin, pp. 86–87, 96, 98; Magill, p. 223; Reichmann in Mosse and Paucker, p. 571; on Germans generally see Hoover, pp. 12, 99, 115, 131; Ferguson, pp. 208–210; on Austrian clergy, see May, pp. 297–298.

62. On Jews in Germany, see Zechlin, pp. 86, 95–96; Magill, pp. 216–217, 220–222; Pulzer, *Jews and the German State*, p. 195. For moving descriptions of how German-Jewish soldiers regarded the war with Russia as a just cause and as a war of revenge for the pogroms, see Tannenbaum, ed., *Kriegsbriefe*, pp. 1, 39, 126, 128.

On the Jews of England, see David Caesarani, "An Embattled Minority: The Jews of Britain during the First World War," in *The Politics of Marginality: Race, the Radical Right and Minorities in Twentieth Century Britain*, T. Kushner and K. Lunn, eds. (London, 1990), p. 62. On France, see Hyman, pp. 52, 57–59.

63. See, for example, *OW*, 21 August 1914, pp. 577–580; 28 August 1914, p. 595; 30 October 1914, pp. 737–739; 22 January 1915, pp. 58–59; 21 May 1915, pp. 382–383; *JVS*, 19 August 1914, p. 2; 10 September 1914, p. 2; 28 September 1914, pp. 1–2; 29 March 1915, p. 2; 29 April 1915, p. 1. German Jews also attacked England and France for allying themselves with evil Russia; see Zechlin, p. 96; Magill, p. 22; Pulzer, p. 195. Germans generally insisted that England was jealous of German economic power, and they attacked the British alliance with Russia; see Hoover, pp. 51–62.

64. Norman Stone, *The Eastern Front, 1914–1917* (New York, 1975), pp. 80–114, 122, 128–144; Kann, *History of the Habsburg Empire*, pp. 484–485; May, pp. 95–99, 107–109.

65. See, for example, *OW*, 4 September 1914, pp. 609–610; 18 December 1914, p. 891; 1 January 1915, pp. 2–3; 12 March 1915, pp. 200–201; 16 April 1915, pp. 289–290, 301; *JZ*, 11 December 1914, p. 1; *Selbstwehr*, 29 January 1915, pp. 1–2; 12 February 1915, p. 1; 19 March 1915, p. 1 (here Ausrottungskrieg); *JVS*, 29 March 1915, pp. 3–4 (also Ausrottungskrieg); *Zweimonats-Bericht . . . der . . . Bnai Brith*, vol. 18, no. 4 (1915), pp. 114–117; *Jung Juda*, 30 April 1915, pp. 115–117; *Jüdisher Nationalkalender . . . 1915/16*, p. 114; *Jüdisches Archiv*, no. 1 (May 1915), pp. 4–12.

66. *OW*, 26 February 1915, p. 154.

67. *OW*, 21 May 1915, p. 381.

68. *JVS*, 29 March 1915, p. 2. See also *Selbstwehr*, 7 May 1915, p. 1.

69. *JVS*, 29 April 1915, pp. 1–2.

70. See, for example, *OW*, 4 September 1914, p. 617; 11 September 1914, pp. 629–630, 634; 14 May 1915, pp. 366–367; *JZ*, 18 September 1914, p. 2; 27 November 1914, pp. 1–2;

JVS, 28 September 1914, pp. 1–2; 18 March 1915, p. 3; *Jüdisches Archiv*, no. 1 (May 1915), p. 13.

71. *OW*, 4 September 1914, pp. 611, 619.

72. *JZ*, 30 October 1914, p. 2. The Russians took Weisselberger hostage to Russia and released him only in November 1915 (see *JZ*, 19 November 1915, p. 3).

73. *OW*, 14 May 1915, p. 367. See also Ludwig Bató, "Das Kriegsjahr 5675," *Jüdischer Nationalkalendar* 1 (1915/16), pp. 28–29.

74. *OW*, 30 April 1915, p. 326; 14 May 1915, p. 368; *Selbstwehr*, 30 April 1915, p. 3; *JVS*, 29 April 1915, p. 1; 28 May 1915, p. 5; *Jüdisches Archiv*, no. 1 (May 1915), pp. 14–15.

75. For vivid first-hand descriptions of Jewish fears about the advancing Russians and about Russian atrocities during the occupation, see Schoenfeld, pp. 134–137; Sperber, pp. 72, 78–97; Lachs, pp. 26, 28–32, 35–36; Mechner, pp. 74–76; Salsitz, p. 31.

76. *OW*, 4 September 1914, p. 610.

77. *OW*, 25 December 1914, p. 895.

78. *OW*, 26 February 1915, p. 154; 5 March 1915, p. 173. See also 30 April 1915, p. 326; *JZ*, 19 March 1915, p. 2; *JVS*, 18 March 1915, p. 1; *Jüdisches Archiv*, no. 2/3 (August 1915), pp. 1–3.

79. See, for example, Dr. Theodor Haas's letter from the field, printed in *JVS*, 18 March 1915, p. 4; and Chaplain Arnold Grünfeld's letter from the field printed in *Selbstwehr*, 24 December 1915, pp. 1–2.

80. *OW*, 18 June 1915, p. 454. See also his letter in 28 September 1915, pp. 713–715.

81. *OW*, 7 May 1915, p. 353. See also *JZ*, 20 August 1915, p. 3.

82. Stone, pp. 128–144, 171–190.

83. *OW*, 21 May 1915, p. 381; 28 May 1915, p. 406; 4 June 1915, p. 423; 11 June 1915, p. 447; 18 June 1915, p. 461; 25 June 1915, pp. 479, 482; 2 July 1915, pp. 497–502, 504–506; 9 July 1915, pp. 520–25; 16 July 1915, pp. 540–545; 23 July 1915, p. 564; *Selbstwehr*, 7 May 1915, p. 4; 11 June 1915, p. 7; 2 July 1915, p. 7; 9 July 1915, p. 5; *JVS*, 16 June 1915, p. 3; *MONOIU*, vol. 27, no. 7–9 (July–September 1915), pp. 1–2; *Jung Juda*, 15 June 1915, p. 177. See also memos, programs, invitations for special prayer services and parades in Vienna, CAHJP, AW 357/2; JMP, IKG-Repräsentanz Prag, Sitzungs-Protokoll 1915, meeting, 23 June 1915.

84. *OW*, 11 June 1915, p. 443.

85. *OW*, 2 July 1915, p. 497.

86. Güdemann, "Aus meinem Leben," diary entries for 27 June and 4 August 1915, pp. 230–232.

87. Herzog, "Dank dem Ewigen," in *Kriegspredigten*, pp. 83–87. See also Aharon Lewin, *Festpredigt anlässlich der Einweihung der Synagoge im k.k. Barackenlager für jüdische Kreigs-flüchtlinge aus Galizien und der Bukowina in Bruck a.d. Leitha gehalten am 27. Juni 1915* (Vienna, 1915).

88. *Jung Juda*, 25 June 1915, p. 177.

89. Telegram, Zionist Party of Austria to the Kaiser, printed in *JZ*, 2 July 1915, p. 2.

90. *Selbstwehr*, 25 June 1915, p. 1.

91. *Selbstwehr*, 17 September 1915, p. 4.

92. *JVS*, 6 August 1915, p. 3.

93. See Lieben, p. 112; Hirsch, *Die Juden und der Krieg*, p. 14.; *Zweimonats-Bericht . . . der . . . Bnai Brith*, vol. 18, no. 5 (1915), p. 153; Zionist Central Committee for Western Austria to Copenhagen office, World Zionist Organization, 22 April 1915, CZA, L6/295.

94. *OW*, 25 June 1915, p. 469.

95. See, for example, *OW*, 18 June 1915, p. 454; 6 August 1915, pp. 585–586; 13 August 1915, pp. 605–607; 8 October 1915, p. 743; *JZ*, 28 May 1915, p. 3; 11 June 1915, p. 2; 27 August 1915, p. 3; 8 September 1915, p. 1; *Selbstwehr*, 18 June 1915, pp. 5–6; 25 June 1915,

pp. 5–6; 2 July 1915, pp. 2–6; 9 July 1915, pp. 5–6; 16 July 1915, pp. 1, 4–6; 30 July 1915, pp. 2–7; 13 August 1915, p. 1; 27 August 1915, pp. 5–6; 7 September 1915, pp. 12–14; 24 December 1915, pp. 1–2; *JVS*, 6 August 1915, p. 3; *MONOIU*, vol. 27, nos. 7-9 (July–September 1915), pp. 7–10; *Jüdisches Archiv*, no. 2/3 (August 1915), pp. 1–11.

96. For a full discussion of this issue, see chapter 5.

97. See, for example, *OW,* 29 October 1915, pp. 797–800; 3 December 1915, pp. 877–879; *MONOIU*, vol. 27, nos. 7–9 (July–September 1915), pp. 2–4; *JZ*, 5 November 1915, p. 1; *Selbstwehr*, 20 August 1915, p. 1; Memorandum, Executive Committee of Austrian Zionists to Minister President, printed June 25, 1915, CZA, Z3/845.

98. Mayor Schutzmann, Boryslaw, to Robert Stricker, head of the Komité jüdisches Kriegsarchiv, CAHJP, INV. 6526/III. See also other reports in the same file; undated letter in INV. 6526/I; Stricker to Central Zionist Office, Berlin, 29 July 1915, CZA, Z3/154; memo to army high command by Zionists, Jewish nationalists, and Aguadath Israel, n.d., probably 1915, CZA, Z3/155 and CAHJP, AW 357/2 complaining about Polish nastiness to Jews in the Austrian zone of occupation in Poland as well as in Galicia.

99. CAHJP, INV. 6526/I (files of Jüdisches Kriegsarchiv); *JZ*, 23 July 1915, p. 1; *OW*, 30 July 1915, p. 575; *Selbstwehr*, 30 July 1915, p. 7.

100. Memorandum, printed June 25, 1915, in CZA, Z3/845; reprinted in *JVS*, 20 August 1915, pp. 4–5; *Selbstwehr*, 20 August 1915, p. 3.

101. *JVS*, 23 July 1915, p. 1. See also *Selbstwehr*, 9 July 1915, p. 1.

102. *JZ*, 18 June 1915, p. 1; 30 July 1915, p. 1; 15 October 1915, p. 1; *Selbstwehr*, 6 August 1915, p. 2; *JVS*, 29 April 1915, p. 2.

103. *OW*, 20 August 1915, pp. 629, 634; 27 August 1915, pp. 646–649; 3 September 1915, pp. 668–669; *JZ*, 20 August 1915, p. 1; speech at plenum of IKG Wien, 18 August 1915, in CAHJP, AW 305/11. For similar views in 1916, see *OW*, 18 August 1916, pp. 541–542; 25 August 1916, p. 563; *JKor*, 18 August 1916, p. 1.

104. Isaak Hirsch, *Die Juden und der Krieg*, pp. 8, 11–12.

105. Speech, Vienna's IKG President Alfred Stern, Festsetzung, IKG Wien, 1 December 1915, CAHJP, AW 71/16; reprinted in *OW*, 3 December 1915, p. 886.

106. *JKor*, 15 April 1916, p. 1; 4 May 1916, p. 1; 18 May 1916, pp. 1–2.

107. May, pp. 120–122; Stone, pp. 235–243, 247–255, 260.

108. *JKor*, 12 June 1916, p. 1; 27 June 1916, p. 1.

109. *JKor*, 6 July 1916, p. 1; 21 July 1916, p. 1; September (n.d.) 1916, p. 1; 21 December 1916, p. 1.

110. *OW*, 8 September 1916, pp. 589–590; 6 October 1916, pp. 657–658; *MONOIU*, vol. 28, nos. 6–8 (June–August 1916), pp. 1–2; *Selbstwehr*, 1 September 1916, p. 1.

111. *Selbstwehr*, 28 May 1915, p. 1; *JZ*, 28 May 1915, p. 1; telegram of Vienna IKG to Kaiser, printed in *OW*, 4 June 1915, p. 423; *MONOIU*, vol. 27, no. 5/6 (May–June 1915), pp. 1–2; *Zweimonats-Bericht . . . der . . . Bnai Brith*, vol. 18, no. 3 (1915), pp. 92–94; *Jung Juda*, 28 May 1915, p. 145. See also, Adolf Altmann, "Der Lügengeist," in *Salzburger Volksblatt*, 10 June 1915, p. 4, clipping in CAHJP, Au 175/2.

112. See, for example, Güdemann, p. 227.

113. Kann, *History of the Habsburg Empire,* p. 472; Stone, p. 243.

114. Erwin A. Schmidl, *Juden in der k. (u.) k. Armee, 1788–1918, Studia Judaica Austriaca* 11 (1989), p. 5.

115. *Jung Juda*, 18 September 1914, p. 229.

116. *Selbstwehr*, 28 November 1914, p. 1.

117. *OW*, 14 August 1914, p. 561; 4 September 1914, p. 609; 30 October 1914, p. 739.

118. *OW*, 8 October 1914, pp. 683–684. See also 7 August 1914, p. 553; 14 August 1914, p. 561; 19 February 1915, p. 134.

119. *JZ*, 5 March 1915, p. 1; 19 March 1915, pp. 1–2; 28 May 1915, p. 1.

120. *OW*, 21 May 1915, p. 389. See also *Jung Juda*, 8 October 1915, inside back cover; 22 October 1915, p. 309 and inside back cover.

121. *OW*, 22 October 1915, p. 789–790.

122. *Selbstwehr*, 14 May 1915, p. 1. See also 15 October 1915, p. 1.

123. *JZ*, 8 October 1915, p. 1; *Selbstwehr*, 15 October 1915, p. 3; *OW*, 8 October 1915, p. 750.

124. *OW*, 29 January 1915, p. 79; *JVS*, 27 January 1915, p. 1; *MONOIU*, vol. 27, no. 1/2 (Jan.–Feb. 1915), p. 14.

125. *OW*, 12 February 1915, p. 117; *Selbstwehr*, 12 February 1915, p. 4; *JVS*, 24 February 1915, p. 5.

126. See, for example, *OW* 11 September 1914, pp. 627–628; 8 October 1914, p. 683; 11 December 1914, pp. 853–855; 30 July 1915, pp. 569–570; *JZ*, 18 September 1914, pp. 1–2; *JVS*, 29 March 1915, p. 3; Isaak Hirsch, *Die Juden und der Krieg*, pp. 6–7; Schwartz, *Der Krieg kommt*, p. 7.

127. *Jüdisches Archiv*, no. 1 (May 1915), pp. 1–2; *Selbstwehr*, 22 January 1915, pp. 3, 6. On IKG Wien subvention aid, see CAHJP, AW 357/2.

128. Ludwig Bató, "Das Kriegsjahr 5675," in *Jüdischer Nationalkalendar*, vol. 1 (1915/16), pp. 20–21.

129. For such views in the first year of the war, see *OW*, 11 December 1914, p. 860; 18 December 1914, p. 876; 19 February 1915, pp. 133–134; *MONOIU*, vol. 27, no. 1/2 (January–February 1915), pp. 1–2, 11–12; no. 3/4 (March–April 1915), p. 1; *Zweimonats-Bericht . . . der . . . Bnai Brith*, vol. 18, no. 4 (1915), p. 116; *Selbstwehr*, 26 February 1915, p. 1; 9 April 1915, pp. 1–2; 23 April 1915, pp. 1–2; *JVS*, 14 May 1915, pp. 1–2; 4 June 1915, pp. 1–2.

130. Zechlin, pp. 2, 86–92, 516–567; Werner Mosse, "Die Krise der europäischen Bourgeoisie und das deutsche Judentum," in Mosse and Paucker, pp. 1–26; Saul Friedländer, "Die politische Veränderungen der Kriegszeit und ihre Auswirkungen auf die Judenfrage," in Mosse and Paucker, pp. 27–65; Jochmann in Mosse and Paucker, pp. 409–415, 436; Reichmann in Mosse and Paucker, pp. 513–520; David Engel, "Patriotism as a Shield—The Liberal Jewish Defence against Antisemitism in Germany during the First World War," *LBIYB*, 31 (1986), pp. 147–171; Magill, pp. 209, 215–216, 222–223; Pulzer, pp. 194–195, 199–200.

Anti-Semitism also grew in England, which did not suffer the same level of war-time privation as Germany and Austria. While anti-Jewish charges and activities never reached the same fevered pitch as they did in the Central Powers, they nevertheless made British Jews profoundly uncomfortable about their place in British society. See Caesarani, pp. 61–76.

131. On German Jewish yearnings to belong utterly to the German *Volk* as a result of the war, see Jochmann, p. 409; Reichmann, pp. 513, 548; Magill, p. 236; Zechlin, pp. 87, 545.

132. Werner T. Angress, "The German Army's 'Judenzählung' of 1916. Genesis—Consequences—Significance," *LBIYB*, 23 (1978), pp. 117–137; Angress, "Das deutsche Militär und die Juden im Ersten Weltkrieg," *Militärgeschichtliche Mitteilungen*, 19 (1976), pp. 77–146; Zechlin, pp. 524–536; Jochmann, pp. 425–427; Reichmann, p. 559.

133. Reichmann, pp. 521–570, 577–584; Mordechai Breuer, *Jüdische Orthodoxie im Deutschen Reich, 1871–1918* (Frankfurt, 1986), p. 346; Zechlin, p. 551.

134. For a full discussion, see chapters 5 and 6.

CHAPTER 3

1. On the home front in World War I, see Arthur Marwick, *The Deluge: British Society and the First World War* (London, 1965); Jean Jacques Becker, *The Great War and the French*

People (Leamington Spa, 1985); Patrick Fridenson, ed., *The French Home Front 1914–1918* (Providence, 1991); John Williams, *The Other Battleground: The Home Fronts: Britain, France and Germany 1914–1918* (Chicago, 1972); J. M. Winter, *The Great War and the British People* (London, 1986); and the classic, E. Sylvia Pankhurst, *The Home Front: A Mirror to Life in England during the First World War* (London, 1932).

2. On Jewish patriotic war work in Germany and France, see Kaplan, *Making of the Jewish Middle Class*, pp. 219–226; and Hyman, *From Dreyfus to Vichy*, pp. 49–54.

3. Open letter, Dr. Alfred Stern, 29 July 1914, CAHJP, AW 357/2; Report on IKG activities, 25 October 1915, AW 372; Vertreter-Sitzung, 1 September 1914, IKG Wien, AW 72/15; JMP, Israelitische Kultusgemeinde-Repräsentanz Prag, Sitzungs-Protokoll 1914, 13 August 1914, 6 September 1914; *Selbstwehr*, 27 August 1914, p. 2; *OW*, 7 August 1914, pp. 550–551, 553, 555.

4. See records of donations to the Red Cross and a host of other organizations, CAHJP, AW 356, 357/2, 357/3; 247/5, 248/4, 248/5.

5. For Vienna, see CAHJP, AW 357/2; AW 357/4.

6. Such activities were regularly reported in *Zweimonatsbericht . . . der . . . Bnai Brith*. The Jewish press presented frequent descriptions of war work by Jewish charitable organizations all over Austria.

7. Protokoll, 17 August 1914 and letter of invitation to the meeting, 7 August 1914, CAHJP, AW 356; *OW*, 18 September 1914, p. 648.

8. "Über Kriegsfürsorge der österreichischen Vereinigung U.O.B.B.," *Zweimonatsbericht . . . der . . . Bnai Brith*, 17, no.5/6 (1914), p. 200; "Die Krieg und die Humanität," 18, no. 3 (1915), p. 106.

9. Letter, JNF Austria to JNF branches, 20 August 1914, CZA, Z3/840; *OW*, 11 September 1914, p. 633.

10. *Selbstwehr*, 27 August, 1914, p. 3; 20 September 1914, p. 6.

11. See, for example, *OW*, 1 January 1916, p. 10; 3 March 1916, p. 164; 12 May 1916, p. 329; 26 May 1916, p. 360; 23 November 1917, p. 742; 25 January 1918, p. 62; 22 February 1918, p. 121; *Jung Juda*, 19 October 1917, inside back cover; 14 June 1918, inside front cover; *JZ*, 26 May 1916, p. 5.

12. Based on lists of contributions, 1914–1918, to IKG Wien, CAHJP, AW 246/5, 247/4; 248/4, 249/4; 250/4.

13. *OW*, 20 August 1915, p. 631.

14. CAHJP, AW 357/1; 357/2; 357/3; 357/4; 250/5; Plenarsitzung, IKG Wien, 19 November 1914, AW 71/15; Plenarsitzung, 25 May 1915, 20 May 1917, AW 71/16; Vertreter-Sitzungen, 12 May 1915, 11 October 1915, 26 April 1916, AW 72/15; Vertreter-Sitzungen, 15 November 1916, 9 May 1917, 6 June 1918, AW 72/16.

15. *OW*, 26 May 1916, p. 361; 2 June 1916, p. 370.

16. JMP, IKG-Repräsentanz Prag, Sitzungs-Protokoll 1914, 22 November 1914; Sitzungs-Protokoll 1915, 17 October 1915; Sitzungs-Protokoll 1916, 7 May 1916, 19 November 1916; Sitzungs-Protokoll 1917, 2 December 1917; Sitzungs-Protokoll 1918, 27 June 1918.

17. *JKor*, 11 January 1917, p. 2; 8 February 1917, p. 3. For other examples, see *XXVII. Jahresbericht des Kranken-Unterstützungs-Vereines "Lewias Chen" pro 1914* (Vienna, 1915), CAHJP, AW 2311/24, p. 3; "Rechenschaftsbericht des Vereines für fromme und wohltätige Werke Chewra Kadischa für die Bezirke XII–XV über das Verwaltungsjahr vom 1. April 1914 bis 31. März 1915," AW 2358/5.

18. *OW*, 27 November 1914, p. 827; *Jung Juda*, 8 October 1915, inside back cover; 22 October 1915, p. 309 and inside back cover.

19. IKG Wien, circular letter, May 1916, CAHJP, AW 357/3.

20. On the ideology of "patriotic motherhood," see Barbara J. Steinson, "'The Mother Half of Humanity': American Women in the Peace and Preparedness Movements in World War I," in Carol Berkin, and Clara Lovett, eds., *Women, War and Revolution* (New York, 1980), pp. 259–281; and Elshtain, *Women and War*. On women and patriotic war work in general, see Daniel, *Arbeiterfrauen in der Kriegsgesellschaft*, pp. 25–26, 81–82; Berkin and Lovett, p. 209. On the lesser significance of the Home Front, see Margaret R. Higonnet and Patrice L. R. Higonnet, "The Double Helix," in Margaret R. Higonnet, Jane Jenson, Sonya Michel, and Margaret C. Weitz, eds., *Behind the Lines: Gender and the Two World Wars* (New Haven, 1987), p. 35.

21. *OW*, 31 July 1914, p. 530.

22. Open Letter, IKG Vienna, 29 July 1914, CAHJP, AW 356 and 357/2; printed in *OW*, 7 August 1914, pp. 550–551.

23. *OW*, 31 July 1914, p. 530; 7 August 1914, pp. 551–552.

24. *OW*, 15 December 1916, p. 820; 26 January 1917, p. 57; 7 September 1917, p. 571; 12 September 1917, p. 644; 19 April 1918, p. 241.

25. See, for example, in Vienna, *OW*, 14 August 1914, p. 565; 5 February 1915, p. 111; 23 April 1915, p. 318.

26. *41. Rechenschafts-Bericht des Vereines zur Errichtung von Volksküchen (nach israelitischem Ritus) für das Jahr 1914* (Vienna, 1915), CAHJP, AW 2286/26; *42. Rechenschafts-Bericht des Vereines zur Errichtung von Volksküchen (nach israelitischem Ritus) für das Jahr 1915* (Vienna, 1916), AW 2286/27; *OW*, 23 July 1915, p. 560.

27. See reports in *Zweimonats-Bericht . . . der . . . Bnai Brith*, 17, no. 5/6 (1914), pp. 202–203; 18, no. 1 (1915), pp. 5, 9, 20, 24, 26, 36.

28. See, for example, *Selbstwehr*, 27 August 1914, pp. 2–3; 13 November 1914, p. 2; 7 May 1915, p. 6; 29 October 1915, p. 6; 3 March 1916, p. 7; *JVS*, 17 September 1914, p. 3.

29. *OW*, 14 August 1914, p. 565; 21 August 1914, p. 585; 1 January 1915, p. 7; 5 February 1915, p. 106; *JVS*, 10 September 1914, p. 4.

30. *OW*, 29 January 1915, p. 91; 26 February 1915, p. 168; "Kundmachung," IKG Vienna, 31 July 1914, CAHJP, AW 356.

31. See, for example, Bertha Landre's description of her mother in "Durch's Sieb der Zeit gefallen," pp. 100–101.

32. Freud, "Vignettes of My Life," p. 14.

33. *OW*, 16 October 1914, p. 703.

34. *OW*, 4 December 1914, p. 835.

35. *OW*, 19 March 1915, p. 225.

36. Many of the requests or thank you notes from soldiers for prayer books or prayer-shawls, often to replace lost or destroyed ones, are quite moving. See CAHJP, AW 362; AW 357/1; 357/2; 357/3; 249/4.

37. See Referatsbogen, August 6, 1916, CAHJP, AW 357/3.

38. Correspondence in CAHJP, AW 356; AW 357/2; 357/3; 357/4.

39. Letter of IKG to Kriegsministerium, 11 August 1914, and response, 19 August 1914, and other correspondence in CAHJP, AW 356. The War Ministry provided 2000 crowns for the project. For a copy of the prayer book itself, see AW 358. On distribution of the prayer book after 1914, see AW 357/2; *OW*, 3 November 1916, p. 720.

40. See discussions in JMP, IKG-Repäsentanz Prag, Sitzungs-Protokoll 1915, meetings 10 October 1915, 21 November 1915, 12 December 1915, which reveal the divisions on the IKG board on this issue. Many felt that there was no reason for the Prague IKG to provide supplies to religious Hungarian soldiers. Of course, the IKG did sometimes provide prayer books without question; see Sitzungs-Protokoll 1917, meeting 15 April 1917.

41. JMP, IKG-Repräsentanz Prag, Sitzungs-Protokolle 1915, 22 August 1915; 10 October 1915; Sitzungs-Protokoll 1917, 16 September 1917.

42. For 1914 and 1915 see CAHJP, AW 368, and response to inquiry by Hermann Wolf, AW 356; for 1916 see *OW*, 3 November 1916, p. 720.

43. *OW*, 3 November 1916, p. 720; 16 November 1917, p. 730.

44. See correspondence and reports of activities of rabbis in Vienna, CAHJP, AW 363.

45. See "Kriegserinnerungen," Album of Rabbi Béla Fischer, 1916–1918, essentially a collection of thank you cards from soldiers and Jewish chaplains, CAHJP, AW 3111.

46. CAHJP, AW 364/2; AW 364/3.

47. See correspondence and reports, CAHJP, AW 364/1; letter from Rothschild Bank to IKG, 20 March 1915 in AW 357/2. On the female volunteers at the soup kitchens, see yearly reports of the Viennese Verein zur Errichtung von Volksküchen (nach israelitischem Ritus) in AW 2286/26, 2286/27, 2286/28, 2286/29.

48. CAHJP, AW 364/2; AW 364/3, 357/2, 357/3.

49. *OW*, 2 April 1915, p. 267; 9 April 1915, pp. 281, 282, 284; 16 April 1915, pp. 303, 305; 23 April 1915, p. 319; 7 May 1915, p. 357; 17 March 1916, p. 195; 28 April 1916, p. 289; 5 May 1916, pp. 304, 305, 309–310; 12 May 1916, p. 326; 26 May 1916, p. 361; 2 June 1916, p. 371; 16 June 1916, p. 409; 20 April 1917, p. 244; 4 May 1917, p. 279; 25 May 1917, p. 334; 19 April 1918, p. 242; *JZ*, 28 April 1916, p. 6; *Selbstwehr*, 12 May 1916, p. 7; 26 May 1916, p. 6.

50. See for example, *OW*, 31 March 1916, p. 266; 5 May 1916, p. 309.

51. Correspondence with Verein zur Errichtung von Volksküchen (nach isr. Ritus), March and April 1916, CAHJP, AW 248/4; report of Verein "Einheit" for 1914–1916 and its correspondence in 1917 and 1918 with the IKG Vienna, AW 249/5; Vertretersitzung, IKG Wien, 8 March 1916, 29 March 1916, 16 May 1916, AW 72/15; *OW* 3 March 1916, p. 266; 5 May 1916, p. 303; 27 April 1917, p. 266; 19 April 1918, p. 238. The army continued to provide money for food, but the Passover food cost about twice as much as the army provided.

52. See *OW*, 5 November 1914, p. 823; 12 November 1915, p. 838; 1 January 1916, pp. 14–15; 18 February 1916, p. 129; 28 April 1916, p. 287; 15 December 1916, p. 820; 16 February 1917, p. 108; 2 November 1917, p. 696; 28 December 1917, p. 826. For a lovely set of thank you notes from soldiers to her, see Max Grunwald, "80 Jahre meines Lebens," handwritten version, ch. 46, CAHJP, P 97/3.

53. *OW*, 19 February 1915, p. 148; *JKor*, 24 August 1916, p. 4.

54. *Selbstwehr*, 10 December 1915, p. 7; *OW*, 23 April 1915, p. 321; 19 November 1915, pp. 856–857; *JZ*, 23 April 1915, p. 3.

55. See *Selbstwehr*, 10 December 1915, p. 6; 3 March 1916, p. 7; *OW*, 10 December 1915, pp. 901, 904, 908, 910; 17 December 1915, pp. 927; 29 December 1916, p. 854; 28 December 1917, pp. 824–825, 827; *JZ*, 7 January 1916, p. 3; 4 May 1917, p. 5; 4 January 1918, p. 5.

56. *OW*, 11 January 1918, pp. 40–41.

57. *XLIII. Jahresbericht der Israelitischen Allianz zu Wien erstattet an die XLIII. ordentliche Generalversammlung am 5. June 1916* (Vienna, 1916), p. 7, CAHJP, AW 2828/35; *XLII. Jahresbericht der Israelitischen Allianz zu Wien erstattet an die XLII. ordentliche Generalversammlung am 17. Mai 1915* (Vienna, 1915), pp. 16–19, AW 2828/34. Earlier in 1915, before the liberation of Galicia, there were 71,062 Jewish refugees in Bohemia and 23,663 in Moravia. For an excellent discussion of the refugee situation in Vienna, see Beatrix Hoffmann-Holter, *"Abreisendmachung:" Jüdische Kriegsflüchtlinge in Wien 1914 bis 1923* (Vienna, 1995); numbers for 1915, p. 36.

On Jewish fear of the Russian advance see Schoenfeld, *Jewish Life in Galicia*, pp. 134–137; Mechner, "My Family Biography," pp. 74–75; and other sources cited below.

58. *XLIV. Jahresbericht der Israelitischen Allianz zu Wien erstattet an die XLIV. ordentliche Generalversammlung am 25. June 1917* (Vienna, 1917), pp. 13–15, CAHJP, AW 2828/36. See also *XLV. Jahresbericht der Israelitischen Allianz zu Wien erstattet an die XLV. ordentliche Gener-*

alversammlung am 10. Juni 1918 (Vienna, 1918), pp. 11–12, AW 2828/37, which puts the 1917 total number of Jewish refugees at 117,115: 41,213 in Vienna, 71,240 in Bohemia, and 29,031 in Moravia.

59. "Uebersicht der mittelosen Kriegsflüchtlinge," 1 November 1917, KA, KM Präs. 1918, 52-3/1.

60. Hoffmann-Holter, pp. 65, 143.

61. Censorship prevented a thorough discussion of the conditions of the camps, but even censored press reports hint at problems. See *MONOIU*, vol. 26, no. 11/12 (November/December 1914), pp. 3–6. Austrian magazines contained rosy descriptions of the camps. For example, see "Oesterreichische Flüchtlingsstädte," an article from an unidentified magazine, CAHJP, PL 474. Private correspondence offers better evidence. Refugee Josef Sattringey(?) described the Nikolsburg refugee camp as "unangenehm" in his letter to Rabbi Moritz Lewin, 4 January 1916, CAHJP, CS 191. When Parliament reopened in 1917, Jewish deputies offered testimony there about the terrible conditions in the refugee camps. See *JZ*, 20 July 1917, pp. 2–3.

62. See description of a cellar for refugees in Karlsbad, Bohemia, with 80 people, some of them with dysentery, sleeping on wet, filthy straw in *JVS*, 13 January 1915, p. 5.

63. Lachs, *Warum schaust du zurück*, pp. 26–65; quotations on pp. 35, 42. Adolf Mechner's family from Czernowitz also relocated itself in Vienna with relative ease (Mechner, pp. 74–78).

64. Sperber, *God's Water Carriers*, p. 72.

65. Sperber, pp. 36, 71–124.

66. See, for example, discussion of Prague IKG-Repräsentanz at its meeting on 17 September 1914, in JMP, Sitzungs-protokoll, 1914; *OW*, 18 September 1914, pp. 643, 649, 655.

67. At first, the government paid 70 heller a day per person, raising it to 90 heller in June 1915, 1.5 crowns at the end of 1916, and to 2 crowns in late 1917. In 1915, refugees received 6.30 crowns per week at a time when the weekly cost of living was 20.87 crowns. See Hoffmann-Holter, pp. 41–50, 79–82.

68. Hoffmann-Holter, pp. 41, 43–44. See also *OW*, 6 November 1914, p. 765; 27 November 1914, p. 823; 1 January 1916, pp. 17–18; 11 February 1916, p. 107.

69. *OW*, 1 January 1916, p. 17. See also 25 October 1918, p. 684. Hoffmann-Holter (p. 71) also praises Schwarz-Hiller for his devotion and long hours of work without remuneration.

70. *XLII. Jahresbericht der Israelitischen Allianz . . . 1915, XLIII. Jahresbericht der Israelitischen Allianz . . . 1916*, CAHJP, AW 2828/34 and 2828/35. See also open letter, Israelitische Allianz zu Wien, September 1914, to all it supporters, AW 356. On schools see *OW*, 9 July 1915, pp. 517–518.

71. *XLIV. Jahresbericht der Israelitischen Allianz . . . 1917*, p. 22, CAHJP, AW 2828/36; *XLV. Jahresbericht der Israelitischen Allianz . . . 1918*, pp. 5–7, AW 2828/37.

72. *XLIII. Jahresbericht der Israelitischen Allianz . . . 1916*, pp. 6–7, CAHJP, AW 2828/35; *XLIV. Jahresbericht der Israelitischen Allianz . . . 1917*, p. 8, AW 2828/36; *XLV. Jahresbericht der Israelitischen Allianz . . . 1918*, pp. 5-6, AW 2828/37.

73. *Zweimonatsbericht . . . der . . . Bnai Brith*, vol. 17, no. 5/6 (1914), pp. 194–199; vol. 18, no. 1 (1915), p. 40; no. 6 (1915), pp. 173–176; *OW*, 23 October 1914, p. 728; 1 September 1916, p. 584; 1 December 1916, p. 806; Hilfsverein für die notleidende jüdische Bevölkerung in Galizien to IKG Vienna, 2 March 1917, CAHJP, AW 249/4.

74. *Zweimonatsbericht . . . der . . . Bnai Brith*, vol. 19, no. 3 (1916), pp. 123-124; vol. 20, no. 1/2 (1917), p. 17; vol. 21, no. 1/2, p. 57; Hilfsverein to IKG Vienna, 2 March 1917, CAHJP, AW 249/4; Hilfsverein to IKG Vienna, 23 February 1918, AW 250/4. The

Hilfsverein received a yearly subvention of 3000 crowns from the IKG. See also *OW*, 1 September 1916, p. 584; 26 January 1917, pp. 58–59; 17 May 1918, p. 301; *JKor*, 21 December 1916, p. 4; 30 January 1917, p. 3.

75. *OW*, 26 May 1916, p. 357; 30 June 1916, pp. 436–437; *JKor*, 12 June 1916, p. 4; *JZ*, 26 May 1916, p. 5.

76. *Tätigkeitsbericht des Zentralbüros zum Schutze der galizischen Flüchtlinge jüdischen Glaubensbekenntnisses in Brünn für die Zeit vom 15. Dezember 1914 bis 31. Oktober 1915* (Brünn, 1915).

77. Ibid., pp. 12–15.

78. *OW*, 29 January 1915, p. 87.

79. *OW*, 9 April 1915, p. 283. For other efforts in Bohemia and Moravia, see *OW*, 27 November 1914, pp. 825–826; 18 December 1914, pp. 885–886; 2 April 1915, p. 263; 7 May 1915, pp. 355–356; 21 July 1916, p. 486; 1 September 1916, p. 584; 3 November 1916, p. 726; *Selbstwehr*, 15 January 1915, p. 4; 22 January 1915, p. 5; 5 February 1915, p. 6; 26 February 1915, pp. 6–7; 12 March 1915, p. 6; 16 April 1915, p. 7; 25 June 1915, pp. 4–5; 13 July 1917, p. 7; *JVS*, 4 June 1915, p. 6.

80. *OW*, 20 July 1917, pp. 466–467. Indeed, Jewish refugees located in regions with no organized Jewish community had a more difficult experience than those where the Jewish community could marshall its resources on their behalf. See, for example, report on situation of refugees in Asch, Bohemia in *OW*, 11 June 1915, p. 447; or in Upper Austria, *OW*, 24 November 1916, pp. 768–769.

81. JMP, IKG-Repräsentanz Prag, Sitzungs-Protokoll 1914, 17 September 1914.

82. Ledger books of the *Hilfskomitee*, JMP, Box 120707, "Sammlungen für galizische Flüchtlinge;" Box 128484, Records of the Finance Committee of the Hilfskomitee.

83. JMP, IKG-Repräsentanz Prag, Sitzungs-Protokoll 1914, 4 October 1914, 6 December 1914, 20 December 1914; Sitzungs-Protokoll 1915, 25 March 1915, 31 October 1915, 12 December 1915; Sitzungs-Protokoll 1916, 6 February 1916, 7 August 1916. See also IKG Prague to kk Statthalterei (Bohemia), 13 April 1916, JMP, Box 147633, "Galizische Hilfskomitee."

84. IKG Prague to kk Polizeidirektion, Prague, 12 November 1915, JMP, Box 147633, "Galizische Hilfskomitee." In the same box, see letters, 17 September 1915, 17 October 1915, 28 October 1915, 11 January 1916, 2 July 1916 requesting or acknowledging additional state funds to cover costs of clothing and shoes, and other reports. The Jewish press reported regularly on the activities of the *Hilfskomitee*: *Selbstwehr*, 28 November 1914, pp. 1–2; 29 December 1914, p. 3; 8 January 1915, pp. 1–2, 4; *JVS*, 8 October 1914, p. 4; 4 March 1915, p. 3; *Zweimonatsbericht . . . der . . . Bnai Brith*, vol. 19, no. 2 (1916), pp. 82–83; no. 3 (1916), p. 109. For a summary of the efforts of this committee, see Jiří Kuděla, "Galician and East European Refugees in the Historic Lands: 1914–1916," *Review of the Society for the History of Czechoslovak Jews* 4 (1991–1992), pp. 15–32.

85. JMP, Box 147633, Inventory of refugees under care of Versorgungskomité für jüdische Flüchtlinge, 1 February 1915.

86. Report of Robert von Fuchs and discussion at 8 October 1916 meeting of IKG-Repräsentanz Prag, JMP, Sitzungs-Protokoll 1916; Isr. Allianz zu Wien to Prague IKG, 21 August, 12 September, and 25 October 1916, JMP, Box 128484.

87. "Stand des Konto, 'Zentralkomitee für jüdische Flüchtlinge in Prag,' 1 February 1917," JMP, Box 128464 (Finance Committee).

88. See correspondence with organizations and individuals, CAHJP, AW 357/1, 357/2, 246/4, 246/5, 247/4, 248/4, 248/5, 249/4, 249/5, 250/4; Plenarsitzung, IKG Wien, 24 March 1915, AW 71/15.

Recent scholarship has criticized the Vienna IKG for not sufficiently extending itself on behalf of the refugees. See Hoffmann-Holter, pp. 98–99, 102, 105; and David Rechter, "Galicia in Vienna: Jewish Refugees in the First World War," *Austrian History Yearbook* 28 (1997), p. 121. While the actual money spent by the IKG on refugees certainly proved inadequate, such criticism does not give enough weight to the significance of direct government refugee aid in Vienna, which naturally convinced the IKG that there was less need for their involvement. Moreover, both scholars underestimate the amount of subvention aid provided by the IKG, not to mention the enormous outlays of other Jewish charities, whose leaders also sat on the IKG board.

89. "Bericht über die Flüchtlingsschule II. Malzgassse 16 erstattet am Ende des Schuljahres 1914/15," CAHJP, AW 357/2; memo, 28 October 1914, AW 357/1.

90. Circular letter, IKG and *Weibliche Fürsorge*, CAHJP, AW 246/5; Report, AW 357/2; Correspondence, AW 371; *OW*, 11 December 1914, p. 863.

91. CAHJP, AW 365.

92. *Zweimonatsbericht . . . der . . . Bnai Brith*, vol. 19, no. 1 (1916), pp. 20–23; no. 2 (1916), p. 82; no. 3 (1916), pp. 98, 101–102; vol. 20, no. 1/2 (1917), p. 16; vol. 21, no. 1/2 (1918), pp. 20–22, 24–25, 29, 34, 40, 46.

93. *OW*, 23 October 1914, p. 729; 13 November 1914, p. 784; 18 December 1914, p. 888; 5 March 1915, p. 182; 28 January 1916, p. 79; *JVS*, 8 October 1914, p. 5; 21 October 1914, p. 3; 19 November 1914, p. 2; 2 December 1914, pp. 5–6; 7 January 1915, p. 6; 20 January 1915, p. 1; 10 February 1915, p. 6; 29 April 1915, p. 6.

94. *OW*, 5 February 1915, p. 108; 12 March 1915, p. 204; 26 March 1915, p. 243; 3 September 1915, p. 670; 17 September 1915, p. 707; 28 January 1916, p. 79; *JVS*, 4 February 1915, p. 6; 29 September 1915, p. 5.

95. *OW*, 16 February 1917, p. 105; 1 February 1918, p. 74. Letter to IKG Vienna, 20 March 1917, CAHJP, AW 249/4; reports, 2286/26, 2286/27, 2286/28, 2286/29.

96. *JKor*, 21 December 1916, p. 2; 6 March 1917, p. 2; 25 October 1917, p. 3.

97. See, for example, *OW*, 20 November 1914, p. 803; 1 January 1915, p. 11; 22 January 1915, p. 68; 29 January 1915, p. 88; 9 April 1915, p. 287; 30 April 1915, p. 336; 2 July 1915, p. 501; 26 November 1915, p. 869; 6 October 1916, pp. 664–665; 3 November 1916, p. 723; 19 January 1917, p. 45; 25 May 1917, p. 334; 7 September 1917, p. 572; *Selbstwehr*, 25 August 1916, p. 7; 12 January 1917, p. 6; *JVS*, 28 September 1914, p. 4; 23 August 1916, p. 5; *JZ*, 30 March 1917, p. 4; letters to IKG Vienna offering apartments to refugees, 11 September 1914, 3 September 1915, CAHJP, AW 357/2; 16 December 1914, AW 246/5.

98. Letters from Austrian authorities thanking Lewin for this effort, 23 July, 2 August, 11 September 1915, CAHJP, CS 191 (Lewin's personal papers). See also *OW*, 9 July 1915, pp. 524–525.

99. Correspondence in CAHJP, CS 191; *JVS*, 18 February 1916, p. 5.

100. See, for example, letter of Abraham Gelber, 4 September 1918, who writes: "Ich wäre mit meinem Los gegenwärtig zufrieden, wenn meine Frau und das Kind gelebt hätten. Diese Wunde ist unheilbar und plagt mich fortwährend" (CAHJP, CS 191).

101. *Selbstwehr*, 30 October 1914, pp. 1–2; 29 December 1914, p. 1; *JVS*, 8 October 1914, p. 4.

102. *Selbstwehr*, 15 January 1915, pp. 3–4.

103. *Selbstwehr*, 21 May 1915, pp. 3–4; 13 August 1915, pp. 6–7; *JVS*, 28 May 1915, p. 3.

104. *Selbstwehr*, 30 July 1915, pp. 1–2; 7 January 1916, pp. 7–8; *JVS*, 7 January 1916, pp. 3–4. In the fall of 1915, after many refugees had returned home, the school in Prague still had 742 students, and in 1916/17 it had between 600 and 700 students (*Selbstwehr*, 3 December 1915, p. 2; 1 September 1916, p. 7; 8 September 1916, p. 6). The Prague IKG provided the school with space and paid for the utilities. See JMP, IKG-Repräsentaz Prag, Sitzungs-Protokoll 1915, 7 March 1915.

105. *Selbstwehr*, 5 November 1915, p. 6; 10 December 1915, p. 5; 24 December 1915, p. 7; 26 May 1916, pp. 1–2; circular letter, Zionistisches Distriktskomitee für Böhmen, April 1915, CZA, L6/295; Moravia-Silesia Zionist District Committee to Berlin office, WZO, 29 October 1914, Z3/827.

106. *JZ*, 13 November 1914, p. 2; 27 November 1914, p. 1; 11 December 1914, p. 2; 25 December 1914, p. 1; 19 February 1915, pp. 1–2; 21 January 1916, p. 4; 14 April 1916, pp. 7–9; *JVS*, 23 July 1915, p. 4. See also pamphlet, "Das Hilfswerk der Wiener Zionisten für die Kriegsflüchtlinge 1914/1916," CAHJP, AW 248/5; Vienna Zionist office to Leo Herrmann, Berlin, 7 October 1914, CZA, Z3/840; report, prob. January 1915, Zionistisches Zentralkomitee für Westösterreich, Z3/841.

107. Report of the Armen-Ambulatorium des zionist. Zentralkomités für Kriegs-flüchlinge, November 1915, and its correspondence with the IKG Wien, CAHJP, AW 247/5. The IKG provided it with subvention aid.

108. *JZ*, 30 October 1914, pp. 1–2; 30 October 1914, p. 2; 23 February 1917, p. 4; 9 March 1917, p. 4; 15 June 1917, p. 2; 22 June 1917, p. 2; 20 July 1917, p. 2; Zionistisches Zentralkomitee, Vienna, to WZO, Berlin, 29 October 1914, CZA, Z3/841.

109. CZA, L6/313, L6/300.

110. Leo Herrmann to Martin Rosenblüth, Copenhagen Zionist headquarters, 23 April 1915, CZA, Z3/842.

111. *JZ*, 25 December 1914, p. 1. Engaging in its usual polemics, the *JZ* claimed that Jewish liberals did not help the refugees, but such was certainly not the case. In his study of Galician refugees in Vienna, Rechter, "Galicia in Vienna," p. 123, argues that the Zionists became "the most active force" on behalf of Galician refugees, but the evidence does not support this contention.

112. WZO wartime headquarters in Copenhagen to Zionistische Zentralkomitee für Westösterreich, 27 January 1916, and to Zionistische Landeskomitee für Böhmen, 19 January 1916, CZA, L6/300. Initially, the WZO had approved the program to help Galician Jews (Arthur Hantke, 25 September 1914, to Vienna Zionists, Z3/840).

113. No statistics exist on the gender or age breakdown of the Jewish refugees. Still, it stands to reason that a disproportionate percentage of them were women, children, or the elderly. After all, most men aged 18 to 45 were drafted. Most reports about refugee aid assume that most recipients of this charity were women, children, and old people. See, for example, *JVS*, 24 May 1917, p. 5, which describes a refugee family in Brünn consisting of a 62-year-old man, his 59-year-old wife, their two daughters in their thirties, their five small grandchildren, and their Ruthenian maid, all in a tiny apartment. Their son and sons-in-law were in military service, one of them missing in action. One partial list of refugees in Prague (JPM, Box 128220) reveals that 45% of the families were headed by women, far higher than would have been true for the Galician Jewish population as a whole before the war.

114. See, for example, *OW*, 1 January 1915, p. 12; 5 February 1915, p. 110; 12 March 1915, pp. 201–202; 27 October 1916, pp. 704, 707; *JKor*, 19 September 1918, p. 4; *Selbstwehr*, 8 January 1915, p. 5; 29 January 1915, p. 6; 5 February 1915, p. 6; 12 March 1915, p. 6; 11 June 1915, p. 6; 25 June 1915, p. 4; 16 March 1917, p. 5; 13 July 1917, p. 7; *JZ*, 5 March 1915, p. 2; 12 March 1915, p. 4; 26 January 1917, p. 10; 23 February 1917, pp. 3, 5; *JVS*, 29 March 1915, p. 5; 10 April 1915, p. 4; 27 July 1916, p. 3; *Zweimonatsbericht . . . der . . . Bnai Brith*, vol. 19, no. 1 (1916), p. 22; no. 2, pp. 83, 94; no. 3, pp. 119, 124; vol. 20, no. 1/2 (1917), p. 17.

115. *OW*, 18 September 1914, p. 647; 6 November 1914, pp. 765–766.

116. *OW*, 30 October 1914, p. 750; 11 December 1914, p. 866.

117. *OW*, 5 February 1915, p. 111; 19 February 1915, p. 143.

118. *OW*, 12 February 1915, pp. 124–125; 19 February 1915, pp. 142–143; 26 February 1915, p. 163; 12 March 1915, pp. 201–202; 2 April 1915, pp. 259–260; 9 April 1915, p. 281.

119. See, for example, *OW*, 11 December 1914, p. 863; 18 December 1914, pp. 884, 887; 25 December 1914, p. 901; 8 January 1915, p. 35.

120. *OW*, 2 April 1915, p. 261; 9 April 1915, p. 287.

121. *OW*, 11 December 1914, p. 862; 12 March 1915, pp. 204–205; 19 March 1915, p. 226; 26 March 1915, p. 246; 9 April 1915, p. 286; 28 September 1915, p. 724. See also Frauen-Wohltätigkeitsverein Philanthropia to Vienna IKG, 22 October 1914, CAHJP, AW 356.

122. *Selbstwehr*, 30 October 1914, pp. 1–2; 15 January 1915, p. 3; 5 February 1915, p. 7; 7 May 1915, p. 6; *JVS*, 28 May 1915, p. 4.

123. *Selbstwehr*, 29 October 1915, p. 6; 20 July 1917, p. 6; 7 September 1917, p. 8.

124. *JZ*, 26 February 1915, p. 2; 16 April 1915, p. 2; "Das Hilfswerk der Wiener Zionisten für die Kriegsflüchtlinge 1914/16," CAHJP, AW 248/5.

125. *OW*, 2 April 1915, p. 261.

126. *OW*, 4 February 1916, pp. 86–87.

127. *OW*, 1 February 1918, pp. 72–74.

128. *Ein Jahr Flüchtlingsfürsorge der Frau Anitta Müller 1914–1915* (Vienna, n.d., prob. 1915), CAHJP, AW 2318. See also *OW*, 30 October 1914, p. 749; 20 November 1914, pp. 803–804; 11 December 1914, p. 862; 22 January 1915, pp. 65, 67; 13 August 1915, p. 614; 19 November 1915, pp. 855–856; 14 January 1916, p. 37; 19 May 1916, pp. 340–341. Many refugees regarded Müller's tea room as a social and cultural center; see Sperber, p. 134.

129. *Ein Jahr Fluchtlingsfürsorge der Frau Anitta Müller*, p. 59, CAHJP, AW 2318.

130. "Zehn Jahre Arbeit des Vereines Soziale Hilfsgemeinschaft Anitta Müller, 1914–24," CAHJP, AW 2317; "Referat über die Institutionen, welche von Frau Anitta Mueller geleitet und aus von ihr gesammelten Mitteln erhalten werden," 25 June 1918, AW 250/5; *OW*, 8 June 1917, pp. 358–360; 26 April 1918, p. 256; 6 September 1918, pp. 558–559. Müller and her organization continued to assist needy Viennese Jews in the interwar period. She migrated to Palestine in 1936 and proceeded to develop child care institutions there.

131. One of the lasting consequences of women's charity during World War I in all of the belligerent countries was the professionalization of social work. See Daniel, p. 262.

132. *OW*, 22 January 1915, p. 67; 13 August 1915, p. 614; 19 November 1915, pp. 855–856; 29 December 1916, p. 849; 8 June 1917, pp. 358–360; 6 September 1918, pp. 558–559.

133. *OW*, 8 June 1917, pp. 358–360.

134. *JKor*, 28 November 1918, p. 4; *Zweimonatsbericht . . . der . . . Bnai Brith*, vol. 21, no. 3/4 (1918), p. 99.

135. Lachs, p. 110.

136. CAHJP, AW 246/5, 247/4, 248/4, 249/4, 250/4.

137. *W*, 18 September 1914, pp. 647, 655; 27 November 1914, p. 824; *41. Rechenschafts-Bericht des Vereines zur Errichtung von Volksküchen (nach israelitischem Ritus) für das Jahr 1914*, p. 4, CAHJP, AW 2286/26; "Brigittenauer israelitischer Frauen-Wohltätigkeits-Verein, Bericht über seine Tätigkeit im Vereinsjahre 1914," CAHJP, AW 247/4.

138. *Selbstwehr*, 8 January 1915, pp. 2–3; *OW*, 1 January 1915, p. 16; 8 January 1915, p. 32; 9 April 1915, p. 284; *JVS*, 23 August 1916, p. 5; *Zweimonatsbericht . . . der . . . Bnai Brith*, vol. 18, no. 3 (1915), pp. 97–99.

139. *OW*, 11 December 1914, p. 864.

140. *Selbstwehr*, 29 December 1914, p. 1; *JVS*, 17 September 1914, p. 2; 10 February 1915, pp. 5–6.

141. See, for example, *OW*, 11 September 1914, p. 625; 18 September 1914, p. 643; 28 September 1914, p. 668; 20 November 1914, p. 796; 5 March 1915, pp. 174–175; 12 March

1915, pp. 196–197; *JZ*, 27 November 1914, p. 1; *Selbstwehr*, 7 May 1915, pp. 1–2; 10 December 1915, p. 1; *JVS*, 8 October 1914, p. 2.

142. *OW*, 2 February 1915, p. 99.

143. *OW*, 20 July 1917, pp. 453–455, quotation on p. 454.

144. JMP, IKG-Repräsentanz Prag, Sitzungs-Protokoll 1914, 17 September 1914.

145. See, for example, *OW*, 18 September 1914, pp. 648–649; *JZ*, 27 November 1914, p. 1; *Selbstwehr*, 20 September 1914, p. 3; 22 January 1915, p. 4; *Zweimonatsbericht . . . der . . . Bnai Brith*, vol. 18, no. 4 (1915), pp. 117–118.

146. *Zweimonatsbericht . . . der . . . Bnai Brith*, vol. 18, no. 4 (1915), p. 118.

147. *OW*, 8 June 1917, pp. 358–360, quotation on p. 359.

148. *Selbstwehr*, 8 January 1915, p. 2; 29 January 1915, p. 6; 5 February 1915, p. 6; *JZ*, 18 September 1914, p. 2; 27 November 1914, p. 1; *Jung Juda*, 4 December 1914, p. 281. Interestingly, in the fall of 1914, *Selbstwehr* only emphasized humanitarianism.

149. Steven E. Aschheim, *Brothers and Strangers: The East European Jew in German and German Jewish Consciousness, 1800–1923* (Madison, 1982); Jack Wertheimer, *Unwelcome Strangers: East European Jews in Imperial Germany* (New York, 1987); Trude Maurer, *Ostjuden in Deutschland, 1918–1933* (Hamburg, 1986).

150. In her otherwise excellent study of Galician refugees in Vienna, Hoffmann-Holter, pp. 95–102, argues that the Viennese Jewish establishment harbored very negative attitudes to the Galician Jews, but I have found virtually no evidence of hostility. Without conducting a thorough analysis of the press or the records of the Jewish community, Hoffmann-Holter assumed that Viennese Jewish liberals behaved like their counterparts in Germany, but they did not.

151. *OW*, 28 September 1914, p. 668.

152. *OW*, 4 August 1916, p. 518. See also 24 November 1916, pp. 768–769.

153. *OW*, 27 September 1918, pp. 610–612.

154. *JZ*, 5 May 1916, p. 1. See also Hoffmann-Holter, pp. 109–117.

155. *OW*, 2 April 1915, pp. 261–262.

156. *Ein Jahr Flüchtlingsfürsorge der Frau Anitta Müller*, p. 4.

157. Letter to IKG Vienna, 9 April 1915, CAHJP, AW 357/2. The IKG did not respond to letters of this kind.

158. *JVS*, 11 November 1914, p. 3.

159. See, for example, IKG to Bezirks-Polizei-Kommissariat, Leopoldstadt, vouching for the good standing of Galician rabbis in CAHJP, AW 357/2; and Rudolf Krausz to IKG president Stern, March 24, 1915, refusing space for Talmud classes, AW 357/2.

160. CAHJP, AW 247/5, 249/4, 250/4, 250/5.

161. JMP, IKG-Repräsentanz Prag, Sitzungs-Protokoll 1914, 17 September 1914. For other examples, see 12 December 1915, 16 April 1916.

162. Prague IKG, 31 July 1916, to a group of refugees in Hostiwitz near Prague, JMP, Box 147633.

163. JPM, IKG-Repräsentanz Prag, Sitzungs-Protokoll 1915, 24 January 1915, 31 January 1915; Sitzungs-Protokoll 1916, 16 April 1916.

164. JMP, IKG-Repräsentanz Prag, Sitzungs-Protokoll 1915, 22 August 1915; 26 September 1915; Sitzungs-Protokoll 1916, 21 September 1916.

165. IKG Smichow to IKG Prague, 8 November 1914, JMP, Box 128484. See also IKG Königliche Weinberge to IKG Prague, 16 March 1916.

166. See correspondence in JMP, Box 128484, records of the Finance Committee of the Hilfskomitee. The committee feared that it would not have enough money; see report in JMP, IKG-Repräsentanz Prag, Sitzungs-Protokoll 1916, 6 February 1916.

167. JMP, Box 120727, "Sammlungen für galizische Flüchtlinge; Monats-Beitrage ab

März 1915 bis März 1917," Part V, Monthly Contributions from Individuals, August 1916–March 1917.

168. JMP, Box 147633, "Galizische Hilfskomitee," Envelope: Bekleidungsangelegenheiten. The same envelope contains a number of formal requests, in German, from refugees to the committee, and it is possible that refugees also had to make such a formal request in order to receive clothing and blankets.

169. IKG Prague to kk Statthalterei, 13 April 1916, JMP, Box 147633. Galician Jews, of course, were not illiterate, merely unable to read German.

170. *Selbstwehr*, 29 December 1914, p. 1; 8 January 1915, p. 3.

171. *Selbstwehr*, 24 September 1915, p. 1; *JVS*, 7 January 1915, pp. 2–3.

172. Menachem Zentner, "Taten—Erlebnisse," unpublished manuscript, Jerusalem, 1987, as quoted in Wlaschek, *Juden in Böhmen*, p. 80. See also Moses Wiesenfeld, "Begegnung mit Ostjuden," in *Dichter, Denker, Helfer: Max Brod zum 50. Geburtstag,* Felix Weltsch, ed. (Mähr. Ostrau, 1934), pp. 54–57. For parallel feelings among Orthodox Jews in Western Hungary, see Katz, *With My Own Eyes*, p. 21.

173. *Zweimonatsbericht . . . der . . . Bnai Brith*, vol. 18, no. 3 (1915), pp. 97–99.

174. *Zweimonatsbericht . . . der . . . Bnai Brith*, vol. 18, no. 4 (1915), pp. 117–124. See also lecture by Dr. Landau to Bielitz chapter, pp. 114–117; Simon Stern (Saaz, Bohemia), "Wie kann den Juden in Galizien geholfen werden?" *OW*, 23 June 1916, p. 414.

175. See, for example, *Jung Juda*, 26 February 1915, pp. 56–58; 31 March 1916, p. 97; *Tätigkeitsbericht des Zentralbüros zum Schutze der galizischen Flüchlinge . . . in Brünn,* p. 18.

176. *Selbstwehr*, 29 December 1914, p. 1; 8 October 1915, p. 1; 17 April 1916, pp. 1–3; *JVS*, 28 September 1914, p. 1; 7 January 1915, pp. 2–3; 13 January 1915, p. 6. See also circular letter, Zionistisches Distriktkomitee für Böhmen, April 1915, CZA, L6/295.

177. *Selbstwehr*, 5 February 1915, p. 1; 5 March 1915, p. 1; 8 October 1915, p. 2; 12 November 1915, pp. 2–3; 21 January 1916, p. 1; 4 February 1916, p. 1; 18 February 1916, p. 1; 16 June 1916, p. 1; 30 June 1916, pp. 3–4. For similar attitudes of German Zionists to *Ostjuden* see Aschheim, pp. 80–120, 185–214.

178. *Selbstwehr*, 11 June 1915, p. 1.

179. *Selbstwehr*, 11 June 1915, p. 1; 25 June 1915, p. 1; 9 July 1915, pp. 1–2; *JVS*, 20 August 1915, pp. 2–3.

180. *Selbstwehr*, 18 June 1915, pp. 4–5; 2 July 1915, pp. 1–3.

181. *Selbstwehr*, 18 June 1915, pp. 4–5.

182. *Selbstwehr*, 23 July 1915, pp. 2–3.

183. *JVS*, 20 August 1915, pp. 2–3.

184. *Selbstwehr*, 20 August 1915, p. 7.

185. *Selbstwehr*, 17 August 1917, pp. 2–3. See also his articles in *Jung Juda*, 28 May 1915, pp. 157–158; 7 January 1916, pp. 12–14.

186. *JVS*, 28 May 1915, p. 3.

187. *JVS*, 10 February 1915, p. 5.

188. *JVS*, 17 February 1915, p. 4.

189. *JVS*, 24 May 1917, p. 5.

190. IKG Prague to IKG Vienna, 25 July 1916; IKG Jechnitz to IKG Vienna, 17 July 1916; IKG Vienna to Prague IKG, 19 July 1916, CAHJP, AW 357/3 and JMP, Box 128484. See also IKG-Repräsentanz Prag, Sitzungs-Protokoll 1916, 7 August 1916.

191. JMP, Box 128484.

192. IKG Bischofteinitz to IKG Prague, 8 August 1916, JMP, 147633.

193. Hoffmann-Holter, pp. 125–140.

194. See *JVS*, 19 November 1914, p. 4; 2 December 1914, p. 5; *Selbstwehr*, 22 January 1915, p. 7; 16 April 1915, p. 1; 7 May 1915, p. 7; 25 June 1915, p. 5; 24 September 1915, p. 1;

MONOIU, vol. 27, no. 3/4 (March/April 1915), pp. 11–14; no. 5/6 (May/June 1915), pp. 10–11; nos. 7–9 (July–September 1915), pp. 15–16.

195. See, for example, *OW*, 10 November 1916, p. 737; 24 November 1916, pp. 768–769; 20 July 1917, pp. 453–455, 467; 31 August 1917, p. 558; 14 September 1917, p. 582; 19 October 1917, pp. 654–655; 30 November 1917, pp. 749–750; *Selbstwehr*, 12 October 1917, p. 5; *JZ*, 31 August 1917, p. 5; 7 September 1917, p. 2; 28 September 1917, p. 2.

196. *OW*, 16 February 1917, p. 106; 23 February 1917, p. 121; 2 March 1917, pp. 136–137; *JVS*, 7 March 1917, p. 4; *Selbstwehr*, 16 February 1917, p. 1; 9 March 1917, p. 5; 16 March 1917, p. 5; *JZ*, 23 February 1917, p. 1; 9 March 1917, p. 2. See also correspondence between Jüdischer Volksverein "Zion," Prague, and Vienna IKG, 3 March 1917, and between Prague and Vienna IKGs, 26 February 1917 and 2 March 1917, CAHJP, AW 357/4.

197. *JZ*, 5 September [*sic;* October] 1917, pp. 1–2. See also 28 September 1917, p. 2; *OW*, 28 September 1917, p. 620.

198. *JZ*, 23 November 1917, pp. 1–2; 14 December 1917, p. 3.

199. *OW*, 20 July 1917, p. 454; 14 December 1917, p. 789; 29 March 1918, pp. 194–196; 27 September 1918, p. 609; *JZ*, 19 April 1918, p. 1; 27 September 1918, p. 1; 22 November 1918, p. 1.

200. Jüdischer Nationalrat, Vienna, to WZO, Copenhagen office, 6 December 1918, CZA, L6/371.

201. JMP, IKG-Repräsentanz Prag, Sitzungs-Protokoll 1918, 13 October 1918, 20 October 1918.

202. JMP, IKG-Repräsentanz Prag, Sitzungs-Protokoll 1918, 18 November 1918, Anhang 1, "Die Grösste allen Gefahren."

203. Arthur Hantke to Ludwig Singer, n.d., prob. November 1918; telegram, WZO, Copenhagen office, to Jewish National Council, Prague, 20 November 1918; telegram, Jüdischer Nationalrat, Vienna, to WZO, Copenhagen, 16 November 1918, CZA, L6/366; "II. Tätigkeitsbericht des jüdischen Nationalrat in Prag," January 1919, p. 2, L6/85 and L6/91; Jüdischer Nationalrat, Vienna, to WZO, Copenhagen, 28 November 1918 and telegram, 7 December 1918, L6/371; Hantke to Singer, 24 November 1918, Z3/217. See also *Selbstwehr*, 15 November 1918, p. 3; 20 December 1918, p. 3.

204. Hoffmann-Holter, pp. 41, 46–47, 62, 68, convincingly demonstrates that while local officials and police might behave in a nasty manner, the Austrian Ministry of Interior always behaved decently and sympathetically toward the refugees, regularly countering local attempts to expel them.

205. See, for example, *OW*, 23 April 1915, p. 317; 24 November 1916, p. 769; 20 July 1917, pp. 453, 467; 19 October 1917, p. 654; 30 November 1917, p. 749; 25 October 1918, p. 684; *Selbstwehr*, 22 January 1915, p. 7; 7 May 1915, p. 7; 24 September 1915, p. 1; 12 October 1917, p. 5; *JVS*, 8 October 1914, p. 2; *JZ*, 25 December 1914, p. 1; 27 September 1918, p. 1; *MONOIU*, vol. 27, no. 1/2 (January/February 1915), pp. 14–15.

206. IKG Prague to IKG Vienna, 25 July 1916; circular letter, *Zentralkomitee für Flüchtlinge*, 27 March 1917, JMP, Box 128484; kk Feldrabbiner Gustav Blau to IKG Prague, 10 October 1915; IKG Bischofteinitz to IKG Prague, 7 April 1916; IKG Prague to IKG Bischofteinitz, 4 May 1916; and other correspondence in JMP, Box 147633.

207. *OW*, 20 April 1917, pp. 238–239; 16 August 1918, pp. 505–506.

CHAPTER 4

1. Schmidl, *Juden in der k. (u.) k. Armee*, pp. 5, 84. It is impossible to ascertain the exact number of Jewish soldiers because the nature of wartime record keeping and the dissolution of the Monarchy precluded the compilation of accurate statistics.

2. Deák, *Beyond Nationalism*, p. 197; Deák "Jewish Soldiers in Austro-Hungarian Society," Leo Baeck Memorial Lecture 34 (New York, 1990), p. 22.

3. See, for example, Paul Fussell, *The Great War and Modern Memory* (New York, 1975); Eric J. Leed, *No Man's Land: Combat and Identity in World War I* (Cambridge, 1979).

4. Marc Bloch, *Memoirs of War, 1914–1915* (Ithaca, NY, 1980), p. 166.

5. See for example, Erich Maria Remarque, *All Quiet on the Western Front* (New York, 1930); Ernst Jünger, *Storm of Steel* (London, 1929). Ferguson, *The Pity of War,* pp. 357–366, certainly exaggerates when he argues that men fought because they enjoyed battle.

6. George L. Mosse, *Fallen Soldiers: Reshaping the Memory of the World Wars* (New York, 1990). Similarly for the American Civil War—another long, bloody war—historian James M. McPherson, *For Cause and Comrades: Why Men Fought in the Civil War* (New York, 1997), has argued that soldiers persevered because of their commitment to their respective causes: to save the union and its republican liberties from the threat of anarchy in the case of Union soldiers or to defend their homeland from occupation and the imposition of an unwanted economic system in the case of Confederate soldiers.

7. Stéphane Audoin-Rouzeau, *Men at War 1914–1918: National Sentiment and Trench Journalism in France during the First World War* (Providence, 1992), pp. 155–188. On comradeship, pp. 46–52. John Horne, "Soldiers, Civilians and the Warfare of Attrition: Representations of Combat in France, 1914–1918," in *Authority, Identity and the Social History of the Great War,* Frans Coetzee and Marilyn Shevin-Coetzee, eds. (Providence, 1995), pp. 223–249, emphasizes the role of anti-German sentiment and the need to defend French "civilization" from German "barbarity."

8. Bill Gammage, *The Broken Years: Australian Soldiers in the Great War* (Canberra, 1974).

9. Stone. On mobility, pp. 92, 94.

10. For a complete description of Austria-Hungary's military efforts in World War I, see the publication of the Austrian War Archives, *Österreich-Ungarns letzter Krieg, 1914–1918* (Vienna, 1930–1938), 8 vols. In English see Stone; May, esp. 88–128, 451–456, 716–720; Gunther E. Rothenberg, *The Army of Francis Joseph* (West Lafayette, IN, 1976), pp. 172–221.

11. István Deák, "The Habsburg Army in the First and Last Days of World War I: A Comparative Analysis," in *East Central European Society in World War I,* Király and Dreisziger, eds., p. 308. See also Kann, *Habsburg Empire*, p. 483.

12. Report on Austrian soldiers at the front, June 1917, based on a reading of censored letters, Evidenzbüro des k.u.k. Generalstabes, KA, KM Präs. 1917, 52-1/3.

13. On their worry about the Czechs, for example, see Stimmungsberichte, KK Militärkommando, Prag, to Kriegsministerium, Vienna, KA, KM Präs. 1915, 52-4/2-49; Report of the kk Militärkommando in Leitmeritz, 52-1/4-2. These reports make clear that the Czechs lacked enthusiasm for the war, but they did not engage in actual opposition to it. Indeed, military reports from Bohemia in late 1916 (KA, KM Präs. 1917, 52-4, especially 52-4/2) indicate that the army now considered Czech behavior acceptable, although throughout 1917 it worried about the impact of growing food shortages on Czech loyalty.

14. Stone, pp. 122, 125, 127, 240.

15. Rothenberg, pp. 184, 186, 188, 194, 200, 205, 217; Deák, *Beyond Nationalism,* p. 192; Deák, "The Habsburg Army," pp. 302, 305, 307; Kann, *Habsburg Empire,* p. 484; Zeman, pp. 39, 49–50; May, pp. 6, 83, 104, 352–353, 716–717, 798–799; Jay Luvaas, "A Unique Army: The Common Experience," in *The Habsburg Empire in World War I: Essays in Intellectual, Military, Political and Economic Aspects of the War Effort,* Robert A. Kann, Béla K. Király, and Paula S. Fichtner, eds. (Boulder, CO, 1977), pp. 87–103. On the Italians, see Laurence Sondhaus, *In the Service of the Emperor: Italians in the Austrian Armed Forces, 1814-1918* (Boulder, CO, 1990), pp. 104–120.

16. Jaroslav Hašek, *The Good Soldier Švejk and His Fortune in the World War* (New York, 1973; orig. Czech, 1921).

17. S. Grübel, *K. und k. Landsturm. Erinnerungen an den Doppeladler* (Berlin, 1930). Grübel, the father of Fred Grubel, the long-time head of the Leo Baeck Institute in New York, was from Brody, Galicia.

18. Deák, *Beyond Nationalism*, pp. 193–195; Déak, "The Habsburg Army," pp. 305–307; Stone, p. 125.

19. See, for example, Käte Frankenthal, a German Jew who served as a doctor in the Austrian army during World War I: *Der dreifache Fluch: Jüdin, Intellektuelle, Sozialistin: Lebenserinnerungen einer Ärtzin in Deutschland und im Exil* (Frankfurt a/M, 1981), p. 60; Olly Schwarz, a Prague-born Viennese Jew who worked as a volunteer nurse during the war: "Lebenserinnerungen," pp. 21–22; and Eric Fischer, a junior officer from Vienna who commanded a squad of Croats and Italians whose languages he did not speak: "Memoirs and Reminiscences," p. 16.

20. Virtually all the books on the Austrian military during World War I deal with politics and strategy, not with the soldiers themselves. The one exception, Deák, *Beyond Nationalism*, focuses only on officers. A study of Austro-Hungarian enlisted men during the war would be most welcome.

21. Fritz Kreisler, *Four Weeks in the Trenches: The War Story of a Violinist* (Boston, 1915).

22. Deák, *Beyond Nationalism*, p. 192; Stone, p. 243; Rothenberg, p. 187; Kann, *Habsburg Empire*, p. 472; May, pp. 104, 193–195, 200, 380; Richard B. Spence, "The Yugoslav Role in the Austro-Hungarian Army, 1914-1918," in *East Central European Society in World War I*, Király and Dreisziger, eds., pp. 354–365, on Italy, esp. p. 361.

23. Höllriegel, "Die Fahrt auf dem Katarakt," p. 212.

24. May, pp. 287–288.

25. For example, see Yiddish (transliterated) letter of Chajim Ohrgut, fall 1914 (4 Marcheshvan 5675), describing his fallen friend in Tannenbaum, *Kriegsbriefe*, pp. 177–181.

26. See, for example, letter by Yisroel Yakov Dobrusz in Tannenbaum, ed., *Kriegsbriefe*, pp. 176–177; *OW*, 7 May 1915, p. 353.

27. "Persönliches aus dem Weltkrieg in 42 Blättern, 1916–19; Album zusammengestellt von M. Pollack, Prostějov (Prossnitz, Mähren)," letter to parents, April 9, 1917, p. 14, CAHJP, CS 190.

28. "Kriegstagebuch" of Sargent Teofil Reiss, KA B/1576: 12. Reiss's handwritten diary, complete with many photographs, is located in a special collection of material gathered by Erwin Schmidl, the author of the book on Jews in the Habsburg army, which he deposited in the Austrian War Archives. I thank Dr. Schmidl for permission to use this material.

29. On medals, see Reiss, "Kriegstagebuch," 7 April, 22 April, 2 May, 29 December 1917; on his pride when his commander praises him for his bravery, see 15 January 1915; 26 February–23 March 1916, passim.

30. Reiss, "Kriegstagebuch," 23 June 1915.

31. Ibid., 19 July 1915.

32. Ibid., 12 November 1915. See also entries for 27 and 29 July 1916; 3 September 1916; 11 September 1916; 1 December 1917.

33. Indeed, Reiss even thanks God that he is not in the infantry, 19 October 1916; 22 November 1916. He also thinks he can save more money at the front than behind the lines (1 December 1917), an issue especially important after his engagement to be married.

34. Ibid., 1 October, 5 October, 6 October, 13 October 1917.

35. Ibid., 22 November 1916. See also Schoenfeld, p. 158.

36. Ibid., 1 September [*sic*: October] 1918.

37. Bernhard Bardach, "Aus meinem Tagebuch," Bernhard Bardach Collection, LBI, AR 6632; entry for August 13, 1914, I, p. 5.

38. Ibid., April 5, 1915, II, p. 77; May 2, 1915, II, p. 83.

39. Ibid., May 5, 6, 7, 8, 16, 28, 30, 1915; June 3, 4, 1915, II, pp. 83-84, 88, 93-94.

40. Ibid., 25 October 1917, 1 November 1917, V, pp. 397, 400.

41. Wolfgang von Weisl, "Skizze zu einer Autobiographie," in von Weisl, *Die Juden in der Armee Österreich-Ungarns,* p. 36.

42. Kohn, *Living in a World Revolution,* pp. 85–86. Kohn was taken prisoner in March 1915 and spent the rest of the war as a POW in Russia. Other Jewish memoirists also contrasted their own desire to fight with the lack of enthusiasm, or even real disloyalty, of many Czechs. Fischer, "Memoirs and Reminiscences," ch. 2, p. 7, ch. 3, p. 16; Mechner, "My Family Biography," p. 124; Bader, "One Life is Not Enough," pp. 96–97.

43. Lieben, "Aus meinem Leben," p. 104.

44. Ibid., p. 112.

45. Mechner, p. 74.

46. Ibid., pp. 75, 87, 92; quotation on p. 92.

47. Ibid., pp. 106–110.

48. Ibid., pp. 124, 126, insert to p. 126. For his experiences in Italy, see pp. 117–126.

49. *Hella,* pp. 31–32.

50. Hindls, "Erinnerungen aus meinem Leben," pp. 61–67.

51. Joseph Floch, unpublished memoir, LBI, pp. 19–25; unpublished memoir of his life by his wife (1980), LBI, pp. 34–41.

52. Salsitz, p. 214; interview with Bella Greenfield, Jerusalem, July 6, 1989.

53. Clare, *Last Waltz in Vienna,* p. 59.

54. Otto Friedman, "Lebenserinnerungen," unpublished memoir, LBI, p. 4. Friedman's memoir, along with excerpts from several interviews with his son and wife, has been published in *Ein ewiges Dennoch: 125 Jahre Juden in Salzburg,* Marko Feingold, ed. (Vienna, 1993), pp. 466–485.

55. Ulrich R. Furst, "Windows to my Youth," unpublished memoir (1984), LBI, pp. 14–15.

56. Grübel, *K. u. k. Landsturm,* Act I, Scene 9, p. 20.

57. Deák, "Jewish Soldiers" pp. 21–22; Deák, *Beyond Nationalism,* p. 196.

58. All the Jewish newspapers published the names of decorated Jewish soldiers every week. So too did wartime publications like *Jüdisches Kriegsgedenkblatt,* Moritz Frühling, ed., and the *Jüdisches Archiv,* published by the Zionists.

59. "Erinnerungen David Neumanns an seine Soldatenzeit im Ersten Weltkrieg," Appendix 5 in Schmidl, *Juden in der k. (u.) k. Armee,* p. 223.

60. Rudolph Pick, "The Ups and Downs of My Life," unpublished memoir, Institut für Wirtschafts- und Sozialgeschichte: "Dokumentation lebensgeschichtlicher Aufzeichnungen," p. 23. I thank Albert Lichtblau, Institut für Geschichte, University of Salzburg, who is preparing a collection of Austrian Jewish memoirs, for sending me Pick's.

61. Ibid., p. 24.

62. Interview with Neumann in Schmidl, p. 225.

63. Fischer, ch. 3, p. 1. Because of his physical infirmities, he served as a clerk behind the lines.

64. Letter to IKG Wien, 10 April 1917, CAHJP, AW 249/4.

65. *OW,* 9 November 1917, p. 708. See also *OW,* 28 August 1914; 18 December 1914, pp. 877–878.

66. See letters in Tannenbaum, ed., *Kriegsbriefe,* p. 20, 27, 114, 124–125, 158–159.

67. Audoin-Rouzeau, pp. 46–52; Leed, pp. 81–88.

68. Reiss, "Kriegstagebuch," 18 March 1915.

69. Ibid., 29 June 1915; 24 October 1917.

70. Ibid., 7 August 1916; 13 and 14 August 1916; 19 November 1916.

71. Furst, p. 12.

72. Pick, p. 21.

73. Lieben, pp. 121–122.

74. Fischer, ch. 5, p. 3.

75. Neumann in Schmidl, p. 224.

76. Reiss, "Kriegstagebuch," 15 January 1915; 16 January 1915; 26 February–23 March 1916. See also his unease with a lieutenant who wanted to slander him, 11 November 1916.

77. Reiss, 11 October 1916.

78. Bader, "One Life is not Enough," pp. 93-94.

79. Dr. N. N., Brünn, to IKG Wien, 28 May 1917, CAHJP, AW 249/4. See also copies of correspondence between Josef Samuel Bloch and officials in the Foreign Ministry (?), 18 December 1917 and 20 December 1917, AW 251/4.

80. CAHJP, INV. 6526/V.

81. Letter of M. Goldberg, 7 January 1917, files of Jüdisches Kriegsarchiv, CAHJP, INV. 6526/V.

82. Deák, *Beyond Nationalism*, pp. 174–178; Deák, "Jewish Soldiers in Austro-Hungarian Society"; Schmidl, pp. 60–76.

83. Schmidl, *Juden in der k.(u.)k. Armee*, pp. 68–71, 76; Deák, *Beyond Nationalism*, esp. pp. 169–187.

84. See, for example, report of Major Stanislaus Ritter von Osniakowski about the situation in Lemberg during the Russian occupation, 2 September 1914–22 June 1915, KA, KM Präs. 1915, 56-2/11; KK Landespräsident in Bukovina to Minister of the Interior, 12 April 1915, KA, KM Präs. 1915, 56-2/10. The Jewish press regularly cited generals who publicly praised Jewish loyalty and valor. See, for example, *OW*, 29 January 1915, p. 79; 12 February 1915, p. 117; *Selbstwehr*, 12 February 1915, p. 4; *JVS*, 24 February 1915, p. 5.

85. Letter to War Minister General Rudolf Stöger-Steiner, 6 September 1917, KA, KM Präs. 1917, 83-7/22.

86. KA, KM Präs. 1916, 34–17/3.

87. Jochmann, "Die Ausbreitung des Antisemitismus," in *Deutsches Judentum in Krieg und Revolution*, Mosse and Paucker, eds., pp. 421–424; Reichman, "Der Bewusstseinswandel der deutschen Juden," in Ibid., p. 516.

88. Angress, "The German Army's 'Judenzählung' of 1916," pp. 117–137; Zechlin, pp. 527–538; Jochman, "Die Ausbreitung des Antisemitismus," pp. 425–427; Reichmann, "Der Bewusstseinwandel," pp. 516–518; Pulzer, pp. 205–206.

89. See Tannenbaum, ed., *Kriegsbriefe*, pp. 32–37, 66–69, 80, 124–125, 146, 148–150, 184.

90. Aschheim, *Brothers and Strangers*, pp. 139–184; Reichmann, "Bewusstseinwandel," pp. 537–545.

91. Reiss, "Kriegstagebuch," 26 February-23 March, 1916; 17 April 1916.

92. "Persönliches aus dem Weltkrieg," p. 14, CAHJP, CS 190. Pollack transliterated Hebrew terms into German according to Central European Ashkenazic pronunciation, which I have preserved here and elsewhere.

93. See report by Moritz Jungwirt about Passover at the front in 1918, *OW*, 19 April 1918, p. 240; report by Dr. Albert Schweiger about the same phrase in the Yom Kippur liturgy, *OW*, 8 October 1915, p. 738.

94. *OW*, 8 December 1916, p. 798.

95. See, for example, *OW*, 15 December 1916, pp. 815–816; *JVS*, 10 April 1915, p. 4;

Comité der jüd. Landsturmmannschaft, Bruck a/L., 1 October 1914, to IKG Wien, CAHJP, AW 356. See also "Gottesdienst unter Geschützfeuer," *Jüdische Front*, 1 September 1937, p. 9.

96. *JVS*, 10 April 1915, p. 4; *OW*, 16 April 1915, p. 290; *OW*, 16 April 1915, p. 293; *OW*, 28 September 1915, pp. 732–733; *OW*, 17 November 1916, p. 750; *Selbstwehr*, 5 May 1917, pp. 2–3.

97. *OW*, 29 December 1916, p. 847.

98. *Gebetbuch für Israelitische Soldaten im Kriege* (1914), CAHJP, AW 358.

99. *OW*, 28 May 1915, p. 405; *Selbstwehr*, 12 November 1915, p. 2; *JVS*, 8 July 1915, p. 6; *Jung Juda*, 17 March 1916, pp. 90–91. Faludi's name only appears in the *OW* version, ostensibly written by him.

100. Schoenfeld, p. 162. See also report in *JZ*, 6 September 1918, p. 11.

101. Card, March 6, 1917, in Kriegserinnerungen (Album) of Rabbi Béla Fischer, CAHJP, AW 3111.

102. *OW*, 26 March 1915, p. 243; 25 October 1916, pp. 140–141; 23 March 1917, pp. 184–185; 1 March 1918, pp. 140–141; *JVS*, 29 March 1915, p. 5; *JKor*, 7 March 1918, p. 4.

103. *OW*, 10 September 1915, p. 688; 10 March 1916, p. 181; 24 March 1916, p. 212; 29 September 1916, pp. 643–644; 30 March 1917, p. 205; 14 September 1917, p. 591; 15 March 1918, p. 173; Fischer, ch. 5, p. 3. The army could not always offer soldiers full leave for the holidays, but did try to give passes for the hours of services. See correspondence in CAHJP, AW 368.

104. Jewish newspapers were filled with reports by chaplains on seders and services they organized and letters from soldiers praising their efforts. See, for example, letter by Chaplain Majer Tauber on the Eastern Front, *OW*, 16 April 1915, pp. 289–291; report by Chaplain Adolf Altmann on his work in South Tyrol, *OW*, 11 May 1917, p. 301 and 19 April 1918, pp. 234–235; report of Chaplain Majer Tauber, then director of chaplains for the Isonzo Army, describing 60 kosher kitchens feeding 7000 soldiers in 1918, *OW*, 19 April 1918, p. 240. On kosher kitchens or Passover seders organized by energetic individuals, see *OW*, 16 April 1915, p. 302; 14 May 1915, p. 374; 21 May 1915, p. 392; 20 July 1917, pp. 463–464.

105. *JKor*, 8 February 1917, p. 3, quoting the War Ministry's orders of 5 January 1916 and 1 April 1916; *OW*, 5 May 1916, pp. 300–301; 23 February 1917, p. 119; *JVS*, 7 March 1917, pp. 4–5. On the history of kosher food in the Austrian army, see Schmidl, pp. 42–44.

106. See, for example, letter from a group of soldiers to Chaplain Majer Tauber, *OW*, 20 April 1917, p. 242; report *OW*, 20 July 1917, p. 463.

107. "Bericht über meine Besprechung mit dem k.k. Landesverteidigungsminister, 7 December 1916," CAHJP, AW 357/3; Appendix to Plenarsitzung, IKG Wien, 17 December 1916, AW 71/16.

108. Schoenfeld, p. 142.

109. Letter, February 21, 1915, CAHJP, AW 364/3. There are many other requests for matzah in this file.

110. CAHJP, AW 364/3. See other similar requests in AW 357/2.

111. Interview with Neumann in Schmidl, p. 223.

112. Letter, 20 January 1915, CAHJP, AW 364/1; see also report by Hugo Weiss, 30 April 1915, about the Passover food effort of the IKG, in ibid.

113. IKG Wien to IKGs of Brünn, Trieste, Mähr. Ostrau, Pilsen, Troppau, Graz, and Olmütz, 1 February 1915, CAHJP, AW 364/2.

114. *OW*, 16 April 1915, p. 289.

115. CAHJP, AW 362; AW 357/2; AW 357/3; AW 357/4. The number of requests tapered off after 1915, presumably because the growing number of Jewish chaplains managed to supply the soldiers with what they needed.

116. See, for example, report, August 6, 1916, CAHJP, AW 357/3.

117. CAHJP, AW 362; AW 357/2.

118. Letter, 26 October (?) 1915 in CAHJP, AW 357/2. Apparently the army allowed soldiers to have beards as long as they did not obscure marks of rank on the soldier's collar (Schmidl, p. 46). Photographs of Jewish soldiers during the war depict many with beards, although only short ones, not the long flowing beards of Jewish Orthodox tradition. (See, for example, *Jung Juda*, 6 October 1916, p. 297.)

119. Card addressed to Frau Dr. Ludwig Reiss (?) in CAHJP, AW 357/2.

120. *Ranglisten des Kaiserlichen und Königlichen Heeres 1916* (Vienna, 1916), p. 1003.

121. *Ranglisten des Kaiserlichen und Königlichen Heeres 1917* (Vienna, 1917), p. 1343; *Ranglisten des Kaiserlichen und Königlichen Heeres 1918* (Vienna, 1918), pp. 1674–1675. There were also nine Jewish chaplains in the Austrian Landwehr and presumably several in the Hungarian Honvéd; see *Ranglisten der k.k. Landwehr und der Gendarmerie* (Vienna, 1918), p. 549.

122. On Viennese rabbis as "subsidiary" chaplains, see voluminous correspondence in CAHJP, AW 363; AW 357/2; AW 357/3; AW 360.

123. *Ranglisten . . . 1916*, p. 1004; *Ranglisten . . . 1917*, p. 1343; *Ranglisten . . . 1918*, pp. 1674–1675. On the significance of university education in the modern rabbinate, see Ismar Schorsch, "Emancipation and the Crisis of Religious Authority—The Emergence of the Modern Rabbinate," in *Revolution and Evolution. 1848 in German-Jewish History*, Werner Mosse, Arnold Paucker, and Reinhold Rürup, eds. (Tübingen, 1981), pp. 205–247; and Alexander Altmann, "The German Rabbi: 1910–1939," *LBIYB* 19 (1974), pp. 31–49. Altmann, a professor of Jewish Studies at Brandeis, was the son of Dr. Adolf Altmann, a Habsburg Army chaplain during World War I.

124. List of Jewish chaplains with the Isonzo Army, December 1917, KA, KM 1917. 9. Abt., 11-30/2,5 (79846).

125. Rabbi S. Funk to IKG Wien, n.d., probably April 1915; Rabbi Moritz Güdemann to IKG Wien, April 1915, CAHJP, AW 360.

126. Correspondence in CAHJP, AW 364/2; 357/1; 357/2; 356, 363; "Diensttätigkeitsbericht" of Dr. Bernard Templer, 17 January 1916, Olmütz, KA, KM 1917, 9. Abt., 11-3/7 (7896); cards from chaplains to Margarethe Grunwald, in CAHJP, P 97/3; and Kriegserinnerungen (album) of Rabbi Béla Fischer, a subsidiary chaplain with the Lower Austrian Red Cross, AW 3111. See also *OW*, 25 December 1914, p. 908; 16 April 1915, pp. 289–291; 8 October 1915, pp. 737–738; 28 April 1916, p. 290; 18 August 1916, p. 551; 6 October 1916, p. 664; 27 October 1916, p. 707; 22 December 1916, p. 831; 9 March 1917, p. 155; 25 May 1917, p. 323; 19 October 1917, p. 661; 19 April 1918, pp. 234–235, 240; 2 August 1918, p. 483; *Selbstwehr*, 5 May 1917, pp. 2–3; Arnold Frankfurther, "Die k.u.k. israel. Militärseelsorge in Wien," *Hickls Wiener jüdischer Volkskalender* (1916/17), pp. 76–80.

127. Protokolle, IKG Wien Sekretariat, 4 August 1914, CAHJP, AW 356. For other requests to Vienna by chaplains see AW 357/2; 357/3; 357/4; 356; for Prague, see JMP, *Sitzungsprotokolle IKG Prag 1915*, 21 November 1915, 12 December 1915.

128. *OW*, 16 April 1915, pp. 289–291; description of services, p. 290.

129. *OW*, 28 June 1918, p. 395.

130. See, for example, summary of letter to KM, April 1917, complaining about Chaplain Bernard Templer, KA, KM 1917, 9. Abt. 11-24 (25925). See also letter of complaint from wounded soldiers in a military hospital in Vienna, n.d., probably February 1917, CAHJP, AW 357/4; *OW*, 26 October 1917, p. 676; *JZ*, 12 July 1918, p. 6; 6 September 1918, p. 11.

131. Neumann, in Schmidl, p. 223.

132. *OW*, 3 November 1916, p. 718.

133. *OW*, 8 December 1916, p. 798.

134. Bernard Templer, for example, defended himself against the complaints made against him, by arguing that the Olmütz IKG had been unwilling to help him (KA, KM 9. Abt. 1917, 11-24/1,3 (30164) and 11-24/1,4 (44406)).

135. Reiss, "Kriegstagebuch," 6 October 1916.

136. In his research on Jews in the Habsburg army, Erwin Schmidl came across several reports written by Catholic chaplains complaining that Jewish chaplains spent all their time cooking kosher food, arranging occasional services, and writing reports (copies in KA B/1576:2). Some of these reports use nasty, anti-Semitic language, but it is not clear whether they reflect prejudice or just a simple misunderstanding of the role of rabbis compared with that of Catholic priests. Moreover, it is impossible to judge either how typical these reports were or how much truth they reflect. In the spirit of wartime brotherhood, the Jewish press published reports about good relations between chaplains of different religions. See, *OW*, 9 July 1915, pp. 514–515; 23 July 1915; 10 September 1915, pp. 686–687.

137. Chaplain Arnold Frankfurter and the Jewish community of Vienna argued in 1914 and 1915, for example, about who had the right to perform marriages and register births (CAHJP, AW 361).

138. Manfred Altmann, "K.u.k. Feldrabbiner Dr. Adolf Altmann an der Kriegsfront (1915–1918) in Begegnung mit Feldmarschall Conrad von Hötzendorf und anderen Armeekommandanten," in Feingold, ed., *Ein Ewiges Dennoch*, pp. 492–495, 502; quotation on p. 495; Alexander Altmann, "Adolf Altmann (1879–1944): A Filial Memoir," *LBIYB* 26 (1981), pp. 145–167. Altmann reported on his own activities in the Jewish press; see, for example, *OW*, 11 May 1917, p. 301. After the war, Altmann returned to Salzburg and in 1920 moved to Trier, Germany. Three of his sons emigrated to England or America after the Nazis came to power, but they could not obtain visas for their parents, who were deported to Theresienstadt and Auschwitz, where they perished in 1944. See Manfred Altmann, pp. 529–535; conversation, Manfred Altmann with the author, September 1992, London.

139. On the Vienna Rite, see Marsha L. Rozenblit, "The Struggle over Religious Reform in Nineteenth-Century Vienna," *AJS Review* 14, no. 2 (Fall 1989), pp. 179–221. On religious modernization more generally, see Michael A. Meyer, *Response to Modernity*.

140. Letter to IKG Wien, 5 August 1915, CAHJP, AW 357/2.

141. "Diensttätigkeitsbericht," 17 January 1916, KA, KM 1917, 9. Abt., 11-3/7 (7896).

142. *JVS*, 11 October 1916, p. 3.

143. Chaplain R. Faerber understood that Orthodox soldiers might have a hard time with a modern rabbi: "Unsere israelitische Militärseelsorge," *Hickls wiener jüdischer Volkskalender* (1917/18), pp. 46–47.

144. Postcard, n.d., in Kriegserinnerungen (Album), CAHJP, AW 3111.

145. *Selbstwehr*, 5 May 1917, pp. 2–3.

146. *OW*, 7 May 1915, p. 353, reprinted from the *Israelitische Familienblatt*, Hamburg.

147. *OW*, 27 August 1915, p. 646.

148. *JVS*, 7 September 1915, p. 3. The *shma* is also supposed to be recited when one expects imminent death.

149. On the important role of myth among soldiers in World War I, see Leed, pp. 115–162; Fussell, pp. 115–139.

150. Mosse, *Fallen Soldiers*, pp. 6–7, 25, 32, 34–35, 49–50, and 74–78.

151. Horne, pp. 233–235.

152. Jay Winter, *Sites of Memory, Sites of Mourning: The Great War in European Cultural History* (Cambridge, 1995). Winter takes issue with all those who argue that the war marked a decisive break with traditional forms and an embrace of modernism. His analysis of art, literature, film, and popular culture during and after the war reveals

the continued power of traditional modes of representation in England, France, and Germany.

153. George L. Mosse, "The Jews and the German War Experience 1914–1918," Leo Baeck Memorial Lecture 21 (New York, 1977); quotation, p. 5.

154. See, for example, reports and letters in *OW*, 25 December 1914, p. 908, 909; 17 March 1916, p. 195; 3 November 1916, p. 718.

155. Nonobservant Christians also found comfort in Christian symbols; see Audoin-Rouzeau, pp. 85–87.

156. Mosse, "Jews and the German War Experience," pp. 7–8.

157. Copy of letter from Magistrat Wien, 9 September 1914, CAHJP, AW 1478. Most Viennese soldiers were buried near the front.

158. IKG Wien to Weisskirchner, 13 September 1914, CAHJP, AW 1477; IKG Wien, Vetreter-Sitzung, 8 September 1914, AW 72/15. It is interesting that the IKG rendered the Hebrew phrase as it did. It could easily be translated "may his soul be bound in the bonds of eternal life." Did they worry that the more literal translation might sound too Christian?

159. Notes attached to IKG letter of 13 September 1914, CAHJP, AW 1477.

160. Protokoll, Vertreter-Sitzung, IKG Wien, 15 September 1915, CAHJP, AW 1477, and AW 72/15.

161. Protokoll, Vertreter-Sitzung, IKG Wien, 15 September 1914, CAHJP, AW 1477; AW 72/15.

162. Letters, CAHJP, AW 1478, all from late 1914 and early 1915.

163. List of Jews buried in the Kriegergrabstätte in group 91, CAHJP, AW 1478.

164. *JVS*, 20 January 1915, p. 5.

165. *OW*, 10 August 1917, p. 507.

166. As reported by Altmann in *OW*, 28 January 1916, pp. 79–80. See also efforts by Chaplain Bernard Hausner to obtain individual graves for Jewish soldiers, *OW*, 3 November 1916, p. 718.

167. *OW*, 18 June 1915, p. 453; 1 December 1916, p. 787; letter to IKG Wien from Rettungs-Komite Jung-Juda in Lezajsk, n.d., received 15 September 1916, CAHJP, AW 248/5; *JVS*, 20 January 1915, p. 5.

168. Letter, 3 September 1914, CAHJP, AW 357/1.

169. *OW*, 8 January 1915, pp. 24–25.

170. *Bericht der Israelitischen Kultusgemeinde Wien über die Tätigkeit in der Periode 1912–1924* (Vienna, 1924), p. 49.

171. *OW*, 12 March 1915, p. 205.

172. In the summer of 1994, I visited the memorial in the Jewish Section of the Central Cemetery of Vienna and was much moved by it and the graves that surround it. I have described the memorial as I found it.

173. On the Bund jüdischer Frontsoldaten, established in 1932 to counteract escalating anti-Semitism, see *Drei Jahre BJF: Festschrift des Bundes jüdischer Frontsoldaten* (Vienna, 1935) and Martin Senekowitsch, *Gleichberechtige in einer grosse Armee; Zur Geschichte des Bundes Jüdischer Frontsoldaten Österreichs, 1932-38* (Vienna, 1994).

174. Mosse, *Fallen Soldiers*, pp. 46–49, 79-106; Winter, *Sites of Memory*, pp. 78–116. Although others have discussed the political significance of war memorials, Winter emphasizes that most of them functioned as "sites of mourning" for the dead. They honored the dead and expressed the hope that there would be no repetition of murderous war. In its function and message, therefore, this Jewish memorial resembled other memorials to fallen soldiers.

CHAPTER 5

1. Sperber, *God's Water Carriers*, p. 114. For a less dramatic expression of worry about the political impact of Franz Joseph's death, see Bernhard Bardach, "Aus meinem Tagebuch," 22 November 1916, IV, pp. 258–259, LBI, AR 6632.

2. Fischer, "Memoirs and Reminiscences," ch. 3, p. 18. See also Arnold Höllriegel's memory of the prediction of a Czech peasant, "Die Fahrt auf dem Katarakt," p. 6.

3. *OW*, 1 December 1916, pp. 777–778; 783–786; 790; 8 December 1916, p. 802; *JZ*, 24 November 1916, pp. 1–2; 1 December 1916, p. 2; *Selbstwehr*, 1 December 1916, pp. 2–3; *JVS*, 22 December 1916, pp. 1–3, 6; 10 January 1917; *MONOIU*, vol. 28, nos. 9-12 (September–December 1916), pp. 1–5; *Zweimonatsbericht . . . der . . . Bnai Brith*, vol. 19, no. 6 (1916), pp. 190–194. See also reports of special services in CAHJP, AW 307, 308; report of IKG Wien to the governor of Lower Austria, 5 January 1917, AW 248/5; Plenarsitzung IKG Wien, 23 November 1916, AW 71/16.

4. Adolf Altmann, "Predigt gehalten bei den feierlichen Trauergottesdiensten anlässlich des Ablebens Sr. apostolischen Majestät des Kaisers und Königs Franz Josef I. am 30. Nov. und 1. Dez. 1916 im israelitischen Tempel zu Meran und im israel. Soldatenbethause zu Bozen," special supplement to *Meraner Zeitung*, no. 276 (1 December 1916), CAHJP, Au 175/3; reprinted in Feingold, ed., *Ein Ewiges Dennoch*, pp. 497–501.

5. *MONOIU*, vol. 29, no. 1–2 (January–February 1917), pp. 5–19; quotation, p. 19.

6. *OW*, 8 December 1916, p. 802; CAHJP, AW 308, "Trauerakten, Kaiser Franz Josef."

7. Güdemann, "Aus meinem Leben," p. 253 (typed transcript). Güdemann began his memoir in 1899, but continued to work on it until his death in 1918. During World War I, the memoir became a diary.

8. Schoenfeld, *Jewish Life in Galicia*, p. 158.

9. Printed Program, "Trauerandacht," November 26, 1916, IKG Wien, CAHJP, AW 308. The memorial service at the Adas Yisroel Schiffschule, the synagogue of Hungarian Orthodox Jews, did not include *kaddish*, even though it too included psalms and *el moleh rachamim* (program in AW 308). The synagogue also lit a memorial candle every day for 30 days in Franz Joseph's memory (letter, 30 November 1916 to IKG Wien).

10. D. Herzog, *Kaiser Franz Josef I.: Gedenkrede, gehalten im israelitischen Tempel zu Graz* (Frankfort, 1917), p. 5.

11. *JZ*, 24 November 1916, p. 1.

12. Adolf Kurrein, "Ein Heldenlied," *JVS*, 22 December 1916, p. 3.

13. JMP, Sitzungsprotokolle, IKG-Repräsentanz Prag, 3 December 1916.

14. CAHJP, AW 309; *OW*, 15 December 1916, pp. 810–812.

15. "Antwort Seiner Majestät des Kaisers," CAHJP, AW 309.

16. *OW*, 15 December 1916, p. 818; *MONOIU*, vol. 28, nos. 9–12 (September–December 1916), pp. 6–7; *Selbstwehr*, 8 December 1916, p. 2.

17. On war weariness, see May, pp. 654–657, 664–669. For an official army report on war weariness among the soldiers in June 1917, see KA, KM Präs., 52-1/3. Jews remarked on the war weariness as well. One Jewish newspaper laconically noted in mid-1918, "Today there is no more enthusiasm for the war" (*JZ*, 21 June 1918, p. 1). In memoirs, see, for example, Vinca Safar, "Aus meinem Leben," unpublished memoir, LBI, p. 57; Segal, "You Shall Never Forget," p. 22.

18. For an compelling albeit tendentious account of food shortages and "hamstering" see Anna Eisenmenger, *Blockade: The Diary of an Austrian Middle Class Woman, 1914–1924* (New York, 1932). In Jewish memoirs, see, for example, Landre, "Durch's Sieb der Zeit gefallen," pp. 101–103; Lachs, *Warum schaust du zurück*, pp. 77–79; Güdemann, "Aus meinem Leben," pp. 259–260, 265–266, 270; Sperber, pp. 133–134.

On the social impact of food shortages and hamstering, see Reinhard J. Sieder, "Behind the Lines: Working-Class Family Life in Wartime Vienna," in *The Upheaval of War: Family, Work and Welfare in Europe, 1914–1918*, Richard Wall and Jay Winter, eds. (Cambridge, 1988), pp. 109–138; and for Germany, Daniel, pp. 167–169, 183–232.

On the disorganized methods of food rationing in Austria, see Horst Haselsteiner, "The Habsburg Empire in World War I: Mobilization of Food Supplies," in *East Central European Society in World War I*, Király and Dreisziger, eds., pp. 87–102; J. Robert Wegs, *Die österreichische Kriegswirtschaft 1914–1918* (Vienna, 1979).

19. Stimmungsberichte aus Böhmen, k.k. Militärkommando, Prague, to Kriegsministerium, 1917 and 1918, KA, KM Präs. 1917, 52-4; KM Präs. 1918, 52-4; Richard G. Plaschka, Horst Haselsteiner, and Arnold Suppan, *Innere Front: Militärassistenz, Widerstand und Umsturz in der Donaumonarchie 1918*, 2 vols. (Vienna, 1974).

20. Pauley, pp. 64–72; Hoffmann-Holter, pp. 125–140. The army made a direct connection between food shortages and rising anti-Semitism; see Stimmungsberichte aus Böhmen, k.k. Militärkommando, Prague, to Kriegsministerium, KA, KM Präs. 1917, 52-4/13, 21, 23, 25-2, 25-4, 30; KM Präs. 1918, 52-4/11. The Jewish press regularly reported anti-Semitic incidents after censorship eased in late 1917. See *OW*, 19 October 1917, p. 654; 15 March 1918, pp. 161, 163–164, 169; 10 May 1918, pp. 278–279; *JZ*, 15 March 1918, p. 4; 12 April 1918, pp. 3–4; 17 May 1918, p. 7; 21 June 1918, p. 1; *Selbstwehr*, 26 February 1915, p. 1; 8 December 1916, p. 1; 27 July 1917, pp. 1–2; 8 March 1918, p. 7; 27 September 1918, pp. 2–4; *JVS*, 19 April 1918, p. 6.

21. In Bohemia, the army regarded anti-Semitic violence, Czech nationalism, and anti-Austrianism all as a direct result of terrible food shortages. See Stimmungsberichte aus Böhmen, k.k. Militärkommando, Prague, KA, KM Präs. 1917, 52-4/21, 23, 25-2, 25-4. See also *JZ*, 17 May 1918, p. 7. On pogroms, see below and chapter 6.

22. Zeman; May; Richard Georg Plaschka and Karlheinz Mack, eds., *Die Auflösung des Habsburgerreiches. Zusammenbruch und Neuorientierung im Donauraum* (Munich, 1970).

23. The following discussion is based on Zeman, pp. 100–110, 152–159, 237–238; May, pp. 154–169, 259–261, 366–377, 505–509, 619–620, 732–734; Fischer, *Germany's Aims in the First World War*, pp. 195–211, 236–244, 245, 322–323, 440–442, 450–456, 526–533.

24. *OW*, 19 March 1915, pp. 213–214.

25. Copy, "Begrüssung des neuen Statthalters von Galizien Excellenz von Colard durch das Exekutivkomitee des österreichischen Zionisten," Jüdisches Kriegsarchiv, CAHJP, INV. 6526/I; *JZ*, 23 July 1915, p. 1; 6 August 1915, p. 2; *Selbstwehr*, 30 July 1915, p. 7; 6 August 1915, p. 2; *OW*, 25 June 1915, p. 469; 30 July 1915, p. 575; 27 August 1915, p. 650.

26. Memorandum of Austrian Zionists to the government, 25 June 1915, CZA, Z3/843; CAHJP, AW 247/5; protocol, meeting between Robert Stricker and Zionist Actions Committee, Berlin, 29 July 1915, CZA, Z3/154; reports (1915) of anti-Semitic behavior of Polish civil servants in Galicia, Z3/155; *Selbstwehr*, 20 August 1915, p. 3; *JVS*, 20 August 1915, pp. 4–5.

27. *OW*, 10 November 1916, pp. 729–731. For similar views, see *Zweimonatsbericht . . . der . . . Bnai Brith*, vol. 19, no. 6 (1916), pp. 204–205.

28. *OW*, 5 January 1917, pp. 1–2.

29. *JKor*, 30 January 1917, p. 1; 6 March 1917, pp. 1–2.

30. *JZ*, 10 November 1916, pp. 1–2; 1 December 1916, p. 1.

31. *Selbstwehr*, 10 November 1916, p. 1; 22 December 1916, p. 1; 9 February 1917, pp. 4–5. For earlier awareness of the significance of Galicia and her nationally conscious Jewry for Jewish nationalism in Austria generally, see 28 January 1916, p. 1.

32. *JZ*, 17 November 1916, p. 1; *Selbstwehr*, 24 November 1916, p. 4; 9 March 1917, p. 4; *OW*, 24 November 1916, p. 767.

33. Max Rosenfeld, *Polen und Juden* (Berlin, 1917); Rosenfeld, *Die polnische Judenfrage: Problem und Lösung* (Vienna, 1918); Rosenfeld, *Nationales Selbstbestimmungsrecht der Juden in Polen* (Vienna, 1918). Quotation from *Die polnische Judenfrage*, p. 169. Naturally, Rosenfeld supported national autonomy for Jews and other nationalities in Poland as well.

34. *Zweimonatsbericht . . . der . . . Bnai Brith*, vol. 18, no. 4 (1915), pp. 125–128, 144–149; 177–182; vol. 19, no. 1 (1916), pp. 7–15; no. 2, pp. 71–76; no. 4, pp. 143–145; no. 5, pp. 158–168; no. 6, pp. 197–198; vol. 20, no. 1/2 (1917), pp. 49–57; vol. 21, no. 1/2 (1918), pp. 58–62; no. 3/4, pp. 90–91. On new chapters, vol. 20, no. 5/6 (1917), p. 154.

35. *XLIII. Jahresbericht der Israelitischen Allianz zu Wien erstattet an die XLIII. ordentliche Generalversammlung am 5. June 1916* (Vienna, 1916), pp. 5–7, 14–18, CAHJP, AW 2828/35; *XLIV. Jahresbericht der Israelitischen Allianz zu Wien erstattet an die XLIV. ordentliche Generalversammlung am 25. June 1917* (Vienna, 1917), pp. 26–32, AW 2828/36; *XLV. Jahresbericht der Israelitischen Allianz zu Wien erstattet an die XLV. ordentliche Generalversammlung am 10. June 1918* (Vienna, 1918), pp. 16–22, AW 2828/37. See also appeal for money from *Allianz*, Bnai Brith, and the Galician *Hilfsverein* to Vienna IKG, October 1915, CAHJP, AW 357/2.

36. CAHJP, AW 357/3, 248/5, 249/4, 249/5; *OW*, 8 September 1916, pp. 597–598; 30 March 1917, pp. 195–200; 15 September 1917, pp. 581–582; *JZ*, 25 February 1916, p. 2.

37. *Zweimonatsbericht . . . der . . . Bnai Brith*, vol. 19, no. 1 (1916), p. 6; vol. 20, no. 5/6 (1917), pp. 161–162; vol. 21, no. 3/4 (1918), pp. 88–90; *Jahresbericht der Israelitischen Allianz . . . 1916*, pp. 21–30, CAHJP, AW 2828/35; *Jahresbericht der Israelitischen Allianz . . . 1917*, pp. 33–35, AW 2828/36; Memo, Alfred Stern, 14 December 1915, about his meeting with Governor General Baron Diller, appended to Plenarsitzung, IKG Wien, 26 December 1915, AW 71/16.

38. Zionistisches Zentralkomitee für Westösterreich to k.u.k. Armee Oberkommando, n.d., CAHJP, AW 357/2; Komitee zur Aufklärung über ostjüdische Fragen to IKG Wien, AW 357/2. See also *OW*, 26 January 1917, pp. 57–58; *JZ*, 29 October 1915, p. 2. For complaints about treatment of Jews in Austrian zone, see files of Jüdisches Kriegsarchiv, CAHJP, INV. 6526; letters of various Zionist and Jewish nationalist groups to the Austrian army in CZA, Z3/155, Z3/149.

39. Jüdisches Kriegsarchiv, CAHJP, INV. 6526/I, 6526/III; 6526/V. For press reports: *JZ*, 17 August 1917, p. 4; 2 November 1917, p. 3.

40. *OW*, 15 March 1918, p. 163; *JZ*, 8 March 1918, p. 1; 22 March 1918, pp. 3–4. For earlier worries about this issue, see *JZ*, 22 February 1918, p. 1.

41. *OW*, 26 April 1918, p. 249; 20 September 1918, p. 600; *JKor*, 25 April 1918, p. 2; *JZ*, 26 April 1918, p. 1; *Selbstwehr*, 3 May 1918, p. 1; *Jung Juda*, 3 May 1918, p. 133; *JVS*, 3 May 1918, pp. 2–3. See also correspondence of IKG Brünn and IKG Vienna, 28 April 1918 and 3 May 1918, CAHJP, AW 250/4; Plenarsitzung, IKG Wien, 24 April 1918, 2 May 1918, with appended report of President Alfred Stern's meeting with Minister of the Interior, AW 71/16.

42. *OW*, 24 May 1918, pp. 309–310; 27 September 1918, p. 619; *JZ*, 24 May 1918, p. 2; 26 July 1918, p. 1; *Selbstwehr*, 30 August 1918, p. 5.

43. See handwritten note on report of the pogrom, 16 April 1918, Zionist Central Committee for West Austria, CZA, L6/342. On the other hand, *OW*, 26 April 1918, p. 249 denied that the pogrom was a food riot.

44. *JKor*, 25 April 1918, p. 2; 2 May 1918, p. 6; 13 June 1918, p. 7. On the position of the Orthodox in Polish politics see Gershon Bacon, "Agudat Israel in Interwar Poland," *The Jews of Poland between Two World Wars*, pp. 20–35.

45. *JZ*, 16 November 1917, p. 1; 15 February 1918, pp. 1–2; 26 April 1918, pp. 2–3; 3 May 1918, pp. 1–2; *Selbstwehr*, 23 November 1917, p. 1; 22 February 1918, p. 1; 1 March 1918, p. 3; *JVS*, 24 May 1917, p. 2.

46. *JZ*, 16 November 1917, p. 1; *Selbstwehr*, 22 February 1918, p. 1; *OW*, 2 August 1918, p. 474.

47. *JZ*, 10 May 1918, pp. 4–5.

48. "Bericht des Präsidiums," CAHJP, AW 357/1.

49. M. Lothringer, "Mi jeloch lefonenu?" *OW*, 9 July 1915, p. 519.

50. Heinrich Schreiber, "Zur Frage des Gemeindebundes," *OW*, 23 July 1915, pp. 549–550. The Bnai Brith also urged such unity: *Zweimonatsbericht . . . der . . . Bnai Brith*, vol. 18, no. 5 (1915), pp. 148–149.

51. *OW*, 3 December 1915, pp. 877–879.

52. *OW*, 7 April 1916, pp. 237–238; 11 August 1916, pp. 525–526; 16 February 1917, p. 105; 8 June 1917, pp. 357–358; 13 July 1917, pp. 437–438; *Zweimonatsbericht . . . der . . . Bnai Brith*, vol. 20, no. 3 (1917), pp. 79–81.

53. Plenarsitzung, 25 July 1916, CAHJP, AW 71/16; memo on Alfred Stern's meeting with the Ministry for Religion and Education, 25 May 1916, AW 357/3.

54. *OW*, 29 September 1916, pp. 638–639; 17 October 1916, pp. 679–680, 688; *JKor*, 18 August 1916, pp. 1–2; *Zweimonatsbericht . . . der . . . Bnai Brith*, vol. 19, no. 5 (1916), pp. 169–181; *Selbstwehr*, 27 September 1916, pp. 2–3.

55. *OW*, 22 September 1916, pp. 621–623.

56. JMP, IKG-Repräsentanz Prag, Sitzungsprotokolle 1916, 17 August 1916, 3 September 1916, 8 October 1916. On Bohemian-Jewish attitudes to Galician Jewish refugees, see chapter 3.

57. *OW*, 17 November 1916, p. 753; *Selbstwehr*, 1 December 1916, p. 1.

58. *JKor*, 4 January 1917, p. 2; 11 January 1917, p. 1; 18 January 1917, pp. 1–2.

59. *JKor*, 11 January 1917, p. 1. Prague's opposition preceeded the German-Austrian announcement about Poland and was not influenced by it.

60. *OW*, 13 July 1917, pp. 437–438; 27 July 1917, pp. 470–471; 19 October 1917, pp. 653–654.

61. *OW*, 27 July 1917, pp. 470–471.

62. *JZ*, 19 February 1915, p. 1; 6 August 1915, p. 4; 3 March 1916, p. 1; 12 April 1918, pp. 2–3; *JVS*, 4 March 1915, p. 3.

63. *JZ*, 3 March 1916, p. 1; *Selbstwehr*, 8 September 1916, p. 2. In 1898, the World Zionist Organization had pledged all Zionists to the goal of "conquering the communities," and Austrian Zionists had eagerly tried, with only limited success, to take control through democratic means of the local Jewish communities. See Rozenblit, *Jews of Vienna*, pp. 185–193.

64. *JZ*, 12 March 1915, p. 1; 3 March 1916, p. 1; 12 May 1916, pp. 1–2; 25 August 1916, p. 1; 18 October 1916, p. 1; *JVS*, 6 August 1915, pp. 3–4.

65. *Selbstwehr*, 7 May 1915, p. 1; 7 September 1915, p. 1; 5 May 1916, p. 1.

66. *JZ*, 25 August 1916, p. 1; 1 August [*sic*: should be 1 September since it is no. 35, which follows the no. 34 of 25 August] 1916, p. 1; *Selbstwehr*, 8 September 1916, p. 2; *JVS*, 20 August 1915, pp. 1–2.

67. *Selbstwehr*, 25 August 1916, pp. 3–4. Others did support the federation: *Selbstwehr*, 8 September 1916, pp. 1–2.

68. Rudolf Taussig, Zionist Central Committee, Vienna, to Zionist Central Office, Berlin, 4 October 1916, CZA, Z3/845. See also *JZ*, 10 May 1918, pp. 1–2.

69. *Selbstwehr*, 15 December 1916, p. 1; Albrecht Hellmann, "Erinnerungen an gemeinsame Kampfjahre," in Felix Weltsch, ed., *Dichter, Denker, Helfer*, pp. 51–52. Hellman was the pseudonym of Sigmund Katznelson, the editor of *Selbstwehr* during the war. On the American Jewish congress movement, see Oskar Janowsky, *Jews and Minority Rights (1898–1919)* (New York, 1933); Arthur A. Goren, *New York Jews and the Quest for Commu-*

nity: The Kehillah Experiment, 1908–1922 (New York, 1970), pp. 218–228; Naomi W. Cohen, *Not Free to Desist: The American Jewish Committee, 1906–1966* (Philadelphia, 1972), pp. 91–98.

70. *Selbstwehr*, 19 January 1917, pp. 1–2; 2 February 1917, p. 1; 23 March 1917, pp. 1–2; 6 April 1917, p. 3; 4 May 1917, pp. 2–3; 25 May 1917, pp. 1–3; 1 June 1917, pp. 4–5; 8 June 1917, p. 5; 6 July 1917, pp. 1–2; 20 July 1917, pp. 1–2; 27 July 1917, pp. 1–2; 3 August 1917, pp. 2–3; 17 August 1917, p. 2; 9 November 1917, pp. 1–2; 23 November 1917, p. 3. Lemberg Zionist Rosa Melzer tried to rally Jewish women to support the congress: *OW*, 24 August 1917, pp. 537–538.

71. *Selbstwehr*, 25 May 1917, pp. 1–3.

72. *Selbstwehr*, 30 March 1917, p. 1; 6 April 1917, pp. 2–3; 12 April 1917, pp. 1–2; 27 April 1917, pp. 1–2; 11 May 1917, p. 2; 15 May 1917, pp. 1–2; 1 June 1917, pp. 4–5; 8 June 1917, pp. 4–5; 13 July 1917, pp. 2–3; 20 July 1917, p. 2; 31 August 1917, p. 2.

73. *JZ*, 11 May 1917, pp. 1–2; 1 June 1917, pp. 2–3; 29 June 1917, pp. 1–2.

74. Berlin Zionist Executive to Zionist Central Committee for Western Austria, 14 June 1917, CZA, Z3/846.

75. Correspondence between Taussig/Zionist Central Committee in Vienna and Zionist Executive in Berlin, 18 June 1917, 22 June 1917, 26 June 1917, 28 June 1917, CZA, Z3/847.

76. Protokoll, Zionist Vertrauungsmänner, 15 July 1917, CZA, Z3/847, L6/328.

77. Jüdischer Nationalverein (Kassner and Stricker) and Executive Committee of Austrian Zionists (Taussig and Stand) to Zionist District Committee for Bohemia, 15 August 1917; Katznelson's return letter, 29 August 1917, CZA, Z3/215.

78. Hantke to Stricker, Hantke to Taussig, 16 September 1917, CZA, Z3/215, Z3/848, L6/328.

79. Zionistisches Zentralkomitee to Hantke, 24 September 1917, CZA, Z3/215. Interestingly, *JZ*, the official paper of the Austrian Zionist organization, barely mentioned the congress in 1917 and 1918.

80. *JZ*, 18 January 1918, p. 1. See also correspondence in CZA, Z3/215.

81. Katznelson to Hantke, 15 November 1917, 17 November 1917, CZA, Z3/215.

82. *MONOIU*, vol. 30, no. 1/2 (January–February 1918), pp. 1–4.

83. Katznelson to Hantke, 5 December 1917, 25 February 1918, 26 February 1918; Katznelson to Leo Herrmann, 6 March 1918, 24 March 1918, 3 April 1918; Katznelson to Hantke, 14 May 1918, CZA, Z3/215.

84. Katznelson to Hantke, 14 May 1918, CZA, Z3/215.

85. *JKor*, 10 January 1918, p. 1; 7 February 1918, p. 1; 14 February 1918, pp. 2–3; 21 February 1918, pp. 1–4; 25 April 1918, p. 2; 16 May 1918, p. 3; *OW*, 1 March 1918, p. 138.

86. *JKor*, 21 February 1918, pp. 1–4; *OW*, 1 March 1918, p. 138; *Zweimonatsbericht . . . der . . . Bnai Brith*, vol. 21, no. 1/2 (1918), p. 63.

87. See, for example, JMP, IKG-Repräsentanz, Prag, Sitzungsprotokolle, 24 June 1917, 7 April 1918, 28 April 1918.

88. JMP, IKG-Repräsentanz, Prag, Sitzungsprotokoll, 28 April 1918.

89. IKG Salzburg to IKG Wien, 21 August 1918, CAHJP, AW 250/5; Vertretersitzung, IKG Wien, 4 July 1918, AW 72/16.

90. Clipping from the German Zionist paper, *Jüdische Rundschau*, 8 February 1918, reporting on conference of West Galician Zionist leaders, in CZA, Z3/815.

91. *JZ*, 12 April 1918, pp. 2–3; 30 August 1918, p. 1.

92. Vienna Zionist office to Zionist District Committee in Bohemia, 10 October 1918, CZA, L6/358.

93. *JZ*, 17 May 1918, p. 1; 24 May 1918, pp. 2–4; *Selbstwehr*, 26 April 1918, pp. 3–4; 3 May 1918, p. 6; 7 June 1918, pp. 3–4; *OW*, 31 May 1918, pp. 332–333. Speakers at the congress included Martin Buber, Robert Weltsch, Siegfried Bernfeld, and Salo Baron.

94. *OW*, 10 May 1918, pp. 278–279; 24 May 1918, p. 316; 7 June 1918, pp. 341–342; 26 July 1918, pp. 458–459; 2 August 1918, pp. 473–474, 482–483.

95. *OW*, 21 June 1918, pp. 375–376; 12 July 1918, p. 436; 19 July 1918, pp. 441–442; *JZ*, 21 June 1918, p. 1; See also report in CZA, L6/350.

96. *OW*, 2 August 1918, pp. 473–474.

97. Öffentliche Plenarsitzung, IKG Wien, 26 July 1918, CAHJP, AW 71/16; reprinted in *OW*, 2 August 1918, pp. 474–475; *Selbstwehr*, 9 August 1918, pp. 1–2; *JKor*, 8 August 1918, pp. 3–4.

98. JMP, IKG-Repräsentanz Prag, Sitzungsprotokolle, 26 July 1918, 2 September 1918.

99. JMP, IKG-Repräsentanz Prag, Sitzungsprotokolle, 13 January 1918, 20 January 1918, 28 April 1918; *Selbstwehr*, 31 May 1918, p. 1; 7 June 1918, pp. 1–2; *OW*, 21 June 1918, p. 384.

100. *MONOIU*, vol. 28, no. 9–12 (September–December 1916), p. 14.

101. *OW*, 5 January 1917, pp. 1–2. See also *JVS*, 10 January 1917, pp. 1–2.

102. *JKor*, 4 May 1916, p. 1; 4 January 1917, p. 1; 11 January 1917, p. 1; 22 February 1917, p. 1.

103. *OW*, 22 June 1917, pp. 389–391; quotation on p. 390.

104. *OW*, 29 June 1917, p. 407.

105. *OW*, 13 July 1917, pp. 437–438. For other indications of support for reform, see *OW*, 17 August 1917, pp. 517–518; 9 November 1917, pp. 701–702.

106. *OW*, 4 January 1918, pp. 1-2; 25 January 1918, p. 49.

107. *OW*, 15 February 1918, pp. 97–98.

108. *OW*, 3 May 1918, pp. 261–262.

109. *OW*, 19 July 1918, pp. 441–442.

110. *OW*, 2 August 1918, pp. 473–474. See also 20 September 1918, pp. 593–594.

111. *OW*, 2 August 1918, p. 475.

112. *JKor*, 20 June 1918, p. 2; 8 August 1918, p. 1.

113. Nathan Birnbaum, *Den Ostjuden ihr Recht* (Vienna, 1915), p. 24. On Birnbaum's transformation, see the insightful analysis in Wistrich, *Jews of Vienna*, pp. 381–420.

114. *JZ*, 28 May 1915, p. 1; 30 July 1915, p. 1; 12 July 1918, p. 1; 26 July 1918, p. 1; *Selbstwehr*, 13 July 1917, p. 1; *JVS*, 31 January 1918, p. 1.

115. Speech in parliament, 16 June 1917, reprinted in *JZ*, 22 June 1917, pp. 1–2; *Selbstwehr*, 6 July 1917, pp. 3–4.

116. *Selbstwehr*, 23 November 1917, p. 4.

117. *JZ*, 14 June 1918, p. 1.

118. Rozenblit, *Jews of Vienna*, pp. 170–178; Gaisbauer, pp. 451–523; Böhm, vol. II, pp. 342–347. On the commitment of the Austrian Social Democratic party to national cultural autonomy, see Karl Renner, *Der Kampf der österreichischen Nationen um den Staat*. The Socialists did not consider the Jews one of the nations of Austria; see Robert S. Wistrich, *Socialism and the Jews: The Dilemmas of Assimilation in Germany and Austria-Hungary* (Rutherford, 1982), pp. 299–348.

119. The conflict between Palestine and diaspora work became a leitmotif of Zionist politics in the interwar period. See Ezra Mendelsohn, *Zionism in Poland*; Mendelsohn, *Jews of East Central Europe*, pp. 43–63 passim; and Freidenreich, pp. 48–83.

120. *Selbstwehr*, 19 February 1915, p. 1; 12 March 1915, p. 1; 9 April 1915, p. 1; 7 May 1915, p. 1; 7 September 1915, p. 1; 5 May 1916, p. 1; *JZ*, 18 June 1915, p. 1; 15 October 1915, p. 1; 14 April 1916, pp. 2–3; 30 June, 1916, p. 1; 1 December 1916, pp. 1–2.

121. *Selbstwehr*, 12 March 1915, p. 1; 5 May 1916, p. 1; *JVS*, 3 November 1915, pp. 1–2; 28 June 1916, pp. 1–2; *JZ*, 14 January 1916, p. 1.

122. *Selbstwehr*, 12 March 1915, p. 1; 7 May 1915, p. 1; 5 May 1916, p. 1; *JZ*, 15 October 1915, p. 1; *JVS*, 3 November 1915, pp. 1–2.

123. *JZ*, 11 February 1916, p. 1; 1 December 1916, pp. 1–2; *Selbstwehr*, 23 June 1916, p. 1.

124. *JZ*, 8 June 1917.

125. Hermann Kadisch, *Die Juden und die österreichische Verfassungsrevision* (Vienna, 1918); quotation on p. 7. This pamphlet reprinted a July 1917 article by Kadisch, originally in *Jüdische Kriegshefte*, vol. 3. Kadisch had made the same point about German in *JZ*, 14 January 1916, p. 1.

126. *Selbstwehr*, 12 April 1918, p. 1.

127. *JZ*, 6 September 1918, pp. 1–2.

128. *JZ*, 21 January 1916, p. 1; 18 October 1916, p. 1; 26 January 1917, pp. 1–2; *OW*, 28 April 1916, pp. 284–285; 27 October 1916, p. 703.

129. On the Jüdischer Nationalverein, see Rozenblit, *Jews of Vienna*, pp. 172–174. On wartime board members see *JZ*, 6 August 1915, p. 4; 18 October 1916, p. 1.

130. *JZ*, 27 July 1917, pp. 1–2.

131. *JZ*, 27 July 1917, pp. 1–2; 14 December 1917.

132. *JZ*, 22 June 1917, pp. 1–2; *Selbstwehr*, 6 July 1917, pp. 3–4; *OW*, 22 June 1917, pp. 389–391; see also *JZ*, 3 August 1917, pp. 1–3; 28 December 1917, pp. 1–2; *Selbstwehr*, 25 May 1917, pp. 1– 3. For an earlier example of Straucher's views, see his "Über Nationaljudentum," *Jüdischer Nationalkalender auf das Jahr 5676, 1915–1916* (Vienna, 1915), pp. 88–93.

133. Rosenfeld, *Die polnische Judenfrage*; Rosenfeld, *Nationales Selbstbestimmungsrecht*. Although these two books focus on Poland and Galicia, Rosenfeld sought autonomy all over Austria. See his *Nationale Autonomie der Juden in Oesterreich* (Czernowitz, 1912). For the official position of Poale Zion on national autonomy see *Die Juden im Kriege: Denkschrift des Jüdischen Sozialistischen Arbeiterverbandes Poale-Zion an das Internationale Sozialistische Bureau*, 2d ed. (Den Haag, 1917).

134. *JZ*, 9 March 1917, p. 4; 13 July 1917, pp. 1–2; 16 November 1917, pp. 1–2; 12 July 1918, p. 1; *Selbstwehr*, 13 July 1917, p. 1; 26 July 1918, p. 1; *JVS*, 12 July 1918, pp. 1–2.

135. "Denkschrift der national organisierten Judenschaft an die österr. Regierung," *JZ*, 22 March 1918, p. 1; *Selbstwehr*, 22 March 1918, p. 1; *OW*, 22 March 1918, p. 180. Zionists interpreted the government's response far too optimistically.

136. Report, Party conference of West Austrian Zionists, 28 April 1918, CZA, Z3/849.

137. *JZ*, 30 August 1918, pp. 4–5. See also Michael Ringel, Zionist Union of Lwów, to Berlin Central Zionist Office, 22 July 1918, CZA, Z3/815.

138. *JZ*, 18 August 1917, p. 1; *Selbstwehr*, 23 November 1917, p. 1.

139. *JZ*, 28 September 1917, pp. 1–2; 5 July 1918, pp. 2–3; *Selbstwehr*, 23 November 1917, p. 1; *OW*, 28 September 1917, p. 628; 3 May 1918, pp. 262–263.

140. *JVS*, 3 May 1918, p. 1; 15 May 1918, p. 2; 12 July 1918, pp. 1–2.

141. Zeman, pp. 72–94, 113–117, 120–127, 168–175, 213–216; May, pp. 262–273, 352–365, 675–678, 737–738, 744–754; H. Louis Rees, *The Czechs during World War I: The Path to Independence* (Boulder, 1992).

142. For a good examples of restrained support for the Austrian *Gesamtstaat*, see *Selbstwehr*, 13 July 1917, p. 1; 31 August 1917, pp. 1–2; 20 September 1918, p 1.

143. *Selbstwehr*, 15 June 1917, p. 1; 6 July 1917, p. 1; 20 July 1917, p. 5. See also Stricker's speech to Prague Zionists, *Selbstwehr*, 23 November 1917, p. 3. The government regularly closed down *Rozvoj*, the newspaper of the "Czech Jews," during the war, presumably because it advocated Czech independence. (See reports in *Selbstwehr*, 26 November 1915, p. 6; *JZ*, 14 January 1916, p. 4.) Unfortunately, no liberal Jewish German-language newspapers existed in the Czech lands, so it is hard to gauge the attitudes of liberal Jews on this issue.

144. *Selbstwehr*, 11 January 1918, p. 4; 25 January 1918, pp. 1, 5–6.

145. *Selbstwehr*, 8 June 1917, pp. 3–4; 20 July 1917, p. 5; 17 August 1917, p. 4; 25 January 1918, p. 1; 16 May 1918, pp. 1–2.

146. *Selbstwehr*, 15 February 1918, p. 1; 1 March 1918, pp. 1–2.

147. *Selbstwehr*, 8 March 1918, p. 7; 15 March 1918, pp. 1–2; 16 May 1918, pp. 1–2; 21 June 1918, pp. 4-5; 16 August 1918, p. 1; 30 August 1918, pp. 1–2; 27 September 1918, pp. 2–4; *JZ*, 10 August 1917, p. 4; 15 March 1918, p. 4; 17 May 1918, p. 7; 30 August 1918, p. 2.

148. *Selbstwehr*, 16 August 1918, p. 1; 30 August 1918, pp. 1–2.

149. *Selbstwehr*, 13 July 1917, p. 1; 3 August 1917, pp. 2-3; 17 August 1917, p. 4; 22 March 1918, p. 1; 5 April 1918, pp. 2–3; 19 April 1918, pp. 1–2; 28 June 1918, p. 6; 26 July 1918, p. 1; 9 August 1918, p. 1.

150. *Selbstwehr*, 5 April 1918, pp. 2–3; 26 July 1918, p. 1; 9 August 1918, p. 1; 20 September 1918, p. 1; *JVS*, 24 May 1917, pp. 1–2.

151. *JVS*, 7 March 1917, pp. 1–2; 24 May 1917, pp. 1–2; 3 May 1918, p. 1; 12 July 1918, pp. 1–2.

152. *Selbstwehr*, 16 November 1917, p. 2.

153. *Selbstwehr*, 9 August 1918, p. 1.

154. Prague District Committee to Zionist Central Committee for West Austria, 24 March 1918; Zionist District Association for Bohemia to Zionist Central Committee, 25 March 1918, CZA, Z3/848.

155. Weltsch to Herrmann, 8 August 1918, in CZA, Z3/850.

156. *Zweimonatsbericht . . . der . . . Bnai Brith*, vol. 21, no. 3/4 (1918), p. 103.

157. *Zweimonatsbericht . . . der . . . Bnai Brith*, vol. 21, no. 3/4 (1918), p. 108.

158. *JKor*, 28 February 1918, pp. 2–3; 13 April 1918, pp. 1–3.

159. *JKor*, 28 Februry 1918, p. 1.

160. *OW*, 23 March 1917, pp. 177–178; 6 April 1917, pp. 213–215; 4 May 1917, pp. 270–272; 4 January 1918, pp. 1–2; 26 July 1918, pp. 457–458; *JKor*, 14 February 1918, pp. 1–2; 13 April 1918, p. 1; *Zweimonatsbericht . . . der . . . Bnai Brith*, vol. 20, no. 3 (1917), pp. 66–68; *JZ*, 30 March 1917, p. 1; 20 April 1917, p. 1; 7 December 1917, p. 1; *Jüdischer Nationalkalender, 1917/18*, pp. 21–23; Jonas Kreppel, *Ins vierte Kriegsjahr. Österreich-Ungarns Bilanz dreier Kriegsjahre* (Vienna, 1917); Sperber, pp. 122–123; Güdemann, pp. 268–269.

161. *OW*, 8 December 1916, p. 793; 15 December 1916, pp. 809–810; *JKor*, 21 December 1916, pp. 1–2.

162. *OW*, 7 December 1917, pp. 765–766; 14 December 1917, pp. 781–783; 4 January 1918, pp. 1–2; 15 February 1918, pp. 97–98; *JKor*, 28 February 1918, p. 1.

163. *OW*, 8 March 1918, pp. 145–146; *JKor*, 7 March 1918, p. 1.

164. *JKor*, 7 March 1918, p. 1.

165. *OW*, 12 April 1918, p. 209; 19 April 1918, pp. 229–230; 26 April 1918, pp. 245–246; 10 May 1918, pp. 277–278.

166. *JZ*, 15 February 1918, p. 1; *OW*, 15 February 1918, pp. 98–99; Austrian Zionists to Copenhagen office of WZO, 12 February 1918, CZA, L6/335; Taussig to Zionist Central Office, Berlin, 12 February 1918, Z3/848. For earlier Zionist support of Ukrainian national independence, see *JZ*, 22 September 1915, p. 3.

167. For example, speech of Alfred Stern, 28 October 1917, *OW*, 2 November 1917, p. 691.

168. The press was filled with such sentiment. See also Güdemann, p. 270; Sperber, p. 147.

169. *OW*, 15 February 1918, p. 97.

170. *OW*, 6 September 1918, pp. 557–558.

171. *JZ*, 18 October 1916, p. 1; 26 January 1917, p. 2; 27 March 1918, p. 6; *Selbstwehr*, 10 March 1916, pp. 1–2; 14 September 1917, p. 2; *Jüdischer Nationalkalender 1917/1918*, pp. 27–33.

CHAPTER 6

1. Segal, "You Shall Never Forget," p. 26.

2. Ibid., pp. 26–27, 30.

3. Lachs, pp. 89–90.

4. István Deák argues even more forcefully that "the ultimate victims of the dissolu-tion of the Habsburg Monarchy have undoubtedly been the Jews." See "The Habsburg Empire," in *After Empire: Multiethnic Societies and Nation-Building,* Karen Barkey and Mark von Hagen, eds. (Boulder, 1997), p. 137. Similarly, Geoff Eley, "Remapping the Nation: War, Revolutionary Upheaval and State Formation in Eastern Europe, 1914–1923," in *Ukrainian-Jewish Relations,* Aster and Potichnyj, eds., pp. 205–246, noted that the postwar successor states, with their "stricter definitions of individual identity" proved especially problematic for the Jews.

5. Here I disagree fundamentally with McCagg, pp. 219–220, who argues that most modern Jews easily accepted the collapse of the Monarchy and the creation of the succes-sor states because they had already assimilated to the dominant cultures of those states. Elsewhere he describes the process as the "melting away" of the Habsburg Jewry; see William O. McCagg, "Jewish Assimilation in Austria: Karl Kraus, Franz Werfel and Joseph Roth on the Catastrophe of 1914–1919," in *Austrians and Jews in the Twentieth Century: From Franz Joseph to Waldheim,* Robert S. Wistrich, ed. (London, 1992), p. 61.

6. There were small Jewish communities outside of Vienna, including Linz, Upper Austria; Graz, Styria; and, after the plebiscite of 1920, several German-speaking, orthodox communities in the Burgenland, an area traditionally in the Kingdom of Hungary, which joined Austria at that time. Even with the addition of the Burgenland, the vast majority of interwar Austrian Jewry lived in Vienna.

7. The discussion here is based on Zeman; May; Macartney; Plaschka and Mack; Sked; and Manfried Rauchensteiner, *Der Tod des Doppeladlers. Österreich-Ungarn und der Erste Weltkrieg* (Graz, 1993).

8. May, p. 772.

9. For an excellent treatment of oppressive Romanianization in interwar Romania, see Irina Livezeanu, *Cultural Politics in Greater Romania: Regionalism, Nation Building and Ethnic Struggle, 1918-1930* (Ithaca, NY, 1995).

10. Franz Theodor Csokor, *November 3, 1918,* in *A Critical Edition and Translation of Franz Theodor Csokor's European Trilogy,* Katherine McHugh Lichliter, ed. (New York, 1995), pp. 27–71.

11. *OW,* 4 October 1918, pp. 625–626; 11 October 1918, pp. 641–642.

12. *JKor,* 3 October 1918, p. 1.

13. *OW,* 18 October 1918, pp. 657–659. See also *JKor,* 22 October 1918, p. 1.

14. *JZ,* 4 October 1918, pp. 1–2; Straucher, the Zionist leader from Bukovina, similarly expressed a desire for Austrian continuity to an almost-empty parliament on October 4 (*JZ,* 11 October 1918, pp. 2–3).

15. Report of Chajes' audience with the emperor, 2 October 1918, and Weltsch to Zionist District Committee for Bohemia, 10 October 1918, CZA L6/358. Chajes spoke of national rights primarily in the East. On Chajes generally, see Moritz Rosenfeld, *Oberrab-biner Hirsch Perez Chajes; Sein Leben und Werk* (Vienna, 1933).

16. Telegram, Viennese Zionists to Berlin Zionist office, n.d., but reporting the Octo-ber 14 meeting, CZA, Z3/850; *JZ,* 18 October 1918, pp. 1–2; *OW,* 18 October 1918, pp. 664–665. The WZO also thought Austrian continuity served Jewish interests; see Berlin Zionist office to Robert Weltsch, Vienna, 8 October 1918, Z3/850.

17. *JZ,* 18 October 1918, p. 1; 25 October 1918, p. 1.

18. *OW*, 25 October 1918, pp. 673–675.

19. *OW*, 25 October 1918, p. 673; 1 November 1918, pp. 689–690; 15 November 1918, p. 721.

20. *JKor*, 1 November 1918, pp. 1–2.

21. *JZ*, 25 October 1918, pp. 1–2; 1 November 1918, p. 1.

22. *OW*, 15 November 1918, p. 721. See also 13 June 1919, pp. 367–368; or statement of loyalty of Linz Jewish community, December 1, 1918, CAHJP, AW 250/5.

23. Neumann in Schmidl, *Juden in der k. (u.) k. Armee*, pp. 227, 228.

24. Safar, "Aus meinem Leben," pp. 33, 59, 76. This sense of confusing uncertainty pervades many memoirs, including Floch and Furst, "Windows to My Youth."

25. Lieben, "Aus meinem Leben," p. 123.

26. Stolper, "Recorded Memories," pp. 37, 51, 64–68, 71.

27. Bardach, "Aus meinem Tagebuch," 21 October 1918, VI, p. 534, LBI, AR 6632.

28. Schwarz, "Lebens-Erinnerungen," pp. 26–30, 76.

29. Ernst Saxonhouse, "Memoirs," unpublished memoir, LBI, pp. 6–7.

30. Sperber, *God's Water Carriers*, p. 149.

31. Lachs, pp. 70, 85.

32. Ibid., pp. 90–92, 96, 104–107, 113.

33. Bernhard Bardach, "Aus meinem Tagebuch," 3 November 1918, VI, pp. 543–544, LBI, AR 6632.

34. Deutsch, *Confrontations with Myself*, p. 68, for example, describes how her parents, who had fled to Vienna during the war, eagerly returned to Przemysl at the end.

35. Hoffmann-Holter, *"Abreisendmachung,"* pp. 143–159.

36. Schoenfeld, *Jewish Life in Galicia*, pp. 173–179.

37. Mechner, "My Family Biography," pp. 126–128, 152–159. For a powerful analysis of how interwar Romania used widespread anti-Semitism as a tool for national mobilization, see Livezeanu, esp. pp. 69–87 and 189–208.

38. Schoenfeld, p. 201.

39. Magocsi, pp. 459–520; Piotr S. Wandycz, *The Lands of Partitioned Poland, 1795–1918* (Seattle, 1974); Joseph Rothschild, *East Central Europe between the Two World Wars* (Seattle, 1974).

40. Magocsi, p. 506, estimates that between 30,000 and 60,000 Jews were killed in 1,236 pogroms in 524 places in Dnieper Ukraine between 1917 and 1921. The standard sources on Polish Jewish history give no specific numbers, presumably because all the sources exaggerate in one direction or the other.

41. For an excellent analysis of this neutrality, see Mendelsohn, *Zionism in Poland*, pp. 97–101.

42. *OW*, 6 December 1918, pp. 772–773. See also *OW*, 22 November 1918, pp. 739–740, 740–746; 29 November 1918, pp. 756–757; 27 December 1918, pp. 829–831.

43. *OW*, 6 December 1918, pp. 773–774. See also *OW*, 22 November 1918, p. 743; 29 November 1918, p. 757.

44. *OW*, 6 December 1918, p. 770. For positive assessments of the Ukrainians see *OW*, 6 December 1918, p. 782; 13 December 1918, p. 790; 21 March 1919, pp. 182–183; 23 May 1919, pp. 320–321.

45. *JKor*, 28 November 1918, pp. 1–3; 5 December 1918, pp. 3–4. On 27 March 1919, p. 3, the paper published the official Jewish statistics on the pogrom damage: 73 dead, 271 wounded, 108 million crowns in material damage.

46. *JZ*, 15 November 1918, p. 1; 22 November 1918, pp. 1–4; 29 November 1918, pp. 1–4; 13 December 1918, pp. 2–3; 31 January 1919, pp. 2–3; *Selbstwehr*, 29 November 1918, p. 1; 13 December 1918, p. 3; *JVS*, 22 November 1918, p. 5; 6 December 1918, pp. 1–3.

47. *JZ*, 8 November 1918, p. 3; 6 December 1918, pp. 3–5.

48. *JZ*, 29 November 1918, p. 1. Despite positive attitudes to Ukrainian independence and Ukrainian recognition of Jewish national status, they also worried about Jews in the Ukraine: *JZ*, 25 October 1918, p. 4; 28 February 1919, p. 1; 21 March 1919; Taussig, Vienna, to Central Zionist Office, Berlin, 12 February 1918, Z3/848; Austrian Zionist Organization to Zionist Office Copenhagen, 12 February 1918, L6/335. On Ukrainians and Jewish national rights, see Jonathan Frankel, "The Dilemmas of Jewish National Autonomism: The Case of Ukraine, 1917–1920," in *Ukrainian-Jewish Relations* , pp. 263–279.

49. Josef Bendow (pseudonym for Joseph Tenenbaum), *Der Lemberger Judenpogrom (November 1918–Jänner 1919)* (Vienna, 1919), quotation on p. 43. For similar views see pogrom reports in CZA, L6/112; L6/116; Z3/178–182.

50. *OW*, 23 May 1919, p. 313; 20 June 1919, p. 375; *JKor*, 19 December 1918, p. 2; 16 January 1919, p. 3; 8 May 1919, p. 2; 15 May 1919, p. 2; 22 May 1919, p. 1; 6 June 1919, p. 3; 13 June 1919, pp. 3–4; *JZ*, 14 February 1919, p. 4; 23 May 1919, pp. 1–2.

51. *OW*, 3 January 1919, pp. 1–2; 20 June 1919, p. 375.

52. *OW*, 23 May 1919, pp. 309–310; 6 June 1919, pp. 341–343; 20 June 1919, pp. 375, 378–379; 27 June 1919, pp. 393–394; *JKor*, 1 May 1919, p. 2; 15 May 1919, p. 1; 6 June 1919, pp. 1, 3; 20 June 1919, pp. 2–3.

53. *JZ*, 4 April 1919, p. 1; 4 July 1919, pp. 3–4; *JVS*, 12 June 1919, pp. 1–4; *Hickls Jüdische Volkskalender, 1919/20*, pp. 17–19.

54. Victor S. Mamatey and Radomír Luža, eds., *A History of the Czechoslovak Republic, 1918–1948* (Princeton, 1973); Carol Skolnick Leff, *National Conflict in Czechoslovakia: The Making and Remaking of a State, 1918–1987* (Princeton, 1988); and Derek Sayer, *The Coasts of Bohemia: A Czech History* (Princeton, 1998).

55. Kieval, *The Making of Czech Jewry*, pp. 183–186, 192.

56. JMP, IKG-Repräsentanz, Prag, Sitzungsprotokoll, 20 October 1918. See also 13 October 1918.

57. JMP, IKG-Repräsentanz, Prag, Sitzungsprotokoll, October 27, 1918.

58. JMP, IKG-Repräsentanz, Prag, Sitzungsprotokoll, November 1, 1918. Unfortunately, the text of the statement of loyalty is not included in the notes of the board meeting.

59. JMP, IKG-Repräsentanz, Prag, Sitzungsprotokoll, 10 November 1918.

60. JMP, IKG-Repräsentanz, Prag, Sitzungsprotokoll, 10 November 1918.

61. Hindls, "Erinnerungen aus meinem Leben," pp. 90–91, 97.

62. Ibid., pp. 98–100, 116; quotation on p. 100.

63. *Hella*, p. 48.

64. Landre, "Durch's Sieb der Zeit gefallen," pp. 22; supplement, p. 15; 98, 118–119, 231–232, 267–268.

65. Kohn, *Living in a World Revolution*, pp. 119, 121–122. Kohn first did Zionist work elsewhere in Europe, but in 1925 settled in Palestine. Upset with Zionist attitudes to the Arabs, he left for the United States in 1933, where he became a professor of history, first at Smith and then at the City College of New York.

66. Brod, *Streitbares Leben*, p. 88.

67. Ibid., pp. 98–99.

68. *Selbstwehr*, 11 October 1918, p. 1; 18 October 1918, p. 1; 25 October 1918, pp. 1–2.

69. Memorandum, Zionistischer Distiktsverband für Böhmen, 23 October 1918, CZA, L6/366; Max Brod to Leo Herrmann, 24 October 1918, L6/366.

70. *Selbstwehr*, 25 October 1918, pp. 1–3. For private concerns about anti-Semitism, see Max Brod to Leo Herrmann, 18 October 1918, CZA, L6/366; Brod, *Streitbares Leben*, pp. 236–238, citing the same letter.

71. *Selbstwehr*, 8 November 1918, pp. 4–5.

72. *Selbstwehr*, 15 November 1918, p. 3.

73. Kieval, pp. 98, 170, 187. From 1918 to 1939 Singer edited a Czech-language Zionist paper, *Zidovské zprávy*.

74. *JVS*, 22 November 1918, p. 5.

75. Hillel Kieval, "Masaryk and Czech Jewry: The Ambiguities of Friendship," in *T. G. Masaryk (1850–1937)*, vol. 1, *Thinker and Politician*, Stanley B. Winters, ed. (New York, 1990), pp. 302–327; Michael A. Riff, "The Ambiguity of T.G. Masaryk's Attitudes on the 'Jewish Question,'" in *T. G. Masaryk (1850–1937)*, vol. 2, *Thinker and Critic*, Robert B. Pynsent, ed. (New York, 1989), pp. 77–87; Christoph Stölzl, "Die 'Burg' und die Juden: T. G. Masaryk and sein Kreis im Spannungsfeld der jüdischen Frage: Assimilation, Antisemitismus und Zionismus," in *Die "Burg": Einflussreich politische Kräfte um Masaryk und Beneš*, vol. 2, Karl Bosl, ed. (Munich, 1974), pp. 79–110.

76. Kieval, "Masaryk and Czech Jewry," pp. 309–315; Kieval, *Making of Czech Jewry*, p. 188. Masaryk supported Jewish nationalism because he regarded the Jews as a separate nation, whose members could not become Czech. On Zionist displays of his picture, see, for example, *Selbstwehr*, 10 January 1919, p. 1.

77. Pogroms occurred in such places as Falkenau, Strakonitz, Pilsen, Deutschbrod, and Prague in Bohemia, and at Holleschau, Ungarisch Brod, Mährisch Ostrau, Lundenberg, and Ungarisch Hradisch in Moravia. See *Selbstwehr*, 29 November 1918, pp. 3–4; 6 December 1918, pp. 1–2; 13 December 1918, p. 1; 20 December 1918, p. 3; 24 January 1919, p. 3; *JVS*, 6 December 1918, p. 3; *OW*, 15 November 1918, p. 738; 22 November 1918, p. 742; 13 December 1918, pp. 800–803; 31 January 1919, p. 74; 23 May 1919, pp. 310–311; *JKor*, 5 December 1918, p. 5; 12 December 1918, p. 2; 16 January 1919, p. 3; 23 January 1919, p. 3; 30 January 1919, p. 3; 22 May 1919, p. 2; *JZ*, 15 November 1918, p. 1; 22 November 1918, p. 5; 29 November 1918, pp. 3, 7; 13 December 1918, p. 4. See also reports in CZA, Z3/217.

78. *Selbstwehr*, 6 December 1918, pp. 1–2.

79. Report of activities of Jüdischer Nationalrat, Prague, 23 December 1918, CZA, Z3/180.

80. *Selbstwehr*, 13 December 1918, p. 1; report, CZA, Z3/217.

81. *Selbstwehr*, 20 December 1918, pp. 4–5; 17 January 1919, p. 1; 24 January 1919, pp. 1–3; *JVS*, 6 December 1918, p. 3; *OW*, 4 April 1919, p. 215. These views were shared by the Viennese Zionist establishment; see *JZ*, 22 November 1918, p. 5; 6 December 1918, p. 4; 13 December 1918, p. 5.

82. *OW*, 24 January 1919, p. 58, reporting on a delegation of Bohemian rabbis to President Masaryk. Non-Zionists in Vienna also shared these views; see *OW*, 22 November 1918, pp. 742–743; 29 November 1918, p. 763; 10 January 1919, p. 17; 23 May 1919, p. 311.

83. *JVS*, 27 June 1919, p. 5; 4 July 1919, p. 6.

84. *Selbstwehr*, 8 November 1918, p. 1; 15 November 1918, p. 1; telegram, Ludwig Singer, Jewish National Council, 6 November 1918, CZA, Z3/217.

85. Report, Jüdischer Nationalrat, Prague, 23 December 1918, CZA, Z3/180.

86. *Selbstwehr*, 20 December 1918, p. 1.

87. *JVS*, 28 March 1919, pp. 3–4.

88. Landre, p. 119.

89. J. Nina Lieberman, "Lost and Found: A Life," unpublished memoir, LBI, p. 23.

90. On their delight on being independent of Stricker and Vienna, see Max Brod to Leo Herrmann, 24 October 1918, CZA, Z3/217, L6/366; 28 October 1918, L6/366.

91. Memo, Zionistischer Distriktsverband für Böhmen, 23 October 1918, CZA, Z3/217, L6/366.

92. Leo Herrmann to Ludwig Singer, 3 December 1918, CZA, Z3/217; Jewish National Council, Prague, to Copenhagen Zionist office, n.d., but certainly November 1918, L6/366. By contrast, Zionists in Czernowitz, Bukovina, demanded the creation of a Jewish constituent assembly, a Jewish voting curia, and proportional representation in all governmental bodies (OW, 8 November 1918, p. 713).

93. Selbstwehr, 8 November 1918, p. 2; 9 May 1919, pp. 5–6; OW, 15 November 1918, pp. 727–728; telegram of Jewish National Council to Czech government in Paris, 18 November 1918, CZA, L6/366.

94. Brod to Herrmann, 28 October 1918, CZA, L6/366; see also Brod to Herrmann, 23 October 1918, 24 October 1918, L6/366, Z3/217.

95. Brod to Herrmann, 4 November 1918, CZA, Z3/217.

96. Report, Jüdischer Nationalrat, Prague, 23 December 1918, CZA, Z3/180. Interestingly, they worried less about the Czech "assimilationists," presumably because the Czech Jews posed less of a threat to their relations with the government.

97. "II. Tätigkeitsbericht des jüdischen Nationalrat in Prag," January 1919, CZA, L6/85; Selbstwehr, 3 January 1919, p. 1; 28 March 1919, p. 2; JVS, 4 April 1919, p. 5.

98. Selbstwehr, 15 November 1918, p. 2; 13 December 1918, p. 2; JKor, 2 January 1919, p. 4.

99. Brod to Zionist office, Copenhagen, 1 February 1919, CZA, L6/91.

100. Report on the national movement in Moravia, n.d., but probably November 1918, CZA, L6/366; Brod to Herrmann, 4 November 1918, Z3/217; Selbstwehr, 8 November 1918, p. 1; 22 November 1918, p. 5; 29 November 1918, pp. 3–4; 6 December 1918, pp. 4 5; 13 December 1918, p. 2; 3 January 1919, p. 7; 10 January 1919, p. 6; 7 February 1919, p. 7; 14 February 1919, p. 7; OW, 22 November 1918, p. 747; 6 December 1918, p. 781; JZ, 8 November 1918, p. 4; 22 November 1918, p. 6; 29 November 1918, p. 6; 6 December 1918, p. 7; 17 January 1919, p. 7.

101. JVS, 22 November 1918, pp. 5, 6–7; OW, 22 November 1918, p. 748; JZ, 15 November 1918, p. 3.

102. Selbstwehr, 10 January 1919, p. 6; 31 January 1919, p. 2.

103. Selbstwehr, 4 April 1919, p. 4; JVS, 28 March 1919, p. 3; JZ, 4 April 1919, p. 5.

104. Selbstwehr, 20 December 1918, p. 3.

105. Selbstwehr, 3 January 1919, p. 3; JVS, 2 June 1919, p. 2.

106. Selbstwehr, 7 February 1919, pp. 3–4; 25 April 1919, p. 6.

107. Open letter, Jewish National Council, CZA, L6/85; L6/91; Selbstwehr, 24 January 1919, p. 3. Naturally, the Zionists were pleased when a group of Slovakian Jews formed a Jewish National Council in Slovakia in March 1919 (Selbstwehr, 4 April 1919, p. 3).

108. Selbstwehr, 10 January 1919, pp. 1–5; JZ, 10 January 1919, pp. 1–2; 17 January 1919, pp. 2–3.

109. Report, Jüdischer Nationalrat, Prague, 23 December 1918, CZA, Z3/180; report, meeting of Jüdischer Nationalrat with Kramář, Z3/217; L6/371; Hantke to Singer, 18 November 1918; Hantke to Zionist organization in Budapest, 20 November 1918, Z3/217; correspondence on violence in Slovakia, L6/96; Selbstwehr, 22 November 1918, p. 5; 13 December 1918, p. 1; JVS, 22 November 1918, p. 7.

110. Report, Jüdischer Nationalrat, Prague, 23 December 1918, CZA, Z3/180; II. Tätigkeitsbericht des jüdischen Nationalrat, Prague, January 1919, L6/85; Hantke to Singer, n.d., probably November 1918, L6/366; Selbstwehr, 10 January 1919, p. 5; 21 March 1919, pp. 1, 4–5; 28 March 1919, p. 2; 4 April 1919, p. 3; JVS, 4 April 1919, p. 5.

111. Correspondence, Siegmund Katznelson, 9 February 1919, CZA, L6/91; Alfred Engel to Rabbi Moritz Lewin, Nikolsburg, 15 February 1919, CAHJP, CS 191; Selbstwehr, 25 April 1919, p. 6.

112. JMP, IKG-Repräsentanz, Prag, Sitzungsprotokoll, 10 November 1918, 17 November 1918.

113. JMP, IKG-Repräsentanz, Prag, Sitzungsprotokoll, 18 November 1918, Anhang 1, "Die Groesste allen Gefahren."

114. JMP, IKG-Repräsentanz, Prag, Sitzungsprotokoll, November 18, 1918.

115. JMP, IKG-Repräsentanz, Prag, Sitzungsprotokoll, November 24, 1918.

116. JMP, IKG-Repräsentanz, Prag, Sitzungsprotokoll, 9 December 1918. Interestingly, the Zionist press did not cover these events.

117. *Selbstwehr*, 6 December 1918, p. 3; JMP, IKG-Repräsentanz, Prag, Sitzungsprotokoll, December 9, 1918.

118. JMP, IKG-Repräsentanz, Prag, Sitzungsprotokoll, December 9, 1918, Report of December 8 meeting of committee to change voting rules for the IKG.

119. Max Brod, "Juden, Deutsche, Tschechen: Ein menschlich-politische Betrachtung," *Im Kampf um das Judentum* (Berlin, 1920), pp. 7–36; quotations on pp. 15, 17. On the need for Jewish nationalists to work for universalist, humanitarian goals, see also Max Brod, "Gegen den Nationalismus und für ihn," *Selbstwehr*, 11 April 1919, pp. 2–3.

On Brod generally, see Margarita Pazi, *Max Brod: Werke und Personlichkeit* (Bonn, 1970), which does not adequately deal with Brod's Jewish activities; Robert Weltsch, "Max Brod and His Age," *Leo Baeck Memorial Lecture* 13 (New York, 1970); and most recently, Claus-Ekkehard Barsch, *Max Brod im Kampf um das Judentum: Zum Leben und Werk eines deutsch-jüdischen Dichters aus Prag* (Vienna, 1992). In addition to writing books and plays, Brod worked as a bureaucrat for the government until 1929, then served as literary and music critic for the *Prager Tagblatt* until he left for Palestine in 1939, where he became the producer for the Hebrew theater company *Habimah*.

120. *Selbstwehr*, 15 November 1918, p. 2.

121. *JVS*, 22 November 1918, p. 2.

122. *JVS*, 1 January 1919, p. 5.

123. Speech of Angelo Goldstein, Jewish National Council, to *Jüdischer Volksrat*, Ung. Hradisch, Moravia, 28 January 1919, *Selbstwehr*, 7 February 1919, p. 7; interview with Hugo Bergmann, *Selbstwehr*, 28 March 1919, p. 4; *JVS*, 23 May 1919, p. 1.

124. *Selbstwehr*, 11 April 1919, p. 3; 18 April 1919, pp. 1, 3; 25 April 1919, pp. 1–4; *JVS*, 2 June 1919, p. 2.

125. *OW*, 13 December 1918, pp. 785–786.

126. *JKor*, 5 December 1918, pp. 4–5.

127. See, for example, appeal of the Jüdischer Volksrat, Brünn, *JVS*, 1 January 1919, p. 5.

128. Report of Jüdischer Nationalrat, Prague, 3 May 1919, CZA, L6/96; *Selbstwehr*, 11 April 1919, pp. 1–2; 18 April 1919, p. 4; *JVS*, 16 May 1919, pp. 2–3.

129. On Jewish lobbying at Versailles, see Janowsky. On Czech resistance to including Jewish national rights in the treaty, see Kieval, *Making of Czech Jewry*, pp. 190–191.

130. Correspondence in CZA, L6/96, especially *Jüdischer Nationalrat* to WZO leader Leo Motzkin in Paris, 28 July 1919; and to Leo Herrmann, then in England, 9 August 1919; *Selbstwehr*, 3 October 1919, pp. 1, 4; 10 October 1919, p. 3.

131. Kieval, *Making of Czech Jewry*, p. 191; Mendelsohn, *Jews of East Central Europe*, pp. 131–169; and Aharon Moshe Rabinowicz, "The Jewish Minority," in *The Jews of Czechoslovakia*, vol. 1, pp. 155–265, which reproduces many relevant texts. Jews could elect to belong to the Jewish nation, but they were not required to do so. Kieval, "Masaryk and Czech Jewry," p. 317, convincingly argues that Czech political leaders recognized the Jews as a nation to reduce the strength of the German minority and also because they did not regard the Jews as Czech.

132. *Selbstwehr*, 2 May 1919, pp. 1–2; 9 May 1919, pp. 1–2; 16 May 1919, p. 1; 30 May 1919, pp. 1–2; 6 June 1919, pp. 1–2; 13 June 1919, pp. 1–5; *JVS*, 12 June 1918, pp. 1, 4, 6.

133. *Selbstwehr*, 30 May 1919, p. 2; 6 June 1919, pp. 2–4.

134. *JVS*, 12 June 1919, p. 3.

135. *Selbstwehr*, 6 June 1919, p. 1; *JVS*, 12 June 1919, p. 4.

136. *Selbstwehr*, 20 June 1919, pp. 1–2; *OW*, 20 June 1919, pp. 379–380.

137. Mendelsohn, *Jews in East Central Europe*, pp. 146, 159; Kieval, *Making of Czech Jewry*, pp. 195–196. For a full discussion and relevant statistics, see epilogue.

138. *OW*, 9 May 1919, p. 282. The notice appeared in the *Reichenberger Zeitung* on April 5. A report in *Zweimonatsbericht . . . der . . . Bnai Brith*, vol. 21, no. 6 (1918), p. 199, also noted that Bohemian Jews considered themselves part of the German nation.

139. Lieberman, p. 140.

140. On the Austrian Republic, see Charles A. Gulick, *Austria from Habsburg to Hitler* (Berkeley, 1948); Heinrich Benedikt, ed., *Geschichte der Republik Österreich* (Vienna, 1954); Karl R. Stadler, *The Birth of the Austrian Republic, 1918–1921* (Leiden, 1966); and Erika Weinzierl and Kurt Skalnik, eds., *Österreich 1918–1938: Geschichte der ersten Republik*, 2 vols. (Graz, 1983).

141. Denkschrift, 4 November 1918, CZA, Z3/214; letter to government of Deutschösterreich, 4 November 1918, L6/366; report, Reich conference of Austrian Zionists, 20 October 1918, L6/366; *JZ*, 25 October 1918, p. 1; 8 November 1918, pp. 1–2.

142. Weltsch to Herrmann, 28 October 1918, CZA, Z3/850; L6/366. See also Weltsch to Herrmann, 16 October 1918, Z3/850.

143. Herrmann to Weltsch, 1 November 1918, CZA, Z3/850; Z3/214; L6/366.

144. *WMZ*, 9 April 1919, pp. 1–2; 13 May 1919, p. 1.

145. IKG Wien, Plenarsitzung, 5 November 1918, CAHJP, AW 71/16; "Bericht über die Tätigkeit des Jüdischen Nationalrates für Deutschösterreich im ersten Monat seines Bestandes," 10 December 1918, p. 3, CZA, L6/93; report on Stern's resignation in L6/366. Interestingly, the Zionist press did not cover this event, and the *Bericht der Israelitische Kultusgemeinde Wien über die Tätigkeit in der Periode 1912–1924* (Vienna, 1924), p. 5, omits any mention of conflict on the issue.

146. On subsequent Zionist efforts to take over the community, see Freidenreich, pp. 48–83. Zionists achieved a majority on the communal board for the first time only in 1932.

147. "Bericht über die Tätigkeit des Jüdischen Nationalrates für Deutschösterreich," 10 December 1918, CZA, L6/93; telegrams and letters from Council to Copenhagen Zionist Office, November 1918, L6/366; L6/371; Weltsch to Herrmann, 16 November 1918, Z3/850; *JZ*, 15 November 1918, p. 3; 29 November 1918, p. 4.

148. Correspondence between Jüdischer Nationalrat, Vienna, and Zionist Office in Copenhagen, November 1918, CZA, L6/366; December 1918, L6/371; with Central Zionist Office, Berlin, December 1918 and January 1919, Z3/184; correspondence between Jüdisches Pressbüro, Vienna, and Central Zionist Office, Berlin, December 1918 and spring 1919, CZA, L6/371, L6/98, L6/99.

149. Telegrams, Jüdischer Nationalrat, Vienna, to Zionist Office, Copenhagen, 26 June 1919, 2 July 1919, CZA, L6/98.

150. *JZ*, 6 December 1918, pp. 1–2.

151. "1. Tätigkeitsbericht der Zentralstelle zur Versorgung jüdischer Kinder im Auslande; Sektion des Vereines `Soziale Hilfsgemeinschaft Anitta Müller in Wien . . . 1919–1920," CAHJP, AW 2320.

152. *JZ*, 21 March 1919, p. 5. For a defense of such Jewish national schools, see Robert Stricker, *Wie können wir unsere Jugend jüdisch erhalten?* (Vienna, 1919).

153. "Bericht über die Tätigkeit des Jüdischen Nationalrates für Deutschösterreich," CZA, L6/93; *JZ*, 8 November 1918, p. 7; 15 November 1918, pp. 4–5. See also description by Zionist activist Isidor Schalit in his memoirs, pp. 216–218, in CZA, A196/62/1.

154. CAHJP, AW 72/17, IKG-Wien, Protokoll der Vertreter-Sitzung, 8 February 1919; Correspondence, Jüdische Gruppe der Wiener Stadtschutzwache and IKG Wien, 6 May 1919 and 26 May 1919, AW 251/4.

155. "Bericht über die Tätigkeit des Jüdischen Nationalrates für Deutschösterreich, 10 December 1918, CZA, L6/93; open letter, 8 December 1918, L6/93; report, Jüdischer Nationalrat für Deutschösterreich, n.d., but obviously November 1918; Karl Renner to Jüdischer Nationalrat, 27 November 1918, L6/371; telegram exchange, December 1918, Z3/851; *JZ*, 22 November 1918, p. 6.

156. *JZ*, 13 December 1918, p. 5; *JKor*, 28 November 1918, pp. 1–2; Hoffmann-Holter, pp. 154–156.

157. Examples of the Hebrew title for the Council on stationery in CZA, Z3/180 and Z3/366.

158. *JZ*, 15 November 1918, pp. 1–2.

159. *JZ*, 6 December 1918, p. 5.

160. Robert Weiss, "Was will die jüdische Jugend," *OW*, 30 May 1919, pp. 330–331; Weiss, "Was wir wollen," *Jüdische Jugendblätter*, vol. 2, no.1 (1 March 1919), pp. 11–13.

161. *WMZ*, 11 February 1919, p. 1.

162. *JZ*, 13 December 1918, p. 1.

163. Robert Stricker, *Die wirksame Abwehr des Antisemitismus* (Vienna, 1919); Stricker, *Schadet der Jüdische Nationalismus den Juden?* (Vienna, 1919).

164. Josef Fraenkel, "Robert Stricker," in Josef Fraenkel, ed., *Robert Stricker* (London, 1950), pp. 13–18, 78–80; Freidenreich, pp. 55–72. During World War II, Stricker was deported to Theresienstadt and Auschwitz.

165. *OW*, 17 January 1919, pp. 34–36.

166. *JZ*, 17 January 1919, pp. 1–2; 31 January 1919, p. 1; 7 February 1919, pp. 1–2; 14 February 1919, p. 1; *WMZ*, 19 January 1919, p. 3; 30 January 1919, p. 3.

167. *WMZ*, 7 February 1919, p. 3; 10 February 1919, p. 1; 13 February 1919, p. 4. See also Robert Stricker, *Die Vertreter des jüdischen Volkes* (Vienna, 1919).

168. *WMZ*, 2 February 1919, p. 7; 13 February 1919, p. 11.

169. *JZ*, 21 February 1919, p. 1; *WMZ*, 17 February 1919, p. 1; 18 February, pp. 1, 4. Even anti-Zionists were pleased that Stricker would represent Jewish interests in parliament; see *OW*, 21 February 1919, p. 113.

170. Fraenkel, "Robert Stricker," p. 14.

171. Robert Stricker, *Jüdische Politik in Oesterreich* (Vienna, 1920?). This book is a collection of Stricker's parliamentary speeches. See also F. R. Bienenfeld, "Robert Stricker in Austrian Politics," in Fraenkel, ed., *Robert Stricker*, pp. 20–24.

172. *JZ*, 25 April 1919, p. 1; 2 May 1919, p. 1; *WMZ*, 16 April 1919, p. 1; 18 April 1919, pp. 5–6; 20 April 1919, p. 10; 22 April 1919, pp. 2–3; 4 May 1919, p. 1.

173. *JZ*, 9 May 1919, p. 1; *WMZ*, 5 May 1919, pp. 1–2; 6 May 1919, pp. 1–2.

174. *JZ*, 30 May 1919, p. 5.

175. Telegram, Jüdischer Nationalrat für Deutschösterreich to Cental Zionist Office, Berlin, 15 January 1918 [*sic*; 1919], CZA, Z3/851; to Zionist Office in Copenhagen, n.d., but probably January 1919, L6/88.

176. *JZ*, 4 April 1919, p. 1; 6 June 1919, p. 1.

177. *WMZ*, 15 February 1919, p. 1; 17 February 1919, p. 1; 19 February 1919, p. 1; 27 February 1919, p. 1; 15 March 1919, p. 1.

178. *WMZ*, 9 May 1919, p. 1; 30 May 1919, p. 1; 3 June 1919, p. 1.

179. *WMZ*, 11 February 1919, p. 1; 17 February 1919, p. 1; 18 February 1919, p. 1; 4 March 1919, pp. 1–2; 19 March 1919, p. 1.

180. Bienenfeld, p. 22.

181. *WMZ*, 28 June 1919, p. 1.

182. *JZ*, 31 January 1919, p. 1; 16 May 1919, p. 1; 20 June 1919, p. 1; 11 July 1919, p. 1; 18 July 1919, p. 4; 8 August 1919, p. 5; *WMZ*, 13 May 1919, p. 1.

183. Zionists in Galicia and in Bukovina in 1918/19 also demanded national rights for the Jews. See CZA, Z3/788 for Bukovina, and Z3/816 for Galicia; *JZ,* 25 October 1918, p. 2; 13 December 1918, p. 6; 3 January 1919, p. 5. On Jewish nationalist politics in interwar Poland, see Mendelsohn, *Jews of East Central Europe*, pp. 11–83; Mendelsohn, *Zionism in Poland*; and Heller, esp. ch. 8.

184. *OW*, 18 October 1918, pp. 659–660. On national rights as an Eastern European solution, see also *OW*, 25 October 1918, pp. 673–674; 1 November 1918, pp. 689–690; *Zweimonatsbericht . . . der . . . Bnai Brith*, vol. 21, no. 6 (1918), pp. 198-203.

185. *OW*, 25 October 1918, pp. 675–676; 1 November 1918, p. 696; 6 December 1918, p. 780.

186. *OW*, 8 November 1918, pp. 705–707; 22 November 1918, pp. 737–738; 6 December 1918, pp. 779–780; 13 December 1918, p. 800; 10 January 1919, pp. 23–24; *MONOIU*, vol. 31, nos. 2–4 (February–April 1919), pp. 3–4; *Zweimonatsbericht . . . der . . . Bnai Brith*, vol. 22, no. 1 (1919), pp. 9–10; *JKor*, 1 November 1918, p. 1; 5 December 1918, pp. 1, 2; 2 January 1919, p. 3.

187. *OW*, 8 November 1918, p. 705; see also pp. 706, 712; 24 January 1919, p. 56; Protokoll, meeting of Bezirkskommission 11/XX of IKG Wien, 14 December 1918, CAHJP, AW 250/5.

188. *OW*, 25 October 1918, p. 675; *JKor*, 12 December 1918, p. 2.

189. *JKor*, 1 November 1918, p. 2.

190. *OW*, 3 January 1919, pp. 8–9.

191. *OW*, 25 October 1918, pp. 673–675; quotations on p. 675.

192. *OW*, 1 November 1918, p. 696. See also *OW*, 10 January 1919, pp. 23–24.

193. *OW*, 6 December 1918, pp. 779–780; *JKor*, 5 December 1918, p. 2.

194. *OW*, 3 January 1919, p. 7. See also 30 May 1919, p. 344.

195. Bader, "One Life is not Enough," p. 101b. (Bader mistakenly began to number her pages again from p. 98 after she finished p. 112; thus 101b is the p. 101 that follows p. 112, not the first p. 101.)

196. Segal, p. 28.

197. Stolper, "Recorded Memoirs," pp. 68–69, 80.

198. *Zweimonatsbericht . . . der . . . Bnai Brith*, vol. 22, no. 1 (1919), pp. 17–46; *OW*, 29 November 1918, p. 764; 6 December 1918, p. 774; 20 December 1918, p. 810–811; 27 December 1918, p. 829; 14 February 1919, p. 104.

199. *OW*, 27 December 1918, p. 829; 25 April 1919, pp. 251–252.

200. *Zweimonatsbericht . . . der . . . Bnai Brith*, vol. 22, no.5 (1919), pp. 154–164; *XLVI. Jahresbericht der Israelitischen Allianz zu Wien erstattet an die XLVI. ordentliche Generalversammlung am 21. Mai 1925* (Vienna, 1925) in CAHJP, AW 2828/38.

201. *OW*, 6 December 1918, pp. 779–780; 3 January 1919, pp. 8–9; *JKor*, 5 December 1918, p. 2.

202. *OW*, 27 December 1918, pp. 821–822.

203. *OW*, 27 December 1918, pp. 823–824.

204. *OW*, 24 January 1919, pp. 55–56.

205. *Zweimonatsbericht . . . der . . . Bnai Brith*, vol. 22, no. 1 (1919), pp. 2–17; quotation on pp. 11–12.

206. *OW*, 27 June 1919, pp. 390–392. Bloch presented his long-held views in the first article and in the weeks that followed provided historical documentation. See *OW*, 4 July 1919, pp. 405–408; 11 July 1919, pp. 421–424; 18 July 1919, pp. 437–439; 25 July 1919, pp. 453–456.

207. *MONOIU*, vol. 31, no. 2–4 (February–April 1919), p. 4.

208. *JKor*, 5 December 1918, p. 1. See also letter from Ed. Deutsch in *OW*, 20 December 1918, pp. 814–815.

209. *JKor*, 2 January 1919, p. 3; *OW*, 27 December 1918, p. 824; *JZ*, 3 January 1919, p. 6.

210. Manfred Altmann, "K.u.k. Feldrabbiner Dr. Adolf Altmann an der Kriegsfront (1915–1918)," in *Ein Ewiges Dennoch,* Marko M. Feingold ed., pp. 527–528.

211. Fischer, "Memoirs and Reminiscences," ch. 5, p. 4.

212. Lachs, pp. 111–112.

213. Eva Reichmann, "Der Bewusstseinswandel der deutschen Juden," in *Deutsches Judentum in Krieg und Revolution,* Mosse and Paucker, eds., esp. pp. 583–612; Michael Brenner, *The Renaissance of Jewish Culture in Weimar Germany* (New Haven, 1996).

EPILOGUE

1. Joseph Rothschild, pp. 27–72; Antony Polonsky, *Politics in Independent Poland, 1921–39: The Crisis of Constitutional Government* (Oxford, 1972); Norman Davies, *God's Playground: A History of Poland* (New York, 1982).

2. Heller; Mendelsohn, *Jews of East Central Europe*, pp. 11–84; Yisrael Gutman, "Polish Antisemitism Between the Wars: An Overview," in *Jews of Poland*, Gutmann, Mendelsohn, Reinharz, and Shmeruk, eds., pp. 97–108; Emanuel Melzer, "Antisemitism in the Last Years of the Second Polish Republic," in ibid., pp. 126–137.

3. Mendelsohn, *Jews of East Central Europe*, pp. 29–32; figures for Galicia on pp. 31–32.

4. Ibid., pp. 43–68; Heller, pp. 249–293.

5. Livezeanu; Rothschild, pp. 281–322.

6. Mendelsohn, *Jews of East Central Europe*, pp. 171–211; statistics on p. 181.

7. Rothschild, pp. 137–199; Mendelsohn, *Jews of East Central Europe*, pp. 85–128; Patai, *Jews of Hungary*, pp. 468–534.

8. Mendelsohn, *Jews of East Central Europe*, pp. 107–112; Patai, *Jews of Hungary*, pp. 480–483, 507–511; Nathaniel Katzburg, "The Jewish Question in Hungary during the Inter-War Period—Jewish Attitudes," in *Jews and Non-Jews in Eastern Europe 1918–1945*, Bela Vago and George Mosse, eds. (New York, 1974), pp. 113–124.

9. Patai, *Jews of Hungary*, p. 507.

10. The discussion in this and the following paragraphs is based on Rothschild, pp. 73–135; Sayer, esp. 163–195; Mamatey and Luža, eds., *A History of the Czechoslovak Republic*; and Leff.

11. In addition to the sources cited above, see also Elizabeth Wiskemann, *Czechs and Germans: A Study of the Struggle in the Historic Provinces of Bohemia and Moravia*, 2d ed. (New York, 1967).

12. Mendelsohn, *Jews of East Central Europe*, p. 142; Rabinowicz, "The Jewish Minority," in *The Jews of Czechoslovakia*, vol. 1, pp. 155–265.

13. Mendelsohn, *Jews of East Central Europe*, p. 146. Gustav Fleischmann, "The Religious Congregation, 1918–1938," in *The Jews of Czechoslovakia* vol. 1, p. 267, notes that 54% of the Jews in 1921 and 57% in 1930 indicated that they belonged to the Jewish nation on the census.

14. Mendelsohn, *Jews of East Central Europe*, pp. 131–169; statistics on pp. 141, 146. In Sub-Carpathian Ruthenia, 87% of the largely orthodox Jews identified as Jews by nationality in 1921.

15. Jan Heřman, "The Development of Bohemian and Moravian Jewry, 1918–1938," in *Papers in Jewish Demography 1969*, U. O. Schmelz, P. Glikson, and S. Della Pergola, eds. (Jerusalem, 1973), p. 201.

16. Mendelsohn, *Jews of East Central Europe*, p. 159; Kieval, *Making of Czech Jewry*, pp. 195–196. Kieval argues that German identity was no longer viable in the interwar period, giving way either to a Czech or a Jewish national identity. I think that a large percentage of Jews—including the Jewish nationalists—retained a German cultural identity.

17. Ibid.

18. Kieval, *Making of Czech Jewry*, pp. 193–194.

19. Barbara Jelavich, *Modern Austria: Empire and Republic, 1800–1986* (Cambridge, 1987), pp. 151–224; Benedikt, ed., *Geschichte der Republik Österreich*; Weinzierl and Skalnik, eds. *Österreich 1918–1938*; Gulick, *Austria from Habsburg to Hitler*; on anti-Semitism specifically, Pauley, *From Prejudice to Persecution*, esp. pp. 75–280.

20. Leo Goldhammer, *Die Juden Wiens: Eine statistische Studie* (Vienna, 1927), p. 7; Hugo Gold, ed., *Gedenkbuch der untergegangenen Judengemeinden des Burgenlandes* (Tel Aviv, 1970); Josef Klampfer, *Das Eisenstädter Ghetto* (Eisenstadt, 1966).

21. Freidenreich, esp. pp. 180–203; Sylvia Maderegger, *Die Juden im österreichischen Ständesstaat, 1934–38* (Vienna, 1973).

22. Freidenreich, pp. 48–83, 147–158.

23. See, for example, Lieberman, "Lost and Found: A Life," p. 28, 74–75; Meir Neeman, "Autobiography," unpublished memoir, LBI; Freda Ulman Teitelbaum, *Vienna Revisited* (Santa Barbara, CA, 1995).

24. *Jüdische Front*, 8 July 1933, p. 5.

25. Michael John, "'We Do Not Even Possess Our Selves': On Identity and Ethnicity in Austria, 1880–1937," *Austrian History Yearbook* 30 (1999), pp. 50–56, 62–64.

Bibliography

Primary Sources

ARCHIVES

Central Archives for the History of the Jewish People, Jerusalem (CAHJP)
AW, Archiv der Israelitischen Kultusgemeinde, Wien
Au, Austria
CS 190, Persönliches aus dem Weltkrieg in 42 Blättern, 1916–19. Album zusammengestellt von M. Pollak, Prostějov
CS 191, Papers of Rabbi Dr. Moritz Lewin, Nikolsberg
P 97, Papers of Rabbi Max Grunwald
P 149, Papers of Dr. Egon Zweig
PL 474, Galician Refugees in an Austrian Camp
INV. 6526, Jüdisches Kriegsarchiv
INV. 6383, Hugo Grünberger postcards, 1916–1918

Central Zionist Archives, Jerusalem (CZA)
Z3, Central Zionist Office, Berlin, 1914–1919
L6, Copenhagen Office of the Zionist Organization, 1914–1919
F1, Austria
A196, Papers of Isidor Schalit

Jewish State Museum, Prague (JMP)
Box 128464, Finanzkomitee des Hilfskomitees für die jüdische Flüchlinge
Box 147633, Galizische Hilfskomitee
Box 120727, Sammlungen für galizische Flüchlinge
Box 128220, Ledger Books, Refugees
Israelitische Kultusgemeinde-Repräsentanz, Prag, Sitzungs-Protokoll, 1914–1918

Kriegsarchiv (War Archives),Vienna (KA)
    KM (Kriegsministerium)-Präs., 1914–1918
    KM, 9. Abteilung (Geistlichkeit), 1917–1918
    B/1576, Nachlass Erwin Schmidl

Leo Baeck Institute, New York (LBI)
Unpublished Memoirs
    Bader, Lillian. "One Life is Not Enough."
    Basch, Egon. "Wirken und Wandern: Lebenserinnerungen," 1952.
    Bergmann, Else. "Familiengeschichte."
    Berliner, Gertrude. "From My Family: Fiction and Truth," 1958.
    Bill, Friedrich. "Kuriose Biographie. Von Franz Josephs und meiner Geburt bis zum
        Tode Mitteleuropas," 1954.
    Ehrentheil, Otto F. "Part of the Honors," 1977–1978.
    Fischer, Eric. "Memoirs and Reminiscences (1898–1985)."
    Flesch, Philipp. "Mein Leben in Deutschland vor und nach dem 30. Januar 1933,"
        1940.
    Floch, Joseph. Untitled.
    Floch, Wife of Joseph. Untitled, 1980.
    Fraenkel, Bela. "Erinnerungen," 1940–1948.
    Freud, Esti D. "Vignettes of My Life," 1979.
    Friedman, David. "Trieb zur Kunst."
    Friedman, Otto. "Lebenserinnerungen," 1940.
    Furst, Ulrich R. "Windows to My Youth," 1984.
    Güdemann, Moritz. "Aus meinem Leben," 1899–1918.
    Herzog, David. "Pathways of My Life."
    Hindls, Arnold. "Erinnerungen aus meinem Leben," 1966.
    Hirsch, Gertrude. "Memories of My Childhood and Early Married Life."
    Höllriegel, Arnold (Richard Arnold Bermann). "Die Fahrt auf dem Katarakt (Auto-
        biographie ohne einen Helden)."
    Kallir, William. Untitled.
    Klein, Margarete. "Brief aus Israel an meine Verwandten in Oesterreich," (1992).
    Kriegsfield, Max. "Ein Schicksal ohne Tragoedie."
    Landre, Bertha. "Durch's Sieb der Zeit gefallen. Jedes Menschenleben ist ein Roman."
    Lederer, Regina Berger. "From Old World to New: Omi's Stories."
    Lieben, Fritz. "Aus meinem Leben," 1960.
    Lieberman, J. Nina. "Lost and Found: A Life."
    Mechner, Adolf. "My Family Biography," 1978–1981.
    Nell, Sidonie. "Kindheitserinnerungen."
    Safar, Vinca. "Aus meinem Leben."
    Saxonhouse, Ernest. "Memoirs," 1985.
    Scheuer-Karpin, Rose. "Unter Kaiser und König und Danach," 1993.
    Schwarz, Olly. "Lebenserinnerungen."
    Segal, Erna. "You Shall Never Forget" (text in German).
    Steiner, Paul. "Autobiography," 1986 (text in German).
    Stolper, Toni. "Recorded Memories," taped and transcribed by her grandson, Alister
        Campbell, 1982.
Personal Papers
    AR 6632   Bernhard Bardach Diaries from World War I.

Institut für Wirtschafts- und Sozialgeschichte, University of Vienna
  Pick, Rudolph. (Unpublished Memoirs): "The Ups and Downs of My Life."

NEWSPAPERS AND PERIODICALS

Blätter aus der jüdischen Jugendbewegung, Vienna, 1918.
Freie Tribune, Organ der jüdischen Sozialdemokratischen Partei "Poale Zion" in Deutschösterreich, Vienna, 1919.
Hickl's Jüdischer Volkskalender, Brünn-Vienna, 1914/15–1919/20.
Jerubbaal, Ein Zeitschrift der jüdischen Judend, Vienna, 1918/19.
Jüdische Front, Offizielles Organ des Bundes jüdischer Frontsoldaten Österreichs, Vienna, 1932–1938.
Jüdische Jugendblätter, Vienna, 1919.
Jüdische Korrespondenz, Vienna, 1916–1919.
Jüdische Volksstimme, Brünn, 1914–1919.
Jüdische Zeitung, National-Jüdisches Organ, Vienna, 1914–1919.
Jüdischer Nationalkalender, Vienna, 1915/16–1919/20.
Jüdisches Archiv, Mitteilungen des Komitees "Jüdisches Kriegsarchiv," Vienna, 1915–1917.
Jüdisches Kriegsgedenkenblatt, Vienna, 1914–1917.
Jung Juda, Illustrierte Zeitschrift für unsere Jugend, Prague, 1914–1919.
Monatschrift der Oesterreichisch-Israelitische Union, Vienna, 1914–1919.
Oesterreichische Wochenschrift or *Dr. Bloch's Oesterreichische Wochenschrift,* Vienna, 1914–1919.
Selbstwehr, Prague, 1914–1919.
Wiener Morgenzeitung, Vienna, 1919.
Zweimonats-Bericht für die Mitglieder der österr. israel. Humanitätsvereine "Bnai Brith," Vienna, 1914–1920/21.

PUBLISHED MEMOIRS

Bloch, Josef Samuel. *My Reminiscences.* Vienna: R. Löwit, 1923.
Bloch, Marc. *Memoirs of War, 1914–15.* Translated by Carole Fink. Ithaca, NY: Cornell University Press, 1980.
Brod, Max. *Streitbares Leben, 1884–1968.* Rev. ed. Munich: F. A. Herbig, 1969.
Clare, George. *Last Waltz in Vienna: The Rise and Destruction of a Family, 1842–1942.* New York: Holt, Rinehart and Winston, 1980.
Deutsch, Helene. *Confrontations with Myself.* New York: Norton, 1973.
Eisenmenger, Anna. *Blockade: The Diary of an Austrian Middle Class Woman, 1914–1924.* New York: R. Long and R. R. Smith, 1932.
Fenyvesi, Charles. *When the World Was Whole: Three Centuries of Memories.* New York: Penguin, 1990.
Frankenthal, Käte. *Der dreifache Fluch: Jüdin, Intellektuelle, Sozialistin: Lebenserinnerungen einer Ärtzin in Deutschland und im Exil.* Frankfurt a/M: Campus, 1981.
Katz, Jacob. *With My Own Eyes: The Autobiography of an Historian.* Translated by Ann Brenner and Zipora Brody. Hanover, NH: Brandeis University Press and University Press of New England, 1995.
Kohn, Hans. *Living in a World Revolution: My Encounters with History.* New York: Trident, 1964.
Kreisler, Fritz. *Four Weeks in the Trenches: The War Story of a Violinist.* Boston: Houghton Mifflin, 1915.

Lachs, Minna. *Warum schaust du zurück. Erinnerungen 1907–1941.*Vienna: Europaverlag, 1986.

Mauthner, Fritz. *Prager Jugendjahre: Erinnerungen.* 1918. Reprint, Frankfurt: S. Fischer, 1969.

Mautner, Hella Roubicek. *Hella.* Transcription of taped reminiscences. Privately printed by Nelly Urbach and Willy Mautner, Washington, DC, 1996.

Mayer, Sigmund. *Ein jüdischer Kaufmann 1831 bis 1911: Lebenserinnerungen.* Leipzig: v. Drucker und Humblot, 1911.

Patai, Raphael. *Apprentice in Budapest: Memories of a World That Is No More.* Salt Lake City: University of Utah Press, 1988.

Salsitz, Norman (as told to Richard Skolnik). *A Jewish Boyhood in Poland: Remembering Kolbuszowa.* Syracuse, NY: Syracuse University Press, 1992.

Schoenfeld, Joachim. *Jewish Life in Galicia Under the Austro-Hungarian Empire and in the Reborn Poland, 1898–1939.* Hoboken, NJ: Ktav, 1985.

Sperber, Manès. *God's Water Carriers.* Translated by Joachim Neugroschel. New York: Holmes and Meier, 1987.

Teitelbaum, Freda Ulman. *Vienna Revisited.* Santa Barbara, CA.: Fithian, 1995.

Wechsberg, Joseph. *The Vienna I Knew: Memories of a European Childhood.* Garden City, NY: Doubleday, 1979.

Weltsch, Robert. "Looking Back over Sixty Years." *LBIYB* 27 (1982): 379–390.

———. "Max Brod and His Age." *Leo Baeck Memorial Lecture* 13 (1970).

Winkler, Wilhelm. *Wir von der Südfront. Ernstes und Heiteres aus den Kämpfen in Serbien und am Isonzo.*Vienna: Monz, 1916.

Zuckerkandl, Bertha. *Österreich intim. Erinnerungen 1892–1942.* Frankfurt: Ullstein, 1970.

Zweig, Stefan. *The World of Yesterday.* New York:Viking, 1943.

SERMONS

Drobinsky, J. *Aus der Enge: Zwei Kanzelrede, gehalten am 1. Neujahrsmorgen des Kriegsjahres 5676 (1915) und an einem Sabbath (zur Propagierung der 3. Kriegsanleihe) im Tempel Wien-Mariahilf.* Vienna: Vorstande des isr. Tempelvereins für die beiden Gemeindebezirke Mariahilf und Neubau in Wien, 1915.

Färber, Rubin. *Heil dir Land, dessen Herrscher ein Edler! gottesdienstliche Festrede gehalten anlässlich des 86. Geburtstages seiner Majestät des Kaisers Franz Josef I., am 18 August 1915* [*sic*: 1916]. Mährisch Ostrau: Selbstverlag, 1916.

———. *Unser Kaiser, ein Sendbote Gottes. Predigten zum Allerhöchsten Geburtstage Sr. Maj. des Kaisers Franz Joseph I. und aus anderen patriotischen Anlässen.* Mährisch Ostrau: Selbstverlag, 1915.

Guttmann, Samuel Wolf. *Festrede anlässlich des 67. Jahrestages der Thronbesteigung unseres allergnädigsten Kaisers und Königs Franz Joseph I. bei dem am 2. Dezember 1915 im Tempel zu Lemberg stattgehalten Festgottesdeinste.* Lemberg: Israelitische Kultusgemeinde in Lemberg, 1915.

Herzog, D. *Kaiser Franz Josef I.: Gedenkrede, gehalten im israelitischen Tempel zu Graz.* Frankfurt: J. Kauffmann, 1917.

———. *Kriegspredigten.* Frankfurt: J. Kauffmann, 1915.

Hirsch, Isaak. *Die Juden und der Krieg. Festpredigt zur Feier des 85. Gebürtstages Sr. Majestät des Kaisers Franz Josef I.* Wiznitz: Sam. L. Ippen, 1915.

Lewin, Aharon. *Festpredigt anlässlich der Einweihung der Synagoge im k.k. Barackenlager für jüdische Kreigsflüchtlinge aus Galizien und der Bukowina in Bruck a.d. Leitha gehalten am 27. Juni 1915.*Vienna: Jos. Schlesinger, 1915?

Rosenmann, M. *In schwerer Zeit: Zwei Predigten über den Krieg.*Vienna: Alfred Hölder, 1914.

Schwartz, Emanuel. *Busspredigt für die Chewra Kedischa, gehalten am Erew R"H Schwat 1916.* Prague: Richard Brandeis, 1916.

———. *Der Krieg kommt, um das gebeugte u. gekränkte Recht herzustellen. Predigt gehalten bei der Chanukkafeier 1915.* Prague: Selbstverlag, 1915.

———. *Wenn du in den Krieg ziehst. Predigt, gehalten am Sabbat den 29. August 1914.* Prague: Jakob B. Brandeis, 1914.

POLITICAL AND INTELLECTUAL TRACTS

Abeles, Otto. *Jüdische Flüchtlinge: Szenen und Gestalten.* Vienna: R. Löwit, 1918.

Bendow, Josef (Joseph Tenenbaum). *Der Lemberger Judenpogrom.* Vienna: M. Hickl Verlag, 1919.

Bergmann, Hugo. *Jawne und Jerusalem: Gesammelte Aufsätze.* Berlin: Jüdischer Verlag, 1919.

Birnbaum, Nathan. *Gottes Volk.* Vienna: R. Löwit, 1918.

———. *Den Ostjuden ihr Recht.* Vienna: R. Löwit, 1915.

———. *Was sind Ostjuden?* Vienna: R. Löwit, 1916.

Brod, Max. *Das gelobte Land. Ein Buch der Schmerzen und Hoffnungen.* Leipzig: Kurt Wolf, 1917.

———. *Im Kampf um das Judentum.* Berlin: R. Löwit, 1920.

Deutsch, Aladar. "Das Kriegswesen nach der Lehrer der Bibel und der Tradition des Judentums," *XVII. Jahresbericht der k.k. III. Deutschen Staatsrealschule in Prag-Neustadt veröffentlicht am Schlusse des Schuljahres 1914–1915.* Prague: Selbstverlag, 1915.

Hirsch, Isidor. *Krieg und Ethik.* Frankfurt: J. Kauffmann, 1916.

Juden im Kriege: Denkschrift des jüdischen sozialistischen Arbeiterverbandes Poale-Zion an das Internationale Sozialistische Bureau, 2nd. ed. Den Haag: Selbstverlag, 1917.

Kadisch, Hermann. *Die Juden und die österreichische Verfassungsrevision.* Vienna: Wm. Berkelhammer, 1918.

Kreppel, Jonas. *Der Friede im Osten.* Vienna: Verlag "Der Tag," 1918.

———. *Ins vierte Kriegsjahr. Österreich-Ungarns Bilanz dreier Kriegsjahre.* Vienna: Selbstverlag, 1917.

———. *Juden und Judentum von heute.* Zurich: Amalthea, 1925.

———. *Der Kampf für und wider den Frieden.* Vienna: Redaktion "Der Tag," 1917.

———. *Österreich-Ungarn nach dem Friedensschlusse (eine Phantasie?).* Vienna: Redaktion "Der Tag," 1915.

———. *Der Weltkrieg und die Judenfrage.* Vienna: Redaktion "Der Tag," 1915.

Renner, Karl. *Der Kampf der österreichischen Nationen um den Staat.* Leipzig: F. Deuticke, 1903.

Rosenfeld, Max. *Nationale Autonomie der Juden in Oesterreich.* Czernowitz: Gutenberg, 1912.

———. *Nationales Selbstbestimmungsrecht der Juden in Polen.* Vienna: R. Löwit, 1918.

———. *Polen und Juden.* Berlin: R. Löwit, 1917.

———. *Die polnische Judenfrage: Problem und Lösung.* Vienna: R. Löwit, 1918.

Stricker, Robert. *Der jüdische Nationalismus.* Vienna: Verlag der Wiener Morgenzeitung, n.d., prob. 1919.

———. *Jüdische Politik in Oesterreich.* Vienna: Verlag der Wiener Morgenzeitung, n.d., prob. 1920.

———. *Schadet der Jüdische Nationalismus den Juden?* Vienna: Verlag der Jüdischen Zeitung, 1919.

———. *Wie können wir unsere Jugend jüdisch erhalten?* Vienna: Verlag der Jüdischen Zeitung, 1919.

———. *Die Vertreter des jüdischen Volkes.* Vienna: Verlag des zionistischen Landeskomitee, 1919.

———. *Die wirksame Abwehr des Antisemitismus*.Vienna:Verlag der Jüdischen Zeitung, 1919.
York-Steiner, Heinrich. *Bedeutet der Krieg einen Ausnahmszustand?*Vienna: Eisenstein, 1915.

OTHER PUBLISHED PRIMARY SOURCES

Austria, k.u.k. Statistische Zentralkommission, *Österreichische Statistik*, N.F., vols. 1–2, Die
Ergebnisse der Volkszählung vom 31. Dezember 1910 in den im Reichsrate vertrete-
nen Königreichen und Ländern (1912-1914).
Bericht der Israelitischen Kultusgemeinde Wien über die Tätigkeit in der Periode 1912–1924.Vienna:
Verlag der Israelitischen Kultusgemeinde Wien, 1924.
Csokor, Franz Theodor. *November 3, 1918*. In *A Critical Edition and Translation of Franz
Theodor Csokor's European Trilogy*, edited by Katherine McHugh Lichliter, 27–71. New
York: Peter Lang, 1995.
Drei Jahre BJF: Festschrift des Bundes jüdischer Frontsoldaten.Vienna: Selbstverlag, 1935.
Frühling, Moritz. *Biographisches Handbuch der in der k. u. k. Österr.-Ungar. Armee und Kriegs-
marine activ gedienten Offiziere, Ärzte, Truppen- und Rechnungs-Führer und sonstigen
Militärbeamten jüdischen Stammes*.Vienna: Selbstverlag, 1911.
Grübel, S. *K. und k. Landsturm. Erinnerungen an den Doppeladler*. Berlin:Vertreibsstelle des
Verbandes Deutscher Bühnenschriftsteller u. Bühnenkomponisten, 1930.
Grunwald, Max. *Gebete in Kriegszeit für israelitische Frauen und Mädchen*. Vienna: Jos.
Schlesinger, 1914.
Hašek, Jaroslav. *The Good Soldier Švejk and His Fortunes in the World War*. New, unabridged
translation by Cecil Parrott. New York:Thomas Y. Crowell, 1973; orig. Czech 1921.
Hungary. Központi Statisztikai hivatal. *Ungarisches Statistisches Jahrbuch* 19 (1911).
Infanterie-Regiment I.R. 14: ein Buch der Erinnerung an Grosse Zeiten, 1914–1918. Linz:
Feichtinger, 1919.
Infanterie-Regiment 94 im Weltkriege. Goblenz: Böhme, 1929.
Das Infanterie-Regiment Nr. 99 im Weltkrieg 1914–1918.Vienna: Kammeradschaft der Offiziere
des ehem. Inf. Reg. 99, 1929.
Das Jüdische Prag: Eine Sammelschrift. Prague:Verlag der Selbstwehr, 1917.
Jünger, Ernst. *Storm of Steel*. Translated by Basil Creighton. London: Chatto & Windus,
1929.
Kriegshagadah, 1914–1915. Brünn: Jüdischer Buch- und Kunstverlag, 1915.
Lamm, Louis. *Verzeichnis jüdischer Kriegsschriften*. Berlin, 1916.
Larisch, Anna. *150 Kochrezepte für die Kriegszeit*. Brünn:Winniker, 1915.
Ranglisten des kaiserlichen und königlichen Heeres 1916.Vienna: K.k. Hof- und Staatsdruckerei,
1916.
Ranglisten des kaiserlichen und königlichen Heeres 1917.Vienna: K.k. Hof- und Staatsdruckerei,
1917.
Ranglisten des kaiserlichen und königlichen Heeres 1918.Vienna: K.k. Hof- und Staatsdruckerei,
1918.
Remarque, Erich Maria. *All Quiet on the Western Front*. Translated by A. W. Wheen. New
York: Milestone Editions, 1930.
Roth, Joseph. *Radetsky March*.Translated by Geoffrey Dunlop. New York:Viking, 1933.
Schematismus für das k. u. k. Heer und für die k. u. k. Kriegsmarine für 1914.Vienna: K.k. Hof-
und Staatsdruckerei, 1914.
Stern, Marianne. *Kriegs Kochbuch der Frauenzeitschrift Wiener Mode*.Vienna: Gesellschaft für
Graphische Industrie, 1915.
Strunz, Franz, and Max Grunwald. *Empor die Herzen! Andachten für Gebildete aller Stände*.
Vienna: L.W. Seidel & Sohn, n.d.

Tannenbaum, Eugen, ed. *Kriegsbriefe deutscher und österreichischer Juden*. Berlin: Neuer Verlag, 1915.

Tätigkeitsbericht des Zentralbüros zum Schutze der galizischen Flüchtlinge jüdischen Glaubens-bekenntnisses in Brünn für die Zeit vom 15. Dezember 1914 bis 31. Oktober 1915. Brünn: Selbstverlag, 1915.

Weltsch, Felix, ed. *Dichter, Denker, Helfer: Max Brod zum 50. Geburtstag*. Mährisch Ostrau: Verlag von Julius Kittls Nachfolger, 1934.

Zuckermann, Hugo. *Gedichte*. Vienna: R. Löwit, 1915.

Select Secondary Sources

Altmann, Alexander. "Adolf Altmann (1879–1944): A Filial Memoir." *LBIYB* 26 (1981): 145–167.

Altmann, Manfred. "K.u.k. Feldrabbiner Dr. Adolf Altmann an der Kriegsfront (1915-1918) in Begegnung mit Feldmarschall Conrad von Hötzendorf und anderen Armeekom-mandanten." Sonderteil, in *Ein Ewiges Dennoch: 125 Jahre Juden in Salzburg*, edited by Marko M. Feingold. Vienna: Böhlau, 1993.

Anderson, Benedict. *Imagined Communities: Reflections on the Origins and Spread of National-ism*. Rev. ed. London: Verso, 1991; orig. 1983.

Angress, Werner. "Das deutsche Militär und die Juden im Ersten Weltkrieg." *Militär-geschichtliche Mitteilungen* 19 (1976): 77–146.

———. "The German Army's 'Judenzählung' of 1916. Genesis—Consequences—Signifi-cance." *LBIYB* 23 (1978): 117–137.

Armstrong, John. *Nations before Nationalism*. Chapel Hill: University of North Carolina Press, 1982.

Aschheim, Steven E. *Brothers and Strangers: The East European Jew in German and German Jewish Consciousness, 1800–1923*. Madison: University of Wisconsin Press, 1982.

———. "Eastern Jews, German Jews and Germany's Ostpolitik in the First World War." *LBIYB* 28 (1983): 351–365.

Aster, Howard, and Peter J. Potichnyj, eds. *Ukrainian-Jewish Relations in Historical Perspective*. 2d ed. Edmonton: Canadian Institute of Ukrainian Studies, University of Alberta, 1990.

Audoin-Rouzeau, Stéphane. *Men at War 1914–1918: National Sentiment and Trench Journalism in France during the First World War*. Translated by Helen McPhail. Providence: Berg, 1992.

Austria, Bundesministerium für Heereswesen und Kriegsarchiv. *Österreich-Ungarns letzter Krieg, 1914–1918*. 8 vols. Vienna: Verlag der Militärwissenschaftlichen Mitteilungen, 1930–1938.

Barany, George. "'Magyar Jew or Jewish Magyar?' Reflections on the Question of Assimi-lation." In *Jews and Non-Jews in Eastern Europe, 1918–1945*, edited by Béla Vago and George L. Mosse, 51–98. New York: Wiley, 1974.

Barkey, Karen and Mark von Hagen, eds. *After Empire: Multiethnic Societies and Nation-Building: The Soviet Union and the Russian, Ottoman, and Habsburg Empires*. Boulder, CO: Westview, 1997.

Barsch, Claus-Ekkehard. *Max Brod im Kampf um das Judentum: Zum Leben und Werk eines deutsch-jüdischen Dichters aus Prag*. Vienna: Passagen, 1992.

Barth, Fredrik. *Ethnic Groups and Boundaries: The Social Organization of Cultural Difference*. Boston: Little, Brown, 1969.

Becker, Jean-Jacques. *The Great War and the French People*. Translated by Arnold Pomerans. Leamington Spa: Berg, 1985.

Beller, Steven. "Patriotism and the National Identity of Habsburg Jewry, 1860–1914." *LBIYB* 41 (1996): 215–238.

Benedikt, Heinrich, ed. *Geschichte der Republik Österreich.* Vienna: Verlag für Geschichte und Politik, 1954.

Berkin, Carol, and Clara Lovett, eds. *Women, War and Revolution.* New York: Holmes and Meier, 1980.

Böhm, Adolf. *Die zionistische Bewegung.* 2d. rev. ed. 2 vols. Tel Aviv: Hozaah Ivrith, 1935–1937.

Braham, Rudolph, ed. *Hungarian-Jewish Studies.* New York: World Federation of Hungarian Jews, 1966.

Brenner, Michael. *The Renaissance of Jewish Culture in Weimar Germany.* New Haven: Yale University Press, 1996.

Breuer, Mordechai. *Jüdische Orthodoxie im Deutschen Reich, 1871-1918: Die Sozialgeschichte einer religiösen Minderheit.* Frankfurt: Jüdischer Verlag bei Athenäum, 1986.

Broszat, Martin. "Von der Kulturnation zur Volksgruppe. Die nationale Stellung der Juden in der Bukowina im 19. und 20. Jahrhundert." *Historische Zeitschrift* 200 (1965): 572–605.

Brubaker, Rogers. *Citizenship and Nationhood in France and Germany.* Cambridge: Harvard University Press, 1992.

Caesarani, David. "An Embattled Minority: The Jews of Britain during the First World War." In *The Politics of Marginality: Race, the Radical Right and Minorities in Twentieth Century Britain,* edited by T. Kushner and K. Lunn, 61–81. London: Frank Cass, 1990.

Coetzee, Frans, and Marilyn Shevin-Coetzee, eds. *Authority, Identity and the Social History of the Great War.* Providence: Berghahn Books, 1995.

Cohen, Gary B. "Jews in German Liberal Politics: Prague, 1880–1914." *Jewish History* 1 (spring 1986): 55–74.

———. "Jews in German Society: Prague 1860–1914." *Central European History* 10 (1977): 28–54.

———. *The Politics of Ethnic Survival: Germans in Prague, 1861-1914.* Princeton: Princeton University Press, 1981.

Daniel, Ute. *Arbeiterfrauen in der Kriegsgesellschaft: Beruf, Familie und Politik im Ersten Weltkrieg.* Göttingen: Vandenhoeck & Ruprecht, 1989.

Deák, István. *Beyond Nationalism: A Social and Political History of the Habsburg Officer Corps, 1848–1918.* New York: Oxford University Press, 1990.

———. "Jewish Soldiers in Austro-Hungarian Society." *Leo Baeck Memorial Lecture* 34 (1990).

———. "Pacesetters of Integration: Jewish Officers in the Habsburg Monarchy." *East European Politics and Society* 3 (winter 1989), pp. 22–50.

Denscher, Bernhard. *Gold gab ich für Eisen: Österreichische Kriegsplakate 1914-1918.* Vienna: Jugend und Volk, 1987.

———. *Das Schwarz-Gelbe Kreuz: Wiener Alltagsleben im Ersten Weltkrieg.* Vienna: Wiener Stadt- und Landesbibliothek, 1988.

Drabek, Anna M., Mordechai Eliav, and Gerald Stourzh, eds. *Prag—Czernowitz—Jerusalem: Der österreichische Staat und die Juden vom Zeitalter des Absolutismus bis zum Ende der Monarchie. Studia Judaica Austriaca* 10 (1984).

Elshtain, Jean Bethke. *Women and War.* New York: Basic Books, 1987.

Engel, David, "Patriotism as a Shield—the Liberal Jewish Defence against Antisemitism in Germany during the First World War." *LBIYB* 31 (1986): 147–171.

Feingold, Marko M., ed. *Ein Ewiges Dennoch: 125 Jahre Juden in Salzburg.* Vienna: Böhlau, 1993.

Ferguson, Niall. *The Pity of War.* New York: Basic Books, 1999.

Fischer, Fritz. *Germany's Aims in the First World War.* 1961. New York: Norton, 1967.

Fraenkel, Josef, ed. *Robert Stricker.* London: Claridge, Lewis & Jordan, 1950.

Frankel, Jonathan. "An Introductory Essay—the Paradoxical Politics of Marginality: Thoughts on the Jewish Situation During the Years 1914–1921." *Studies in Contemporary Jewry* 4 (1988): 3–21.

Freidenreich, Harriet Pass. *Jewish Politics in Vienna, 1918–1938.* Bloomington: Indiana University Press, 1991.

Fridenson, Patrick, ed. *The French Home Front 1914–1918.* Providence: Berg, 1991.

Fussell, Paul. *The Great War and Modern Memory.* New York: Oxford University Press, 1975.

Gaisbauer, Adolf. *Davidstern und Doppeladler. Zionismus und jüdischer Nationalismus in Österreich, 1882–1918.* Vienna: Böhlau, 1988.

Gammage, Bill. *The Broken Years: Australian Soldiers in the Great War.* Canberra: Australian National University Press, 1974.

Gellner, Ernest. *Nations and Nationalism.* Ithaca, NY: Cornell University Press, 1983.

Gold, Hugo, ed. *Gedenkbuch der untergegangenen Judengemeinden des Burgenlandes.* Tel Aviv: Olamenu, 1970.

———. *Geschichte der Juden in der Bukowina.* 2 vols. Tel Aviv: Olamenu, 1958–1962.

———. *Die Juden und Judengemeinden Böhmens in Vergangenheit und Gegenwart.* Brünn and Prague: Jüdischer Buch- und Kunstverlag, 1934.

———. *Die Juden und Judengemeinden Mährens in Vergangenheit und Gegenwart.* Brünn: Jüdischer Buch- und Kunstverlag, 1929.

Goldhammer, Leo. *Die Juden Wiens: Eine statistische Studie.* Vienna: R. Löwit, 1927.

Grebler, Leo, and Wilhelm Winkler. *The Cost of the World War to Germany and to Austria-Hungary.* New Haven: Yale University Press, 1940.

Gulick, Charles A. *Austria from Habsburg to Hitler.* 2 vols. Berkeley: University of California Press, 1973.

Gutman, Yisrael, Ezra Mendelsohn, Jehuda Reinharz, and Chone Shmeruk, eds. *The Jews of Poland Between Two World Wars.* Hanover, NH: Brandeis University Press and University Press of New England, 1989.

Hanák, Péter. "Die Volksmeinung während des letzten Kriegsjahres in Österreich-Ungarn." In *Die Auflösung des Habsburgerreiches: Zusammenbruch und Neuorientierung im Donauraum,* edited by Richard Georg Plaschka and Karlheinz Mack, 58–66. Munich: R. Oldenbourg, 1970.

Häusler, Wolfgang. "Assimilation und Emanzipation des ungarischen Judentums um die Mitte des 19. Jahrhunderts." *Studia Judaica Austriaca* 3 (1976): 33–79.

Havránek, Jan. "The Development of Czech Nationalism." *Austrian History Yearbook* 3, pt. 2 (1967), 223–260.

Heller, Celia S. *On the Edge of Destruction: Jews of Poland Between the Two World Wars.* New York: Schocken, 1977.

Heřman, Jan. "The Development of Bohemian and Moravian Jewry, 1918–1938." In *Papers in Jewish Demography 1969,* edited by U. O. Schmelz, P. Glikson, and S. Della Pergola, 191–206. Jerusalem: World Union of Jewish Studies and the Institute of Contemporary Jewry, Hebrew University, 1973.

Higonnet, Margaret. R., Jane Jenson, Sonya Michel, and Margaret C. Weitz, eds. *Beyond the Lines: Gender and the Two World Wars.* New Haven: Yale University Press, 1987.

Hobsbawm, E. J. *Nations and Nationalism since 1780: Programme, Myth, Reality.* 2nd ed. Cambridge: Cambridge University Press, 1992; orig. 1990.

Hoffmann-Holter, Beatrix. *"Abreisendmachung": Jüdische Kriegsflüchtlinge in Wien 1914 bis 1923.* Vienna: Böhlau, 1995.

Hoover, A. J. *God, Germany, and Britain in the Great War: A Study in Clerical Nationalism.* New York: Praeger, 1989.

Horwitz, Rivka. "Voices of Opposition to the First World War among Jewish Thinkers." *LBIYB* 33 (1988): 233–259.

Hyman, Paula E. *From Dreyfus to Vichy: The Remaking of French Jewry, 1906–1939.* New York: Columbia University Press, 1979.

Iggers, Wilma A. *Die Juden in Böhmen und Mähren: Ein historisches Lesebuch.* Munich: C. H. Beck, 1986.

———. *Women of Prague: Ethnic Diversity and Social Change from the Eighteenth Century to the Present.* Providence: Berghahn, 1995.

Janowsky, Oskar. *Jews and Minority Rights (1898–1919).* New York: Columbia University Press, 1933.

Jászi, Oscar. *The Dissolution of the Habsburg Monarchy.* Chicago: University of Chicago Press, 1929, 1961.

Jelavich, Barbara. *Modern Austria: Empire and Republic, 1800–1986.* Cambridge: Cambridge University Press, 1987.

The Jews of Czechoslovakia: Historical Studies and Surveys, 3 vols. Philadelphia: Jewish Publication Society and New York: Society for the History of Czechoslovak Jews, 1968–1984.

John, Michael. "'We Do Not Even Possess Our Selves': On Identity and Ethnicity in Austia, 1880–1937." *Austrian History Yearbook* 30 (1999): 17–64.

Judson, Pieter M. *Exclusive Revolutionaries: Liberal Politics, Social Experience, and National Identity in the Austrian Empire, 1848–1914.* Ann Arbor: University of Michigan Press, 1996.

———. "'Not Another Square Foot!' German Liberalism and the Rhetoric of National Ownership in Nineteenth-Century Austria." *Austrian History Yearbook* 26 (1995): 83–97.

———. "'Whether Race or Conviction Should Be the Standard': National Identity and Liberal Politics in Nineteenth-Century Austria." *Austrian History Yearbook* 22 (1991): 76–95.

Kann, Robert A. *A History of the Habsburg Empire, 1526-1918.* Berkeley: University of California Press, 1974.

———. "Hungarian Jewry During Austria-Hungary's Constitutional Period (1867–1914)." *Jewish Social Studies* 7 (1945): 357–386.

———. *The Multinational Empire: Nationalism and National Reform in the Habsburg Monarchy, 1848–1918.* 2 vols. New York: Columbia University Press, 1950.

Kann, Robert A., Béla K. Király, and Paula S. Fichtner, eds. *The Habsburg Empire in World War I: Essays in Intellectual, Military, Political and Economic Aspects of the War Effort.* East European Monographs, 23. Boulder, CO.: East European Quarterly, 1977.

Kaplan, Marion A. *The Making of the Jewish Middle Class: Women, Family, and Identity in Imperial Germany.* New York: Oxford University Press, 1991.

Kassner, S. *Die Juden in der Bukowina.* 2nd ed. Vienna: R. Löwit, 1917.

Katzburg, Nathaniel. "The Jewish Question in Hungary during the Inter-War Period— Jewish Attitudes." In *Jews and Non-Jews in Eastern Europe 1918–1945,* edited by Béla Vago and George L. Mosse, 113–124. New York: Wiley, 1974.

Kestenberg-Gladstein, Ruth. *Neuere Geschichte der Juden in den böhmischen Ländern. Erster Teil: Das Zeitalter der Aufklärung 1780–1830.* Tübingen: J. C. B. Mohr, 1969.

Kieval, Hillel J. "Caution's Progress: The Modernization of Jewish Life in Prague, 1780-1830." In *Toward Modernity: The European Jewish Model,* edited by Jacob Katz, 71–105. New Brunswick: Transaction Books, 1989.

————. *The Making of Czech Jewry: National Conflict and Jewish Society in Bohemia, 1870–1918.* New York: Oxford University Press, 1988.

————. "Masaryk and Czech Jewry: The Ambiguities of Friendship." In *T. G. Masaryk (1850–1937).* Vol. 1, *Thinker and Politician,* edited by Stanley B. Winters, 302–327. New York: St. Martin's, 1990.

Király, Béla and Nándor F. Dreisziger, eds. *East Central European Society in World War I.* Boulder and Highland Lakes: Social Science Monographs and Atlantic Research and Publications, 1985.

Kisch, Guido. "Das jüdische Prag vor zwei Generationen: Zur fünfzigsten Wiederkehr des Todestages von Rabbiner Alexander Kisch." *Judaica Bohemiae* 3, no.2 (1967): 87–100.

Kocka, Jürgen. *Facing Total War: German Society 1914–1918.* Translated by Barbara Weinberger. Cambridge, MA: Harvard University Press, 1984; German orig. 1973.

Kohn, Hans. *Nationalism: Its Meaning and History.* Princeton: D. Van Nostrand, 1955, 1965.

————. *The Idea of Nationalism: A Study in Its Origins and Background.* New York: Macmillan, 1944.

————. "Was the Collapse Inevitable?" *Austrian History Yearbook* 3, pt.3 (1967): 250–263.

Kořalka, Jiří. *Tschechen im Habsburgerreich und in Europa, 1815–1914. Sozialgeschtliche Zusammenhang der neuzeitlichen Nationsbildung und der Nationalitätenfrage in den böhmischen Ländern.* Vienna: Verlag für Geschichte und Politik and Munich: R. Oldenbourg, 1991.

Kuděla, Jiří. "Galician and East European Refugees in the Historic Lands: 1914–1916." *Review of the Society for the History of Czechoslovak Jews* 4 (1991–1992): 15–32.

Kushner, Tony. "Sex and Semitism: Jewish Women in Britain in War and Peace." In *Minorities in Wartime: National and Racial Groupings in Europe, North America and Australia during the Two World Wars,* edited by Panikos Panayi. Oxford: Berg, 1993.

Leed, Eric J. *No Man's Land: Combat and Identity in World War I.* Cambridge: Cambridge University Press, 1979.

Leff, Carol Skolnick. *National Conflict in Czechoslovakia: The Making and Remaking of a State, 1918–1987.* Princeton: Princeton University Press, 1988.

Leslie, John. "Der Ausgleich in der Bukowina von 1910: Zur österreichischen Nationalitätenpolitik vor dem Ersten Weltkrieg." In *Geschichte zwischen Freiheit und Ordnung: Gerald Stourzh zum 60. Geburtstag,* edited by Emil Brux, Thomas Fröschl, and Josef Leidenfrost, 113–144. Graz: Verlag Styria, 1991.

Livezeanu, Irina. *Cultural Politics in Greater Romania: Regionalism, Nation Building and Ethnic Struggle, 1918–1930.* Ithaca, NY: Cornell University Press, 1995.

Macartney, C. A. *The Habsburg Empire 1790–1918.* New York: Macmillan, 1969.

Maderegger, Sylvia. *Die Juden im österreichischen Ständestaat, 1934–38.* Vienna: Geyer, 1973.

Magill, Stephen. "Defense and Introspection: German Jewry, 1914." In *Jews and Germans from 1860 to 1933: The Problematic Symbiosis,* edited by David Bronsen, 209–233. Heidelberg: Carl Winter Universitätsverlag, 1979.

Magocsi, Paul Robert. *A History of Ukraine.* Seattle: University of Washington Press, 1996.

Mamatey, Victor S., and Radomír Luža, eds. *A History of the Czechoslovak Republic, 1918–1948.* Princeton: Princeton University Press, 1973.

Markovits, Andrei S., and Frank E. Sysyn, eds. *Nation Building and the Politics of Nationalism: Essays on Austrian Galicia.* Cambridge, MA: Harvard Ukrainian Research Institute, 1982.

Marwick, Arthur. *The Deluge: British Society and the First World War.* London: The Bodley Head, 1965.

Matthäus, Jürgen. "Deutschtum und Judentum under Fire—The Impact of the First World War on the Strategies of the Centralverein and the Zionistische Vereinigung." *LBIYB* 33 (1988): 129–147.

Maurer, Trude. *Ostjuden in Deutschland, 1918–1933*. Hamburg: Hans Christians Verlag, 1986.

May, Arthur J. *The Passing of the Hapsburg Monarchy, 1914–1918*. 2 vols. Philadelphia: University of Pennsylvania Press, 1966.

McCagg, William O, Jr. *A History of Habsburg Jews, 1670–1918*. Bloomington: Indiana University Press, 1989.

———. "On Habsburg Jewry and Its Disappearance." *Studies in Contemporary Jewry* 4 (1988): 84–95.

———. "Jewish Assimilation in Austria: Karl Kraus, Franz Werfel and Joseph Roth on the Catastrophe of 1914–1919." In *Austrians and Jews in the Twentieth Century: From Franz Joseph to Waldheim*, edited by Robert S. Wistrich, 58–81. London: Macmillan and New York: St. Martin's Press, 1992.

McPherson, James M. *For Cause and Comrades: Why Men Fought in the Civil War*. New York: Oxford University Press, 1997.

Mendelsohn, Ezra. *The Jews of East Central Europe between the World Wars*. Bloomington: Indiana University Press, 1983.

———. *Zionism in Poland: The Formative Years, 1915–1926*. New Haven: Yale University Press, 1981.

Monk, Ray. *Ludwig Wittgenstein: The Duty of Genius*. New York: Free Press, 1990.

Mosse, George L. *Confronting the Nation: Jewish and Western Nationalism*. Hanover, NH: Brandeis Unviersity Press and University Press of New England, 1993.

———. *Fallen Soldiers: Reshaping the Memory of the World Wars*. New York: Oxford University Press, 1990.

———. "The Jews and the German War Experience, 1914–1918," *Leo Baeck Institute Memorial Lecture* 21 (1977).

Mosse, Werner E. and Arnold Paucker, eds. *Deutsches Judentum in Krieg und Revolution 1916–1923*. Tübingen: J. C. B. Mohr, 1971.

Niewyk, Donald L. "The German Jews in Revolution and Revolt, 1918–19." *Studies in Contemporary Jewry* 4 (1988): 41–66.

Pankhurst, E. Sylvia. *The Homefront: A Mirror to Life in England during the First World War*. London: Cresset, 1932.

Patai, Raphael. *The Jews of Hungary: History, Culture, Psychology*. Detroit: Wayne State University Press, 1996.

Paul-Schiff, Maximilian. "Teilnahme der österreichisch-ungarischen Juden am Weltkrieg. Eine statistische Studie." *Mitteilungen zur jüdischen Volkskunde* 26/27 (1924–1925): 151–56.

Pauley, Bruce F. *From Prejudice to Persecution: A History of Austrian Anti-Semitism*. Chapel Hill: University of North Carolina Press, 1992.

Pazi, Margarita. *Max Brod: Werke und Persönlichkeit*. Bonn: H. Bouvier, 1970.

Plaschka, Richard G., Horst Haselsteiner, and Arnold Suppan. *Innere Front: Militärassistenz, Widerstand und Umsturz in der Donaumonarchie 1918*. 2 vols. Vienna: Verlag für Geschichte und Politik, 1974.

Plaschka, Richard Georg, and Karlheinz Mack, eds. *Die Auflösung des Habsburgerreiches: Zusammenbruch und Neuorientierung im Donauraum*. Munich: R. Oldenbourg, 1970.

Polonsky, Antony. *Politics in Independent Poland, 1921–39: The Crisis of Constitutional Government*. Oxford: Clarendon, 1972.

Pribram, Alfred. *Urkunden und Akten zur Geschichte der Juden in Wien*. Vienna: Wilhelm Braumüller, 1918.

Pulzer, Peter. *Jews and the German State: The Political History of a Minority, 1848–1933*. Oxford: Blackwell, 1992.

Rauchensteiner, Manfried. *Der Tod des Doppeladlers. Österreich-Ungarn und der Erste Weltkrieg*. Graz: Styria, 1993.

Rechter, David. "Galicia in Vienna: Jewish Refugees in the First World War." *Austrian History Yearbook* 28 (1997): 113–130.

Rees, Louis H. *The Czechs during World War I: The Path to Independence.* Boulder, CO: East European Monographs, 1992.

Reichmann, Eva G. "Der Bewusstseinswandel der deutschen Juden." In *Deutsches Judentum in Krieg und Revolution, 1916–1923,* edited by Werner Mosse and Arnold Paucker, 511–612. Tübingen: J. C. B. Mohr, 1971.

Renan, Ernst. "What Is a Nation." In *Nation and Narration,* edited by Homi K. Bhabha, 8–21. London: Routledge, 1990.

Riff, Michael A. "The Ambiguity of Masaryk's Attitudes on the 'Jewish Question'." In *T. G. Masaryk (1850–1937).* Vol. 2, *Thinker and Critic,* edited by Robert B. Pynsent, 77–87. New York: St. Martin's, 1989.

Robertson, Ritchie and Edward Timms, eds. *The Habsburg Legacy: National Identity in Historical Perspective. Austrian Studies* 5. Edinburgh: Edinburgh University Press, 1994.

Rosenfeld, Moritz. *Oberrabbiner Hirsch Perez Chajes; Sein Leben und Werk.* Vienna: Selbstverlag, 1933.

Rothenberg, Gunther E. *The Army of Francis Joseph.* West Lafayette, IN.: Purdue University Press, 1976.

Rothschild, Joseph. *East Central Europe between the Two World Wars.* Seattle: University of Washington Press, 1974.

Rozenblit, Marsha L. *The Jews of Vienna, 1867–1914: Assimilation and Identity.* Albany: State University of New York Press, 1983.

———. "The Jews of Germany and Austria: A Comparative Perspective." In *Austrians and Jews in the Twentieth Century: From Franz Joseph to Waldheim,* edited by Robert S. Wistrich, 1–18. New York: St. Martin's Press, 1992.

Rürup, Reinhard. "Der 'Geist von 1914' in Deutschland. Kriegsbegeisterung und Ideologisierung des Krieges im Ersten Weltkrieg." In *Ansichten vom Krieg. Vergleichende Studien zum Ersten Weltkrieg in Literatur und Gesellschaft,* 1–30. Königstein/Ts: Forum Academicum, 1984.

Rutkowski, Ernst. "Das Schicksal des Oberleutnants in der Reserve Dr. Leon Lebensart im Weltkrieg 1914–1918." *Zeitschrift für die Geschichte der Juden* 1 (1967): 231–246.

Sayer, Derek. *The Coasts of Bohemia: A Czech History.* Princeton: Princeton University Press, 1998.

Schmidl, Erwin A. "Jews in the Austro-Hungarian Armed Forces, 1867–1918." *Studies in Contemporary Jewry* 3 (1987): 127–146.

———. *Juden in der k. (u.) k. Armee 1788–1918. Studia Judaica Austriaca* 11 (1989).

———. "200 Jahre jüdische Soldaten in Österreich." *Truppendienst* 28, no. 3 (June 1989): 228–231.

Senekowitsch, Martin. *Gleichberechtige in einer grosse Armee. Zur Geschichte des Bundes Jüdischer Frontsoldaten Österreichs 1932–38.* Vienna, 1994.

Silber, Michael. "The Historical Experience of German Jewry and Its Impact on Haskalah and Reform in Hungary." In *Toward Modernity: The European Jewish Model,* edited by Jacob Katz, 107–157. New Brunswick and Oxford: Transaction Books, 1989.

———, ed. *Jews in the Hungarian Economy, 1760–1945.* Jerusalem: Magnes Press, 1992.

Sked, Alan. *The Decline and Fall of the Habsburg Empire, 1815–1918.* London: Longman, 1989.

Smith, Anthony D. *The Ethnic Origins of Nations.* Oxford: Basil Blackwell, 1986.

———. *Nationalism and Modernism: A Critical Survey of Recent Theories of Nations and Nationalism.* London: Routledge, 1998.

———. *Theories of Nationalism.* New York: Harper and Row, 1971.

Sondhaus, Laurence. *In the Service of the Emperor: Italians in the Austrian Armed Forces 1814–1918*. Boulder, CO: East European Monographs, 1990.

Stölzl, Christoph. "Die 'Burg' und die Juden: T. G. Masaryk und sein Kreis im Spannungsfeld der jüdischen Frage: Assimilation, Antisemitismus und Zionismus." In *Die "Burg": Einflussreich politische Kräfte um Masaryk und Benes*, edited by Karl Bosl, vol. 2, 79–110. Munich, 1974.

Stone, Norman. *The Eastern Front, 1914–1917*. New York: Charles Scribner's Sons, 1975.

Stourzh, Gerald. "Galten die Juden als Nationalität Altösterreichs?" *Studia Judaica Austriaca* 10 (1984): 73–116.

Taylor, A. J. P. *The Habsburg Monarchy, 1809–1918*. Chicago: University of Chicago Press, 1948, 1976.

Thon, Jakob. *Die Juden in Oesterreich*. Berlin: Bureau für Statistik der Juden, 1908.

Timms, Edward. *Karl Kraus: Apocalyptic Satirist: Culture and Catastrophe in Habsburg Vienna*. New Haven: Yale University Press, 1986.

Vincent, C. Paul. *The Politics of Hunger: The Allied Blockade of Germany, 1915-1919*. Athens: Ohio University Press, 1985.

Wall, Richard and Jay Winter, eds. *The Upheaval of War: Family, Work and Welfare in Europe, 1914–1918*. Cambridge: Cambridge University Press, 1988.

Wandruszka, Adam and Peter Urbanitsch, eds. *Die Habsburgermonarchie 1848–1918*. Vol. 3, *Die Völker des Reiches*. Vienna: Verlag der österreichischen Akademie der Wissenschaften, 1980.

————. *Die Habsburgermonarchie 1848–1918*. Vol. 4, *Die Konfessionen*. Vienna: Verlag der österreichischen Akademie der Wissenschaften, 1985.

Wandycz, Piotr S. *The Lands of Partitioned Poland, 1795–1918*. Seattle: University of Washington Press, 1974.

Wank, Solomon. "The Nationalities Question in the Habsburg Monarchy: Reflections on the Historical Record." In *Working Papers in Austrian Studies*, Center for Austrian Studies, University of Minnesota, April 1993, pp. 1–18.

Weinzierl, Erika, and Kurt Skalnik, eds. *Österreich 1918–1938: Geschichte der Ersten Republik*. 2 vols. Graz: Styria, 1983.

Weisl, Wolfgang von. *Die Juden in der Armee Österreich-Ungarns*. Tel Aviv: Olamenu, 1971.

Wertheimer, Jack. *Unwelcome Strangers: East European Jews in Imperial Germany*. New York: Oxford University Press, 1987.

Whiteside, Andrew. "The Germans as an Integrative Force in Imperial Austria: The Dilemma of Dominance." *Austrian History Yearbook* 3, pt. 1 (1967): 157–200.

Williams, John. *The Other Battleground: The Home Fronts: Britain, France and Germany 1914–1918*. Chicago: H. Regnery, 1972.

Williamson, Samuel, Jr. *Austria-Hungary and the Origins of World War I*. New York: St. Martin's, 1991.

Williamson, Samuel, R. Jr., and Peter Pastor, eds. *Essays on World War I: Origins and Prisoners of War*. New York: Social Science Monographs, Brooklyn College Press, 1983.

Winkler, Wilhelm. *Berufsstatistik der Kriegstoten der öst.-ung. Monarchie*. Vienna: Deutsch-österreichischen Staatsamtes für Heereswesen, 1919.

————. *Die Totenverluste der öst.-ung. Monarchie nach Nationalitäten*. Vienna: Deutschösterreichischen Staatsamtes für Heereswesen, 1919.

Winter, J. M. *The Great War and the British People*. London: Macmillan, 1986.

————. *Sites of Memory, Sites of Mourning: The Great War in European Cultural History*. Cambridge: Cambridge University Press, 1995.

Wiskemann, Elizabeth. *Czechs and Germans: A Study of the Struggle in the Historic Provinces of Bohemia and Moravia*. 2d ed. New York: St. Martin's, 1967, orig. 1938.

Wistrich, Robert S. *The Jews of Vienna in the Age of Franz Joseph.* Oxford: Oxford University Press, 1989.

———. "Liberalism, *Deutschtum* and Assimilation." *Jerusalem Quarterly* 42 (Spring 1987): 100–118.

———. "The Modernization of Viennese Jewry: The Impact of German Culture in a Multi-Ethnic State." In *Toward Modernity: The European Jewish Model,* edited by Jacob Katz, 43–70. New Brunswick, NJ: Transaction Books, 1987.

———. ed. *Austrians and Jews in the Twentieth Century: From Franz Joseph to Waldheim.* New York: St. Martin's, 1992.

Wlaschek, Rudolf M. *Juden in Böhmen: Beiträge zur Geschichte des europäischen Judentums im 19. und 20. Jahrhundert.* Munich: R. Oldenbourg, 1990.

Wróbel, Piotr. "The Jews of Galicia under Austrian-Polish Rule, 1869–1918." *Austrian History Yearbook* 25 (1994): 97–138.

Zechlin, Egmont. *Die deutsche Politik und die Juden im ersten Weltkrieg.* Göttingen: Van den Hoeck & Ruprecht, 1969.

Zeman, Z. A. B. *The Break-Up of the Habsburg Empire 1914–1918: A Study in National and Social Revolution.* London: Oxford University Press, 1961.

Zipperstein, Steven J. "The Politics of Relief: The Transformation of Russian Jewish Communal Life during the First World War." *Studies in Contemporary Jewry* 4 (1988): 22–40.

Zöllner, Erich. "The Germans as an Integrating and Disintegrating Force." *Austrian History Yearbook* 3, pt. 1 (1967): 201–233.

Index

Altmann, Adolf, 48, 100, 104, 107, 160
Anschluss, 132, 150, 155, 158, 168
anti-Semitism, 4, 9, 36, 109
  in Austrian Republic, 11, 134, 136, 150,
    152, 154, 156, 157, 160, 168
  in Czechoslovakia, 139, 141, 142, 146,
    147, 168
  among Czechs, 22, 26, 124, 125, 139, 141,
    142, 210 n. 21
  in Galicia, 11, 29, 30, 50, 52, 108
  among Germans, 22, 136, 177 n. 41
  in Germany during World War I, 44, 56,
    94
  in Habsburg army, 82, 92–93
  Habsburg Austria as only protection
    against, 54, 56, 80, 105, 106, 109,
    111, 120, 128, 163
  in Hungary, 11, 31, 165
  Jewish activity to dispel during World
    War I, 39, 44, 54,55–56, 59, 79, 91,
    102, 113–115, 117, 119, 127, 162
  and Jewish identity, 21, 170, 181 n. 98
  and Jewish refugees, 65, 78–79, 108, 139,
    146
  during last two years of war, 10, 56–57,
    60, 73, 78–80, 105, 106, 107,
    108–109, 119, 120–121, 163
  among Poles, 11, 52, 111, 112–113,
    137–138, 163–164

  in Prague, 79
  in successor states, 4, 10, 128–129, 163,
    165
  in Vienna, 33, 181 n. 95
army, Habsburg, 85–86, 133
  and anti-Semitism, 82, 92–93, 95, 163
  attitudes toward Jews, 93–94
  and integration of Jews, 82, 91–92
  and Jewish religious ritual, 96–97,
    192 n. 51
Association of Jewish Front Soldiers,
    104–105, 169, 208 n. 173
Austria, Habsburg
  Jewish desire for continuity of, 109-110,
    119-126
  Jewish loyalty toward, 4, 9, 24, 25, 57, 59,
    80, 82–83, 93–94, 102, 119, 129, 134,
    169, 172
  Jewish identity in, 9, 22, 23–24, 127, 128
  and national identity, 17–18, 162, 172
  nationality conflict in, 17, 19, 57, 107,
    109, 112, 129
  proposals for national autonomy in, 109,
    131
  and supranationalism, 17
  and wartime patriotism, 39–40
Austria-Hungary
  Jews in, 14–15, 21-23
  and national identity, 3, 8, 17–18

Austrian brotherhood, 54, 60
Austrian Israelite Union, 35–36, 113, 117,
    118, 120, 157, 159, 160
Austrian Republic, 132, 168
Austrian Republic, Jews in, 11, 12, 129, 135,
    150–161, 168
    and attitudes to German nation, 150,
        152–153, 155–158, 163, 168
    and attitudes to the state, 152–153,
        155–156, 163, 168
    and crisis of identity, 150, 155, 156
    and Jewish identity, 150, 153–159, 163
    and Jewish national rights, 151–155
    and opposition to Jewish nationalism,
        156–157
autonomy, Jewish national, 37, 55, 111–112,
    115, 116–118, 120, 121–126, 134,
    138, 141, 144, 151

Bar Kochba, 37
Benedikt, Clothilde, 62, 63, 71
Beneš, Edward, 131, 149
Bergmann, Hugo, 148
Birnbaum, Nathan, 121
Bloch, Josef Samuel, 35–36, 75, 111, 159,
    182 n. 120
Bohemia, Jews in, 15, 25–28
    and Austrian loyalty, 28, 124, 139
    and Czech identity, 11, 26–28, 124, 141,
        146-147, 149, 167-168
    and Galician/Bukovinian refugees,
        68–69, 70–71, 72
    and German identity, 25–28, 146–147,
        149, 177–178 n. 41
    and Jewish nationalism, 117, 124, 125,
        167
Bnai Brith, 60, 62, 68, 69, 70, 77, 112, 126,
    147, 157, 160
Brest-Litovsk, Treaty of, 126
Brno. See Brünn
Brod, Max, 37, 117, 140, 144, 146–147,
    222 n. 119
Brünn, 68, 141, 145
Brünn Platform, 182 n. 127
Brusilov Offensive, 49, 53, 66, 84
Bukovina, 18-19, 48, 50, 131–132, 164
Bukovina, Jews in, 11, 15, 23, 28, 30
    and Austrian loyalty, 50, 52
    and German culture, 30
    and Jewish nationalism, 30, 37, 123

refugees from. See refugees
    and Zionism, 37, 124
Burgenland, 169, 217 n. 6
Burgfrieden, 52, 56, 78, 108

camaraderie, 82, 84, 91–92
Chajes, Hirsch Perez, 134, 158
chaplains, Jewish, 63, 83, 96, 97, 98–101,
    102, 205 n. 115, 207 n. 136
Cracow, pogroms in, 112–113
Cracow Program, 37, 121
Csokor, Franz Theodor, 132–133
Czechoslovakia
    anti-Semitism in, 142, 166
    creation of, 131, 132
    and Czechoslovak identity, 132, 166,
        172-173
    Jewish attitudes toward, 138–143, 163
    Jewish identity in, 11, 129, 133, 143–150,
        167–168, 173
    Jewish national rights in, 143–149, 163,
        167, 222 n. 131
    Jews in, 167–168
        and Czechoslovak identity, 167–168,
            173
        and mourning Habsburg collapse,
            138–139, 141
    nationality conflicts in, 166–167
Czechs, 17, 18, 176 n. 28, 181 n. 95
    and anti-Semitism, 22, 26, 124, 125, 139,
        141, 142, 210 n. 21
    and struggle for independence, 124
    war time loyalty of, 40, 85, 88, 89, 201 n.
        13, 203 n. 42

Deutschösterreich. See Austrian Republic

Eastern Front, 48, 49, 84–85, 87–88, 90, 163
Ehrlich, Jakob, 154
Engel, Alfred, 71
Entente, 109, 111, 124, 129
ethnic identity, 3, 7–8, 170
ethnocultural nationalism, 7, 8, 170

Fischer, Béla, 64, 96, 101
Fourteen Points, 109, 111, 131, 137
France, Jews in, 20–21, 47
Franz Ferdinand, 10, 41
Franz Joseph, 17, 28, 41–42, 47, 53, 54, 86,
    143, 184 n. 11

cult of, 28–29, 32, 107, 179 n. 68
  death of 10, 88, 106
  Jewish response to death of, 106,
    107–108, 209 n. 9
von Fuchs, Robert, 76, 79, 108, 116

Galicia, 17, 18, 19
  assistance to Jews in, 112, 113
  fighting in, 48, 49, 50, 53, 84, 88, 101
  Jewish concerns about, 4, 48, 110–113
  and Jewish desire to keep Austrian,
    52–53, 110–113, 163
  liberation of, 51–52, 88, 110
  pogroms in, 109, 110, 136, 137–138
  Polish-Ukrainian conflict in, 131, 136,
    137
  refugees from. See refugees
  status of, 110–111, 114, 118, 120, 123, 126,
    131
Galicia, Jews in, 15, 22, 23, 25, 28–30, 112,
    114–115, 164, 179 n. 70
  and Austrian identity, 29, 50–51, 121
  and cult of Franz Joseph, 28–29, 179 n.
    68
  and Polish culture, 29–30
  and Polish nationalism, 30, 112
  and reactions to outbreak of war, 42,
    43
  and Russian persecution, 50
  and wartime patriotism, 50–51
  and Zionism, 30, 36, 37, 112, 113, 118,
    124
Galician Jewish soldiers, 51, 90, 101
Germans (in Austria), 18
  and anti-Semitism, 119, 121, 125
  in Bohemia and Moravia, 18, 131, 176 n.
    28, 177 nn. 31, 41
  in Bukovina, 18
  in Czechoslovakia, 166–167
  and Habsburg collapse, 132
  and nationalism, 17, 170
Germany, Jews in, 20–21, 23, 47, 56–57, 74,
    91, 95, 102, 135, 160, 176 n. 24,
    186 n. 62
graves, soldiers', 102–103
Grünfeld, Sofie, 71–72, 75
Grunwald, Margarethe, 65, 72
Grunwald, Max, 107
Güdemann, Moritz, 34, 35, 51, 55, 97, 98,
    104, 107

Habsburg Monarchy, 15
  dissolution of, 4, 109, 127, 128, 131–133
  national identity in, 3, 8, 17–18, 19,
    172–173, 175 n. 12
Hantke, Arthur, 116, 117
Hasidism, 22, 77–78, 98, 107
Herrmann, Leo, 125, 144, 151
Home Front, 9–10, 54, 58, 59–74, 163
  and dispelling anti-Semitism, 59
  and Habsburg loyalty, 59
  helping Jewish soldiers, 63–65
  refugee aid, 71–73
  role of women, 62–63, 71–73
Hungary, 8, 15, 17, 18, 132, 165–166,
    174 n. 19
Hungary, Jews in, 15, 22, 23, 25, 30-32,
    165–166
  and German culture, 31–32
  and Habsburg loyalty, 32
  and Hungarian identity, 11, 22, 30–32,
    129, 165–166, 180 n. 83

Israelitische Allianz, 67-68, 69, 70, 72, 112
Israelitische Kultusgemeinde, (IKG), Prague,
    61, 64, 69, 118, 191 n. 40
  and attitudes toward Czechoslovakia,
    139–140
  and efforts against anti-Semitism, 119
  and efforts to unite Austrian Jews, 114,
    119
  and expelling refugees, 79–80, 139
  and Jewish National Council, 145–146
  and refugee aid, 69, 76, 78, 80,
    195 n. 104
Israelitische Kultusgemeinde (IKG), Vienna,
    36, 51, 56, 60, 61, 64, 118
  and assistance to religious Jewish sol-
    diers, 63, 98
  and common graves for soldiers, 103
  and efforts against anti-Semitism, 119,
    121
  and efforts to unite Austrian Jews,
    113–114
  and emperor Karl, 108
  and Jewish National Council, 151–152
  and refugee aid, 69–70, 76, 194 n. 74,
    194–195 n. 88
Israelitische Kultusgemeinden, other
  and Jewish nationalism in Moravia and
    Silesia, 145

Israelitische Kultusgemeinden, other (*continued*)
   and new emperor Karl, 108
   and work on behalf of Galician
       refugees, 67, 68, 69–70
   and work on behalf of Jewish soldiers,
       64
Italian Front, 53–54, 84, 85, 86, 126
   Jewish attitudes toward, 53-54, 86–89,
       126–127

Jewish congress, 115–118
Jewish ethnic identity, 4–5, 8–9, 21, 23,
       24–25, 38, 57, 107, 127, 129,
       149–150, 160, 170-–71, 177 nn. 34,
       35, 181 n. 98
   in Galicia, 29–30
   in Vienna, 33–36, 150, 156, 157, 158, 159,
       160, 169
Jewish identity
   in army, 83, 94–98, 105
   in Austria, 3–4, 9, 22, 23, 24, 25, 38,
       40–41, 57, 83, 105, 106, 109, 115,
       120, 127, 162, 181 nn. 96, 98
   in Austrian Republic, 129, 150–160,
       168
   crisis of after Habsburg collapse, 129,
       156, 162
   in Czechoslovakia, 129, 133, 144,
       146–148, 149–150, 160
   in France and Germany, 4, 20–21
   in Hungary, 11, 22, 30–32, 129
   in Poland, 11, 129
Jewish liberals, 113, 114, 126, 133, 156–160,
       162, 198 n. 150
Jewish National Association, 123, 125
Jewish National Council
   in Austrian Republic, 151–153
   in Brünn, 141, 145
   in Czechoslovakia, 142, 148,
   in Moravia and Silesia, 145
   in Prague, 79, 141, 144, 145–146
   in successor states, 129
   in Vienna, 151–153, 155
Jewish nationalism, 11, 30, 36–37, 107,
       127, 129, 133, 147, 155, 162, 182 n.
       127
   and Austrian loyalty, 37
   in Austrian Republic, 150–155
   in Czechoslovakia, 143–149 , 167–168,
       227 n. 16

and desire for recognition of Jews as a
       nation in Austria, 111–112, 115, 120,
       121–126
   and German culture, 37, 147, 149
   in Poland, 164
   in Romania, 165
Jewish soldiers, 9, 54, 82, 200 n. 1
   and anti-Semitism, 91, 92–94, 102
   attending to the religious needs of, 63–65
   attitudes toward Russia, 86–89
   attitudes toward Italy, 86–89
   and Austrian loyalty, 93–94, 102, 105
   from Galicia, 87, 91, 99, 101
   graves for, 102–103
   and Jewish honor, 90–91, 102
   and Jewish identity, 94–98, 101, 102, 105,
       163
   and Jewish religious observance, 94–98,
       101
   and Jewish religious symbols, 101
   as Maccabees, 46–47, 65, 102
   and memorials for, 104–105
   religious soldiers, 55, 91, 94, 97, 98, 99,
       101, 105, 206 n. 118
   and social isolation, 91–92, 102
   and war time ideology, 86–89, 102
Jewish solidarity, 9, 59–60, 63, 64, 65–66,
       70, 71, 73-74, 80–81, 95, 101, 102
Jewish valor, 51, 55, 82, 87, 90, 101, 102
Jewish war memorials, 104–105
Jews
   attitudes toward Russia, 44–48, 51–53,
       86–89, 185 n. 38
   Austrian identity, 24, 25, 38, 57–58, 65,
       73–74, 79–80, 94, 105, 106, 107, 109,
       120–121, 127, 139, 155, 157, 158,
       169, 181 n. 96
   Austrian loyalty, 4, 9, 50, 53, 94, 106, 127,
       163
   and Austrian Republic, 134–135, 152,
       156, 157–158
   and Austrian victories, 51, 88, 89, 126
   and collapse of Habsburg Monarchy, 10,
       128–129, 133–143, 159, 160, 163,
       217 nn. 4, 5
   and Czech culture, 9, 22, 26–28, 129,
       146–147, 149, 167
   and Czech nation, 110, 124, 129,
       146–147, 149, 167–168, 215 n. 143,
       227 n. 16

and desire to keep Galicia Austrian,
110–113, 163
and efforts to unite, 107, 113–119, 133
and German culture, 9, 22, 23–28, 30,
31–32, 34, 122, 129, 146–147, 149,
150, 153, 155, 156, 157–158, 159, 168,
169, 177–178 n. 41, 227 n. 16
and German nation, 20–21, 23, 110, 150,
152, 153, 155–156, 157–158, 168,
169, 176 n. 29, 227 n. 16
and German *Volk,* 9, 11, 21, 23, 26, 30,
34, 56, 129, 146–147, 159, 168, 169
and Habsburg continuity, 10, 38, 54, 58,
60, 81, 105, 106, 109–110, 113,
119–126, 133, 163
as a nation, 19–21, 30, 34, 36, 115–118,
121–126, 147–148
and Polish culture, 9, 23, 29, 129, 164
and Polish nation, 110, 113, 129, 136, 164
as a religio-ethnic group, 20, 34, 36, 38,
107, 158, 159, 162, 170
as a religious community, 19–21, 22, 147,
158, 159, 162
and Socialism, 38, 169
and wartime patriotism, 4, 9, 38, 40,
43–48, 50–56, 82, 94, 102
Joseph II, 15, 25, 31
Jüdische Nationalrat. See Jewish National
Council

Kadisch, Hermann, 115, 122–123, 124
Kadisch, Hermine, 62
Karl, 42, 50, 108, 109, 121, 124, 131, 132,
134
Kassner, Salomon, 123
Katznelson, Sigmund, 116, 117
Kohn, Gustav, 60
Kohn, Hans, 5, 27, 28, 43, 89, 140, 173 n. 2,
219 n. 65
Koserak, Alois, 139–140, 146
Krauss, Karl, 181 n. 96

Lemberg
liberation of, 51, 52
pogrom in, 137–138, 147
Lewin, Moritz, 70
Lwów. *See* Lemberg

Magyarization, 18, 19, 23, 30–32
Magyars, 8, 11, 31, 165

Masaryk, Thomas, 124, 131, 139, 142, 143,
144, 149, 220 n. 76
minority rights, 148, 151, 154, 164, 166
modernization, Jewish, in the army, 82–83
Moravia, Jews in, 15, 25–28, 178 n. 59
and Austrian loyalty, 28
and Czech identity, 147, 167–168
and Galician/Bukovinian refugees, 68,
70, 71
and German identity, 25–28, 147, 148,
168, 177–178 n. 41
and Jewish nationalism, 144, 147–148, 168
Moravia, pogroms in, 109, 220 n. 77
Müller, Anitta, 72–73, 75, 112, 153, 154,
197 n. 130

Národní Výbor, 139, 144, 145
nation-states
creation of, 109
and Jewish identity, 110, 127, 128–129,
150
and national identity, 4–5
national identity
in Habsburg Monarchy, 3, 8, 19
in successor states, 3, 129
national self-determination, 106, 109, 122,
131, 133, 141
nationalism
definitions of, 5–6, 173 n. 2
civic nationalism, 6, 171, 172
and ethnic loyalty, 6, 170
ethnocultural nationalism, 7, 8, 170
in France and Germany, 6–7, 174 n. 13
history of, 6, 173 n. 10
nationality conflict, in Austria, 17, 19, 57,
107, 109, 112
Nazis, 167, 170, 173

Ofner, Julius, 154, 157
Orthodox Jews
attitudes toward Poles, 111, 113, 126, 138
attitudes toward Russia, 53
and Austrian continuity, 120, 121
and Austrian Jewish unity, 118
and Habsburg collapse, 133
in Hungary, 165
and Jewish identity, 159
and Jewish nationalism, 126, 144–145,
148, 156, 157
and Jewish soldiers, 65

Orthodox Jews (*continued*)
   and refugee aid, 70
   and soldiers' graves, 103
   and successor states, 134
   and war bonds, 61
Österreichisch-israelitische Union. See Austrian Israelite Union

Passover in the field, 94, 95, 96–98, 102
Passover food for soldiers, 64–65, 192 n. 51
Patak, Erna, 153, 154
patriotic war work, 60–63
   and female patriotism, 63
patriotism, Jewish, 9, 39–41, 43–48, 50–51, 54–56, 59, 63, 82, 89
   and aid to Galician refugees, 65, 71, 73–74
   in Galicia, 50–51
Plaschkes, Leopold, 153, 154
Poalei Zion, 112, 123, 124, 148
pogroms
   in Bohemia and Moravia, 109, 142, 220 n. 77
   in Galicia, 11, 29, 109, 110, 112–113, 136, 137–138, 142, 163
   in Russia, 45, 51, 126
   in Slovakia, 142, 152
   in Ukraine, 137, 218 n. 40
Poland
   anti-Semitism in, 136
   creation of, 131, 136–137
   pogroms in, 137–138
   war-time discussions of future status, 110–111
Poland, Jews in, 138, 148, 163–164
Poles, 18, 29, 110, 111
   Jewish attitudes towards, 111, 112, 163
Polish Legion, 137–138
Prague, Jews in, 26–27, 79, 139
   and refugees, 66, 69, 71, 72, 76–80
   and Czechoslovakia, 139–141
   and Jewish national rights, 144–146, 148–149
   See also Israelitische Kultusgemeinde, Prague, and Zionists in Prague

Red Cross, 59, 60, 62, 63, 64, 80, 101
refugees (from Galicia and Bukovina), 66–67, 153, 192 n. 57, 194 n. 80, 196 n. 113
   Austrian identity of, 65, 73–74, 79, 80, 158

camps for, 66, 68, 70, 193 n. 61
   and collapse of Habsburg Monarchy, 133, 135–136
government assistance to, 67, 193 n. 67, 195 n. 88, 200 n. 204
Jewish assistance to, 9–10, 58, 59, 65–74
   in Bohemia and Moravia, 68–69, 70–71, 195 n. 104
   in Vienna, 69–70, 71, 72–73, 152, 194 n. 74, 194–195 n. 88, 196 n. 111
   by women, 71–73
   by Zionists, 70–71, 72–73, 145, 152
Jewish attitudes toward, 74–81
   in Bohemia and Moravia, 76–80, 114–115, 199 n. 169
   in Vienna, 74–76, 198 n. 150
   and Jewish solidarity, 58, 59, 65–66, 73–74, 163
   and Jewish unity, 113–114
   return home, 53, 136, 146
   and significance for Zionists, 115, 123
Reiss, Teofil, 87–88, 92, 95
Renner, Karl, 153, 182 n. 127
Romania, 132
Romania, Jews in, 11, 163, 164–165
   Jewish attitudes toward, 53, 126, 136
Romanians (in Bukovina), 19, 131, 164
Rosenfeld, Max, 112, 123, 125
Russia, Jewish attitudes toward, 4, 43–48, 50–53, 83, 86, 185 n. 38
Ruthenes, 18–19, 29, 85, 88, 111, 112 , 131, 137, 165, 179 n. 75. *See also* Ukrainians

Schwarz-Hiller, Rudolf, 67, 80, 116, 133
Silesia, Jewish nationalism in, 144, 147–148
Singer, Ludwig, 125, 141, 144, 149
Slovakia, 131, 132, 142, 166
Slovakia, Jews in, 31, 32, 143, 145, 147, 167
Socialists, 182 n. 127, 185 n. 38, 214 n. 118
Sonnenschein, Theodor, 116, 147–148
soup kitchens, 62, 70, 72
spirit of 1914, 39–43, 162, 183 n. 1
Stand, Adolf, 37, 116
Stern, Alfred, 51, 108, 113, 116, 119, 152
Straucher, Benno, 37, 52, 112, 115, 121, 123, 124, 125
Stricker, Robert, 52, 116–117, 121, 123, 124, 125, 143, 150, 151, 153, 154, 169
Sub-Carpathian Ruthenia, 167, 226 n. 14

successor states, 130, 131–132
  anti-Semitism in, 128, 163
  and crisis of Jewish identity, 4, 128, 162, 163
  and national identity, 3, 132, 172

Tauber, Majer, 51, 98, 99
Taussig, Rudolf, 116, 117
tripartite identity
  in Austrian Republic, 150, 160, 168, 169
  in Czechoslovakia, 143, 149, 160, 167-168
  in Habsburg Austria, 4–5, 9, 23, 24, 25, 33, 38, 41, 105, 107, 127, 128, 155, 162
  in successor states, 10, 12, 127, 128, 163

Ukraine, 111, 126, 137, 218 n. 40, 219 n. 48
Ukrainians, 131, 137–138, 164. See also Ruthenes
Ulmann, Regine, 71–72
Umgangssprache, 18, 26

Versailles Peace Conference, 138, 148, 152, 154, 155, 164
Versailles Treaty, 10
Vienna
  and Austrian identity, 33
  and German identity, 32–33, 181 n. 95
Vienna, Jews in, 15, 23, 32–36, 169, 217 n. 6
  and Austrian Republic, 134–135, 150
  and elections of 1919, 153–154
  and Habsburg collapse, 128, 133, 134–136
  and Jewish identity, 32-36, 157–160
  and Jewish nationalism, 151–154, 156–157
  and patriotic war work, 60–64
  and refugees, 66–68, 69–70, 71–73, 74–76, 79–80

war bonds, 55, 61, 80
war memorials, 104–105, 208 n. 174
war weariness, 108
Weibliche Fürsorge, 62, 70, 71–72, 112
Weisselberger, Salo, 50
Weltsch, Robert, 89, 125, 151, 213 n. 93
Western Front, 83–84, 108
women, Jewish
  and elections of 1919, 154
  and Jewish nationalism, 153

  and Passover food for soldiers, 64–65
  and refugee aid, 71–73
  and response to outbreak of war, 43
  and war work, 59, 62–63, 197 n. 131
World War I
  Austrian attitudes toward, 86
  Austrian victories in 51–52, 120, 126
  and Christian symbolism, 101–102
  enthusiasm for, 39–43, 162
  and Jewish desire to liberate East European Jews, 40, 44, 51, 126, 162
  and Jewish desire to liberate Galicia, 48
  as a Jewish holy war, 4, 40, 43–48, 51–53, 54, 58, 83, 89, 126, 162
  Jewish reactions to outbreak, 42–43
  Jewish soldiers in, 9, 10, 82–105
  and Jewish support for Austrian war effort, 40–41, 43–48, 50, 89–90
  and Jewish war memorials, 104–105
  and Jewish wartime ideology, 44–48, 50–51, 86–89, 126, 162–163
  as a just cause, 84
  origins, 41, 183 n. 4
  and war memorials, 208 n. 174
  and war weariness, 108, 209 n. 17
World Zionist Organization, 71, 116, 117, 145, 148, 151, 152, 154

Yiddish, 18, 19, 22, 29, 30, 31, 72, 164

Zionism, 36–37, 127, 162, 171
  and German culture, 37, 122
  in Hungary, 32, 165–166
  in Poland, 11, 164
  post-World War I success, 155, 156, 160
  See also Zionists
Zionists
  and attitudes to Galician refugees, 75, 77–78, 79–80
  attitudes toward Russia, 46, 48
  and Austrian loyalty, 55, 121, 122
  and Austrian Republic, 150-153
  in Bohemia and Moravia, 36–37, 124–125, 143–149
  in Bukovina, 37, 124
  and collapse of Habsburg Monarchy, 134, 138, 140–141
  and Czech-German conflict, 124–125, 143, 146–147
  and Czech nationalism, 124–125, 141

Zionists (*continued*)
  and Czechoslovakia, 140–149
  and death of Franz Joseph, 107–108
  and desire to keep Galicia Austrian,
    52–53, 111–112
  and efforts to combat anti-Semitism, 56,
    79–80, 116, 154
  and elections of 1919, 148–149, 153–
    154
  in Galicia, 30, 36–37, 118, 124
  and Habsburg continuity, 53, 55, 111,
    113, 120, 121, 134
  and help for Jews in Galicia, 112
  and Jewish national rights, 115–118,
    121–126, 129, 133, 134, 140,
    143–149, 151–154, 169,
    221 n. 92
  and Jewish national rights in Austrian
    Republic, 150–153
  and Jewish national rights in Czechoslo-
    vakia, 143–149
  and Jewish unity in Austria, 113, 115–118
  and patriotic war work, 61, 65
  and pogroms, 138, 145, 152
  and Poles, 113, 138
  in Prague, 37, 115, 116, 117, 124, 125 ,141,
    144, 146, 148–149
  and refugee aid, 70–71, 72–73, 80, 145,
    152, 195 n. 104, 196 n. 111
  and Ukraine, 126
  in Vienna, 34, 36, 116, 117, 151, 169
  and wartime ideology, 46, 48, 52
Zionist women, 62, 65, 71–73
Zweig, Stefan, 33, 42–43